PALGRAVE MACMII
GREAT DEBATES IN LAW

PALGRAVE MACMILLAN
GREAT DEBATES IN LAW

Series editor
Jonathan Herring
Professor of Law,
University of Oxford

Contract Law
Jonathan Morgan

Criminal Law
Jonathan Herring

Employment Law
Simon Honeyball

Family Law
Jonathan Herring, Rebecca Probert and Stephen Gilmore

Property Law
David Cowan, Lorna Fox O'Mahony and Neil Cobb

Other titles are in course of preparation.

If you would like to comment on this book, or on any other law text published by Palgrave Macmillan, please write to lawfeedback@palgrave.com.

PALGRAVE MACMILLAN
GREAT DEBATES IN LAW

GREAT DEBATES IN
FAMILY LAW

JONATHAN HERRING
Fellow in Law,
Exeter College, Oxford

REBECCA PROBERT
Professor of Law,
University of Warwick

STEPHEN GILMORE
Senior Lecturer in Law,
King's College, London

This edition first published 2012 by PALGRAVE MACMILLAN

Palgrave Macmillan in the UK is an imprint of Macmillan Publishers Limited, registered in England, company number 785998, of Houndmills, Basingstoke, Hampshire RG21 6XS.

Palgrave Macmillan in the US is a division of St Martin's Press LLC, 175 Fifth Avenue, New York, NY 10010.

Palgrave Macmillan is the global academic imprint of the above companies and has companies and representatives throughout the world.

Palgrave® and Macmillan® are registered trademarks in the United States, the United Kingdom, Europe and other countries.

ISBN: 978–0–230–29291–8 paperback

This book is printed on paper suitable for recycling and made from fully managed and sustained forest sources. Logging, pulping and manufacturing processes are expected to conform to the environmental regulations of the country of origin.

A catalogue record for this book is available from the British Library.

10   9   8   7   6   5   4   3   2   1
21 20 19 18 17 16 15 14 13 12

Printed and bound in Great Britain by
CPI Antony Rowe, Chippenham and Eastbourne

CONTENTS

INTRODUCTION

This is a fascinating time to be studying family law. It is widely agreed that significant changes are taking place in the way we understand family life. Concepts such as marriage, parenthood and childhood are changing at an extraordinary pace. For many people these changes are liberating, the strictures of these old-fashioned concepts being reworked so that people are free to live the personal life they lead, without censure or blame. But for other people these are frightening times, with the 'bedrocks' of society, such as marriage and parenthood, being challenged, with who knows what consequences.

This book is designed to help you think more deeply about some of the great debates in family law at the moment. The book does not cover every issue there is to discuss, but does cover most of the major themes. It assumes you are familiar with the main principles of family law, although there are summaries of the law at the relevant places.

The book does not tell you the 'correct answer' to these various issues. Of course, there are no 'correct answers'. It is hoped that by reading this book you will come to understand how sensible people can disagree on these questions. Maybe you will come to see at least some merit in views you previously thought were untenable.

At the end of each chapter there is a list of further reading. You can use this to gain further perspectives and to help you think through the issues yourself. Soon you will find there are a wide range of views on many of these controversial issues. The more you read the more you will be able to develop your own point of view.

CASES

ix

LEGISLATION

1

THE NATURE OF FAMILIES AND FAMILY LAW

INTRODUCTION

At the heart of family law are some very basic questions: what is a family, and how should the rights and responsibilities of family members be regulated by the law? Indeed, one might take this question further and ask whether they should be regulated by law at all: one very important current debate is just how far families should be expected to resolve their disputes without recourse to law. Assuming that the law is to play some role – at least in establishing what individuals are entitled to, and what they are expected to do – a further question presents itself: what criteria should be used in deciding these points? Should the law make moral judgments about who is a good parent, or a good wife or husband, and use these judgments to determine individuals' entitlements? And, if so, how do judges decide what makes a good parent or partner?

First, however, we should tackle the most basic questions of all: what do we mean by the term 'family'?

Debate

What is a family?

Families come in all kinds of shapes and sizes. There is little consistency about the way the term is used. Sometimes it is taken to refer to a 'nuclear family' (parents and their dependent children); sometimes it is taken to refer to kinship (a larger group of people related by blood or marriage, of the kind found in a family tree); or households (a group sharing accommodation). In some communities it is common to refer to a close family friend as an uncle or cousin, even though there is no blood tie. One of the difficulties in defining 'family' is the power of the definition and especially the stigma that follows from denying that a certain group of people is a family.[1] In part this explains the strong objections from the

---

[1] G. Douglas, *An Introduction to Family Law* (Oxford University Press, 2005), p. 3.

gay and lesbian community to the now repealed s 28 of the Local Government Act 1988, which referred to gay and lesbian relationships as 'pretended family relationship[s]'.[2]

How we describe and classify the family for the purposes of statistical analysis is a matter for debate in its own right. If, for example, we define the 'traditional' family as one consisting of a married couple with two or more children, then it is very easy to say that few families match this model. A study in 2011[3] found that only 16 per cent of the population believed they fitted into such a traditional model, and that even in 1961, only 38 per cent of families matched the traditional model. Yet the narrowness of this definition makes it inevitable that only a small proportion of families will fall within its scope: does the fact that a married couple have only one child, or even no children, make them any less traditional?

If we focus on the more neutral concept of 'household', then we can see that in 2010 29 per cent of all households consisted of people living on their own; 28 per cent of couples with no children; 27 per cent of a couple with children; 10 per cent of a lone parent with children; 3 per cent of two or more unrelated adults; and 1 per cent of multi-family households. Looking at just families with children: 63 per cent were a married couple family; 13.4 per cent were a cohabiting couple family, and 23.6 per cent were a lone-parent family.[4] Given the regular headlines about the decline of marriage, it is striking that most couples with children are married.

At the same time, it is clear that there has been considerable change in family life over the past 40 years, with more individuals living alone (possibly with a partner elsewhere); an increasing proportion of births taking place outside marriage (largely but not exclusively to cohabiting couples); and higher rates of relationship breakdown. Attitudes have changed radically as well. As late as 1989 a sizeable majority – 70 per cent – of respondents to the British Social Attitudes Survey took the view that 'people who want children ought to get married'.[5] By contrast, in a recent survey 77 per cent of people believed that single parents can be a proper family; and 59 per cent believed that same-sex couples can be a family. Only 36 per cent of those questioned believed that a couple with children had to be married to be a proper family.[6]

The significance of the changes in family life is a matter of some debate. There are certainly many who are concerned about changes in family life. 83 per cent of those questioned blamed 'family breakdown' as the source of the problems leading to the riots in London in the summer of 2011.[7] Family breakdown can also

---

[2] The section was repealed by the Local Government Act 2003, sch 8(1), para 1.

[3] Centre for the Modern Family, *Family* (Centre for the Modern Family, 2011).

[4] National Statistics, *Social Trends 2011* (National Statistics, 2011).

[5] J. Scott, 'Women and the Family' in R. Jowell, S. Witherspoon and L. Brook with B. Taylor (eds), *British Social Attitudes: The 7th Report* (Gower, 1990), pp. 60, 61.

[6] Centre for the Modern Family, *Family*.

[7] Centre for Social Justice, *Strengthening the Family and Tackling Family Breakdown* (Centre for Social Justice, 2011), p. 1.

cause enormous personal hardship.[8] The Centre for the Modern Family found 43 per cent of people over 60 lived alone and 25 per cent of the over-60s lived alone with no family nearby.[9]

Alison Diduck[10] notes the differences between 'the families we live by and the families we live with', suggesting that we hold on to an ideal of what family life is like (the traditional nuclear family) that is at odds with the realities of family life. She goes on to examine further our reasons for holding on to the 'ideal' of traditional family life:

> When we mourn the loss of the 'traditional family', therefore, we may be grieving for the loss of more than the values we ascribe to it like loyalty, stability, co-operation, love and respect; we must also remain aware of its underlying values of patriarchy, heterosexism and race and class hierarchy.[11]

Others argue that the changes in family life should not produce concern. Katherine Rake, for example, suggests that:

> Modern family life obviously has its challenges. But, the modern family is also testament to a rise in tolerance and choice which was not there for generations before. No longer do people have to live with abusive partners, be punished with social stigma if they are lone parents or have to hide their gay relationships. Family form has changed throughout history but what remains constant is that families are the most important social institution in UK society.[12]

Further, whatever claims may be made about the so-called 'decline' in family life, it is clear that for the vast majority of people families, whatever their form, are important. In one survey 92 per cent of people felt very or fairly close to their families.[13]

All of these changes have thrown up into the air the question of what family is. Much of what may have been taken for granted about 'normal family life' has shifted. The question of what makes a family has therefore become a very difficult question.

THE LAW

'Family' is presently a term that is of limited legal significance. While much effort has been spent in attempting a legal definition of 'marriage', 'parent' and 'parent-hood', relatively few cases have defined 'a family'. Nonetheless, the concept of

---

[8] See e.g. R. Probert and J. Miles, *Sharing Lives and Dividing Assets* (Hart Publishing, 2009).

[9] Centre for the Modern Family, *Family*.

[10] A. Diduck, *Law's Families* (Butterworths, 2003), p. 23.

[11] Ibid, p. 23.

[12] Quoted in Diduck, *Law's Families*, p. 24.

[13] Centre for the Modern Family, *Family*.

'family life' is central to rights under the European Convention on Human Rights, leading to renewed debate on the meaning of family in recent years.

The meaning of family in domestic legislation

In *Fitzpatrick v Sterling Housing Association Ltd,*[14] the House of Lords had to consider the meaning of 'family' for the purposes of the Rent Act 1977. The case involved a Mr Thompson and a Mr Fitzpatrick who had lived together in a flat for 18 years before the former's death. The flat was in Mr Thompson's name, but under the Rent Act 1977 Mr Fitzpatrick could succeed to the tenancy if he could show he was a member of Mr Thompson's family. In short, the question was whether a gay couple could be a family for the purposes of the Rent Act 1977. By three to two the House of Lords held they could.[15]

For Lord Slynn, writing in the majority, the hallmarks of family life were 'that there should be a degree of mutual inter-dependence, of the sharing of lives, of caring and love, or commitment and support'.[16] He added that it was crucial was that the relationship was not 'a transient superficial relationship.'[17] Applying this to the facts of the case, their relationship was of long standing and Mr Fitzpatrick had cared for Mr Thompson for the last six years of his life. They could therefore be regarded as family.

Lord Clyde argued that a sexual element or at least the potential for one, needed to be shown.[18] His concern was that a criterion was needed to distinguish between a family relationship and one based on friendship. This reflected the earlier decision of the House of Lords in *Joram Developments Ltd v Sharratt,*[19] in which a 24-year-old man and a 75-year-old woman shared a flat, enjoying each other's company and living communally, although there were no sexual relations. The House of Lords was willing to say they shared a household, but not that they were members of a family. Was that the right decision?

The approach of the minority in *Fitzpatrick* was interesting. They started with what they regarded as two paradigm family relations: those created by law – marriage or adoption – and those created by blood tie – parent or child. As Mr Fitzpatrick and Mr Thompson were not analogous to either of these they could not be regarded as family members. As we shall see, this more formalist approach to defining the family still has its advocates.

Following *Fitzpatrick*, the law uses a fairly broad understanding of family, one that is not restricted to blood relations or those who have formalized their relationship in law through, for example, civil partnership or marriage. The case might seem to suggest that it is intimacy and stability which are seen as the hallmarks of family life. However, it would be wrong to suggest that the courts look

---

[14] [2000] 1 FCR 21.

[15] See further *Mendoza v Ghaidan* [2004] UKHL 30 (holding that a same-sex couple could be regarded as living together as husband and wife) and see now Civil Partnership Act 2004.

[16] [2000] 1 FCR 21, at p. 32.

[17] [2000] 1 FCR 21, at p. 32.

[18] [2000] 1 FCR 21, at p. 47.

[19] [1979] 1 WLR 928.

only at the quality of the actual relationship. Where a couple are in a formal legal relationship or blood tie (e.g. marriage, parenthood) that will usually be sufficient to render them members of the same family. It is generally only those who are not related in this way who have to evidence the quality of their relationship.

Despite these developments recognizing a variety of family forms it can be argued that there is a hierarchy of families in family law, with the top position being taken by married couples, civil partners now coming a close second and couples who have not formalized their relationship below them.[20] Certainly the closer a relationship is to the 'ideal' of marriage the more likely it is to be recognized as a family.

Family law and the European Convention on Human Rights

Under Article 8 of the ECHR everyone has the right to respect for his private and family life. In *Secretary of State for Work and Pensions v M*,[21] Lord Bingham, in considering the meaning of family life for the purposes of the ECHR, suggested that 'love, trust, confidence, mutual dependence and unconstrained social inter-course...are the essence of family life'.

This clearly is a broader understanding of families beyond the traditional understanding. Indeed, as Lord Hope noted in *EM (Lebaonon) v Secretary of State for the Home Dept*:[22] 'there is no pre-determined model of family or family life to which Article 8 must be applied'.

Arguably the European Court of Human Rights (ECtHR) itself has been less progressive, while still rejecting a formal approach to the definition of family life. In defining family life, it is clear that the paradigm of family life for the ECtHR has been a husband and wife and children.[23] This can be seen in *B v UK*,[24] in which the ECtHR explained that there could be a variety of kinds of *un*married father, ranging from an ignorant or indifferent father to the relationship with the child being 'indistinguishable from the conventional family-based unit'. Clearly, here the court regarded the 'conventional family-based unit' as a married couple with children and took the quality and nature of their relationship for granted.[25] As a result, although mothers inevitably have family life with their children,[26] this is not true of fathers. As the European Court in *Lebbink v Netherlands*[27] stated: 'The court does not agree with the applicant that a mere biological kinship, without any further legal or factual elements indicating the existence of a close personal relationship, should be regarded as sufficient to attract the protection of Art 8'.

---

20 R. Bailey-Harris, 'Same-Sex Partnerships in English Family Law', in R. Wintemute and M. Andenæs (eds) *Legal Recognition of Same-Sex Partnerships* (Hart Publishing, 2001).
21 [2006] UKHL 11, para 5.
22 [2008] UKHL 64, para 37
23 J. Liddy, 'The Concept of Family Law Under the ECHR' (1998) 1 *European Human Rights Law Review* 15.
24 [2000] 1 FCR 289.
25 In *Ahmut v The Netherlands* (1997) 24 EHRR 62 it was stated that once two people have family life, only in exceptional circumstances will that be lost.
26 *Re B (Adoption by One Natural Parent to Exclusion of Other)* [2001] 1 FLR 589.
27 [2004] 3 FCR 59, at para 37.

It explained that in considering a claim of a father the court would consider 'the nature of the relationship between the natural parents and the demonstrable interest in and commitment by the father to the child both before and after its birth'.[28]

At the same time, it should be noted that Article 8 has been found to cover same-sex couples;[29] unmarried couples;[30] siblings;[31] uncle/nephew;[32] grandparents/grandchild;[33] and foster parents/foster-child.[34] However, it appears that the further the relationship departs from the paradigm (i.e. the more remote the blood relationship from that of the parent–child relationship), the more evidence is needed to show that there was a close *social* relationship between the parties. So in *Boyle v UK*[35] the uncle and nephew had 'family life' because the uncle proved he was a father figure to the boy.

It should be added that if the relationship does not fall within family life, it may still be protected by Article 8 as an aspect of the parties' private life.[36] Article 8 protects rights to respect for both private and family life and so it may just be of symbolic significance whether a relationship is seen as one of family or private life.

SEEKING A DEFINITION OF THE FAMILY

With these points in mind we should turn to consider the different approaches that could be taken to defining the term 'family'.

1. A formalistic definition

The arguments in favour

A formalistic definition would rely on compliance with certain formalities in order for a relationship to be a family. It is crucial for the law to be certain. That is an aspect of the rule of law. The law must also use a definition which is susceptible to proof. We cannot expect the courts to be poking into people's bedrooms to try and find out exactly what is going on. For these reasons a formalist approach has a number of advantages. It focuses on objective criteria that can be observed and proved. Typically this might include whether the couple are married or in a civil partnership; or whether they have children. It would avoid all references to difficult questions about whether the relationship was intimate or committed. It provides a definition which can be effectively used in courts as it is quick (and therefore cheap), not intrusive, and is clear.

---

[28] At para 36. See further *Anayo v Germany* [2011] 1 FLR 1883.
[29] *Schalk and Kopf v Austria* [2010] ECHR 995.
[30] *X, Y, Z v UK* [1997] 3 FCR 341.
[31] *Senthuran v Secretary of State for the Home Department* [2004] 3 FCR 273.
[32] *Boyle v UK* (1994) 19 EHRR 179.
[33] *Adam v Germany* [2009] 1 FLR 560.
[34] *X v Switzerland* (1978) 13 DR 248.
[35] (1994) 19 EHRR 179. See also *Jucius and Juciuvienė v Lithuania* [2009] 1 FLR 403.
[36] *Znamenskaya v Russia* [2005] 2 FCR 406, at para 27.

Problems
The primary difficulty with the formalist approach is that it can appear technical. It will mean some groups are treated as a family which should not be; and some are not who should. Some people argue that it would be bizarre if the law treated an unmarried couple who had lived together for 20 years any differently from a married couple who had been married 20 years. Should the fact that the married couple undertook a short ceremony 20 years previously make a difference? Even more bizarrely, the married couple who had not seen each other for 20 years might be treated as a family, but not the unmarried couple who had shared their lives for 20 years. While the formalist approach might have the benefits of certainty and ease of proof, these are outweighed by the disadvantages of it producing results which seem at best arbitrary and at worst unjust.

Of course, in deciding on the weight to be accorded to these objections, we might also want to know how many cohabiting couples had been together for 20 years, and how many married couples had separated for such a period. A formalist approach could serve as a proxy for other more empirically based approaches if it was established that the vast majority of families fell within a certain model. But are there other approaches that would better recognize the variety of modern families?

2. A function-based definition

In favour
A function-based definition focuses on what we want families to do in our society.[37] If a group of people perform these functions then the law can treat them as a family. Under this approach, it matters not what the formal nature of their relationship is (e.g. whether they are married); what matters is whether their relationship performs the kind of functions we seek from a family. In short what is important is what they do, rather than what they are. A parent is a person who looks after a child in a parental way, whether or not there is a blood tie. It is the person actually caring for the child who needs the rights, duties and support of the law; not a person with a blood tie who has no day-to-day relationship with the child.

This has led David Morgan to argue that although we may not be able to define what a family is, we can identify what 'family practices' are.[38] Waite LJ in *Fitzpatrick v Sterling Housing Association Ltd*[39] provided judicial support for this approach:

> The question is more what a family does than what a family is. A family unit is a social organisation which functions through its linking its members closely together. The functions may be procreative, sexual, sociable, economic, emotional. The list is not exhaustive.

---

[37] L. Glennon, 'Fitzpatrick v Sterling Housing Association Ltd – An Endorsement of the Functional Family' (2000) 14 *International Journal of Law, Policy and the Family* 226.
[38] D. Morgan, *Rethinking Family Practices* (Palgrave Macmillan, 2011).
[39] [1998] 1 FLR 6.

This raises the tricky issue of what we regard as being the key functions of a family. Waite LJ's suggestions could be amplified to include the following: providing security and care for its members; producing children; socializing and raising of children; providing economically for its members;[40] a sexual relationship;[41] or a relationship revealing caring and sharing.[42] We would need to decide which combination of these would be essential for a functioning family.

Problems

One difficulty in adopting that approach is apparent from the statement in favour of it: how can we decide what are the central functions of a family? There is a long list in the previous paragraph and it is difficult to identify any as essential for a family. Does a family really require children? Must it involve a sexual relationship? The approach does not really get us any closer to finding a definition of a family. It reframes the question, that is all.

There is also the difficulty of proof. If we decide that caring and intimacy are key to the concept of family, how might this be proved? Absent highly invasive investigations exploring the details of their relationship, it is hard to see how this could be used in a court.

Another objection is that there is a danger that the approach presupposes that the traditional family is the ideal, and only permits other family forms to be included within the definition if they are sufficiently close to the functions of that ideal.[43] It has, for example, been argued that it is only because of the dominant position marriage has held in our society that a sexual element is seen as important to the definition of family,[44] although this element obviously plays an important part in reproducing the family.

3. The normal meaning of the word

In favour

An alternative approach would be to define family in the sense that it understood by the person in the street. This has many advantages. The principal one is that 'family' is essentially a social construct: it is a word we use to define a group of people in our society whom we regard as family. The circularity of this is obvious: there is no 'objective truth' in the definition and it will change from society to society and age to age depending on what is regarded as a family. By relying on the 'normal' meaning of the word family the law can keep up to date with fast-changing understandings of what it means to be a family in a modern society.

---

[40] See P. Rusk, (1998) 'Same Sex Spousal Benefits' (1998) 52 *U T Fac L Rev* 170.

[41] See Lord Clyde in *Fitzpatrick v Sterling Housing Association Ltd* [2000] 1 FCR 21, at p. 35.

[42] See S. Wong, 'Caring and Sharing: Interdependency as a Basis for Property Redistribution', in A. Bottomley and S. Wong (eds) *Changing Contours of Domestic Life, Family and Law* (Hart Publishing, 2009).

[43] Harvard Law Review, 'Looking for a Family Resemblance: The Limits of the Functional Approach to the Legal Definition of Family' (1991) 104 *Harv LR* 1640.

[44] M. Fineman, *The Autonomy Myth* (The New Press, 2004).

Problems

There is much to be said in favour of this definition when used by sociologists. It is less helpful for lawyers.[45] In borderline cases the person in the street may say: 'I don't know if this is a family or not'. Or we might find a range of views on whether a group of people is a family, reflecting religious and cultural diversity. Moreover, how is the view of the person in the street to be elicited? The approach, in short, provides no answer in the cases where we most need one: difficult cases.

4. A self-definition approach

In favour

We could take the view that a particular group or pair are a family if they say they are. Eekelaar and Nhlapo[46] have suggested that societies are gradually accepting an increasing variety of family forms and are reaching the position that a family is any group of people who regard themselves as a family. The benefit of such an approach is that it does not stigmatize people as 'not family' unless they do not wish to be regarded as a family.

There may be political merits in this. Describing a group of people as not being a family has stigmatizing overtones. It is not surprising, therefore, that politicians tend to avoid excluding people from the concept of a family. In 2008 the then government accepted there was no ideal family:

> There is no single family form that guarantees happiness or success. All types of family can, in the right circumstances, look after their family members, help them get on in life and, for their children, have high hopes and the wherewithal to put them on the path to success.[47]

Against

While the law could adopt a self-definition approach, it would be difficult for the law to attach any kind of significance or rights to being part of a family. It would mean that the word would cease to have much legal significance. It is inconceivable that any government would provide fiscal advantages or social security benefits to individuals simply on the basis that they had defined themselves as being 'family'.

Some would argue such a DIY definition fails to recognize there are some families that are much better than others. The Centre for Social Justice argues:

> Politicians and policy makers have typically shied away from distinguishing between family structures. They have become scared they might upset someone if they talk about two-parent families. Too many hide behind the mantra that it is just about personal choice and that Government has no

---

[45] Indeed it was expressly rejected by Lords Slynn and Nicholls in *Fitzpatrick v Sterling Housing Ltd* [2000] 1 FCR 21.
[46] J. Eekelaar and T. Nhlapo, 'Introduction', in J. Eekelaar and T. Nhlapo (eds) *The Changing Family: International Perspectives on the Family and Family Law* (Hart Publishing, 1998), p. ix.
[47] Cabinet Office (2008) *Families in Britain* (The Stationery Office, 2008), p. 5.

opinion…. The difference in stability between marriage and cohabitation is of fundamental importance, yet Government policy has failed to recognise that [there is] a 'marriage effect'.[48]

5. Care-centred family law

In favour

Traditionally family law has been particularly focused on sexual relations between adults: marriage or cohabitation. These have been the focal point of family law for some time. However, a strong argument can be made for a 'sexless family law': where the central focus is on relationships of care and dependency, rather than sex. One of us has argued:

> … we must ask what kinds of relationship require the ministrations of family law with its protective; adjustive; and supportive functions. The answer is not marriage, civil partnership and cohabitation. In other words a sexual relationships is not what marks a relationship as one requiring the functions of the law. Rather it is relationships marked by care and interdependency. These are the relationships which are of greater importance to society and need promotion. These are the relationships which are likely to cause the greatest disadvantage, especially in economic terms and, therefore need the protective and adjustive work of family law.[49]

Alison Diduck, arguing along similar lines, claims:

> For me, 'family' is one way to describe forms or expressions of intimate or private living based upon care and interdependence. And so, family could include a couple, of the same or different sexes with or without children, co-habiting with or without legal formality, or, indeed not co-habiting at all. Family also means an adult caring for a child or other dependent relative. What makes a relationship familial to me then is not necessarily a biological, legal, or conjugal connection, rather it is what people do in it, it is a relationship characterized by some degree of intimacy, interdependence, and care. These important social and personal aspects of life are tied, if not always for the 'right' reasons, to family and family relations.[50]

The argument here is essentially taking a functional approach but focusing on a particular function: the care of dependants.[51] The claim is that it is the care of dependants which marks a relationship as deserving the support of the law. Two independent adults living together and having sex together are hopefully

---

[48] Centre for Social Justice, *Every Family Matters* (Centre for Social Justice, 2009), pp. 8–9.
[49] J. Herring, 'Sexless Family Law' (2010) 11 *Lex Familiae* 3, p. 16.
[50] A. Diduck, 'What Is Family Law For?' (2011) *Current Legal Problems* 287.
[51] J. Millbank, 'The Role of "Functional Family" in Same-Sex Family Recognition Trends' [2008] *CFLQ* 255.

having fun, but what they are doing is not of much benefit to the rest of society. It is not likely their relationship will cause either severe economic harm. Caring relationships, by contrast, do deserve encouragement by the state and are liable to economic disadvantage which the law needs to address.

Problems

Much weight is placed in this approach on the notion of care. There are two particular difficulties with this. The first is that it is not readily susceptible to proof. What exactly counts as care: are we talking about physical tasks, or is it the emotional dimension that is important? Must the care work be done with a caring attitude? Even leaving these issues aside most acts of care take place in private and cannot be readily proved in retrospect.

The second problem is that within the context of an apparently caring relationship significant abuse can take place. The issues surrounding child or elder abuse demonstrate that very well. Many of those supporting a care-based approach emphasize that they are talking about just or non-abusive caring relationships, but defining exactly what constitutes a just caring relationship is far from straightforward and can be controversial.

6. No definition

In favour

As there is no real agreement over what constitutes a family or what family practices are, one solution is to throw up our hands in despair and declare there is no definition of a family for legal purposes. As noted when we discussed the law, in fact, there are relatively few circumstances in which it is necessary to define the family for legal purposes. The law could rely on terms such as marriage, civil partnership, parenthood and cohabitation; and avoid having to define the term.

Against

While the law certainly could operate without a formal legal definition, that is not necessarily desirable. First, many people do regard their families as important personally and the institution of families as being socially significant. It would be odd if the law did not engage with such a sociologically significant concept. Second, the concept of 'family-friendly' policies is one which does carry some political weight. If the law did not engage with the definition of the family the political weight that such arguments would carry would be lost.

CONCLUSION

What this demonstrates is that there are dangers in seeking to promote family life or talk about family law unless we are clear what it is we mean by families. We need to be precise about what aspect of the family a law is seeking to promote, or which group of people is intended to be covered by a particular law. Indeed, it may be that some parts of family law will apply to some families and not to others. It is not that some groups are family and some are not, but that some family groups may need the benefits of a particular law and others not.[52] The search for one perfect definition is likely to be doomed, but what we can strive for is the definition of 'family' best suited to the particular circumstances.

Debate 2

Should family law be about morality?

At one time the courts seemed very willing to make moral judgments. The courts would regularly declare what had caused the breakdown of a marriage; who was a good mother or a good father; or what was the best way to raise a child.[53] However, increasingly the courts have been unwilling to do this, and have accepted that there is not necessarily one right answer in difficult cases.[54] In particular, the courts are more and more reluctant to accept that a party's bad conduct should affect the outcome of a case. At one time the question of whether a party had engaged in bad conduct was highly relevant in divorce cases, custody disputes and financial cases. Nowadays it is rarer to find such explicit blame-finding.[55] In this debate we will consider the extent to which family law is still based, or should be based, on moral judgments.

THE LAW

We will not go through all of the areas where fault is or is not relevant, but will mention here some key examples.

1 *Divorce* At one time divorce was only available on proof of serious misconduct by one's spouse. Nowadays divorce is only available on proof of a non-fault based ground: irretrievable breakdown (see Chapter 8). While it is true that three of the facts that are relied upon are fault-based, following the special procedure (see Chapter 8) where the divorce is undefended there is no effective investigation of the alleged facts and the application is, in essence, done on the paperwork.

2 *Financial Orders* At one time the conduct of the parties could play a major role in the financial orders. A spouse who had behaved 'badly' could expect to have a substantial reduction in the award that they might receive, or an increase in the award if they had behaved particularly well. Since the early 1970s, however, it has been accepted that conduct should only be taken into account where

---

[52] P. Ghandhi and E. MacNamee, 'The Family in UK Law and the International Covenant on Civil and Political Rights' (1991) 5 *International Journal of Law and the Family* 104.

[53] For a wide-ranging discussion on the role of fault in family law see A. Bainham, 'Men and Women Behaving Badly: Is Fault Dead in English Family Law?' (2001) 21 *OJLS* 219.

[54] *Piglowska v Piglowski* [1999] 2 FLR 763.

[55] A. Bainham, 'Men and Women Behaving Badly: Is Fault Dead in English Family Law?' (2001) 21 *OJLS* 219.

it is 'obvious and gross'[56] or (in the words of the statute) where it would be 'inequitable to disregard it'.[57] But what is regarded as conduct that it would be inequitable to disregard? In *Miller v Miller*,[58] the House of Lords rejected the argument that the bad conduct of the husband in committing adultery after just a couple of years of marriage justified increasing the award. In another case, Burton J suggested that to be taken into account the conduct had to be such that to ignore it would produce a 'gasp'.[59] Conduct which only led to a 'gulp' would be insufficient. So the cases where it has been taken into account tend to be of the most serious kind. In *K v K (Financial Provision: Conduct)*[60] the wife helped her depressed husband's suicide attempt as she wished to acquire his estate and to set up a new life with her lover. Her conduct was such that it should be taken into account and her award was reduced from the £14,000 she would have received but for her misconduct to £5,000.[61] In *K v L*[62] the husband sexually abused the wife's grandchildren. The Court of Appeal agreed that this entitled the judge awarding the husband nothing, even though the wife owned property valued at over £4 million. It was explained that his conduct was so appalling and its 'legacy of misery' so profound that a nil award was appropriate.

3   It could also be argued that the fact that the House of Lords or Court of Appeal will only overturn a lower court's decision if it is shown that the judgment was clearly outside the range of decisions that the court could reasonably make is an example of the law's reluctance to impose moral standards.[63] The higher courts will not overturn a ruling simply because it is not the decision that they would have made. A similar attitude may be seen in the courts' encouragement of the parties to reach their own agreement.[64]

4   Baroness Deech[65] makes the controversial point that we have been happy to attach responsibilities and make moral judgments about some areas of life – the environment, diet or smoking – but not, she believes, in relation to intimate family life. That might be questioned. Parents certainly report feeling they are failures.[66] The government has promoted the use of parenting classes and holds

---

[56] *Wachtel v Wachtel* [1973] Fam 72, discussed in G. Douglas, 'Bringing an End to the Matrimonial Post Mortem: *Wachtel v Wachtel* and Its Enduring Significance for Ancillary Relief', in S. Gilmore, J. Herring and R. Probert (eds), *Landmark Cases in Family Law* (Hart Publishing, 2011).

[57] Matrimonial Causes Act 1973, s. 25(2)(g).

[58] [2006] UKHL 24.

[59] *S v S (Non-Matrimonial Property: Conduct)* [2006] EWHC 2793 (Fam).

[60] [1990] FCR 372.

[61] *HM Customs and Excise and another v A* [2002] 3 FCR 481 held that the fact that the husband was a convicted drug dealer was conduct which it was inequitable to ignore.

[62] [2010] EWCA Civ 125.

[63] *Re C (A Minor) (Adoption: Parental Agreement: Contact)* [1993] 2 FLR 260, at p. 273.

[64] E.g. J. Pearce, G. Davis and J. Barron, 'Love in a Cold Climate – Section 8 Applications under the Children Act 1989' [1999] *Family Law* 22.

[65] R. Deech, 'Cohabitation' [2010] *Family Law* 39.

[66] <http://www.telegraph.co.uk/news/uknews/8262695/School-gate-mums-make-each-other-feel-like-failures.html>

parents to account for the truancy and criminal behaviour of their offspring. It is far from clear there is not a moral blaming culture surrounding parenting.

ARGUMENTS IN FAVOUR OF IGNORING MORALITY

There are many good arguments in favour of the law not using moral judgments in its assessments. First, if ever our society was one which had a shared set of moral values, it is difficult to claim that that is still true today.[67] In a society marked with such cultural and religious diversity should the courts start making moral judgments? In doing so they would, inevitably, be reinforcing the moral values of a particular group and seeking to impose them on everyone. This is reflected in the fact that generally our society has become one in which it is regarded as inappropriate to make moral judgments about the ways in which other people live their lives.

Linked to this is the difficult issue of how we determine what the values of society actually are. Andrew Bainham,[68] for example, questions whether it can be said that society accepts that adultery is morally wrong. He argues: 'It seems likely that if we were to concentrate on the practice rather than the theory of matrimonial obligations, at least as strong a case could be made for identifying a community norm of marital infidelity'. Yet if one looks at the results of successive British Social Attitudes surveys over the last 18 years, one finds a consistent proportion – 84–85 per cent – agreeing with the statement that 'extra-marital sex is mostly or always wrong'.[69] Should we judge the values of our society by what people say, or by what individuals do?

Some sociologists believe we are witnessing an increase in individualization, with personal development being a key aspect of people's lives.[70] Elisabeth Beck-Gernsheim explains the individualization thesis in this way:

> On the one hand, the traditional social relationships, bonds and belief systems that used to determine people's lives in the narrowest detail have been losing more and more of their meaning…. New space and new options have thereby opened up for individuals. Now men and women can and should, may and must, decide for themselves how to shape their lives – within certain limits, at least.[71]

In an influential book Antony Giddens has argued that we have seen a move away from the romantic ideal of a relationship for life, the idea that once you have

---

[67] A. Bainham, 'Family Law in a Pluralistic Society' (1995) 23 *Journal of Law and Society* 234, p. 239.

[68] A. Bainham, 'Family Rights in the Next Millennium' (2000) 53 *Current Legal Problems* 471.

[69] S. Duncan and M. Phillips, 'New Families? Tradition and Change in Modern Relationships', in A. Park, J. Curtice, K. Thomson, M. Phillips, M. Johnson and E. Clery (eds) *British Social Attitudes: the 24th Report* (London: Sage, 2008), table 1.1.

[70] See e.g. U. Beck, *Individualization* (Sage, 2000) but see J. Eekelaar, 'Law, Family and Community', in G. Douglas and N. Lowe (eds), *The Continuing Evolution of Family Law* (Family Law, 2009) for a questioning of this.

[71] Beck, *Individualization*, p. iv.

found Mr or Ms Right you stay with them for life. Rather he sees a growth in the pure relationship:

> a situation where a social relation is entered into for its own sake, for what can be derived by each person from a sustained association with another; and which is continued only in so far as is thought by both parties to deliver enough satisfaction for each individual to stay within it.

The growth of individualism is also seen as influencing the development of the law. Alison Diduck writes of:

> the newly important place of the individual in society and, by extension, in families. The autonomous, free-willed individual, the paradigmatic legal subject in the spheres of the market and political and civil society, has now become a part of the sphere of the family, and family law has had to accommodate this intrusion. It thus asserts norms extolling control guilt-free and altruistic relationships based upon love, at the same time as it acknowledges that individual family members have rights and may act in irrational, self-interested ways to claim them.

A second argument is that even if we were in a position to find a collective morality, there is a question whether or not the court is, in practical terms, the right place to make such an assessment. For one thing, there is the difficulty of assessing the evidence. Imagine for a moment it was thought appropriate to make an assessment of who was to blame for the ending of a marriage. Could the court receive the evidence that would be necessary to make such a judgment? Even if it was practically possible it would take so much time and therefore such expense that it would be a hugely uneconomical exercise, especially bearing in mind that one suspects that in most cases the answer would be that both parties were at least partly to blame.

A third point is that even if there was a collective set of moral judgments we may still decide that the courts were an inappropriate place to make those judgments because of their public nature. The courts tend to communicate in terms of an 'order' whereas it may be that a better form of moral judging would take place through a conversation. Also, a court judgment carries with it a huge weight of state authority. In the criminal context it carries the mark of state censure. It must be questioned whether it is appropriate for state-sanctioned blame to be needed, rather than the comments of friends and relatives.

In favour of moral judgments

The first point to make might be said to be a technical one, but it is not. Regan has argued that the law cannot avoid making moral judgments.[72] The view that we should not make moral judgments in the family courts is itself a form of moral judgment. That is not an argument against this approach, but it does highlight

---

[72] M. Regan, *Family Law and the Pursuit of Intimacy* (New York University Press, 1993).

that it should not be imagined that failing to make moral judgments involves a kind of neutrality.[73]

A second point is that the law does still make moral judgments in a whole variety of contexts. Although it is true that certain kinds of moral judgments, especially in terms of sexual behaviour, are no longer made, morality covers a wider range of issues than sex! Naomi Cahn argues that we have seen a shift in the focus of moral values underpinning family law, away from fault, sexuality and privilege, with a new focus on caring, commitment and equality.[74] What we are seeing, and is very welcome, is the shift from 'traditional morality' upholding certain codes of sexual behaviour in particular, to upholding the new 'morality of caring', to use Carol Smart's phrase.[75] This argues that weight should be given to caring practices and what parents do. Indeed, although, there is much more that family law could do, we have already seen in this chapter an argument that a major role for family law should be to facilitate care work and to protect the interests of those undertaking care work.[76] That will involve making moral judgment, in ensuring that there is fairness in care work, but they will be different kinds of judgments than used to be made in the past.

Similarly, if we look at moral obligations towards children, in terms of financial and physical protection, we see a strong line still being taken by the law. The notion of responsibility is a key one in family law.[77] Also, as Bainham argues, the courts are willing to use bad behaviour as evidence of how an individual may behave in the future. So, although a father who has been violent may not be denied contact with his child on the basis that he has behaved immorally, he might be denied contact on the basis that his past bad conduct indicates that he might pose a risk to the child in the future.[78]

Jane Murphy summarizes what she sees as the changes in moral language in this way:

> Contemporary family law has replaced the emphasis on limiting sexual relations to marriage that characterized the fault era with an emphasis on other values – equality, fairness, responsibility for dependent spouses and, most especially, emotional and financial commitment to children. The language of the laws embodying these new values contains fewer explicit references to morality. But, this new discourse – with its emphasis on obligations, protection, duty, and equality – is the language of an expanded meaning of morality informed by the concept of practicing virtues. Individuals lead

---

[73] Regan, *Family Law and the Pursuit of Intimacy.*
[74] N. Cahn, 'The Moral Complexities of Family Law' (1997) 50 *Stanford L Rev* 225.
[75] C. Smart, 'The Legal and Moral Ordering of Child Custody' (1991) 19 *Journal of Law and Society* 485.
[76] P. Laufer-Ukeles, 'Reconstructing Fault: The Case for Spousal Torts' (2010) 79 *U Cin L Rev* 207.
[77] J. Bridgeman, H. Keating and C. Lind, *Responsibility, Law and the Family* (Ashgate, 2008).
[78] A. Bainham, 'Men and Women Behaving Badly: Is Fault Dead in English Family Law?' (2001) 21 *OJLS* 219.

moral lives by meeting their duties, treating others fairly and protecting the vulnerable.[79]

In a similar vein, Helen Reece has written of the emphasis on the 'responsible post-liberal' individual. Her observations, made initially in the context of the Family Law Act 1996, are just as pertinent to some more recent reforms to family law. She explains:

> The responsible post-liberal individual is judged, not by what he does but by how profoundly he has thought about what he does. The old view of responsibility was clear-cut; there just were certain actions that you should or should not take: 'good behaviour is simple. It is about easy things. The choice may be difficult but the distinction is easy. Stealing is wrong; lying is wrong; telling the truth is right.' The new form of responsibility is no longer about discrete decisions – responsible behaviour has shifted to a way of being, a mode of thought. Faced with the decision whether to tell a lie, we can no longer say with confidence that the responsible individual is the one who tells the truth. Now, the individual shows his responsibility by the attitude with which he approaches the decision, the extent to which he reflects on the implications of what he chooses.[80]

The gender implications of Giddens' 'pure' relationship also need to be considered. As Diduck argues:

> the 'self' he assumes seems to be profoundly gendered: the free-moving autonomous individual resembles more closely the lived realities of men, who more easily than women are able to move from one pure relationship to the next in search of self-fulfilment.[81]

Whether one accepts that it is gendered or not, it certainly seems that despite the individualistic account there is still a strong sense of obligation that family ties do generate.[82] John Eekelaar and Mavis Maclean, for example found extensive evidence of a sense of obligation among both married and unmarried couples.[83] What does seem to be changing is the need to formalize these perceived obligations. As Ulrich Beck and Elisabeth Beck-Gernsheim argue. 'Biographies are removed from the traditional precepts and certainties, form external control and

---

[79] J. Murphy, 'Rules, Responsibility and Commitment to Children: The New Language of Morality in Family Law' (1999) 60 *U Pitt L Rev* 1111.

[80] H. Reece, 'Divorcing Responsibly' (2000) 8 *Feminist Legal Studies* 65.

[81] Diduck, *Law's Families*, p. 6.

[82] C. Smart, *Personal Life* (Polity, 2007).

[83] J. Eekelaar and M. Maclean, 'Marriage and the Moral Bases of Personal Relationships' (2004) 31(4) *Journal of Law and Society* 510

general moral laws, becoming open and dependent on decision-making, and are assigned as a task for each individual.'[84]

Interestingly this causes them to suggest that relationships with children are more secure and therefore more important than relationships with adults that come and go.[85]

CONCLUSION

It would probably be impossible to create a family law which was amoral. Even seeking to take a neutral stance between moral arguments, is itself a moral approach. What we have seen in recent years is a change in the kind of moral values that underpin court decisions. Gone have been approaches based on moral blame for 'sinful' conduct and instead an emphasis on the values of responsibility, care and autonomy.

Debate 3

Should resolution of family disputes be left to the individuals involved?

THE LAW

For the past few decades in family law there has been a clear push towards encouraging couples to resolve their disputes for themselves. The current proposals over legal aid will severely restrict access to legal advice, leaving couples with little option but to resolve their disputes themselves. The *Family Justice Review* saw encouraging parties to resolve their disputes themselves as a clear advantage:

> Generally it seems better that parents resolve things for themselves if they can. They are then more likely to come to an understanding that will allow arrangements to change as they and their children change. Most people could do with better information to help this happen. Others need to be helped to find routes to resolve their disputes short of court proceedings.[86]

The routes to resolving disputes include mediation, defined by an earlier government White Paper on divorce reform as 'a process in which an impartial third person, the mediator, assists couples considering separation or divorce to meet together to deal with the arrangements which need to be made for the future'.[87] The core goal in mediation is 'to help separating and divorcing couples to reach their own agreed joint decisions about future arrangements; to improve communications between them; and to help couples work together on the practical

---

[84] U. Beck and G. Beck-Gernsheim, *The Normal Chaos of Love* (Polity Press, 1995), p. 5.
[85] Ibid, p. 35.
[86] D. Norgrave, *Family Justice Review* (Ministry of Justice, 2011), para. 104.
[87] Lord Chancellor's Department, *Looking to the Future: Mediation and the Ground for Divorce* (HMSO, 1995), para 5.4.

consequences of divorce with particular emphasis on their joint responsibilities to co-operate as parents in bringing up their children'.[88] Most mediators hold a screening meeting before starting mediation and if, for example, it becomes clear that there has been serious violence in the past, they will refuse to go ahead with the mediation. Further, if during the course of the mediation the mediator is concerned that one party is being taken advantage of, it is always open to the mediator to stop the mediation and suggest that the parties seek legal advice.[89] Baroness Hale in *Holmes-Moorhouse v Richmond-Upon-Thames London Borough Council*[90] set out the potential advantages of private ordering, whether with the assistance of a mediator or not:

> The reality is that every effort is made, both before and during any family proceedings, to encourage the parents to agree between themselves what will be best for their children. There are many good reasons for this. The parents know their own children better than anyone. They also know their own circumstances, what will suit them best, what resources are available and what they can afford. Agreed solutions tend to work much better and last much longer than solutions imposed by a court after contested proceedings. The contest is likely to entrench opposing viewpoints and inflame parental conflict. Conflict is well known to be bad for children. Not only that, the arrangements made when the couple separate are bound to have to change over time, as the children grow up and their own and their parents' circumstances change. Parents who have been able or helped, through mediation or in other ways, to agree a solution at the outset are more likely to be able to negotiate those changes for themselves, rather than to have to return to court for further orders.

Of course, it would be better for all of us if we could resolve our disputes without litigation, so one might well ask why this argument is specifically used in the context of family law.

Another way in which the law is encouraging the private resolution of family disputes is by giving greater weight to agreements entered into by the parties themselves. *Radmacher v Granatino*[91] (see Chapter 10) indicated that greater weight will be attached to pre-marriage contracts, bringing them closer in line to the enforcement of cohabitation contracts. It would be wrong, however, to think that the law is willing to leave all disputes to the decision of the couple concerned. In *Radmacher v Granatino*, the Supreme Court made it clear that it would not give effect to a contract which was unjust. Similarly, in disputes over the upbringing of children, the courts will rely on assessment of a child's best interests, regardless of the views of the parties.

---

[88] Lord Chancellor's Department, *Looking to the Future*, para 6.17.
[89] The contents of mediation are to be kept privileged and cannot usually be referred to in later proceedings: *DB v PO* [2004] EWHC 2064 (Fam).
[90] [2009] 1 FLR 904, para 31.
[91] [2010] UKSC 42.

Jonathan Herring[92] has suggested three reasons why the government has been keen to encourage couples to resolve their own disputes. First, it ties in well with a commitment to reduce government spending, including a drastic reduction in the legal aid budget. Second, it deflects the ferocious campaigns by groups relating to family law. For example, there has been a strong campaign by fathers' rights groups in relation to contact cases. Encouraging couples to make decisions themselves deflects the criticisms made against the government for not intervening in this area to enhance fathers' rights. Third, there is an assumption that family disputes are 'private matters'. One explanation is that this is a matter of freedom: people should be free to divorce when they wish; couples should be free to contract what agreements they wish; parents should be free to raise their children as they wish.[93]

Arguments in favour

At the heart of the argument in favour of allowing couples to make decisions about their family life is the notion of autonomy. Autonomy at its most simple is a recognition that individuals should be allowed to make decisions for themselves. Joseph Raz defines it in this way:

> The ruling idea behind the ideal of personal autonomy is that people should make their own lives. The autonomous person is a (part) author of his own life. The ideal of personal autonomy is the vision of people controlling, to some degree, their own destiny, fashioning it through successive decisions throughout their lives.[94]

Arguments such as these have led Stephen Cretney to promote what he describes as the principle of private ordering:

> 'Private ordering' is based on the philosophy that individuals should have the right to organise their lives as they wish, free from intervention by the state and by the courts, and that, accordingly, they should have the right to create legal obligations, enforceable by the courts, either in substitution for what the state prescribes as the default option, or to provide for situations in which the state makes no regulatory provision.[95]

Nor is it just at the level of principle that the argument can be made in favour of getting the parties to resolve their own disagreements.

First, there is the issue of cost. In many family disputes, as family lawyers will quickly attest, there is no right answer. The judge can produce one answer, but another judge on another day will produce another. Allowing the parties to reach

---

[92] J. Herring, 'Relational Autonomy and Family Law', in J. Wallbank, S. Choudhry and J. Herring, (eds) *Rights, Gender and Family Law* (Routledge, 2010).

[93] N. Woolcock, 'It's No Nanny State, More an Extended Family, Minister Says', *The Times*, 26 November 2004.

[94] J. Raz, *The Morality of Freedom* (Oxford University Press, 1986), p. 369.

[95] S. Cretney, 'Private Ordering and Divorce – How Far Can We Go?' [2003] *Family Law* 399, p. 399.

their own agreement is likely to produce an answer which is just as good as the one a judge should reach, but at just a fraction of the cost to the state.

Second, encouraging private ordering will allow the couple to use their own moral principles to resolve the issues. As already mentioned in this chapter, our country is divided in terms of the moral and religious values that people hold. Why should a couple not use the values which are important to them and which they live their lives by, rather than have the values of a judge imposed upon them?

Third, couples who are separating often complain that the result reached by the courts does not work in the circumstances of the family. The couple know their family better than anyone else. A one-size-fits-all solution, which the court will typically impose, might work for most families, but not for a particular family. Further, allowing the couple to resolve their own disputes means they can focus on the issues that matter for them. Too often lawyers and judges select the agenda and focus on matters of little relevance to the couple. If the couple are left to resolve their own disputes they can focus on the dispute over who keeps the teddy bear collection, if that is crucial for them, even if to outsiders that seems a trivial matter.

Fourth, and this is an important point, encouraging couples to resolve their disputes themselves encourages the couple to develop their own communication skills. The message of the current law is that if the couple cannot agree they should consult a lawyer and go to court. That is a recipe for bankruptcy for the couple and enrichment for the lawyers! A better message is that couples must learn to resolve these issues alone.

Arguments against

There are several major flaws with the argument in favour of encouraging all couples to sort matters out for themselves. Of course, there are some cases where the couple can easily resolve their dispute and they would be permitted and encouraged to do so. But for the following reasons we should not assume that to be the norm.

First, family law cases are not simply private matters but often involve important social issues. In Chapter 10 we shall see an argument that the form of financial redistribution, if any, on divorce can have major repercussions on decisions about child care during marriage. As Martha Fineman has pointed out in her book *The Autonomy Myth*, care for those who are unable to look after themselves is one of the most important jobs within society. She demonstrates how this care of dependants has been delegated to 'families' and thus been unacknowledged in the public sphere. Women in particular have, as a result, had their crucial societal contribution unrecognized and unrewarded. Fineman thus argues:

> [T]he family in [the traditional 'separate spheres' understanding of society] is positioned as a unique and private arena. I argue that this is an incorrect and unsustainable conception. The family is contained within the larger

society, and its contours are defined as an institution by law. Far from being separate and private, the family interacts with and is acted upon by other societal institutions. I suggest the very relationship is not one of separation, but of symbiosis. It is very important to understand the roles assigned to the family in society – roles that otherwise might have to be played by other institutions, such as the market or the state.[96]

The state, then, has a major interest in what happens to property on divorce because of the practical and symbolic value that is thereby granted to care work. The current law, as we shall see, enables care work in some cases to be recognized and valued in financial orders on divorce. However, that would be lost if financial orders simply became the product of mediation.[97] Hale LJ (as she then was) recognized this clearly in *SRJ v DWJ (Financial Payments)*:

> It is not only in [the child's] interest but in the community's interests that parents, whether mothers or fathers, and spouses, whether husbands or wives, should have a real choice between concentrating on breadwinning and concentrating on home-making and childrearing, and do not feel forced, for fear of what might happen should their marriage break down much later in life, to abandon looking after the home and the family to other people for the sake of maintaining a career.[98]

Similarly, where children are involved there is a hugely important state interest in ensuring that the interests of children are promoted. If we leave issues over children simply to be resolved by agreements between parents we are abandoning children to the decisions of their parents, who may be emotionally wrought and ill-prepared to assess the well-being of children. As already mentioned, there are concerns over whether mediation affects children's interests. As Richards explains:

> ...while mediation may do much to help parents reach agreements and set up workable arrangements for children, it cannot protect children's interests. It must rely on the information about children that the parties bring to the sessions. Necessarily this information will be presented in the light of parental perceptions, hopes, fears, anxieties, and guilt. In most cases this will serve children's interests well enough, but it cannot be termed protection as it is not based on an independent view[99]

A second major issue is that if couples are left to resolve issues between themselves there may be inequality of bargaining power. MacLellan argues that negotiated

---

[96] Fineman, *Autonomy Myth*, p. xviii.
[97] J. Herring, 'Why Financial Orders on Divorce Should Be Unfair' (2005) 19 *International Journal of Law, Policy and the Family* 218.
[98] [1999] 2 FLR 176.
[99] M. Richards, 'But What About the Children? Some Reflections on the Divorce White Paper' [1995] *CFLQ* 223, 225.

agreements are likely to reflect disadvantage to women that is experienced generally in society.[100] He argues:

In a society where power is systematically distributed asymmetrically, contract is likely to reinforce such an asymmetry...inequality of bargaining power means that the construction and enforcement of contracts are likely to be symptoms of such inequality rather than its remedy.[101]

Women, it is argued by some, are by nature, in general, conflict-averse.[102] They may more readily agree rather than argue, partly as a result of being socially conditioned to avoid conflict.[103] It may well be that the wife's primary concern is that she keeps the children, and is willing to agree to anything in order to achieve that goal.[104] One survey of the research concluded that generally women were not putting their own interests first in mediation and therefore were losing out to men, who were.[105] There is some evidence that women are more likely to suffer depression than men at the end of a relationship, and this may also affect their bargaining ability.[106]

It would be wrong to assume that women as negotiators are necessarily inferior to men, but in any couple there may be one party who is more experienced at negotiations (e.g. in the course of their employment), or more knowledgeable about financial affairs or their legal rights, or is simply a more forceful personality. One party may be suffering depression; one may be obsessed with a single issue and not able to negotiate reasonably on other issues; or one may not be convinced that the marriage is over and their hope for a reconciliation may thus impede their bargaining position. There are particular concerns about using mediation where the relationship has been characterized by violence.[107] In such cases mediators themselves accept that mediation is unsuitable because co-operation and proper negotiations can only take place where there is no abuse or fear.[108] The concern is whether the mediators can always ascertain those cases where there has been domestic violence.[109] Particularly difficult are cases where the parties do not regard

---

[100] See also M. Neave, 'Resolving the Dilemma of Difference: A Critique of 'The Role of Private Ordering in Family Law' (1994) 44 *University of Toronto Law Journal* 97.

[101] D. McLellan, 'Contract Marriage – The Way Forward or Dead End?'(1996) 23 *Journal of Law and Society* 234, p. 239.

[102] J. Doughty, 'Identity Crisis in the Family Courts? Different approaches in England and Wales and Australia' (2009) 31 *Journal of Social Welfare and Family Law* 231.

[103] L. Trinder, Firth, A., and C. Jenks, ' "So presumably things have moved on since then?" The management of risk allegations in child contact dispute resolution' (2010) 24 *International Journal of Law, Policy and the Family* 29.

[104] S. Tilley, 'Recognising Gender Differences in all Issues Mediation' [2007] *Family Law* 352.

[105] S. Tilley, 'Recognising Gender Differences in all Issues Mediation' [2007] *Family Law* 352.

[106] A. Bottomley, 'What is Happening to Family Law? A Feminist Critique of Conciliation', in J. Brophy and C. Smart (eds) *Women in Law: Explorations in Law Family and Sexuality* (Routledge and Kegan Paul, 1985); P. Bryan, 'Killing us Softly: Divorce Mediation and the Politics of Power' (1992) 40 *Buff L Rev* 441.

[107] F. Kaganas and C. Piper, 'Domestic Violence and Divorce Mediation' (1994) 16 *Journal of Social Welfare and Family Law* 265.

[108] Where mediators detect a clear imbalance of power which they cannot counter they should terminate the mediation: Law Society, *Code of Practice* (Law Society, 2004), paras 6.2–6.4.

[109] J. Murphy, 'Revitalizing the Adversary System in Family Law' (2010) *U Cin L Rev* 891.

themselves as victims of domestic violence.[110] In a recent study of mediation it was found that mediators used a variety of techniques to put domestic violence issues to one side.[111]

A third concern that arises in relation to mediation specifically is whether it is as neutral as it purports to be.[112] The mediator may influence the discussion by the tone they use in response to proposals and even body language.[113] Piper,[114] in her study of mediation, notes that a mediator's summaries of what has been said during the mediation play a crucial role in the mediation and yet often exclude what the mediator believes to be 'non-relevant matters'.[115] Dingwall and Greatbatch found that mediators had 'the parameters of the permissible',[116] in other words a band of orders they thought acceptable. There would be no intervention as long as the negotiations were within that band, but if the mediation appeared to be going beyond that band the mediator would seek to influence the discussion.[117] If these concerns are at all valid we have the worrying result that, although it appears the parties are reaching the agreement, in effect we are having adjudication by the mediator. Adjudication that is secret, without reasons and lacking accountability.

A further issue surrounds disclosure. Every family lawyer would say that it is common for rich spouses to portray themselves as impoverished. Indeed a large part of a solicitor's job can be to ascertain the true wealth of the other party, through requesting disclosure of the necessary documentation. As mediation has less effective methods of checking levels of wealth compared with disclosure mechanisms used by lawyers, it is likely to work against the interests of the less well-off spouse.

There are also doubts whether mediators have the expertise to consider the complex tax and financial issues which may have to be dealt with on divorce.[118] For many couples the most valuable asset that a couple own is their pension. Yet most couples will not appreciate that, or if they do, will not be able to understand its value or the range of ways a pension might be divided on divorce. Many

---

[110] G. Davis, S. Bevan, G. and Z. Cumming, *Monitoring Publicly Funded Family Mediation* (Legal Services Commission, 2000), p. 5 found that 41per cent of women and 21per cent of men in their sample stated that fear of violence made it difficult to resolve issues in their case.

[111] Trinder, Firth and Jenks, ' "So Presumably Things Have Moved on Since Then?" The Management of Risk Allegations in Child Contact Dispute Resolution'.

[112] R. Dingwall and D. Greatbatch, 'Family Mediators – What Are They Doing?' (2001) 31 *Family Law* 379.

[113] M. Richards, 'Private Worlds and Public Intentions: The Role of the State at Divorce', in A. Bainham, D. Pearl and R. Pickford (eds) *Frontiers of Family Law* (John Wiley & Co, 1995).

[114] C. Piper, 'Norms and Negotiation in Mediation and Divorce' in M. Freeman (ed.) *Divorce: Where Next?* (Dartmouth, 1996).

[115] See also E. Kruk, 'Power Imbalance and Spouse Abuse in Domestic Disputes' (1998) 12 *International Journal of Law, Policy and the Family* 1.

[116] Dingwall and Greatbatch, 'Family Mediators – What Are They Doing?'.

[117] One example given was that the mediator did not mind whether the father saw the children one weekend in three or four, but would not be happy if the father was to have no contact.

[118] Dingwall and Greatbatch, 'Family Mediators – What Are They Doing?'.

solicitors struggle with the complexities of pension sharing, so to assume a couple or mediator can adequately deal with the pension is unrealistic.

It would be wrong to assume that the choice is between mediation and litigation in court.[119] Even in cases involving lawyers, it is very rare for cases to reach court.[120] In a major study by Ingleby not one case in his sample resulted in a contested final hearing.[121] Davis et al. similarly noted:

> ... some solicitors gave us the impression that they regarded trials of the ancillary relief issue in much the same light as they viewed the white rhino – a possibly mythical creature which was outside their immediate experience.[122]

A subsequent study of clients' experiences of solicitors and mediators found no evidence of lawyers as 'aggressive troublemakers'.[123]

A particularly popular form of negotiation through lawyers relies on 'collaborative law'. Lawyers who sign up to this agree to work together to find a solution that works for both parties. It has received judicial endorsement.[124] It has been defined in this way:

> Each person appoints their own lawyer but instead of conducting negotiations between you and your partner by letter or phone you meet together to work things out face to face.
> Each of you will have your lawyer by your side throughout the entire process and therefore you will benefit from legal advice as you go. The aim of collaborative law is to resolve family disputes without going to court.[125]

To some this combines the benefits of mediation with the benefits of having independent legal advice. The difficulty is that it involves legal fees, while paying a single mediator may be seen as cheaper.

Supporters of a lawyer-based approach argue that negotiations between lawyers ensure that the bargaining process is on an equal footing and that values which the law wishes to promote can infiltrate the negotiations. The lawyer also plays an important role in being partisan – being on the side of the client.[126] To many clients, having someone to take their side and fight their corner is of great psychological benefit during the trauma of divorce. Interestingly, of clients who had used both lawyers and mediators in one study, 60 per cent stated that their lawyers had been helpful, but only 35 per cent said this of their mediators.[127] In a further

---

[119] J. Eekelaar, M. Maclean and S. Beinart, *Family Lawyers* (Hart Publishing, 2000).

[120] G. Davis, 'Informing Policy in the Light of Research Findings' (2001) 31 *Family Law* 31, 822.

[121] R. Ingleby, *Solicitors and Divorce* (Oxford University Press, 1992).

[122] G. Davis, S. Cretney, and J. Collins, *Simple Quarrels* (Clarendon Press, 1994).

[123] G. Davis, S. Finch, and R. Fitzgerald, 'Mediation and Legal Services – The Client Speaks' (2001) 31 *Family Law* 110.

[124] *S v P (Settlement by Collaborative Law Process)* [2008] 2 FLR 2040.

[125] Resolution, *Collaborative Family Law* (Resolution, 2011).

[126] Davis, Finch and Fitzgerald, 'Mediation and Legal Services – The Client Speaks'.

[127] G. Davis, S. Clisby, and Z. Cumming, p. 11.

study[128] 67 per cent of those who had divorced said they were satisfied or fairly satisfied with their solicitors; only 22 per cent were dissatisfied or very dissatisfied. The complaints particularly centred on the failure of solicitors to take account of the stressful and emotional aspects of the divorce. Satisfaction with solicitors was notably higher than with mediators.[129] This suggests the attempts to persuade all couples to mediate will not necessarily increase the sum of human happiness.

CONCLUSION

There can be little doubt that the changes to legal aid will lead to a dramatic increase in the use of mediation and a decrease in the amount of legal aid work performed by family lawyers. As the debates in this chapter show, the arguments in favour of doing this are based primarily on encouraging autonomy. However, there are grave concerns that in fact encouraging couples to resolve their own disputes will not give adequate attention to the interests of children or the wider community. Further, that mediation is likely to work in the interests of the stronger party, be that the party with better financial skills, negotiation skills or emotional strength.

Further Reading

A. Bainham, 'Family Law in a Pluralistic Society' (1995) 23 *Journal of Law and Society* 234.
A. Bainham, 'Men and Women Behaving Badly: Is Fault Dead in English Family Law?' (2001) 21 *OJLS* 219.
A. Diduck, *Law's Families* (Butterworths, 2003).
A. Diduck, 'What is Family Law For?' (2011) *Current Legal Problems* 287.
M. Fineman, *The Autonomy Myth* (The New Press, 2004).
J. Herring, 'Relational Autonomy and Family Law', in J. Wallbank, S. Choudhry and J. Herring (eds) *Rights, Gender and Family Law* (Routledge, 2010).
J. Herring, 'Sexless Family Law' (2010) 11 *Lex Familiae* 3.
L. Trinder, A. Firth and C. Jenks, ' " So Presumably Things Have Moved on Since Then?" The Management of Risk Allegations in Child Contact Dispute Resolution' (2010) 24 *International Journal of Law, Policy and the Family* 29.

---

[128] Newcastle Centre for Family Studies, *Picking up the Pieces* (DCA, 2004).
[129] For a more negative view of the relationship between solicitors and clients see C. Wright, 'The Divorce Process: A View from the Other Side of the Desk' (2006) 18 *CFLQ* 93 who finds that clients and solicitors face difficulties in communicating.

2

PARENTS

INTRODUCTION

The question of 'who or what is a parent?' is one that has been the subject of much debate in recent years, largely as the result of developments in assisted reproduction that allow the roles of genetic, gestational and social mother to be split in a way previously confined to the pages of science fiction and fantasy. While it has been possible for biological *parentage* to be decoupled from legal *parenthood*[1] since adoption was first put on a legal footing in 1926, the questions raised by donor insemination, egg donation and surrogacy arrangements are even more complex. A key distinction between them is that the transfer of parenthood in adoption cases rests upon a decision as to the fitness of the individuals concerned, whereas the allocation of parenthood in the context of assisted reproduction depends on strict rules and abstract categories. The allocation – and, perhaps more crucially, the exercise – of parental responsibility in such cases will, however, depend in many cases on judicial evaluation of the family dynamics and the roles played by different individuals.

Assisted reproduction not only raises the question of who should be regarded as the child's parent, but also, from the perspective of a child born from donated gametes, the very practical question of 'who *is* my parent?' Until relatively recently this was a question to which no answer could be supplied, but in 2005 legal policy on donors changed from a position in which only non-identifying information would be available to one in which only those willing to provide identifying information would be allowed to donate. Subsequently, the Human Fertilisation and Embryology Act 2008 was passed, making important changes to the law's concept of parenthood and the ability of some of the parties involved to access various kinds of information about their biological kin.[2] At the same time

---

[1] See e.g. A. Bainham, 'Parentage, Parenthood and Parental Responsibility: Subtle, Elusive Yet Important Distinctions', in A. Bainham, S. Day Sclater and M. Richards (eds), *What Is a Parent? A Socio-Legal Analysis* (Hart Publishing, 1999).

[2] See further C. Jones, 'The Identification of "Parents" and "Siblings": New Possibilities Under the Reformed Human Fertilisation and Embryology Act', in J. Wallbank, S. Choudhry and J. Herring (eds), *Rights, Gender and Family Law* (Routledge, 2009).

the informal use of sperm donors and surrogate mothers *outside* licensed clinics has generated case-law on the role and responsibilities of the parties concerned,[3] as has the far from uncommon situation where the man recorded on the child's birth certificate is not the biological father.

This chapter will look first at the debates on what makes someone a parent in the eyes of the law, and consider the weight that should be attached to biological parentage in the allocation of legal parenthood. It then goes on to look at the debates on the allocation of parental responsibility: there are sharply conflicting views on whether all parents should have parental responsibility, and on who besides legal parents should be entitled to exercise it. Finally, it considers the question of whether a child has a right to knowledge of his or her genetic origins, and – if so – what the law could and should do to ensure that such knowledge is available to those who want it.

Debate

What makes someone a parent: biological or social parenthood?

In recent decades various different models have been put forward to try to provide an overarching test of legal parenthood. Chris Barton and Gillian Douglas, for example, suggested back in 1995 that 'the extent to which legal recognition is given to a person's intention or desire to be regarded as a parent, and to fulfil the functions of a parent, has increased over time, so that it is now the primary test of legal parentage'.[4] They had in mind the examples of adoption, and the provisions of the original legislation in this area, the Human Fertilisation and Embryology Act 1990.

This perhaps does not give sufficient weight to the fact that the cases in which becoming the parent of a child was not intended and perhaps even unwanted are likely to be more numerous than those where parenting is purely based on intention rather than biology: after all, it is estimated that about one-third of conceptions are unplanned. These latter cases could be better accommodated within a 'responsibility' model that identifies as the legal parents those causally responsible for bringing about the birth of a child.[5] This has the advantage of providing a principled explanation for the exclusion of those who donate sperm or eggs, but does not of course include social parents and so cannot be the *sole* test of legal parenthood.

---

[3] See e.g. *R v E and F (Female Parents: Known Father)* [2010] EWHC 417 (Fam); *T v T* [2010] EWCA Civ 1366.

[4] C. Barton and G. Douglas, *Law and Parenthood* (Butterworths, 1995), p. 51. See also J. Hill, 'What Does It Mean to Be a "Parent"? The Claims of Biology as the Basis for Parental Rights' (1991) 66 *NY U L Rev* 353.

[5] See e.g. R. Probert, 'Families, Assisted Reproduction and the Law' (2004) 16 *Child and Family Law Quarterly* 273.

The difficulty of finding one model to fit all rules on the allocation of legal parenthood has been highlighted by Judith Masson, who draws a distinction between parenting by being and parenting by doing.[6] This has the advantage of covering the different situations in which legal parenthood is accorded to different individuals, but is less helpful in resolving those cases where there is more than one candidate for the title of parent. If we have one who is, and one who does, how does the law decide which is to be described as a parent? And why, one might also ask, when parenthood is no longer based exclusively on biological parentage, is it still assumed that there should be no more than two parents?

We will set out the way in which the law currently allocates legal parenthood between competing candidates, and then go on to look at the debates on whether the current law has moved too far away from the biological focus of the common law.

THE LAW

At common law, the position was simple: legal parenthood was determined by biological parentage. While there might be difficulties in proving this, necessitating the use of various presumptions (for example that the mother's husband was the father of her child), the rule itself was not in doubt.

In the context of assisted reproduction, by contrast, matters become a little more difficult. Sperm donors were specifically excluded from legal parenthood,[7] raising the possibility that the child might have no legal father at all. Moreover, the legal mother is no longer necessarily the genetic mother, but rather the woman who gives birth to the child[8] – who may, of course, be doing so as part of a surrogacy arrangement and have no intention to bring up the child. Similarly, while there will be many cases in which the legal father is also the genetic father, the Human Fertilisation and Embryology Act 2008 extended the circumstances in which a social parent would be regarded as a legal parent of the child. It conferred the identity of mother, father, and 'parent' on various actors within the process of creating a child by means of assisted reproduction, and for the first time made it possible for a child to have two legal parents of the same sex from birth.

Under the Act the female civil partner of the mother undergoing treatment will be treated as the parent of the child in the same way as a husband who is not the biological father of the child would be treated as the father of the child.[9] This reflected the government's policy of providing 'same-sex couples who form a civil partnership with parity of treatment in a wide range of legal matters with opposite-sex couples who enter into a marriage'.[10]

---

[6] J. Masson, 'Parenting by Being; Parenting by Doing – In Search of Principles for Founding Families', in J.R. Spencer and A. Du Bois-Pedain (eds), *Freedom and Responsibility in Reproductive Choice* (Hart Publishing, 2006).

[7] See now Human Fertilisation and Embryology Act 2008, s. 41(1).

[8] Ibid, s. 33(1).

[9] Ibid, s. 42.

[10] *Review of the Human Fertilisation and Embryology Act – A Public Consultation*: para. 8.21.

Similarly, a female cohabitant may now acquire the status of parent by satisfying agreed female parenthood conditions just as a male cohabitant becomes a father by satisfying agreed fatherhood conditions. These agreed conditions replaced the old provision under the 1990 Act whereby the male cohabitant of the mother would be deemed the legal father of the child where donated sperm was used 'in the course of treatment services' provided for the man and a woman 'together'.[11] The phrasing of this posed problems, since the level of involvement expected of the man in question was unclear. The 2008 Act therefore tightened the criteria that must be satisfied. The 'agreed fatherhood/ parenthood conditions' require that consent to the man being treated as the father has been expressed by both the man and the mother in a set form and has not been withdrawn prior to the embryo being placed in the mother or the mother being artificially inseminated.[12] After this has occurred, consent cannot be withdrawn by either party (unless of course the treatment proves unsuccessful and a new cycle begins).

Male couples who commission a surrogate mother to bear a child for them may now acquire the status of parents by means of a parental order: such an order may be made on the application of any couple (whether married, civil partners, or 'living as partners in an enduring family relationship'), as long as the gametes of at least one of the parties were used to bring about the creation of an embryo.[13]

The 2008 Act also extended the possibility of social parenthood beyond the grave, following the precedent set by the Human Fertilisation and Embryology (Deceased Fathers) Act 2003. This amended the 1990 Act so that a man could (at the mother's election) be posthumously registered as a child's father, as long as he had consented to the use of his sperm after his death and to being treated as the father of any resulting child.[14] Less obviously, the 2003 Act also allowed a husband or partner who had not provided sperm to be posthumously registered as the child's father as long as they had consented to being so registered. The 2008 Act includes similar provisions[15] and extends them to the civil partner or female cohabitant of the mother.[16] It is now possible, therefore, for an earlier female cohabitant of a woman to be accorded post-mortem status as the legal parent of a child she never bore or knew.

Much of the debate in this area has focused on the challenge of deciding between competing candidates for the status of parent. A child might, however, have only *one* parent in the eyes of the law as a result of the provisions outlined above. The initial provisions of the 1990 Act directed clinics to consider the child's need for a father in deciding whether to provide treatment; the 2008 Act

---

[11] Human Fertilisation and Embryology Act 1990, s. 28(3). However, this provision remains applicable to conceptions that took place prior to 6 April 2009.
[12] Human Fertilisation and Embryology Act 2008, s. 37.
[13] Ibid, s. 54(1)(b).
[14] Human Fertilisation and Embryology Act 1990, s. 28(5A) and (5B).
[15] Human Fertilisation and Embryology Act 2008, s. 40.
[16] Ibid, s. 46.

amended this so that clinics will now have to consider the need for 'supportive parenting'.[17] But there is no *requirement* that the child should have a second parent of either sex.

Criticisms of separating parenthood from biology

It was noted by the Joint Committee that considered the provisions of the draft Bill that became the Human Fertilisation and Embryology Act 2008 that the Bill 'seeks to take a new approach to parenthood, moving towards the concept of parenthood as a legal responsibility rather than a biological relationship.'[18] These changes have been welcomed by many, and deplored by others. One of the more thoughtful and sustained criticisms comes from Andrew Bainham, who has questioned whether the provisions of the 2008 Act are consistent with the emphasis elsewhere in this area of the law on biological truth. He argues that legal parenthood should be coterminous with biological parentage, and that the role of social parents should be reflected via a grant of parental responsibility rather than by the allocation of legal parenthood,[19] even if this does not satisfy their desire for status.[20]

One head-on challenge to this argument is that legal parenthood need not be linked to biological parentage at all. It would be possible to have a simple register of genetic origins that by itself conferred no rights or responsibilities. Nor is the link between biological parentage and legal parenthood always an obvious one. Emily Jackson has pointed out that 'it is not necessarily self-evident whether the genetic mother or the woman who gives birth is properly described as the child's mother' and that '[i]f parenthood is not a fact waiting to be discovered, we are going to have to make some decisions about the relative importance of various different aspects of motherhood and fatherhood'.[21]

A further counterargument is that a child's biological inheritance is a more complex matter than is sometimes appreciated. Johnson, for example, has noted the impact of not only genetics but gestation (in that the mother's diet and behaviour during and even before pregnancy will have an impact on the child's development) and even post-natal contributions. He contends that 'the pervasive, and at times misplaced, emphasis on genetics in modern culture is driving an unbalanced overly genetic view of parenthood as dominant'.[22]

---

[17] Human Fertilisation and Embryology Act 1990, s. 13(5), as amended.
[18] *Joint Committee on the Human Tissue and Embryos (Draft Bill) – First Report* (2006–7), HL 169-I/ HC 630-I, para. 263.
[19] A. Bainham, 'Arguments about Parentage' (2008) 67 *CLJ* 322.
[20] A. Bainham, 'Status Anxiety? The Rush for Family Recognition', in F. Ebtehaj, B. Lindley and M. Richards (eds), *Kinship Matters* (Hart Publishing, 2006), p. 58.
[21] E. Jackson, 'What Is a Parent?' in A. Diduck and K. O'Donovan, *Feminist Perspectives on Family Law* (Routledge-Cavendish, 2006), p. 67.
[22] M. Johnson, 'A Biomedical Perspective on Parenthood', ch. 3 in A. Bainham, S. Day Sclater and M. Richards (eds) *What Is a Parent?* p. 49.

The different influences that shape us are considered further below, but before examining them we should turn to Callus' criticism of the provisions of the 2008 Act. Her suggestion is that they are perpetuating a deception:

> By recognising the status of two female parents, the child's identity is thrown into disarray because the recognition of two female parents conceals the necessary heterosexual element of human existence.[23]

But in terms of the child's *identity*, will the fact that two females are recorded on the birth certificate have an impact above and beyond that of being brought up by two women? Moreover, the language of deception and concealment assumes the possibility that anyone will be deceived. The very fact that the conception of a child requires both male and female gametes is assurance that the discrepancy between legal parenthood and biological parentage cannot be concealed in this context. And finally, the birth certificate will not record two female parents, it will record the child's mother and the child's parent, thus clearly differentiating biological and social parents.

This is not to say that knowledge of one's biological origins is not important, merely that recording a lesbian co-parent as a parent is not incompatible with that aim. In fact, it is the labelling of the mother's husband or partner as 'father' despite his lack of biological relatedness that perhaps should be questioned. Callus acknowledges that this too can lead to deception: the evidence is that it often *does* lead to deception. Most heterosexual couples whose child was conceived as a result of donor insemination (DI) do not disclose the fact to the children, even if they have been encouraged to do so by the clinic.[24]

Despite the proliferation of the ways in which it is possible to become a parent, no child can have more than two legal parents. To this extent the biological model still constrains the legal imagination. So, for example, if the woman receiving treatment is in a civil partnership, she cannot agree that anyone other than her civil partner is to be the other parent of her child. Where she is not a party to a formal relationship, her consent to a certain person being treated as a parent of the child will override any earlier consent relating to a different person, assuming that it was given before the embryo was placed in her or artificial insemination carried out. Emily Jackson has criticized the insistence that a child can only have two legal parents, arguing that:

> Transparency and descriptive accuracy demand that the law relinquish its principle of parental exclusivity in favour of a model of parenthood that is capable of accommodating its social and technical fragmentation.[25]

---

[23] T. Callus, 'First "Designer Babies", Now *À La Carte* Parents' [2008] *Family Law* 143, 146.

[24] E. Lycett, K. Daniels, R. Curson and S. Golombok, 'School-Aged Children of Donor Insemination: A Study of Parents' Disclosure Patterns' (2005) 20 *Human Reproduction* 810, 818.

[25] Jackson, 'What Is a Parent?' ch 4 in Diduck and O'Donovan (eds), *Feminist Perspectives on Family Law*, p. 74.

We should therefore consider the debate as to whether the law should confer legal parenthood on social parents not only in terms of the justifications for the current law, but also in terms of whether the law should in fact go further and recognize a wider range of social parents.

Should we confer legal parenthood on social parents?
We will focus here on the position of the partner who is involved in the parenting process from the start. Why should the infertile husband or the female partner of the mother be classified as the parent of the resulting child?

The law has, of course, long been willing to ascribe parenthood to men who may not be the biological father of their supposed child. But the novelty of conferring legal parenthood on female partners should not obscure the basic similarity between the two situations. As a matter of logic, the female partner who accompanies the would-be mother to the clinic where the fertility treatment is to be carried out is plays exactly the same role as the infertile husband or cohabitant. Neither has a biological link to the child; each intends to be a parent to the child. While the presumption that a husband was the father of his wife's child was based on an inference as to the most likely state of affairs, its application in some fairly unlikely situations indicates that likelihood was not the sole determinant.

There are three arguments that may be put forward to justify the imposition of legal parenthood on a social parent: wishes, reality, and legal consequences.

Wishes
Using the term 'parent' is more likely to resonate with the views of the parties involved, whether biological or social parents. Caroline Jones, interviewing lesbian couples before the Human Fertilisation and Embryology Act (HFEA) 2008, noted their concern regarding the co-mother's lack of status under the law as it then stood.[26] Leanne Smith similarly found that lesbian parents made a clear distinction between 'mother' and 'parent', but also between *father* and parent. In their view, the mother's partner was not a mother, but she was a parent; the father, by contrast, was not a parent.[27] Another study of a group of embryo donation parents – i.e. couples within which neither party was genetically related to the child – found that they were significantly different from adoptive parents: the latter knew and had some ongoing relationship with the birth parents, while the former gave the donors little thought and were happy not to know any more about them.[28]

What of the donors themselves? Richards, writing before the change in the law on anonymity, noted that donated gametes tended to be regarded solely as biological tissue and 'not accorded with the symbolic properties that those

---

[26] C. Jones, 'Parents in Law: Subjective Impacts and Status Implications around the Use of Licensed Donor Insemination', ch. 5 in Diduck and O'Donovan, *Feminist Perspectives on Family Law*, p. 74.

[27] L. Smith, 'Is Three a Crowd? Lesbian Mothers' Perspectives on Parental Status in Law' [2006] 18 *Child and Family Law Quarterly* 231.

[28] F. MacCallum, 'Embryo Donation. Parents' Attitudes towards Donors: Comparison with Adoption' (2009) 24 *Human Reproduction* 517.

conceived with them are likely to perceive'.[29] Nor does the evidence suggest that different attitudes are found among those who donate knowing that there is a possibility that they will one day be contacted by donor-conceived offspring. A West Australian study of potential sperm donors who responded to a newspaper advertisement found that a high proportion – 78 per cent – were content for non-identifying information to be revealed; almost half – 49 per cent – thought that children born from sperm donation should be told about the manner of their conception and a slightly smaller proportion – 44.5 per cent – thought that such children should have the right to receive identifying information upon achieving adulthood. But only 22 per cent said that they would be interested in meeting a child that had been conceived using their sperm, and 40 per cent of these envisaged that contact would be a one-off event. On the basis of this study at least, then, there is no evidence that those who donate in the knowledge that their identity may someday be revealed regard themselves as the 'real father' or desire a future relationship with the child.[30]

This casts a rather different light on Bainham's argument that under the current law 'the biological father drops out of the legal picture as do everyone in what would have been the paternal family'. It would seem that the sperm donor was never really envisaged as being *in* the picture; similarly, one might question whether being related to someone who donated sperm is really constitutive of 'family' relations. After all, the genetic tie is not necessarily sufficient to create 'family life' for the purposes of the European Convention on Human Rights.[31]

And what of the children? Here, of course, opinions vary. Some donor-conceived children do regard the biological parent as the *real* parent. Tom Ellis, a donor-conceived person who gave evidence to the Joint Committee, argued that the terminology of parent should not be used to refer to a social parent. But this depends on what we understand by the term 'parent'. An interesting distinction was drawn in one study of Australian adolescents who were not donor-conceived, who were interviewed as to the values underpinning the process: 'Some maintained the "fact" of genetic antecedence as defining a "real" father, although consensus was achieved in all discussions that a *parent* was the one who raised and loved the child.'[32] Identifying a person involved in bringing up the child as a parent is not incompatible with recognizing and valuing the genetic contribution of the biological father.

So the classification of the social parent as a parent is in line with the views not just of the adult parties but also, one might argue, the children.

---

[29] M. Richards, 'Assisted Reproduction and Parental Relationships', ch. 15 in A. Bainham, B. Lindley, M. Richards and L. Trinder (eds) *Children and Their Families: Contact, Rights and Welfare* (Hart Publishing, 2003), p. 303.

[30] K. M. Godman, K. Sanders, M. Rosenberg and P. Burton, 'Potential Sperm Donors', Recipients' and Their Partners' Opinions towards the Release of Identifying Information in Western Australia' (2006) 21 *Human Reproduction* 3022.

[31] See e.g. *Lebbink v The Netherlands* [2004] 2 FLR 463.

[32] M. Kirkman, D. Rosenthal and L. Johnson, 'Families Working It Out: Adolescents' Views on Communicating about Donor-Assisted Conception' (2007) 22 *Human Reproduction* 2318.

Reality

Of course, there is an argument that the law should respond to reality rather than reflecting the parties' own definitions of their situation. Eekelaar, for example, has noted that '[t]he modern quest for authenticity is associated with openness about the physical facts of one's birth rather than constructed legal truths'.[33] But what is the reality of the situation? One could reverse the question 'what is a parent?' and ask 'what is a child?' Are we simply the product of our genetic heritage, or are we shaped by our environment, by the values and practices of those that bring us up? The debate as to how far we are shaped by nature and how far by nurture is a long-standing one, but it is clear that the care that a child receives, particularly in the early years, will have an important impact on his or her development.

Gerhardt, for example, describes a baby as 'incomplete' or 'an interactive project', and points out that the infant's relationships with others will affect not only their reactions to social events but the very development of the brain, since the 'orbitofrontal cortex, which is so much about being human, develops almost entirely post-natally'.[34] As she puts it: 'Babies are like the raw material for a self. Each one comes with a genetic blueprint and a unique range of possibilities.'[35] Those who care for us in our early years make an important contribution to who we are. As the novelist A.M. Homes, who was adopted as a baby, put it: I am a product of each of my family narratives – some more than others. But in the end it is all four threads that twist and rub against one another, the fusion and friction combining to make me who and what I am. And not only am I a product of these four narratives – I am also influenced by another narrative; the story of what it is to be the adopted one, the chosen one, the outsider brought in.[36]

The counterargument that the law should reflect the truth is a powerful one. But there are different layers of truth. The love and care that a social parent may provide for a child is just as true as the child's genetic heritage from an unknown donor. In short, it can be argued that to reflect reality the law also needs to reflect the contribution of those who care for the child in its early years.

Legal consequences

It should also be borne in mind that to confer legal parenthood is not simply to confer rights on the parent; it also confers very significant responsibilities. One could argue that the social parent acquires the right to inherit from the child, but in most cases this is going to be a rather illusory right. More relevant will be the parent's responsibility to support the child, should the relationship with the mother or father break down – a responsibility that benefits both the state and the child. And other family relationships flow from the fact of parenthood – for example, the parent's own parents are the child's grandparents – thus cementing the relationship of the child within this wider network of kin.

---

[33] J. Eekelaar, *Family Law and Personal Life* (Oxford University Press, 2007), pp. 70–71.
[34] S. Gerhardt, *Why Love Matters: How Affection Shapes a Baby's Brain* (Routledge, 2004), p. 37.
[35] Ibid, p. 18.
[36] A.M. Homes, *The Mistress's Daughter: A Memoir* (Granta Books, 2007), p. 234.

This emphasis on that particular type of responsibility suggests why parental responsibility alone might not be sufficient. One argument that might convince those who fear that recognizing social parents endangers the family is that to use the terminology of parent is to send a message about the responsibilities of the other party. Of course, it would be possible to use the mechanism of a joint residence order to confer parental responsibility on that other. But parental responsibility granted in such a way can be lost upon the revocation of the order. Its continuance after the relationship between the adults has come to an end may depend to a great extent on whether the social parent wishes to retain a relationship with the child. Parental responsibility may be appropriate for the partner of a parent who arrives on the scene long after the child was born, who does not make the same commitment to the child. But in the context of the HFEA we are not talking about a person who simply happens to be caring for the child, we are talking about someone who has engaged in the process of bringing about the birth of the child, who has agreed that they will be the legal parent of the child.

It might be straining language to describe them as responsible for the birth of that child – but if one thinks of responsibility in prospective, rather than causative terms, that person has certainly indicated willingness to assume responsibility for the child. This is far clearer under the HFEA 2008 than it was under the old law, with the shift from being 'treated together' with the mother to agreed fatherhood conditions – or agreed female parenthood conditions. A parallel would be the ancient status of god-parent, who at the child's baptism makes a vow before God to ensure that the child is brought up in a particular manner. The agreed fatherhood conditions, or the agreed female parenthood conditions, could be seen as the modern secular alternative.[37]

Given the evidence as to the attachments that a child makes in infancy, that person is likely to be an important figure in the life of the child. In Gabb's study of 18 households involving lesbian couples and children, one adolescent clearly missed his mother's previous partner, and felt sad that the relationship was now one of friendship rather than a parent–child relationship.[38] Granting parenthood to that person is both a message that they are making a lifelong commitment to the child and a guarantee that responsibility will continue even if the relationship with the mother or father has come to an end.

The issue of who else should have that responsibility will be considered later; before doing so, however, we need to consider the more difficult question of how social parents who fall outside the scope of the HFEA should be treated.

How should social parents outside the licensed clinic be treated?

Where the mother is in a formal relationship with either a man or a woman, then it matters not whether the treatment takes place in a licensed clinic or not:

---

[37] Although the analogy is not exact, as the role of god-parents was to support rather than supplant the biological parents.

[38] J. Gabb, 'Lesbian M/Otherhood: Strategies of Familial-linguistic Management in Lesbian Parent Families' (2005) 39 *Sociology* 585.

the husband will be the father of the child, or the civil partner the other parent, unless it is shown that he or she did not consent to the treatment.[39] Outside such formal relationships, however, matters become more difficult.

At present it is possible that a male partner of the mother will be registered as the father even though he is not, either because he believes that he is the father or because the couple have agreed to bring up the child as if he were the father. Of course, if it is later established that he is not in fact the father of the child, then the register can be amended; his name would be removed and that of the biological father inserted.

There is of course no such option for the female co-parent of the mother to be registered. Given that many lesbian couples prefer informal arrangements to those organized through a clinic – Dunne, for example, in her study of 37 households involving lesbian couples and children, found that 75 per cent of households had children conceived as a result of donor insemination, and that 86 per cent of these had occurred outside a licensed clinic[40] – this means that there are many more children born to couples where at present there is no scope for the co-parent to be recognized as a parent.

If conferring the status of parent on such women in the context of assisted reproduction is regarded as justifiable because it reflects reality and encourages responsibility (and requires responsibility in the narrow sense of financial liability), then do the same arguments apply to births that occur without the assistance of a licensed clinic? One argument in favour of distinguishing the two situations might be that there is no official assumption of responsibility where the child is conceived outside the framework of the HFEA, no opportunity to sign agreed fatherhood/parenthood conditions. The partner of the mother may well have provided care and support throughout the latter's pregnancy, but cannot be seen as assuming any responsibility for the future child. Difficult questions might also arise where there has been a turnover of partners: should the legal parent be the mother's partner at the time of conception or the time of birth? Moreover, if it is the partner's role in bringing up the child that is relied upon as a justification of parenthood, why should not later partners also acquire that status?

The fact that difficult questions arise does not mean that there is no answer. It would be possible to devise a system whereby couples register their intention to parent before embarking on the process, and are then entitled to register the birth of the child jointly. Given current developments in this area, this is not as radical as it might sound: the courts have shown themselves willing to confer parental responsibility on a lesbian co-parent through the medium of a joint residence order, and to protect what has been described as the 'homo-nuclear' family from undue interference by the biological father.[41]

---

[39] Human Fertilisation and Embryology Act 2008, ss. 35 and 42 respectively.
[40] G. Dunne, 'Opting in to Motherhood: Lesbians Blurring the Boundaries and Transforming the Meaning of Parenthood' (2000) 14 *Gender and Society* 11.
[41] See e.g. *R v E and F (Female Parents: Known Father)* [2010] EWHC 417 (Fam); *Re B (Role of Biological Father)* [2007] EWHC 1952 (Fam).

CONCLUSION

It will be clear from the preceding discussion that there is a vigorous debate about the appropriate allocation of legal parenthood, and the intention has been to set out the different positions rather than advance any particular view. The debate shows the importance of terminology as well as status: perhaps, rather than talking about parents, or about mothers and fathers, we should couch these debates in terms of gestators, progenitors and carers, to refocus attention on the specific contribution each has made or will make.[42]

There is, however, one advantage of the responsibility model that should be noted. By explaining the allocation of legal parenthood in terms of responsibility rather than intention, we move family law away from the wishes of the adults towards a commitment to the child. Couching social parenthood in terms of that person's willingness to assume responsibility for the child is subtly different from the intention model. Intentions can change; responsibilities will not. The problem with the intention model is that it treats the child as a commodity; it is the adult's intention to be a parent that is determinative. It also implies that the parent can intend not to be a parent and thus not take on the responsibility.[43] The responsibility model puts the child back at the heart of the process. It signals that it is, as Samuel Butler once put it, a monstrous freedom to bring a human being into the world,[44] and that the decision to do so carries with it important legal and social consequences.

Debate 2

Who should get parental responsibility?

THE LAW

Under the current law, the only persons who have parental responsibility from the time of the child's birth are the mother and (if he is married to her) the father. A father who is not married to the mother can acquire parental responsibility by registering the birth jointly with her, marrying her, entering into a parental responsibility agreement with her, or applying to the court for a parental responsibility order. A step-parent (whether by marriage or civil partnership) may also acquire parental responsibility by a parental responsibility agreement (which will need the consent of all parents with parental responsibility) or by a parental responsibility order. The transfer of legal parenthood (e.g. by adoption or parental order) also operates to end the parental responsibility of the birth parents and confer it upon the adoptive parents. Any other individuals – including the unmarried partner of

---

[42] See further J. Shapiro, 'Changing Ways, New Technologies and the Devaluation of the Genetic Connection to Children' in M. Maclean (ed.), *Family Law and Family Values* (Hart Publishing, 2005), p. 90.
[43] See e.g. G. Douglas, 'The Intention to Be a Parent and the Making of Mothers' (1994) 57 *MLR* 636, 640.
[44] S. Butler, *Erewhon* (1872).

a parent[45] – can only acquire parental responsibility if a residence order is made in their favour.

Should all fathers have parental responsibility?

The main focus of the debate has been whether fathers who are not married to the mother should have parental responsibility automatically, rather than, as now, needing to take steps to acquire it.

As long ago as 1979 the Law Commission advocated removing all distinctions affecting children born outside marriage, which would have had the result of conferring parental rights (in the terminology of the time) on all fathers, regardless of their relationship with the mother.[46] In the debate that followed, the focus was very much on the relationship between the father and the mother, with concern being expressed that vulnerable mothers and those who had entered into new relationships might be harassed and distressed by the father being able to exercise parental responsibility, and that the likely outcome was an increase in the number of mothers who would refuse to identify the father of their child.[47] The Commission therefore revised its recommendations, with the result that fathers not married to the mother had to take active steps to acquire parental responsibility.[48]

The reasons given by the Law Commission for not conferring parental responsibility on all parents automatically have been described as 'parent-centred' and did not convince its Scottish counterpart.[49] Andrew Bainham similarly argued that it was erroneous to identify the best interests of the child with the wishes of the mother in this way, and suggested that:

> A better approach to the whole matter would be to start from the optimistic position that full parenthood should arise from proof of paternity but to accept that it would be necessary for this to be judicially removed in those cases in which it can be demonstrated that the father is unfit to be involved with the child.[50]

Even this, it should be noted, acknowledges that it may be necessary to remove parental responsibility from some fathers. The shadowy but threatening figure of the rapist-father loomed large in the parliamentary debates, and Bainham noted that 'a specific statutory exception could be created excluding convicted rapists from the status of parenthood'.[51]

---

[45] See e.g. *T v T* [2010] EWCA Civ 1366.

[46] Law Commission, *Illegitimacy*, WP No. 74 (HMSO, 1979).

[47] Law Commission, *First Report on Illegitimacy*, Law Com. No. 118 (HMSO, 1982).

[48] For commentary see A. Bainham, 'The Illegitimacy Saga', in R. Probert and C. Barton (eds) *Fifty Years in Family Law: Essays for Stephen Cretney* (Intersentia, 2012).

[49] For discussion see N. Lowe, 'The Meaning and Allocation of Parental Responsibility – A Common Lawyer's Perspective' (1997) 11 *International Journal of Law, Policy and the Family* 192, 200.

[50] A. Bainham, 'When Is a Parent Not a Parent? Reflections on the Unmarried Father and His Child in English Law' (1989) 3 *International Journal of Law and the Family* 208, 232.

[51] Ibid, 231.

So the issue in debate can be narrowed to the question of whether fathers need to take steps to acquire parental responsibility, or whether the onus should be on the mother (or perhaps the state) to show why a particular father should not have parental responsibility.

One way of approaching the debate is to look at the problems with the current ways of acquiring parental responsibility. Jens Scherpe has noted that the central role of the mother – whose consent is necessary for the father to acquire parental responsibility by birth registration or parental responsibility agreement – does not necessarily serve the purpose of ensuring that undeserving fathers do not acquire parental responsibility, since 'her criteria for making her decision will not necessarily be based on what is in the best interest of the child'.[52] Nor, indeed, does the fact that parental responsibility is accorded to those fathers who are married to the mother of their child necessarily ensure that no undeserving fathers acquire it. Equally problematically, when one examines the justifications given by the courts for making parental responsibility orders, the fact that there appears to be 'no clear and consistent position on the allocation of parental responsibility'[53] reinforces the case for side-stepping such debates altogether and conferring parental responsibility on all fathers automatically.

Another way of approaching the issue would be to note the existing options for constraining the inappropriate exercise of parental responsibility. If parental responsibility were to be conferred on all fathers automatically, doubtless this would include some that the law would regard as unfit to exercise it, but the possibility of imposing conditions or obtaining orders to constrain its misuse reduces any potential risk to the child.[54] Moreover, given that most applications for parental responsibility orders are granted – over 90 per cent in 2010, with most of the remainder being withdrawn rather than rejected – it would arguably be more cost-efficient to require action to be taken to divest unmeritorious fathers of parental responsibility than require the meritorious to take steps to acquire it. This is not, however, unproblematic, since those mothers who might need to take steps to constrain the father's parental responsibility may be the very ones who are most vulnerable and least equipped to take legal proceedings.

A further argument in favour of conferring parental responsibility on all fathers is that this would be consistent with the UK's obligations under international human rights conventions. Attempts have already been made by disgruntled fathers to argue that the current law is in breach of their right to private and family life under the European Convention on Human Rights, and discriminates against them on the basis of their sex and marital status. Such arguments have, however,

---

[52] J. Scherpe, 'Establishing and Ending Parental Responsibility: A Comparative View', in Probert, Gilmore and Herring (eds) *Responsible Parents and Parental Responsibility*, p. 56.

[53] S. Gilmore, 'Parental Responsibility and the Unmarried Father – A New Dimension to the Debate' [2003] *Child and Family Law Quarterly* 21, 38.

[54] See e.g. *B v A, C and D (Acting By Her Guardian)* [2006] EWHC 2 (Fam); H. Reece, 'The Degradation of Parental Responsibility', in Probert, Gilmore and Herring (eds) *Responsible Parents and Parental Responsibility*.

B v UK

been rejected by the European Court of Human Rights, which held that distinctions between mothers and fathers, and between fathers who are married to the mother and those who are not, can be justified. Emphasis was placed on the wide range of circumstances in which a child might be conceived outside marriage.[55] Moreover, the fact that English law did provide some means for a father to acquire parental responsibility meant that there was no breach of the right to respect for private and family life.

More specific is Article 18(1) of the UN Convention on the Rights of the Child, which requires State Parties to '[u]se their best efforts to ensure recognition of the principle that both parents have common responsibilities for the upbringing and development of the child'. However, as Nigel Lowe has noted, although this strongly suggests that the law should treat mothers and fathers equally in this respect, the lack of any sanctions should the UK be in breach has reduced its impact on the development of the law.[56]

In any case, the phrasing of the article hints at the limitations of the law: the state will never be able to ensure that *every* child's parents assume responsibility for his or her upbringing and development. The number of fathers who are positively unfit to exercise parental responsibility may be relatively small, to judge from the number of applications that are rejected by the courts, but the number who are simply uninterested is likely to be considerably larger. When hearing applications for parental responsibility orders, the courts have emphasized the value to the child of knowing 'that their father was concerned enough to make an application to be recognised as their father, and that his status as their father has the stamp of the court's approval'.[57] It is less clear that children will benefit from knowing that their father has parental responsibility if it is never exercised in practice. Nor, it should be noted, can it be assumed that granting parental responsibility to all fathers would encourage them to take responsibility. As Sally Sheldon has noted:

> On balance, it seems rather improbable that a status of which the vast majority of the population has remained demonstrably in ignorance, which accords limited advantages and which gives no right to contact with children is likely to have much influence on men's commitment towards parenting.[58]

Yet it could be argued that debates about whether or not fathers are deserving or disinterested rather misses the point. Surely the key question is: why are they treated differently to mothers? The fact that the mother has undergone pregnancy is obviously a reason for granting her parental responsibility, but it is, it should be noted, a reason rooted in biology rather than her capacity to parent the child satisfactorily. A mother who abuses drugs and alcohol may harm her unborn child

---

[55] *B v UK* [2000] 1 FLR 1.
[56] Lowe, 'The Meaning and Allocation of Parental Responsibility – A Common Lawyer's Perspective', 202.
[57] *Re M (Contact: Family Assistance: McKenzie Friend)* [1999] 1 FLR 75.
[58] S. Sheldon, 'Unmarried Fathers and Parental Responsibility: A Case for Reform?' (2001) 9 *Feminist Legal Studies* 93, 107.

far more significantly than the father has the power to do, but she still has parental responsibility when the child is born.

However, one weakness of the arguments in favour of conferring parental responsibility on all fathers automatically is that they tend to be couched in terms of equality between parents, rather than on the basis of a father's positive contribution to the welfare of his child. Julie Wallbank has noted that this reflects 'the ethics of justice and fairness as opposed to the ethics of care'.[59] Indeed, it is those arguing against any automatic acquisition of parental responsibility who invoke the empirical evidence to show that mothers continue to be the main care-givers. Sheldon, for example, makes the point that:

> whilst it is reasonable to make an assumption that women should get automatic P.R. – on the basis of the demonstrably high probability that they will be primary carers and thus in a better position to make important decisions regarding the child's welfare – rather more research is necessary before it is possible to make the same assumption regarding any category of fathers.[60]

Of course, if this argument were taken to its logical conclusion, then the starting point of the law might be that no father, whether married to the mother or not, should have parental responsibility automatically. But requiring a father to show his active involvement in the child's upbringing and development as a prerequisite for acquiring parental responsibility would pose difficulties, not least in deciding when such an application could be made. How many nappies would a father have to change, how many night-time feeds would he have to provide, before qualifying? The fact that the allocation of parental responsibility currently tends to occur at a very early stage in the child's life means that the focus has to be on the father's intentions (as indicated by his marriage to the mother, willingness to be identified on the birth register, or specific agreement) rather than on what he actually does. Of course, it does not necessarily have to be this way – parental responsibility could be extended at a later date – but the idea of 'earning' parental responsibility in this way sits a little uneasily with the courts' insistence that parental responsibility is not 'a reward for the father, but an order which should only be made in the best interests of [the child]'.[61]

This leads on to a further element of the debate: what would automatically conferring parental responsibility on all fathers actually achieve? When the last government published its proposals for mechanisms to encourage joint registration of births, it was clearly hoped that the fact of registration would bring about a greater sense of responsibility. Indeed, the initial Green Paper was entitled *Joint Birth Registration: Promoting Parental Responsibility*, and the subsequent White Paper expressed the hope that joint birth registration would bring about 'a wider

Welfare Reform Act 2009

---

[59] J. Wallbank, 'Clause 106 of the Adoption and Children Bill: Legislation for the "Good" Father?' [2002] *Legal Studies* 277, 279.

[60] Sheldon, 'Unmarried Fathers and Parental Responsibility: A Case for Reform?', 104.

[61] *Re M (Contact: Parental Responsibility)* [2001] 2 FLR 342, FD, at 365–66.

Eekelaar; some ppl w/o PR act more like prats they those who actually do have it.

cf factual receipts of of state of affr

stamp of pp approval

cultural shift so that more fathers see their child as their responsibility'.[62] That joint registration will confer parental responsibility is clear; that it will encourage responsible parenting less so. While the government pointed out that in 45 per cent of those cases where the birth was registered by the mother alone, the father had regular contact with the child, this simply serves to underline the fact that joint registration is not a prerequisite for a parental relationship. The more pertinent questions are surely: in how many of the other 55 per cent of cases would contact be established if the birth was registered jointly, and in how many cases of joint registration does the father cease to have contact with the child?

It is also significant that these proposals emanated not from the Department for Children, Schools and Families but from the Department for Work and Pensions. They were very clearly linked to one specific manifestation of responsible parenting, namely the payment of child support/maintenance. This leads us on to a further point of debate: should parental responsibility be linked to the payment of child maintenance? Three different perspectives can be identified. The first is the broad argument that if all legal fathers have the obligation to pay child support, then it is only right that they should also have parental responsibility. The second focuses on the individual father, and takes the view that a father who does not pay child support does not deserve parental responsibility. The third is the converse of this, being that an undeserving father should not be able to buy parental responsibility by paying child maintenance. *Herring*

In examining the different arguments that have been put forward, it is worth bearing in mind that most new fathers, whether married to the mother or not, *do* now have parental responsibility. The majority of births outside marriage are to cohabiting couples, and all but a handful of such couples register the birth jointly.[63] High rates of joint registration were also observed among those who were closely involved with, or alternatively separated or divorced from the father.

Moreover, until recently the courts have shown themselves willing to award parental responsibility to almost any interested father. But in the last few years there have been a number of cases in which the courts have refused to make parental responsibility orders in favour of a biological father where the child is being brought up by the mother and a female co-parent, which adds a new twist to the debate. The avowedly 'creative' option of conferring parental responsibility on the father but limiting his exercise of it was adopted in *B v A, C and D (Acting By Her Guardian)*,[64] but in subsequent cases the courts have preferred simply to deny the father parental responsibility altogether.[65] These later cases are consistent with a shift away from parental responsibility as a pure matter of status to

Rob.

---

[62] DWP/DCSF, *Joint Birth Registration: Recording Responsibility*, Cm. 7293, June 2008, para. 10.
[63] K. Kiernan and K. Smith, 'Unmarried Parenthood: New Insights from the Millennium Cohort Study' (2003) 114 *Population Trends* 23.
[64] [2006] EWHC 2 (Fam). For discussion see Reece, 'The Degradation of Parental Responsibility', in Probert, Gilmore and Herring (eds) *Responsible Parents and Parental Responsibility*.
[65] See e.g. *Re B (Role of Biological Father)* [2007] EWHC 1952 (Fam); *R v E and F (Female Parents: Known Father)* [2010] EWHC 417 (Fam).

parental responsibility as involving an active relationship with the child. In *Re B (Role of Biological Father)*[66] the judge reasoned that either the father accepted that the two women should comprise the nuclear family and would not undermine this – which would be wholly inconsistent with him exercising parental responsibility – or he would seek to exercise parental responsibility, thereby undermining their care and creating conflict, which would not be in the best interests of the child. In short, for the father to possess parental responsibility was either unnecessary or undesirable. Nor was there any perceived benefit in a restricted grant of parental responsibility in this case: it was thought that this would lead to false hopes for the father and a lack of security for the mother and her civil partner.

In the end, the most powerful argument against conferring parental responsibility on all fathers automatically may be that of certainty. The current system now confers parental responsibility on the vast majority of known[67] fathers, and all but a tiny proportion of those who have an ongoing relationship with the child. If a man does not even know that he is the father, is there any point in conferring parental responsibility upon him?

Should social parents have parental responsibility?

In considering whether parental responsibility should be conferred on social parents, we should distinguish between those men who believed at the outset that they were the father of the child, and the mother's subsequent partners who take on a caring role for the child.

At present the position of the social parent who only realizes he is not the biological parent at a later date is stark. Re-registration means that he is no longer either a father *or* a legal parent, even though he may have genuinely believed that he was the father of the child and wish to continue to play a role in the child's life. Some men, of course, will wish to divest themselves of parenthood and any responsibilities once they discover the truth, as the applications for damages for deceit indicate. Others will want their parenting role recognized.

If the register were to have different categories for 'parent' and 'father', as discussed above, it would be possible for a man in this position to elect to remain on the register as a parent, even if another man was registered as the father. This may be some consolation to the children involved. In *Re D (Paternity)*,[68] for example, the boy was very hostile to the idea of the truth of his paternity being ascertained: the potential impact of this might have been mitigated if there was still the possibility that the man he thought was his father would remain his parent.[69] It would also ensure that the wider family relationships established through supposed legal parenthood would remain in place.

---

[66] [2007] EWHC 1952 (Fam).
[67] Or rather those who are assumed to be fathers, given the reliance on birth registration or the marriage certificate rather than DNA testing. See e.g. *Re R (Parental Responsibility)* [2011] EWHC 1535 (Fam) for a case in which the mother's husband subsequently discovered that he was not the father.
[68] [2006] EWHC 3545 (Fam).
[69] [2006] EWHC 3545 (Fam).

At present the only real option in such cases is to confer parental responsibility by means of a joint residence order. This was the option taken in *Re A (Joint Residence: Parental Responsibility)*.[70] One can see the same desire to ensure that the child had at least two parents with parental responsibility, and, indeed, the same focus on the interests of the adults as is evident in the cases on lesbian co-parents. The biological father had had no contact with the child; it was Mr A who had been registered as the father on the birth certificate and who had acted as a parent to the child while living with the mother. And the joint residence order was explicitly made 'for the purpose of conferring upon A the parental responsibility which went with it and which the recorder considered was merited by Mr A, whose role he did not wish to see marginalised or diminished'.[71] The same reasoning has been used to justify the award of a joint residence order where a relationship between the mother and her lesbian partner broke down.[72]

However, some commentators have been strongly critical of the proliferation of parental responsibility that this allows. Reece has noted the way in which courts focus on the feelings and emotions of the adults involved when deciding whether or not to grant parental responsibility, and contends that it 'should not be granted in order to prevent adults feeling that the law has emotionally neglected them: parental responsibility should be awarded to adults if and only if they deserve parental responsibility'.[73] Moreover, as Bainham points out, caution is all the more necessary to avoid a swift turnover of adults with parental responsibility:

> The case of step-parenthood perhaps illustrates that caution is requiring in assuming too readily that what looks like a parent must be a parent, or that it is appropriate to hand out a full status to all those looking after children who may, given the propensity for serial relationships, be only in that position for a limited time before being replaced by another parent figure.[74]

Debate 3

Is there a right to know your genetic origins?

We tend to think of the debate about the right to know one's genetic origins as a modern one, but even though previous generations would not have been familiar with the terms they would certainly have been familiar with the underlying issue. Foundlings, for example, might never discover their true parentage. Before the twentieth century, children born outside wedlock might never know their father (and might not even know that their mother *was* their mother). And even children

---

70 [2008] EWCA Civ 867.
71 Ibid, para. 65.
72 *Re G (Residence: Same-Sex Partner)* [2005] EWCA Civ 462.
73 Reece, 'The Degradation of Parental Responsibility', in Probert, Gilmore and Herring (eds) *Responsible Parents and Parental Responsibility*, p. 101.
74 Bainham, 'Status Anxiety? The Rush for Family Recognition', in Ebtehaj, Lindley and Richards (eds), *Kinship Matters*, p. 61.

apparently born in wedlock might be under a misapprehension as to their true parentage.

But the advent of new reproductive technology has certainly added a new dimension to the debate. So too has the increased importance attached to children's rights: Article 7 of the UN Convention on the Rights of the Child provides that a child has 'as far as possible, the right to know and be cared for by his or her parents'. This section will look at the emerging idea that children have a right to know their genetic origins and then at the debates as to how this right should be vindicated, first in the context of birth registration, then in that of assisted reproduction, and finally in the case-law on the ordering of blood tests.

SHOULD THE STATE TRY TO ENSURE THE COMPLETENESS OF THE REGISTER AND, IF SO, HOW?

The law and proposals for reform

When civil registration of births was first introduced, little attempt was made to secure the completeness of the official record. Registrars were delicately advised that 'if the informant declines stating the name of the father, or there shall be reason to believe that the child is illegitimate, the Registrar shall not press inquiry on that subject'.[75] Legislation in 1874 further tightened the rules on who could register what information: the father of an illegitimate child was no longer entitled to register the birth, and his name could only be recorded at the joint request of both parents.[76]

This remains the case under the current law, but the huge increase in the number and proportion of births occurring outside marriage in recent decades has largely been driven by the rise in cohabitation, and joint registration is correspondingly common.[77] The idea that children have the right to know the identity of their parents has led to increased scrutiny of those few remaining cases in which no father is named. There are high rates of joint registration among parents who, although not living together, are still closely involved, but – understandably – joint registration falls to 27 per cent where the parents are no longer in a relationship at the time of the child's birth.[78] However, policy-makers attached more weight to the statistic that the father had regular contact with the child in almost half – 45 per cent – of those cases where the birth was registered by the mother alone. It was therefore proposed that the father's name should be recorded on the birth certificate in all but exceptional cases,[79] and the subsequent

[75] General Record Office, *Regulations for the Duties of Registrars of Births and Deaths and Deputy Registrars* (GRO, 1838), p. 10.
[76] See further R. Probert, 'Recording Births: From the Reformation to the Welfare Reform Act', in F. Ebtehaj, J. Herring, M. H. Johnson and M. Richards (eds) *Birth Rites and Rights* (Hart Publishing, 2011).
[77] S. Smallwood, 'Characteristics of Sole Registered Births and the Mothers who Register Them' (2004) 117 *Population Trends* 20.
[78] Kiernan and Smith, 'Unmarried Parenthood: New Insights from the Millennium Cohort Study'.
[79] Department of Work and Pensions, *Joint Birth Registration: Promoting Parental Responsibility* (2007).

+Bainham (jrnal)

White Paper explicitly justified this by reference to the desirability of children knowing their genetic origins: 'At the heart of our reforms is a desire to promote child welfare and *the right of every child to know who his or her parents are.*'[80]

One might debate whether this was the real reason for the reforms. After all, if children are having contact with a non-resident parent, they will be perfectly well aware of his or her identity, regardless of the gap on the birth certificate. It might rather be suspected that the intended beneficiary of the information was not the child but the state, in that fathers whose names are recorded on the birth certificate are easier to pursue for child support.

The debates

The proposals, and the subsequent terms of the Welfare Reform Act, also led to considerable debate as to what the appropriate balance between parent and child should be in this context. On the one hand, if the right of the child to know who his or her parents are is the most important factor, then this would suggest that a parent's refusal to provide information should be challenged and perhaps even overridden. The White Paper did indeed seem to envisage that paternity testing could be compulsory:

> Where a mother wants the identity of a father to be recorded but this is against the wishes of the father, or the wishes of the father are not known, mothers will be allowed to identify the father of their child independently. At this point the father will be contacted and required to sign the birth register. Where the issue of paternity is denied or challenged, a paternity test will be required and the man concerned will be recorded as the father if his paternity of the child is established by such a test.[81]

More radical still would be the suggestion that there should be paternity testing in all cases, not merely where the man wishes to dispute it. Estimates as to the extent of misattributed paternity vary widely, largely because some are based on samples of men who specifically sought a paternity test – presumably because they had some doubts as to their child's paternity. But even the more modest and convincing estimate that paternity is misattributed in about 4 per cent of cases[82] would amount to approximately 27,600 births per year on current figures. As Bainham has noted, 'whether or not the system "works well" rather depends on whether the aim is to secure registration in virtually every case of birth to a married woman, in which case doubtless it does, or whether the aim is to establish where possible the biological parentage of the child, in which case the success of the system is more questionable'.[83]

---

[80] Department of Work and Pensions/Department for Schools, Children and Families, *Joint Birth Registration: Recording Responsibility* (2008), para. 6 (emphasis added).

[81] DWP/DSCF, 2008: [28].

[82] M. Bellis, K. Hughes, S. Hughes and J. Ashton, 'Measuring Paternal Discrepancy and its Public Health Consequences' (2005) 59 *Journal of Epidemiology and Community Health* 749.

[83] A. Bainham, 'What Is the Point of Birth Registration?' (2008) 20 *Child and Family Law Quarterly* 449.

Some, however, took the view that more weight should to be given to the welfare of the mother – who may also be a child in the eyes of the law. What if the conception was the result of rape, or of a violent and abusive relationship that the mother has finally left? Should a mother be compelled to tell the name of the father in cases such as these? Under the Welfare Reform Act 2009 a number of exceptions were envisaged to the requirement that a mother should provide information about the father. These were that the child had no legal father by virtue of s. 41 HFEA 2008, or the father had died, or the mother did not know the father's identity or whereabouts, or the father lacked capacity (as defined by the Mental Capacity Act 2005) and so was unable to confirm whether he is the father, or the mother had reason to fear for her safety or that of the child if the father was contacted in relation to the registration of the birth.

These exemptions in turn sparked debate as to whether the legislation had moved too far from the right of the child to know his or her parents. As Mark Harper put it in the course of the passage of the Bill through Parliament:

> If it is important to the child to know who both the parents are, allowing the mother not to disclose, or not putting an obligation on disclosing who the father is just because the mother does not know his whereabouts, does not seem a terribly powerful reason .... If it is important for the child to know who its parents are and important to send out this message, there seem to be far too many reasons why the mother can avoid disclosing who the father is.[84]

What was lacking, as Bainham forcefully pointed out, was any attempt 'to evaluate how the many exemptions which would lead to sole registration might be squared with any independent rights which the child or father might have'.[85] He questioned why the child's right to know his or her origins should be any less compelling where the truth – that the birth was the result of rape or incest – might be disturbing.

It is, however, worth remembering that what is at issue is not what the child might want to know, but what the state wants to record. There are other ways of ensuring that the name of the father is recorded for the benefit of the child that do not involve the father being contacted by the state.

SHOULD THE STATE TRY TO ENSURE THAT CHILDREN BORN FROM DONATED GAMETES ARE AWARE OF THEIR BIOLOGICAL PARENTAGE?

The law
Until relatively recently those born as the result of assisted reproduction were not entitled to any information that might identify the donor. However, following a

---

[84] *House of Commons Public Bill Committee on the Welfare Reform Bill*, col 250.
[85] Bainham, 'Arguments about Parentage', 330.

legal challenge by two donor-conceived children,[86] the rules were changed so that anyone donating sperm, eggs or embryos after 1 April 2005 could only do so on the basis that identifying information would be available to the resulting children when they reached the age of 18. The HFEA 2008 made provision for means by which additional information about an individual's biological parentage and other relationships would be available.

The increasing range of provisions could be seen as an indication that one's blood relationships do matter. Yet it is really only where the child's social parents take the view that such relationships matter that these provisions will have any relevance: there is no requirement that donor-conceived children be informed of the circumstances of their conception. The Joint Committee noted that 'many of the provisions...are illusory if the fact of donor-conception are not known'[87] but rejected calls for a statutory duty to be imposed on parents to tell their children that they were donor-conceived, and resiled from proposing that the fact of donor conception be recorded on the child's birth certificate.

The question that should be posed, therefore, is whether the law should do more to ensure disclosure.

Arguments in favour

To require the identity of the donor to be recorded does not necessarily indicate that we are in thrall to our biology. But to obscure the genetic lineage of the child might have real future public health consequences. It has been pointed out that 'more links between genetics and individuals' health are identified every day and consequently the case for the child to be informed is strengthened. Increasingly, the knowledge of genetic inheritance is not just of use to clinicians but informs the lifestyle choices of the person, the decision to procreate, and in some cases access to insurance.'[88]

In other contexts, moreover, the law endorses the importance of establishing the truth of one's genetic origins. A decade ago Thorpe LJ declared in *Re H and A (Children)* that 'the paternity of any child is to be established by science and not by legal presumption or inference'.[89] While the past couple of years have seen a number of cases in which testing of a child's paternity has been refused or where the disclosure of unexpected paternity has not been required,[90] each of these cases turned on its own facts. Moreover, it was stressed in *Re F (Paternity: Jurisdiction)*[91] that the family justice system was entitled to take responsibility for deciding

---

[86] *Rose and EM (a child represented by her mother as litigation friend) v Secretary of State for Health and HFEA* [2002] EWHC 1593 (Admin).

[87] At para 272.

[88] M. Bellis, K. Hughes, S. Hughes and J. Ashton 'Measuring Paternal Discrepancy and Its Public Health Consequences' (2005) 59 *Journal of Epidemiology and Community Health* 749.

[89] [2002] EWCA Civ 383, para. 30.

[90] See e.g. *London Borough of Lambeth v S, C and Others* [2006] EWHC; *Re D (Paternity)* [2006] EWHC 3545 (Fam); *Re J (Paternity: Welfare of Child)* [2006] EWHC 2837 (Fam).

[91] [2007] EWCA Civ 873.

whether a child should be told of their true biological origins. If this is the case where such disclosure has the potential to reveal the mother's infidelity with the consequent damage to the relationship between mother and partner, why is it not the case where the parties have colluded in hiding the truth from the child?

As John Eekelaar has pointed out, whenever the law manipulates the truth, 'it is always important to try to understand whose interests are being served by the manipulation'.[92] There have been a number of studies into why those caring for donor-conceived children usually choose not to tell. One of the child-centred reasons for non-disclosure – the fact that no identifying information would be available to the child even if he or she was told[93] – has now vanished. In its place, however, there may be a new spectre: the fear that a knowable donor may supplant the parent in the affections of the child.

Yet while a knowable donor may seem more threatening than an unknow-able donor, solid fact is likely to be less threatening than the fantasies that the donor-conceived child may weave about their genetic parent. The novelist A.M. Homes, who was adopted as a baby, wrote about making contact with her birth parents: what comes across most clearly in her account is that her birth parents were extremely ordinary and actually quite annoying.[94]

Similarly, a US study of donor-conceived adolescents who had open-identity sperm donors found that most were comfortable with the fact, and that learning that they were donor-conceived had not had a negative effect on their relationship with either the birth mother or the co-parent.[95] They emphasized that what mattered to them was the people who brought them up, and that they felt loved and wanted and (positively) unique. Two said that it was preferable to being conceived as a result of casual sex. Nor did their desire to know more about the donor indicate that they regarded him as the 'real' father: the researchers concluded that 'the youths were mostly hoping for a donor who was simply a good, open-minded person, who would be open to contact and not necessarily be heavily involved in their life'. None of the adolescents seemed to regard the donor as their 'ideal father'; when they envisaged a future relationship it was on terms of friendship rather than wanting a 'dad'.

By contrast, those who do not tell their children that they are donor-conceived should take warning from the evidence that withholding information may compromise the functioning of the family,[96] and from the anger of those who learn as adults that they were donor-conceived.

---

[92] Eekelaar, *Family Law and Personal Life*, p. 58.

[93] Lycett, Daniels, Curson and Golombok, 'School-aged Children of Donor Insemination: A Study of Parents' Disclosure Patterns', 811.

[94] Homes, *The Mistress's Daughter: A Memoir*.

[95] J.E. Scheib, M. Riordan and S. Rubin, 'Adolescents with Open-identity Sperm Donors: Reports from 12–17 Year Olds' (2005) 20 *Human Reproduction* 239. The sample included children of heterosexual couples as well as lesbian couples.

[96] M. S. Paul and R. Berger, 'Topic Avoidance and Family Functioning in Families Conceived with Donor Insemination' (2007) 22 *Human Reproduction* 2566.

Arguments against

Some, however, suggest that the arguments in favour of disclosure simply attach too much weight to genetics. Richards has noted that 'the claim that a knowledge of parentage may be essential to a person's "genetic identity" ... seems to be based on a version of genetic exceptionalism that increasingly pervades our culture in this "century of the gene" '.[97] In practice, of course, genetic differences between individuals are minute: we each share 99.9 per cent of our genes with each other. The fact that we can ascertain genetic links does not necessarily advance our knowledge of ourselves or our kin: 'family history is about the lives and actions of our forebears, not the transmission of DNA sequences.'[98] Carol Smart has similarly argued that bonds based on affection may be just as important as those based on genetics.[99]

A second and more pragmatic argument is that the supply of donated sperm, eggs and embryos may depend on the preservation of anonymity. Having carried out research into the views of would-be parents, Turkmendag, Dingwall and Murphy pose the question thus:

> What is the value of a right to openness for a child who is never conceived because of the reluctance of gamete donors to take on a long-term commitment from which they may reasonably only expect to derive emotional costs rather than benefits?[100]

Others, however, have challenged the idea that removing anonymity has led to a collapse in donor recruitment and have noted that the concerns of at least some potential donors 'can be addressed by better information, counselling and support'.[101]

The way forward?

One final question is: what *can* the law do to ensure that the the truth is disclosed? Various different options have been suggested, such as stating 'by donor' on the birth certificate, dual certificates (as for adopted children), or including a 'warning' on all birth certificates that it is no guarantee of biological parentage.[102]

---

[97] Richards, 'Assisted Reproduction and Parental Relationships', ch. 15 in Bainham, Lindley, Richards and Trinder (eds) *Children and Their Families: Contact, Rights and Welfare*, p. 306.

[98] T. Freeman and M. Richards, 'DNA Testing and Kinship: Paternity, Genealogy and the Search for the 'Truth' of our Genetic Origins' in Ebtehaj, Lindley and Richards (eds), *Kinship Matters*, p. 88. For a discussion of the impact of DNA testing in the USA, see M. A. Rothstein, T. H. Murray, G. E. Kaebnick and M. Anderlik Majunder (eds), *Genetic Ties and the Family. The Impact of Paternity Testing on Parents and Children* (Johns Hopkins University Press, 2005).

[99] C. Smart, 'Family Secrets: Law and Understandings of Openness in Everyday Relationships' (2009) 38 *Journal of Social Policy* 551.

[100] I. Turkmendag, R. Dingwall and T. Murphy, 'The Removal of Donor Anonymity in the UK: The Silencing of Claims by Would-be Parents' (2008) 22 *International Journal of Law, Policy and the Family* 283, 305.

[101] L. Frith, E. Blyth and A. Farrand, 'UK Gamete Donors' Reflections on the Removal of Anonymity: Implications for Recruitment' (2007) 22 *Human Reproduction* 1675.

[102] See e.g. Bainham, 'What Is the Point of Birth Registration?'.

None of these are entirely satisfactory, but the HFEA 2008 may point a way forward. It was noted above that a female partner is just as much a parent as is the infertile husband or cohabitant; the corollary is that he is no more a father than she is. One way forward would be to use the term parent in *both* cases: i.e. a husband who is not the biological father of the child is a parent but not a father. This would address the concern that the current system does not do enough to ensure that the truth is known, while being less intrusive than recording 'by donor insemination' on the birth certificate. It would also ensure that same-sex couples do not feel stigmatized. Moreover, the designation of one of the adults as a 'parent' would not necessarily indicate that the child was conceived as a result of DI, since the term is already in use in the context of adoption. The birth certificate of a child adopted by a same-sex couple shows two *parents*, rather than two mothers or two fathers. Again, it would be logical for this to be extended to adoptions by heterosexual couples.

ARE TESTS TO ASCERTAIN CHILDREN'S GENETIC PARENTS ALWAYS IN THEIR BEST INTERESTS?

Even where a child was not born as a result of assisted reproduction, there may well be uncertainty over the identity of his or her genetic father. Under the current law, a court can direct that DNA tests be carried out in order to ascertain the paternity of a child; the decision whether to do so rests on whether the test would be against the child's interests.[103] Consent for the necessary samples to be taken is also of course necessary: if those with parental responsibility for the child do not consent to a sample being taken, then the court can make the decision that it is in the best interests of the child for this to be done.

The case-law illustrates the changing views on the importance attached to knowledge of one's genetic origins. In the earlier case-law, the stability of the family unit was regarded as being of key importance, and knowledge that might destabilize this was seen as a dangerous thing.[104] In recent years, by contrast, ascertaining the truth has been prioritized above the stability of the existing family unit.[105]

More recent cases have, however, raised a more difficult question. What if the child is of an age to express a view and does not want to know the truth? Here we may need to pay more attention to the distinction between children's rights and children's welfare, all too often blurred or referred to indiscriminately in this area.[106] If it is deemed to be in the child's best interests to learn of his or her true genetic parentage, then the wishes of the individual child, while a weighty factor, cannot be determinative. If, however, children have a right to know, then

---

[103] Family Law Reform Act 1969, s. 20; see e.g. *Re L (A Child)* [2009] EWCA Civ 1239.

[104] See e.g. J. Fortin, '*Re F*: The Gooseberry Bush Approach' (1994) 57 *MLR* 296.

[105] See e.g. *Re H and A (Children)* [2002] EWCA Civ 383.

[106] See further J. Fortin, 'Children's Right to Know Their Origins – Too Far, Too Fast?' [2009] 21 *Child and Family Law Quarterly* 336.

it is possible to argue that they also have a right not to know – that the exercise of this right is a matter on which they are entitled to exercise a judgment. To date the courts have not been willing to concede that there might be a right not to know, or that knowledge might not be in the best interests of the child, although it has been accepted that timing is crucial and that it may be in the child's best interests for the ascertainment of the truth to be postponed to a later date.[107]

Still more difficult are those cases where children do not know that there is any issue over their parentage and so do not have the opportunity of indicating whether they wish to know or not. On the one hand there is the salutary warning issued by John Eekelaar that adults may wish to create legal fictions that disguise physical truths, and to do so in their own interests rather than those of the child.[108] If a mother argues that it would be devastating for her child to learn that that he had no blood tie to the man that he thought was his father, whose interests are being protected here? On the other hand it has been suggested that the current emphasis on the truth does not necessarily give sufficient weight to the values of different communities: should a different approach be taken if the child belongs to a community in which illegitimacy still carries a stigma?[109] Or should the child bear the brunt of challenging the 'oppressive norms' that underpin the concept of illegitimacy?[110]

That potential clash between rights and welfare does, however, require further consideration of both, and this will be examined further in the next chapter.

Further Reading

A. Bainham, S. Day Sclater and M. Richards (eds), *What Is a Parent? A Socio-Legal Analysis* (Hart Publishing, 1999).

A. Bainham, 'What Is the Point of Birth Registration?' [2008] 20 *Child and Family Law Quarterly* 449.

A. Bainham, 'Arguments about Parentage' (2008) 67 *CLJ* 322.

C. Barton and G. Douglas, *Law and Parenthood* (Butterworths, 1995).

A. Diduck and K. O'Donovan (eds), *Feminist Perspectives on Family Law* (Routledge-Cavendish, 2006).

F. Ebtehaj, B. Lindley and M. Richards (eds), *Kinship Matters* (Hart Publishing, 2006).

F. Ebtehaj, J. Herring, M.H. Johnson and M. Richards (eds), *Birth Rites and Rights* (Hart Publishing, 2011).

J. Fortin, 'Children's Right to Know Their Origins – Too Far, Too Fast?' [2009] 21 *Child and Family Law Quarterly* 336.

J. Herring and C. Foster, 'Please Don't Tell Me' (2012) *Cambridge Quarterly of Healthcare Ethics* 21.

---

[107] *Re D (Paternity)* [2006] EWHC 3445 (Fam).
[108] Eekelaar, *Family Law and Personal Life*, ch. 3.
[109] A. Hasan, 'To Tell or Not To Tell: That Is The Question' [2007] *Family Law* 458.
[110] Eekelaar, *Family Law and Personal Life*, p. 76.

R. Probert, S. Gilmore and J. Herring (eds) *Responsible Parents and Parental Responsibility* (Hart Publishing, 2009).

M. Shultz, 'Reproductive Technology and Intent-Based Parenthood: An Opportunity for Gender Neutrality' (1990) *Wis L Rev* 297.

C. Smart, 'Family Secrets: Law and Understandings of Openness in Everyday Relationships' (2009) 38 *Journal of Social Policy* 551.

L. Smith, 'Is Three a Crowd? Lesbian Mothers' Perspectives on Parental Status in Law' [2006] 18 *Child and Family Law Quarterly* 231.

J.R. Spencer and A. Du Bois-Pedain (eds), *Freedom and Responsibility in Reproductive Choice* (Hart Publishing, 2006).

I. Turkmendag, R. Dingwall and T. Murphy, 'The Removal of Donor Anonymity in the UK: The Silencing of Claims by Would-be Parents' (2008) 22 *International Journal of Law, Policy and the Family* 283.

J. Wallbank, 'Too Many Mothers? Surrogacy, Kinship and the Welfare of the Child' [2002] *Medical Law Review* 271.

J. Wallbank, S. Choudhry and J. Herring (eds), *Rights, Gender and Family Law* (Routledge-Cavendish, 2009).

3
CHILDREN'S RIGHTS

INTRODUCTION

There must be few people who would not concede that children must have at least some rights: as persons, children must have the most fundamental of human rights.[1] Many perhaps would go further and say that, because of their vulnerability, children should be entitled to some rights which adults may no longer have. Nevertheless, as a matter of theory the issue of children's rights is hotly debated, both as to the sense in which children can be regarded as rights-holders, and the extent to which they should be accorded rights. In practice difficult questions can arise as to the extent to which children's rights should be recognized in law. This chapter examines some of the theoretical and practical debates surrounding recognition of children's rights.

Debate  1

Should children have rights?

CONCEPTIONS OF RIGHTS

A difficulty that any discussion of children's rights encounters is that the notion of a right is an essentially contested concept.[2] It raises a question prior to whether children should have rights, namely whether children (or at least some children) are capable of being rights-holders. There are two main theories of rights, the Will Theory and the Interest Theory, with different implications for accommodating children as rights-holders. The will theory holds that one can only talk meaningfully about a person having a right if the person can waive, or exercise,

---

[1] As Michael Freeman has observed, one does not, for example, see 'any purported defences of the torture of children': M. Freeman, 'Why It Remains Important to Take Children's Rights Seriously' (2007) 15 *International Journal of Children's Rights* 5, 9.
[2] See e.g. J. Waldron (ed.), *Theories of Rights* (Oxford University Press, 1985); M. H. Kramer, N. E. Simmonds and H. Steiner, *A Debate Over Rights: Philosophical Enquiries* (Oxford University Press, 1998).

enforcement of the right. By contrast the interest theory holds that rights derive from persons' interests, so that a person will have a right simply if that person's interest is sufficient ground for holding another to be subject to a duty. The interest theory protects a person's interests independently of his or her choices, whereas the will theory draws a necessary connection between a person's capacity to exercise his or her will with respect to the right and the idea of being a rights-holder. Babies and very young children will not have the necessary capacities to exercise their will in this way, so the will theory conceptually denies some children the very possibility of having rights. Indeed, Professor Neil MacCormick used the case of children's rights to test the appropriateness of these general theories of rights,[3] and concluded that the interest theory should be preferred because of its greater ability to accommodate children's rights. As Michael Freeman has explained, 'Children have interests to protect before they develop wills to assert, and others can complain on behalf of younger children when those interests are trampled on'.[4]

The interests that children might plausibly claim

If an interest theory of rights is adopted, the next logical question becomes: what are the various interests that children might plausibly claim? This is of course closely linked to the question whether children should be accorded rights, since the answer may need to address the various different kinds of claims children might make. One leading family law commentator, John Eekelaar, has usefully identified three general categories of interests that children might plausibly claim: what he calls the basic, developmental and autonomy interests.[5] A child's basic interests are concerned with a minimal expectation of general physical, emotional and intellectual care. The developmental interests are concerned that children have 'equal opportunity to maximise the resources available to them during their childhood (including their own inherent abilities) so as to minimize the degree to which they enter adult life affected by avoidable prejudices incurred during childhood', in other words that their capacities are developed to best advantage. The autonomy interest is about 'children's freedom to choose their own lifestyle and to enter social relations, according to their own inclinations uncontrolled by the authority of the adult world, whether parents or institutions'.

It is important that these claims are those that the child him or herself might make. As Eekelaar has observed, there is a difference between 'welfarism' (i.e. actions motivated solely by the purpose of promoting another's welfare) and the idea of a person having a right, which is related to the perception that people

---

[3] N. MacCormick, 'Children's Rights: A Test Case for Theories of Rights', ch. 7 in N. MacCormick, *Legal Right and Social Democracy* (Oxford University Press, 1982). For analysis and criticism of the Will Theory, see also J. Dwyer, 'The Conceptual Possibility of Children Having Rights', appendix in *The Relationship Rights of Children* (Cambridge University Press, 2006).

[4] M. D. A. Freeman, 'Taking Children's Rights More Seriously', in P. Alston, S. Parker and J. Seymour (eds), *Children, Rights and the Law* (Clarendon Press, 1992), p. 52, at p. 58.

[5] J. Eekelaar, 'The Emergence of Children's Rights' (1986) 6 *OJLS* 161.

make claims.[6] Thus even in the case of very young (incompetent) children it 'could never be enough to assert simply that an action will be in the child's welfare'. If we are to talk of a child's right in the context of such actions, we 'need to think how the action could be one which the child might plausibly want'.[7]

The danger of 'welfarism' has led Katherine Federle to suggest that we should move beyond the will and interest theories and reconceptualize the meaning of (children) having and exercising rights.[8] Federle contends that having a right

> means the power to command respect, to make claims and to have them heard. But if having a right is contingent upon some characteristic, like capacity, then holding the right becomes exclusive and exclusionary: thus only claims made by a particular group of (competent) beings will be recognised.[9]

She argues that while the interest theory 'does not automatically exclude children from the class of rights-holders, it does define children's interests in terms of their incapacities'[10] and there is a tendency to empower adults to intervene in children's lives rather than empowering children.[11] Thus the kinds of rights that Federle envisions are 'not premised upon capacity but upon power or more precisely, powerlessness'. In other words, rights exist to remedy powerlessness and should flow downhill to the least powerful. Paternalistic justifications thus become unacceptable.

Childhoods

A second difficulty which discussion of children's rights encounters is the fact that childhood is socially constructed.[12] Children may have different experiences of childhood at different times in different societies. This raises several issues.

First, the dominant vision of childhood within a particular society is likely to affect how children are perceived, and therefore perhaps how arguments

---

[6] J. Eekelaar, 'The Importance of Thinking That Children Have Rights', in Alston, Parker and Seymour (eds), *Children, Rights and the Law*, p. 221. Eekelaar adds that 'a claim simply that people should act to further my welfare as they define it is in reality to make no claim at all'. See also his discussion of isolating interests pertaining to the child, in 'The Emergence of Children's Rights', 169.

[7] Eekelaar, 'The Importance of Thinking That Children Have Rights', in Alston, Parker and Seymour (eds), *Children, Rights and the Law*, p. 230 (i.e. via an hypothetical *process*). See also J. Eekelaar, 'The Interests of the Child and the Child's Wishes: The Role of Dynamic Self-Determinism' (1994) 8 *International Journal of Law and the Family* 42.

[8] K. Federle, 'On the Road to Reconceiving Rights for Children: A Post-Feminist Analysis Of The Capacity Principle' (1993) *De Paul L Rev* 983; K . H. Federle, 'Rights Flow Downhill' (1994) 2 *International Journal of Children's Rights* 343; K. H. Federle, 'Looking Ahead: An Empowerment Perspective on the Rights of Children' (1995) 68(4) *Temple L Rev* 1585. Federle's treatment of power may require further refinement: see H. Lim and J. Roche, 'Feminism and Children's Rights', in J. Bridgeman and D. Monk (eds), *Feminist Perspectives on Child Law* (Cavendish, 2000), pp. 238–41.

[9] Federle, 'Rights Flow Downhill', 344.

[10] Ibid, 354.

[11] Ibid, 365.

[12] See A. James, C. Jenks, and A. Prout, *Theorizing Childhood* (Polity, 1998); C. Jenks, *Childhood* (Routledge, 1996); A. James and A. Prout (eds), *Constructing and Reconstructing Childhood* (Falmer Press, 1997); P. Ariès, *Centuries of Childhood: A Social History of Family Life* (Jonathan Cape, 1962).

concerning children's rights are received. If the dominant vision of childhood is as a vulnerable and dependent period, then seeing children as persons with potential to exercise autonomy may be more difficult. The dominant vision may also render less visible children's role as active members of society (e.g. acting as carers for others, such as parents[13]). Furthermore, how children are perceived goes to the very heart of how adults perceive themselves as different from children. As Carole Smith[14] has explained, our vision of the childhood/adulthood distinction may offer some explanation for resistance to granting children rights to take decisions which would lead to their irreparable harm or death. As she comments:

> we are not prepared to withdraw our protection or to abandon the legal distinction between children and adults. To do so would strike at the very heart of the adult-child relationship which enables adults to locate themselves emotionally, as being affectionate, caring, protective, and socially, as being responsible for moulding the next generation of citizens.[15]

Secondly, the social construction of childhood raises difficulties for any universal vision of children's rights, such as the United Nations Convention on the Rights of the Child. How are universal visions of children's rights to be reconciled with the notion of cultural pluralism?[16]

Thirdly, the fact that childhood is socially constructed raises questions as to whether the adulthood/childhood distinction is an artificial one and can be justified. The boundary between childhood and adulthood was challenged by child liberationist ideology in the 1960s and 1970s, which placed great emphasis on individual autonomy, and proposed an extension of adults' rights to children (such as the right to live independently, the right to drive, to take drugs and to have sex).[17] Although this movement should be seen as a product of its time and may seem politically naïve, the rhetoric of the child liberationists was important in raising the profile of the issue of children's rights.[18] More moderate versions of this perspective might now argue that children should not be discriminated against simply on the basis of their age.

---

[13] See e.g. V. Morrow, 'Responsible Children and Children's Responsibilities? Sibling Caretaking and Babysitting by School-age Children', in J. Bridgeman, H. Keating and C. Lind (eds), *Responsibility, Law and the Family* (Ashgate, 2008), p. 105, and generally part 2 of that book.

[14] C. Smith, 'Children's Rights: Judicial Ambivalence and Social Resistance' (1997) 11 *International Journal of Law, Policy and the Family* 103.

[15] Ibid, 135.

[16] See e.g. A. An-Na'im, 'Cultural Transformation and Normative Consensus on the Best Interests of the Child' (1994) 8 *International Journal of Law and the Family* 62–81; M. Freeman, 'Children's Rights and Cultural Pluralism', in M. Freeman (ed.), *The Moral Status of Children* (Martinhus Nijhoff, 1997), ch. 7.

[17] See e.g. R. Farson, *Birthrights* (London: Macmillan, 1974) and J. Holt, *Escape from Childhood* (Harmondsworth, 1975). For a cross-section of the diverse origins of this ideology, see P. Adams, L. Berg, N. Berger, M. Dunne, A. S. Neill and R. Ollendorff, *Children's Rights* (Panther, 1972) and for an overview, see D. Archard, *Children: Rights and Childhood* (Routledge, 2004), ch. 5, and L. Fox Harding, *Perspectives in Child Care Policy* (Prentice Hall, 1997), ch. 5.

[18] Freeman, *The Rights and Wrongs of Children*.

It is important to appreciate that children's liberation is one, rather extreme, approach to children's rights. It is easy to attack children's rights if the focus is on child liberationist ideology. For example, Laura Purdy[19] argues, contrary to the liberationist approach, that children should not have rights equal to those of adults. She argues that there are sufficiently large differences in instrumental reasoning between most children and most adults to justify different treatment of adults and children, and that the child liberationists' 'overly-individualistic' approach is unable to provide children with the intellectual and emotional pre-requisites for that kind of co-operation and sacrifice that is required for a decent society.[20] As Anne McGillivray points out, however, Purdy falls into the trap of conflating children's liberation with children's rights,[21] and this leads Purdy to 'cast rights as the antithesis rather than the essence of relationships and responsibility'.[22] Furthermore, as Tom D. Campbell observes, Purdy's argument needs to make clearer that it is really about children having rights without responsibilities.[23] In contrast to Purdy's position, and more in line with McGillivray's, Michael Freeman has argued that rights protect the integrity of a person in leading his or her life, based on a belief in equality and respect for autonomy. For Freeman, to 'believe in autonomy is to believe that anyone's autonomy is as morally significant as anyone else's'. Freeman thus argues that we should respect a child's autonomy, treating the child as a person and as a rights-holder, (although Freeman also acknowledges that children's autonomy must be seen in the context of their sometimes lesser abilities/capacities).

Reconciling conflict between children's interests

As we have already seen, liberationist ideology has been tempered by more mature and moderate academic criticism, which takes account not only of children's autonomy, but various other interests that children might claim, and how those interests are to be reconciled. The value of Eekelaar's categorization of children's interests (and indeed similar categorizations by others)[24] is that it draws attention to the potential interaction of the various interests. The child's developmental interest is likely to be promoted by exercises of autonomy, perhaps especially if those exercises of autonomy are accompanied by learning from mistakes. But equally, some mistakes in the exercise of autonomy can seriously impinge on the basic interests and developmental interests. Thus the various interests can conflict. Take, for example, the competent adolescent who wishes to refuse medical

---

19 L. Purdy, *In Their Best Interest?* (Cornell University Press, 1992); L. Purdy, 'Why Children Shouldn't Have Equal Rights' (1994) 2 *International Journal of Children's Rights* 223.
20 Ibid, at 236–37.
21 A. McGillivray, 'Why Children Have Equal Rights: In Reply to Laura Purdy' (1994) 2 *International Journal of Children's Rights* 243–58, 245.
22 Ibid, 243.
23 T. Campbell, 'Really Equal Rights? Some Philosophical Comments on "Why Children Shouldn't Have Equal Rights" by Laura M. Purdy' (1994) 2 *International Journal of Children's Rights* 259, 261.
24 See, e.g. Freeman, *The Rights and Wrongs of Children*, categorizing children's rights as: right to welfare, right of protection, right to be treated like adults, rights against parents.

treatment where the refusal will lead to irreparable harm or death. The autonomy and basic interests are in stark conflict in such cases. Theorists have reflected on ways of addressing these types of conflict.

Eekelaar suggested that in seeking to reconcile a conflict between children's basic interests and their decisions, 'some kind of imaginative leap may be required' to 'guess what a child might retrospectively have wanted once it reaches a position of maturity'.[25] Eekelaar acknowledges that the values of the adult world may intrude but that is to be openly accepted, encouraging debate about them.[26] Eekelaar suggests it is possible that some adults might not approve of the fact that their autonomy was thwarted in childhood so as not to leave them at a disadvantage as against other children in realizing their life chances in adulthood, although he considers that this is likely to be a minority viewpoint. Hence, the autonomy interests may be ranked 'subordinate to the basic and developmental interests', but 'where they may be exercised without threatening these two interests, the claim for their satisfaction must be high'.[27]

Michael Freeman, drawing on John Rawls' theory of justice,[28] reaches a similar view, his version of 'liberal paternalism'.[29] Rawls derived his theories of justice by thinking about what would be considered just by persons who were deciding behind a veil of ignorance of their own position within a society. This led him to suggest principles of equal liberty and opportunity, and social/economic arrangements to the greatest benefit of the least advantaged. Applying such an approach to the case of children, Freeman suggested that if the persons participating in this hypothetical social contract did not know whether or not they were children, it is probable that most would wish to mature to an independent adulthood. He concluded:

> The question we should ask ourselves is: what sort of action or conduct would we wish, as children, to be shielded against on the assumption that we would want to mature to a rationally autonomous adulthood and be capable of deciding on our own system of ends as free and rational beings? We would ... choose principles that would enable children to mature to independent adulthood. One definition of irrationality would be such as to preclude action and conduct which would frustrate such a goal. Within the constraints of such a definition we would defend a version of paternism ... .

These discussions are concerned principally with the negative impact that exercises of autonomy might have on child welfare. In other work, however, John Eekelaar has explored the positive implications of the child's interest in self-determination

---

[25] Eekelaar 'The Emergence of Children's Rights', 170.
[26] Ibid.
[27] Ibid. See also Eekelaar, 'The Importance of Thinking That Children Have Rights', in Alston, Parker and Seymour (eds), *Children, Rights and the Law*, pp. 230–31.
[28] J. Rawls, *A Theory of Justice* (Oxford University Press, 1973).
[29] See Freeman, *The Rights and Wrongs of Children*, and Freeman, 'Taking Children's Rights More Seriously' in Alston, Parker and Seymour (eds), *Children, Rights and the Law*, pp. 66–69.

upon welfare decision-making, a process which Eekelaar calls dynamic self-determinism.[30] The purpose of dynamic self-determinism 'is to bring a child to the threshold of adulthood with the maximum opportunities to form and pursue life-goals which reflect as closely as possible an autonomous choice'.[31] It envisages that within a stable environment the child is exposed to a range of influences and in his or her development is given scope to influence the outcome. The method does not primarily seek to elicit decisions from children, but its aim is, through awareness of the child's wishes and feelings, 'to establish the most propitious environment for the child further to develop the personality growing within him or her and in this way to fashion the outcome'.[32] As Eekelaar explains:

> The very fact that the outcome has been, at least partly, determined by the child is taken to demonstrate that the outcome is in the child's best interests. The process is dynamic because it appreciates that the optimal course for a child cannot always be mapped out at the time of decision, and may need to be revised as the child grows up. It involves self-determinism because the child itself is given scope to influence the outcomes.[33]

While these are all useful methods of seeking to reconcile some of children's conflicting interests, there is a danger of seeing children merely in terms of their capacity to become future adults. By contrast, Tom Campbell classifies minors' interests in such a way as to highlight some interests which are distinctively children's, referring to the rights of the minor as person, as child, as juvenile, and as future adult. This recognizes the interests that children may have at different stages of their development, such as the right as a child to play as a child for its own sake.[34]

Resistance to children's rights

Some commentators have argued that rights talk does not represent the most appropriate way of dealing with children. On one view, 'rights talk is morally impoverished and neglects an alternative ethical view of the world, in which the affectionate, caring interdependence which ideally characterises the parent-child relationship assumes an exemplary significance'.[35] By contrast, Michael Freeman argues that this criticism idealizes adult–child relations and presents a myth of childhood as a golden age,[36] yet the realities of many children's lives are different.

---

[30] Eekelaar, 'The Interests of the Child and the Child's Wishes: The Role of Dynamic Self-Determinism'.

[31] Ibid, 53.

[32] Ibid, 54.

[33] Ibid, 48.

[34] See Campbell, 'The Rights of the Minor: as Person, as Child, as Juvenile, as Future Adult', in Alston, Parker and Seymour (eds), *Children, Rights and the Law*, pp. 21–22.

[35] As explained by Archard, *Children: Rights and Childhood*, ch. 8, p. 112, and for criticism of the point, see pp. 118–23.

[36] Freeman, 'Taking Children's Rights More Seriously' in Alston, Parker, and Seymour (eds), *Children, Rights and the Law*, p. 52, at pp. 55–56.

Furthermore, as Martha Minow has pointed out, rights language is not wholly antithetical to notions of dependency and connection with others.[37] Indeed, as she argues, having rights can provide a procedural basis for communication with others.

Another argument is that there is little point or value in talking about children's rights. Onora O'Neill has argued[38] that if we care about children's lives we may have good reasons to focus on adults' obligations to children rather than appealing to children's fundamental rights.[39] O'Neill views children as unlike other oppressed groups claiming rights: they are 'more fundamentally but less permanently powerless; their main remedy is to grow up'.[40] By contrast, Michael Freeman doubts that children's dependency is quite as different from other oppressed groups as O'Neill suggests, in that childhood (as socially constructed) can be artificially prolonged and is determined by those in authority.[41]

O'Neill's preference for a focus on obligations, however, is founded on her observation that there are some obligations, such as being kind and helping to develop others' capacities, which are imperfect obligations because the precise obligations and to whom they are owed are not specified. For O'Neill, such obligations have no allocated right-holders and therefore no counterpart set of rights. Her analysis provides the insight that a shift to the idiom of rights risks excluding and neglecting some things that may matter to children[42] because such things drop out of the picture if, approaching from a rights perspective, no right-holder can be identified. However, as David Archard has queried: 'why should rights not correspond to imperfect as well as perfect obligations?'[43] In other words, it might be argued that each and every child is entitled to demand of all adults that he or she is treated properly by any one of them.[44]

Debate 2

To what extent does, and should, English law recognize a child's autonomy interest?

Perhaps the most controversial children's rights issue which arises in practice is the extent to which the law should allow children to make their own decisions. The issue acquires its sharpest focus in cases where children wish to take decisions which would lead to their irreparable harm or death. This problem has tended to arise in case-law in the context of children's consent, or refusal of consent,

---

[37] M. Minow, 'Interpreting Rights: An Essay for Robert Cover' (1987) *Yale Law Journal* 1860.
[38] O. O'Neill, 'Children's Rights and Children's Lives' (1988) 98 *Ethics* 445.
[39] O'Neill in Alston, Parker and Seymour (eds), *Children, Rights and the Law* 1992), p. 39.
[40] Ibid.
[41] Freeman, 'Taking Children's Rights More Seriously' in Alston, Parker and Seymour (eds), *Children, Rights and the Law*, p. 52, at p. 56.
[42] Ibid, pp. 35–36.
[43] Archard, *Children: Rights and Childhood*, p. 124.
[44] Ibid.

to medical treatment. The case-law has proved controversial and difficult to interpret.

The leading case is the House of Lords' decision in *Gillick v West Norfolk and Wisbech Area Health Authority and Department of Health and Social Security*.[45] Mrs Victoria Gillick objected to a DHSS Memorandum of Guidance[46] which advised that in exceptional circumstances a doctor could prescribe contraception to a girl under 16 without her parents' knowledge or consent. She sought a declaration in the courts that the guidance was unlawful, contending that a doctor could not lawfully prescribe contraceptives to a girl under 16 without parental consent because: (1) the girl could not consent to medical treatment; (2) to do so would infringe parental rights, which entitled her to an absolute veto over her children's medical treatment.[47] Mrs Gillick lost her case in the House of Lords by a majority of three to two.[48] Lord Fraser and Lord Scarman each delivered opinions on the substantive issues and Lord Bridge agreed with both opinions. However, the case has produced considerable debate as to its overall effect because of the different emphases in the opinions of Lords Fraser and Scarman.

The House was clear that a girl under 16 could lawfully consent to contraceptive advice, examination and treatment, provided 'she has sufficient understanding and intelligence to know what they involve'.[49] Also rejecting Mrs Gillick's argument on parental rights, Lord Fraser held as a matter of general principle that:

> parental rights to control a child do not exist for the benefit of the parent. They exist for the benefit of the child and they are justified only in so far as they enable the parent to perform his duties towards the child, and towards other children in the family.[50]

He noted that:

> In practice most wise parents relax their control gradually as the child develops and encourage him or her to become increasingly independent. Moreover the degree of parental control actually exercised over a particular child does in practice vary considerably according to his understanding

---

45 [1986] 1 AC 112.

46 HN(80)46, Section G (as revised). See [1986] 1 AC 112, 179–80.

47 Mrs Gillick's third argument that the doctor would be aiding the offence of sexual intercourse with a girl under 16 contrary to the Sexual Offences Act 1956, ss. 5, 6 and 28(1) is not really material to the children's rights discussion here and is not pursued further.

48 Lord Fraser of Tullybelton, Lord Scarman, and Lord Bridge of Harwich; Lord Brandon of Oakbrook and Lord Templeman dissenting. Mrs Gillick had been unsuccessful before Woolf J at first instance ([1984] QB 581) but had won a unanimous victory in the Court of Appeal ([1986] 1 AC 112, C.A. Eveleigh, Fox and Parker LJJ).

49 [1986] 1 AC 112, 170A.

50 [1986] 1 AC 112, 170 D–E, supporting this view, if necessary, by reference to *Blackstone's Commentaries*, 17th edn (1830), Vol. 1, at p. 452; rejecting the approach in *In Re Agar-Ellis* (1883) 24 ChD 317 and preferring instead that in *Hewer v Bryant* [1970] 1 QB 357, at 369: 'the legal right of a parent to the custody of a child ends at the 18th birthday: and even up till then, it is a dwindling right which the courts will hesitate to enforce against the wishes of the child, and the more so the older he is. It starts with a right of control and ends with little more than advice.'

and intelligence and it would, in my opinion, be unrealistic for the courts not to recognise these facts.[51]

However, Lord Fraser did not appear to translate this description of good practice into a corresponding legal principle recognizing children's independence based solely on developing intelligence and understanding, since he saw the solution in the appeal as depending on an assessment of the child's best interests. For Lord Fraser the 'only practicable course [was] to entrust the doctor with a discretion to act in accordance with his view of what is best in the interests of the girl who is his patient'.[52] He identified five conditions of which the doctor would need to be satisfied if he were to be justified in proceeding without a parent's consent or knowledge:

> (1) that the girl (although under 16 years of age) will understand his advice; (2) that he cannot persuade her to inform her parents or to allow him to inform the parents that she is seeking contraceptive advice; (3) that she is very likely to begin or to continue having sexual intercourse with or without contraceptive treatment; (4) that unless she receives contraceptive advice or treatment her physical or mental health or both are likely to suffer; (5) that her best interests require him to give her contraceptive advice, treatment or both without the parental consent.[53]

Lord Fraser's approach thus seems to require the doctor to mediate the relationship between parental duties and children's interests in decision-making by reference to child welfare; the doctor must ensure, in what is an extension[54] of his clinical judgment, that the parents' duty of protection can be safely abandoned.

While Lord Scarman agreed with Lord Fraser, his expression of principle and application of it to the medical issue in the case focused more on children's evolving capacities and their relationship with parental rights. He concluded that:

> parental right yields to the child's right to make his own decisions when he reaches a sufficient understanding and intelligence to be capable of making up his own mind on the matter requiring decision.[55]

He saw 'a clue to the true principle of the law'[56] in earlier case-law on the age at which children were permitted to live independently of their father ('age of discretion' cases), specifically *R v Howes*.[57] These were cases in which the courts would refuse to return a child to a parent if the child had 'sufficient intelligence

---

[51] Ibid, 171 D–F.

[52] Ibid, 174 B–C.

[53] Ibid., 174 D–E.

[54] For detailed arguments supporting the view that Lord Fraser extends the doctor's role see I. Kennedy, 'The Doctor, the Pill and the 15-year-old Girl', in I. Kennedy, *Treat Me Right, Essays in Medical Law and Ethics* (Oxford University Press, 1988), at pp. 94–95.

[55] [1986] 1 AC 112, 186D.

[56] [1986] 1 AC 112, 183F.

[57] (1860) 3 E & E 332.

and understanding to make up his own mind'.[58] Lord Scarman agreed with the principle of law there expressed, namely the attainment by a child of an age of sufficient discretion to exercise 'a *wise choice in his or her interests*'.[59]

Applying these principles to the medical context of the case, Lord Scarman concluded that:

> as a matter of law the parental right to determine whether or not their minor child below the age of 16 will have medical treatment terminates if and when the child achieves a sufficient understanding and intelligence to enable him or her to understand fully what is proposed. It will be a question of fact whether a child seeking advice has sufficient understanding of what is involved to give a consent valid in law.[60]

However, he added a stringent test for the child's capacity, commenting:

> There are moral and family questions, especially her relationship with her parents; long-term problems associated with the emotional impact of pregnancy and its termination; and there are the risks to health of sexual intercourse at her age, risks which contraception may diminish but cannot eliminate. It follows that a doctor will have to satisfy himself that she is able to appraise these factors before he can safely proceed upon the basis that she has at law capacity to consent to contraceptive treatment.[61]

A human rights challenge to *Gillick* was rejected in *R (Axon) v Secretary of State for Health and the Family Planning Association* (hereafter *Axon*)[62] in which it was argued that a failure to inform a parent that a child was receiving abortion advice and treatment would constitute a breach of a parent's right to respect for family life under Article 8 of the European Convention on Human Rights (ECHR). Silber J held that any such parental right 'dwindles as their child gets older and is able to understand the consequence of different choices and then to make decisions relating to them'[63] and that 'this autonomy must undermine any article 8 rights of a parent to family life'.[64] This might be interpreted as giving increased emphasis to children's autonomy. However, Silber J also held that Lord Fraser's guidelines in *Gillick* applied, and that these are legal pre-conditions[65] to be strictly observed.

---

[58] Ibid, 187D.

[59] Ibid, 187H–188A (emphasis added). Jane Fortin argues that Lord Scarman's statement that the age of discretion was the attainment of 'sufficient discretion to enable him or her to exercise a *wise* choice' was merely a factual description of how the ages of discretion were chosen and did not suggest that he himself confined the notion of *Gillick* competence to those with a capacity for wisdom: see J. Fortin, 'The *Gillick* Decision – Not Just a High-water Mark', in S. Gilmore, J. Herring and R. Probert (eds), *Landmark Cases in Family Law* (Hart Publishing, 2011), at pp. 206–07.

[60] [1986] 1 AC 112, at 188–89.

[61] Ibid, at 189D.

[62] [2006] EWHC 37 (Admin); [2006] QB 539.

[63] Ibid, at para [129].

[64] Ibid, at para [130]. For criticism, see R. Taylor, 'Reversing the retreat from *Gillick*? *R (Axon) v Secretary of State for Health*' (2007) *Child and Family Law Quarterly* 81.

[65] *Axon*, at paras [110] and [111].

He also indicated that Lord Fraser's first condition, that the child understands the advice, was to be read in the light of Lord Scarman's stringent test for capacity (above).

Debate surrounding a children's rights interpretation of *Gillick*

The differences of emphasis in the majority opinions in *Gillick v West Norfolk and Wisbech Area Health Authority and Department of Health and Social Security*[66] led one commentator to ask at the time of the decision, 'just what has *Gillick* decided?',[67] and there has been considerable academic debate about what it achieved.

An influential children's autonomy rights interpretation of *Gillick* is to be found in the writings of John Eekelaar.[68] Eekelaar seized upon Lord Scarman's references to parental rights yielding[69] or terminating[70] upon the child's achievement of sufficient intelligence and understanding, and concluded that 'where a child has reached capacity, there is no room for a parent to impose a contrary view, *even if this is more in accord with the child's best interests*'.[71] Thus in Eekelaar's view *Gillick* had conferred on children 'in wider measure than ever before, that most dangerous but most precious of rights: the right to make their own mistakes'.[72] Eekelaar maintained that Lord Fraser should be taken to have adopted the same general approach, and that his discussion of parental rights with reference to his five conditions should be seen as confined to the solution required by the medical context. On this view, *Gillick* represented a 'fundamental shift in legal doctrine' with 'potentially far-reaching implications'.[73] For example, Eekelaar suggested that the case would apparently require a re-orientation of the court's approach to wardship and to custody disputes on divorce where welfare would now have to defer to the competent child's wishes .[74]

Another leading commentator, Andrew Bainham, interpreted the decision less radically, suggesting that *Gillick* should not be equated with 'a policy of legal autonomy or independence for children'.[75] For Bainham, the majority speeches in *Gillick* 'support a participatory model of decision making, ... according to parents *and* children qualified or relative autonomy'.[76]

---

[66] [1986] 1 AC 112.

[67] P. Parkinson, 'The *Gillick* Case – Just What Has it Decided?' [1986] *Family Law* 11.

[68] J. Eekelaar, 'The Eclipse of Parental Rights' (1986) 102 *LQR* 4 and 'The Emergence of Children's Rights'.

[69] [1986] 1 AC 112, 186D.

[70] Ibid, 188H.

[71] 'The Emergence of Children's Rights', 181, emphasis in original.

[72] 'The Emergence of Children's Rights', 182. It is a view that he thought may not ultimately find favour with the judiciary: J. Eekelaar, '*Gillick*: Further Limits on Parents' Rights to Punish' (1986) 28 *Childright* 9.

[73] S. M. Cretney, '*Gillick* and the Concept of Legal Capacity' (1989) 105 *LQR* 356.

[74] Eekelaar, '*Gillick* in the Divorce Court' (1986) 136 *New Law Journal* 184 , and see also J. Eekelaar, 'Wider Implications of Gillick' (1986) 26 *Childright* 17.

[75] Ibid.

[76] A. Bainham, *Children, Parents and the State* (Sweet and Maxwell, 1988), p. 72.

Stephen Gilmore has questioned more directly whether an autonomy rights interpretation is the most plausible,[77] making the following arguments.

1 The focus in *Gillick* was on children's welfare, not children's autonomy inter-ests. This can be seen in the public debate surrounding the litigation, counsel's arguments and their Lordships' characterization of the issues, all of which focused on resolving the potentially conflicting claims of doctors and parents to know what was in a child's best interests.[78]

2 Lord Scarman expressly agreed with Lord Fraser's opinion (not the reverse), and therefore Lord Scarman's opinion should be read in the light of that agreement. It is therefore at least as plausible, if not more plausible, to see Lord Fraser's welfare approach to the solution in the appeal as *reflecting* their Lordships' earlier general conclusions as to the point at which parental right yields (namely when parental protection is no longer required). Although Jane Fortin[79] has observed that Lord Scarman's 'words of agreement with Lord Fraser's opinion were unsurprising, given their joint view that Mrs Gillick's application was unfounded' and that 'he clearly agreed with much of Lord Fraser's assessment of the preceding case law',[80] Lord Scarman agreed with Lord Fraser's *speech*, not just the outcome, and he did not qualify his agreement,[81] so he should on the face of it be taken to have agreed with all of it.

3 Lord Scarman drew on case-law on the ages of discretion, the underlying rationale of which was to protect children from making decisions harmful to their welfare. This makes it difficult to suppose that Lord Scarman envisaged children making decisions that would lead to their irreparable harm. It might also be argued that Lord Scarman appeared to require that children be able to make a wise choice in their own interest. However, against that view Jane Fortin has argued that Lord Scarman's statement that the age of discretion was the attainment of 'sufficient discretion to enable him or her to exercise a wise choice' was merely a factual description of how the ages of discretion were chosen and did not suggest that he himself confined the notion of Gillick competence to those with a capacity for wisdom.[82]

4 In terms of establishing a precedent, at its most abstract *Gillick* merely endorses a child's power to accept an adult's bona fide, yet possibly mistaken, view of what is in a child's interests. Put simply, the 'reasoning of Lords Fraser and

---

[77] S. Gilmore, 'The Limits of Parental Responsibility', in R. Probert, S. Gilmore and J. Herring, *Responsible Parents and Parental Responsibility* (Hart Publishing, 2009).

[78] See also Eekelaar's own comment: '[t]he public debate which surrounded the litigation tended to revolve around the competing claims of parents and doctors to determine children's interests' in 'The Emergence of Children's Rights', 178.

[79] Fortin, 'The *Gillick* Decision – Not Just a High-water Mark', in Gilmore, Herring and Probert (eds), *Landmark Cases in Family Law*, p. 199.

[80] Ibid, 206.

[81] Except by saying that the issues were so important that he wished to express his opinion in his own words.

[82] Fortin, 'The *Gillick* Decision – Not Just a High-water Mark', in Gilmore, Herring and Probert (eds), *Landmark Cases in Family Law*, pp. 206–07.

Scarman was built upon a consideration of the best interests of the sexually active minor, not upon the right of the minor to be sexually active',[83] or indeed to demand contraceptive treatment.

5 The *Axon*[84] case makes it more difficult to argue a children's autonomy rights reading of *Gillick* because the Fraser guidelines now require both a very high level of understanding *and* a finding that it is in the child's best interests to have treatment without parental consent.

That is not to say that *Gillick* was not a groundbreaking decision. It clearly emancipated children from the nineteenth-century view of absolute parental authority, and Lord Scarman's statements of general principle are clearly an important launch-point for development of legal recognition of the child's autonomy interest. Fortin contends that, in terms of *Gillick*'s landmark status 'it does not matter what the precise effects of the majority decision were',[85] and it is true that *Gillick* 'undeniably placed the idea of children's autonomy rights in the legal consciousness in a way which had not previously existed'.[86] However, against Fortin's opinion, it can still be contended that it is important to distinguish between what is established binding law, and mere dicta in judgments.

Case-law and debates surrounding children's refusal of medical treatment

Gillick v West Norfolk and Wisbech Area Health Authority and Department of Health and Social Security[87] was concerned with whether a competent child could *consent* to medical treatment. In two subsequent Court of Appeal decisions, *Re R (A Minor) (Wardship: Consent to Treatment)*[88] and *Re W (A Minor) (Medical Treatment: Court's Jurisdiction)*,[89] the issue of children's autonomy arose in the context of refusal of consent.

In *Re R* a girl, R, aged 15 years 10 months, was in the care of a local authority, and being treated in an adolescent psychiatric unit. When, in one of her lucid periods, R refused her anti-psychotic medication, the local authority was unhappy

---

[83] S. Gilmore, J. Herring and R. Probert, 'Introduction: Parental Responsibility – Law, Issues and Themes', in Probert, Gilmore and Herring (eds), *Responsible Parents and Parental Responsibility*, p. 4.

[84] [2006] EWHC 37 (Admin); [2006] QB 539.

[85] Fortin, 'The *Gillick* Decision – Not Just a High-water Mark', in Gilmore, Herring and Probert (eds), *Landmark Cases in Family Law*, pp. 199, 222.

[86] Gilmore, Herring and Probert, 'Introduction: Parental Responsibility – Law, Issues and Themes', in Probert, Gilmore and Herring (eds), *Responsible Parents and Parental Responsibility*, p. 6. See H. Teff, *Reasonable Care, Legal Perspectives on the Doctor/Patient Relationship* (Oxford University Press, 1994) p. 152: it was undeniable that *Gillick* 'came to be seen as a symbolic milestone in the enfranchisement of children'.

[87] [1986] 1 AC 112.

[88] [1992] Fam 11 (Lord Donaldson MR, Staughton and Farquharson LJJ), hereafter *Re R*.

[89] [1993] Fam 64 (Lord Donaldson MR, Balcombe and Nolan LJJ), hereafter *Re W*. See J. Eekelaar, 'White Coats or Flak Jackets? Doctors, Children and the Courts – Again' (1993) 109 *LQR* 182; H. Houghton-James, 'The Child's Right to Die' [1992] *Family Law* 550; N. Lowe and S. Juss, 'Medical Treatment – Pragmatism and the Search for Principle' (1993) 56 *MLR* 865; J. Masson, '*Re W*: Appealing from the Golden Cage' (1993) 5(1) *Journal of Child Law* 37; M. Mulholland, '*Re W (A Minor)*: Autonomy, Consent and the Anorexic Teenager'(1993) 9(1) *Professional Negligence* 21; R. Thornton, 'Minors and Medical Treatment – Who Decides?' [1993] *CLJ* 34.

to consent to its administration, and initiated wardship proceedings to determine the issue. The Court of Appeal confirmed that a court in wardship, applying as it must the child's welfare as its paramount consideration, has power to override the wishes of a child, whether competent or otherwise. However, Lord Donaldson went on to make controversial obiter comments on the relationship between a child's competence to consent and parental powers. Referring to the *Gillick* case, he commented:

> Lord Scarman was discussing the parents' right '*to determine* whether or not their minor child below the age of 16 will have medical treatment' [my emphasis] and this is the 'parental right' to which he was referring at p. 186D. A right of determination is wider than a right to consent. The parents can only have a right of determination if *either* the child has no right to consent, that is, is not a keyholder, *or* the parents hold a master key which could nullify the child's consent. I do not understand Lord Scarman to be saying that, if a child was '*Gillick* competent'…the parents ceased to have an independent right of consent as contrasted with ceasing to have a right of determination, that is, a veto. In a case in which the '*Gillick* competent' child refuses treatment, but the parents consent, that consent *enables* treatment to be undertaken lawfully, but in no way determines that the child shall be so treated. In a case in which the positions are reversed, it is the child's consent which is the enabling factor and again the parents' refusal of consent is not determinative. If Lord Scarman intended to go further than this and to say that in the case of a '*Gillick* competent' child, a parent has no right either to consent or to refuse consent, his remarks were obiter, because the only question in issue was Mrs Gillick's alleged right of veto. Furthermore, I consider that they would have been wrong.[90]

This dictum attracted considerable criticism[91] and an opportunity to reconsider it came in *Re W*. A local authority sought leave to invoke the inherent jurisdiction of the High Court to determine the treatment of a 16-year-old girl who was suffering from anorexia nervosa. Lord Donaldson again doubted 'whether Lord Scarman meant more than that the *exclusive* right of the parents to consent to treatment terminated',[92] a doubt now shared by Balcombe LJ,[93] although Lord Donaldson

---

[90] [1992] Fam 11, 23 E–H.
[91] See A. Bainham, 'The Judge and the Competent Minor' (1992) 108 *LQR* 194; G. Douglas, 'The Retreat from *Gillick*' (1992) 55 *MLR* 569; P. Fennell, 'Informal Compulsion: The Psychiatric Treatment of Juveniles under Common Law' [1992] *Journal of Social Welfare and Family Law* 311; J. Masson, 'Adolescent Crisis and Parental Power' [1991] *Family Law* 528; J. Montgomery, 'Parents and Children in Dispute: Who Has the Final Word?' (1992) 4 *Journal of Child Law* 85; J. Murphy, 'Circumscribing the Autonomy of "*Gillick* Competent" Children' (1992) 43(1) *Northern Ireland Legal Quarterly* 60; S. Parker and J. Dewar, [1992] *Journal of Social Welfare and Family* Law 143; R. Thornton, 'Multiple Keyholders – Wardship and Consent to Medical Treatment' [1992] *CLJ* 34; J. Urwin, '*Re R*: The Resurrection of Parental Powers?' (1992) 8 *Professional Negligence* 69.
[92] [1993] Fam 64, at p. 76C.
[93] Ibid, p. 87 E–F.

now acknowledged that he 'may well be wrong'.[94] But he reiterated his view that there could be concurrent consents, preferring however the analogy of the legal flak-jacket (providing the doctor with a shield against a claim in battery) to his earlier keyholder analogy, since keys are capable of both locking and unlocking.[95] Nolan LJ appeared to have some reservations, indicating that the case did not directly concern this point, and that in any case of conflict between a competent child and parent, the court's jurisdiction should always be invoked.[96]

Importantly, W's case differed materially from *Re R* in two respects: she had attained the age of 16; and by section 8 of the Family Law Reform Act 1969 had a statutory power to consent to medical treatment. So far as material, section 8 provides:

> (1) The consent of a minor who has attained the age of 16 years to any…medical treatment, which in the absence of consent would constitute a trespass to the person, shall be as effective as it would be if he were of full age; and where a minor has by virtue of this section given an effective consent to any treatment it shall not be necessary to obtain any consent for it from his parent or guardian; …
>
> (3) Nothing in this section shall be construed as making ineffective any consent which would have been effective if this section had not been enacted.

W contended that section 8 had provided her with an absolute statutory power to determine whether or not she received medical treatment, and the inherent jurisdiction of the court could not be exercised to override that statutory power.[97] The Court of Appeal rejected this interpretation of section 8.[98] Lord Donaldson noted that if parental power to consent was extinguished upon a child's acquisition of capacity to consent, then not only would it not be necessary to obtain a parent's consent as section 8(1) provides, it would be legally impossible. He further argued that section 8(3) 'would create problems since, if the section had not been enacted, a parent's consent would undoubtedly have been effective *as*

---

[94] Ibid.

[95] Ibid, at p. 78 D–E. For commentary, see Eekelaar, 'White Coats or Flak Jackets? Doctors, Children and the Courts – Again'; Houghton-James, 'The Child's Right to Die'; N. Lowe and S. Juss, 'Medical Treatment – Pragmatism and the Search for Principle' (1993) 56 *MLR* 865; Masson, '*Re W*: appealing From the Golden Cage'; Mulholland, '*Re W (A Minor)*: Autonomy, Consent and the Anorexic Teenager'; Thornton, 'Minors and Medical Treatment – Who Decides?'; J. Bridgeman, 'Old Enough to Know Best?' (1993) 13 *Legal Studies* 69; L. Edwards, 'The Right to Consent and the Right to Refuse; More Problems with Minors and Medical Consent' [1993] *Juridical Review* 52; A. Grubb, 'Treatment Decisions: Keeping It in the Family' in A. Grubb (ed.), *Choices and Decisions in Health Care* (Chichester, 1993) p. 37; J. K. Mason, 'Master of the Balancers; Non-Voluntary Therapy under the Mantle of Lord Donaldson' [1993] *Juridical Review* 115; J. Murphy, 'W(h)ither Adolescent Autonomy?' [1992] *Journal of Social Welfare and Family Law* 529.

[96] [1993] Fam 64, at 92.

[97] Under the principle in *A v Liverpool City Council* [1982] AC 363.

[98] [1993] Fam 64, 77 B–C, per Lord Donaldson MR, at 87H, per Balcombe LJ, at 92 E–H, per Nolan LJ.

a consent'.[99] The Court of Appeal thus held that a judge exercising the inherent jurisdiction had power to override the wishes of a competent 16- or 17-year-old.

The idea that there can be concurrent consents in parent and child which can result in a child's refusal of consent to medical treatment being lawfully overridden by parental consent has proved extremely controversial. The case-law has been seen by many commentators as making an illogical distinction between consent and refusal. They ask: how can a child have capacity to consent, yet not have capacity to refuse?[100] Indeed, Balcombe LJ in *Re W* commented that '[i]n logic there can be no difference between an ability to consent to treatment and an ability to refuse treatment'.[101]

Commentators have also observed that the case-law seems to produce some unusual results in practice. Margaret Brazier has commented:

> In practical terms legal principles which result in a mother having no say as to whether her teenage daughter agrees to an abortion, no right even to know of the operation, but being able to require that same daughter to undergo abortion against her will, are odd in the extreme.[102]

Similarly, Jo Bridgeman has noted the allegedly odd position of a 17-year-old mother, who can refuse consent to her child's medical treatment, but can have her own refusal of consent overridden by her own parents.[103]

However, this anomaly really arises from the fact that a child mother falls into both categories of 'parent' and 'child', and it might be counter-argued that this example shows that the law consistently requires of a parent, whether adult or child, that powers of consent are exercised in the child's best interests. Indeed, Nigel Lowe and Satvinder Juss have argued that the approach in *Re W* consistently seeks to protect children by facilitating medical treatment easily when it is in a child's best interests, whilst at the same time protecting children from their own, and their parents', 'wrong-headed decisions'.[104] However, as Gillian Douglas observes, the position is not quite so straightforward, since there may be

---

99 [1993] Fam 64, at 77, reiterating arguments made in *Re R* [1992] Fam 11, at 24 G–H (emphasis in original). Additionally he described s. 8(3) as 'preserving the common law immediately before the Act, which undoubtedly gave parents a power to consent for all children up to the age of 21'.

100 Bridgeman, 'Old Enough to Know Best?', 80; Urwin, '*Re R*: The Resurrection of Parental Powers?', 72: 'It is absurd to say that a child who is competent can consent but cannot refuse treatment.'; S. Cretney, *Elements of Family Law* (Sweet & Maxwell, 1992): 'How can it be argued that a young person who has satisfied the demanding tests of comprehension and maturity required to attain *Gillick* capacity to *consent* does not have the capacity to *refuse* to be subjected to treatment?' (at para 11.28); Grubb, 'Treatment Decisions: Keeping It in the Family', in A. Grubb (ed.), *Choices and Decisions in Health Care* (John Wiley, 1993), at p. 62: 'Both legally and morally, consent or refusal of consent by a competent child must be opposites of the same coin'; J. Harris, 'Consent and End of Life Decisions' (2003) 29 *Journal of Medical Ethics* 10, 15: 'The idea that a child (or anyone) might competently consent to a treatment but not be competent to refuse it is palpable nonsense'.

101 [1993] Fam 64, 88 B–C.

102 M. Brazier, *Medicine, Patients and the Law* (Penguin Books, 1992), p. 346.

103 Bridgeman, 'Old Enough to Know Best?', 80.

104 N. Lowe and S. Juss, 'Medical Treatment – Pragmatism and the Search for Principle' (1993) 56 *MLR* 865, 871–72.

more than one recognized body of medical opinion and a choice of treatments. She also argues that a refusal of consent should be given greater weight because overriding it involves both 'intellectual and bodily' interference with a person's autonomy.[105]

Against the tide of most academic commentary, Stephen Gilmore and Jonathan Herring have sought to show that in some circumstances it is possible that a child could have capacity to consent to treatment, yet not necessarily have capacity to refuse all treatment.[106] Their analysis demonstrates some support for Lord Donaldson's concurrent consents approach. They argue that it is important to distinguish the following two ways of saying 'no' to treatment:

(1) A 'rejection of proposed treatment'. Here the child is offered the option of consenting to a particular treatment. The child considers the proposed treatment and indicates that he or she does not consent to it; or, in other words, declines to provide consent to that particular treatment.

(2) A 'refusal of treatment'. Here the child has decided not to have any treatment whatsoever. It is not merely the patient's wish to decline particular treatment, but a decision to refuse all treatment, a conscious decision to incur the consequences of a total failure to treat.[107]

Gilmore and Herring maintain that these definitions carry at least two significant distinctions: first, as to the capacity required of the child in each case; and second, that they involve asking two different questions. Rejection of proposed treatment involves asking, 'do I assent or not to the treatment proposed?'; a refusal of treatment involves the question 'do I refuse all treatment, understanding all the consequences which ensue from that decision?' Gilmore and Herring conclude that:

it does not necessarily follow from the fact that a child has capacity to consent (and/or capacity to decline consent) to certain specific treatment, X, that he or she will have capacity to refuse all treatment...the child considering whether or not to consent will not necessarily have addressed the 'refusal of treatment' question (not least because he or she may only have been told by the doctor about the proposed treatment). In a case in which the child has capacity to consent to X but does not fully understand the consequences of a total failure to treat, parental responsibility to consent is not fully extinguished by the child's capacity and it is necessary for a parent to have the power to consent to treatment, including, if necessary, treatment X.[108]

---

[105] Douglas, 'The Retreat from *Gillick*', 576.

[106] S. Gilmore and J. Herring, '"No" Is the Hardest Word: Consent and Children's Autonomy' [2011] *Child and Family Law Quarterly* 3; S. Gilmore and J. Herring, 'Children's Refusal of Medical Treatment: Could *Re W* be distinguished?' [2011] *Family Law* 715.

[107] Gilmore and Herring, 'Children's Refusal of Medical Treatment: Could *Re W* Be Distinguished?'.

[108] Ibid, at p. 716. Gilmore and Herring proceed to argue that *Re W* might be distinguished in a future case of a fully competent child on the basis that the expert evidence in *Re W* only showed the adolescent to have capacity to consent and not to refuse all treatment. For criticism, see E. Cave and J. Wallbank, 'Minors' Capacity to Refuse Treatment: A Reply to Gilmore and Herring' [2012] *Medical Law Review*;

Several arguments can also be made at a more general level for treating consent to treatment and refusal of treatment differently.[109] One argument is that there are different levels of autonomous decision-making.[110] For example, some decisions may merely reflect a person's immediate inclinations, whereas others may be the product of greater reflection on the person's overall desire given his own values, even if this runs contrary to his immediate desire.[111] An argument might then be made that the former, weaker notion of autonomy may be regarded as sufficient to authorize routine medical treatment which can only benefit the patient, yet insufficient to amount to a legally effective refusal of treatment, where the refusal will interfere with a person's overall life goals and those matters have not been fully considered. Another argument is that the interconnectedness of persons cannot be ignored when considering the exercises of autonomy. For example, a refusal of treatment may leave parents with a child who is severely disabled, obliging the parents to undertake a heavy burden of care.[112] While one can imagine a parent suffering emotional distress at a child being given a treatment of which he or she did not approve, this is unlikely to have as significant an impact as a decision not to give treatment.[113]

Has there been a 'retreat from *Gillick*'?

The dominant characterization of the developing case-law in academic commentary is that *Gillick West Norfolk and Wisbech Area Health Authority and Department of Health and Social Security*[114] represented a high-water mark for children's autonomy rights, from which there has since been a retreat. This view is evident, for example, in Gillian Douglas' oft-cited commentary on *Re R (A Minor) (Wardship: Consent to Treatment)*, proclaiming in its title 'the retreat from *Gillick*',[115] but Douglas is not alone in this characterization of the case-law, which is evident in other articles in law journals,[116] and in law textbooks.[117] It is a view which has spread unquestioned to commentators in other disciplines: sociology,[118] social work,[119]

---

and for a response, S. Gilmore and J. Herring, 'Children's Refusal of Treatment: The Debate Continues' [2012] Family Law 973.

109 For detailed discussion, see Gilmore and Herring, ' "No" Is the Hardest Word: Consent and Children's Autonomy', 19 et seq.

110 See J. Coggon, 'Varied and Principled Understandings of Autonomy in English Law: Justifiable Inconsistency or Blinkered Moralism?' (2007) 15 *Health Care Analysis* 235, 236.

111 Ibid.

112 Gilmore and Herring, ' "No" Is the Hardest Word: Consent and Children's Autonomy', p. 23.

113 Ibid, 24.

114 [1986] 1 AC 112.

115 [1992] Fam 11; Douglas, 'The Retreat from *Gillick*'.

116 See e.g. Bridgeman, 'Old Enough to Know Best?', 80 ('leaps and bounds away from the approach in *Gillick*'), and J. Roche, 'Children's Rights: In the Name of the Child' [1995] *Journal of Social Welfare and Family Law* 281, 282.

117 See e.g. J. Masson, R. Bailey-Harris, R. Probert, *Cretney's Principles of Family Law* (8th edn, London: Sweet and Maxwell, 2008), at p. 507; C. Lyon and P. de Cruz, *Child Abuse* (2nd edn), at p. 379 ('the already very marked retreat from the principles of the *Gillick* decision').

118 E.g. V. Bell, 'Governing Childhood: Neo-liberalism and the Law' (1993) 22(3) *Economy and Society* 390); J. Pilcher, 'Contrary to *Gillick*: British Children and Sexual Rights since 1985' (1997) 5 *International Journal of Children's Rights* 299.

119 Smith, 'Children's Rights: Judicial Ambivalence and Social Resistance', 110–20.

psychology,[120] and child psychiatry.[121] Yet, as the foregoing account of the case-law and its possible interpretations should have revealed, the existence, nature and extent of any so-called retreat from *Gillick* is a matter which can be much debated. The idea of retreating from earlier (? fixed) decisions is complicated by the nature of the common law, which develops by applying and distinguishing earlier cases. Thus the earlier cases in part *acquire* their meaning from interpretation in later cases. There is therefore another viewpoint: that the *Gillick* case was not setting in stone for all time a general account of the legal recognition of children's autonomy. Indeed, as Lord Scarman himself acknowledged in *Gillick*, it was 'the beginning, not the conclusion, of a legal development in a field glimpsed by one or two judges in recent times...but not yet fully explored'.[122]

Further Reading

General

P. Alderson, *Young Children's Rights* (London: Jessica Kingsley, 2nd edn, 2008).

P. Alston, S. Parker and J. Seymour (eds), *Children, Rights and the Law* (Oxford: Clarendon Press, 1992).

D. Archard, *Children: Rights and Childhood* (London and New York: Routledge, 2004) and the works cited in his bibliographical essay at pp. 231–42.

B. Franklin (ed.), *The New Handbook of Children's Rights Comparative Policy and Practice* (London: Routledge, 2002).

M. D. A. Freeman, *The Rights and the Wrongs of Children* (London, 1983).

M. Freeman, *The Moral Status of Children: Essays on the Rights of the Child* (Martinhus Nijhoff, 1997).

J. Fortin, *Children's Rights and the Developing Law* (Cambridge: Cambridge University Press, 3rd edn, 2009).

For a detailed practitioner work, see Alistair MacDonald, *The Rights of the Child Law and Practice* (Family Law, 2011).

Assessments of the *Gillick* case

A. Bainham, 'The Balance of Power in Family Decisions' (1986) 45(2) *CLJ* 262.

J. Eekelaar, 'The Eclipse of Parental Rights' (1986) 102 *LQR* 4.

J. Eekelaar 'The Emergence of Children's Rights' (1986) 6 *OJLS* 161.

S. Gilmore, 'The Limits of Parental Responsibility', in R. Probert, S. Gilmore and J. Herring, *Responsible Parents and Parental Responsibility* (Hart Publishing, 2009).

J. Fortin, 'The *Gillick* Decision – Not Just A High-water Mark', in S. Gilmore, J. Herring and R. Probert, *Landmark Cases in Family Law* (Hart Publishing, 2011).

---

[120] D. Dickenson and D. Jones, 'True Wishes: The Philosophy and Developmental Psychology of Children's Informed Consent' (1995) 2(4) *Philosophy, Psychiatry and Psychology* 287, 291: 'it seems *clear* that the English courts, through case-law, are swinging towards care and protection' (emphasis added), although there is no real analysis of *Gillick* in the paper.

[121] J. Pearce, 'Consent to Treatment During Childhood, The Assessment of Competence and Avoidance of Conflict' (1994) 165 *British Journal of Psychiatry* 713.

[122] [1986] 1 AC 112, 176C.

I. Kennedy, 'The Doctor, the Pill and the 15-year-old Girl', in I. Kennedy, *Treat me Right, Essays in Medical Law and Ethics* (1988) ch. 5.

S. Lee, 'Towards a Jurisprudence of Consent', in J. Eekelaar and S. Ball (eds) *Oxford Essays in Jurisprudence* (3rd Series) (Oxford, 1987) ch. 9.

J. Montgomery, 'Children as Property?' (1988) 51 *MLR* 323;

P. Parkinson, 'The *Gillick* Case – Just What Has It Decided?' [1986] *Family Law* 11.

G. Williams, 'The *Gillick* Saga' [1985] *NLJ* 1156–58 and 1179–82.

On post-*Gillick* cases

A. Bainham, 'The Judge and the Competent Minor' (1992) 108 *LQR* 194.

E. Cave and J. Wallbank, 'Minors' Capacity to Refuse Treatment: A Reply to Gilmore and Herring' [2012] Medical Law Review.

G. Douglas, 'The Retreat from *Gillick*' (1992) 55 *MLR* 569.

J. Eekelaar, 'White Coats or Flak Jackets? Doctors, Children and the Courts – Again' (1993) 109 *LQR* 182.

S. Gilmore and J. Herring, ' "No" Is the Hardest Word: Consent and Children's Autonomy' [2011] *CFLQ* 3.

S. Gilmore and J. Herring, 'Children's Refusal of Treatment: The Debate Continues' [2012] Family Law 973.

N. Lowe and S. Juss, 'Medical Treatment – Pragmatism and the Search for Principle' (1993) 56 *MLR* 865.

Other commentaries are contained in the footnotes of the chapter.

4

DISPUTES OVER CHILDREN

INTRODUCTION

In this chapter we explore some debates which have arisen in the context of parental disputes about children's upbringing. One issue that has been very hotly contested over the last two decades and continues to stimulate vigorous debate on law and policy is the courts' approach to the allocation of parenting time on the breakdown of parents' relationships. Non-resident parents' concerns that the courts' general approach of awarding residence to one parent (usually the child's mother) and contact to the other does not adequately value the potential input of both parents on separation, have been given voice by the campaigns of fathers' rights organizations.[1]

It has been argued that shared residence should be the norm, or, when putting the argument at its highest, that there should be a presumption of equal division of the child's time.[2] It is also contended that the law has failed to acknowledge non-resident parents' rights to contact with their children and that, at the least, the law should recognize a presumption of ongoing contact. The law on contact in cases of domestic violence has proved particularly controversial, stimulating, by contrast, a debate about whether there should be a presumption *against* contact in cases of domestic violence. Concerns have also been expressed about the efficiency of the courts and their seeming ineffectiveness in enforcing contact in intractable disputes.[3]

---

[1] See R. Collier and S. Sheldon (eds), *Fathers' Rights Activism and Law Reform in Comparative Perspective* (Hart Publishing, 2006).

[2] This is a phenomenon going beyond England: see H. Rhoades, 'The Rise and Rise of Shared Parenting Laws: A Critical Reflection' (2002) 19 *Canadian Journal of Family Law* 75; H. Rhoades and S. Boyd, 'Reforming Custody Laws: A Comparative Study' (2004) 18(2) *International Journal of Law, Policy and the Family* 119.

[3] See for judicial acknowledgement of the problems: *V v V (Children) (Contact: Implacable Hostility)* [2004] EWHC 1215 (Fam); [2004] 2 FLR 851 [7]–[12]; *Re D (Intractable Contact Dispute: Publicity)* [2004] EWHC 727; [2004] 1 FLR 1226.

The latter concerns gained momentum in policy debate around the turn of the millennium,[4] and eventually led to procedural changes to improve court processes and efficiency,[5] and to the passing of the Children and Adoption Act 2006, which introduced new measures for facilitating and enforcing contact. As yet, however, there has been no change to the law's substantive approach to contact and residence disputes, and the recent Family Justice Review recommended no change in the law to establish a presumption of shared parenting.[6] However, the debates remain topical: the government has recently indicated, in response to the Review, its belief 'that there should be a legislative statement of the importance of children having an ongoing relationship with both their parents after family separation, where that is safe, and in the child's best interests',[7] and has issued a consultation paper on how this should be expressed in legislation.[8] For the time being, however, the statutory guidance by which the courts decide residence and contact cases remains the same as it was when the current legislation, the Children Act 1989 (CA 1989), was enacted. The courts must in each case be guided by the child's welfare as the paramount consideration, as enjoined by section 1(1) of the 1989 Act, having regard also to a checklist of factors in section 1(3). The use of 'welfare' as a decision-making criterion and the elevation of the child's welfare to the paramount consideration, however, are themselves not uncontroversial matters and have provoked significant academic debate. The debates in this chapter will look first, therefore, at whether the use of the 'welfare principle' in section 1 of the CA 1989 is satisfactory. The chapter then turns to examine whether there is, and should be, a norm of shared residence. The final section examines the law relating to contact, debates surrounding how that law is properly characterized, and whether the law should adopt presumptions in this context.

origin: Symington v Symington ; Lord Cairns L duty to look to the natural of the father .. JvC. — Lord MacDermott.

Debate 1
The welfare principle: is it any good?

What could possibly be wrong with the idea of focusing on a child's welfare when making a decision with respect to him or her? As Jonathan Herring has pointed

4 *Making Contact Work: A Consultation Paper from the Children Act Sub-Committee of the Lord Chancellor's Advisory Board on Family Law (CASC) on the facilitation and enforcement of contact* (Lord Chancellor's Department, 2001); *Making Contact Work: A Report to the Lord Chancellor on the Facilitation of Arrangements For Contact Between Children and their Non-residential Parents and the Enforcement of Court Orders For Contact* (Lord Chancellor's Department, 2002); *Government's Response to the Report of the Children Act Sub-Committee of the Lord Chancellor's Advisory Board on Family Law 'Making Contact Work'* (2002); HM Government, *Parental Separation: Children's Needs and Parents' Responsibilities* (Cm 6273, 2004).
5 Practice Direction: Revised Private Law Programme [2010] 2 FLR 717.
6 *Family Justice Review Final Report* (November 2011), at 4.27 and 4.28.
7 Ministry of Justice and Department for Education, *The Government Response to the Family Justice Review: A System with Children and Families at Its Heart* (February 2012, Cm 8273), at p. 18, para 61.
8 Department for Education and Ministry of Justice consultation paper, *Co-operative Parenting Following Family Separation: Proposed Legislation on the Involvement of Both Parents in a Child's Life* (13 June 2012).

out, making arguments against the welfare principle may at first blush appear a bit like arguing with 'rhubarb crumble',[9] and that will no doubt be the reaction of some readers when confronting this question for the first time. However, as might be expected, there are arguments both for and against the 'welfare principle' as set out in section 1 of the CA 1989. The debates can be divided into two strands: first, examining the various advantages and disadvantages which attend the use of 'welfare' as a decision-making criterion per se; and secondly, debates surrounding English law's elevation of children's welfare to the paramount consideration on matters of child upbringing. *+p 38 Eekelaar. undalloyable dogma*

'Welfare' as a decision-making criterion

Several points can be made in favour of the welfare principle. It can be argued that it has an important rhetorical function, representing 'an important social and moral value that children, being vulnerable, impressionable and dependent, must be protected from harm'.[10] In addition, as Jonathan Herring has observed, it:

> focuses the court's attention on the person whose voice may be the quietest both literally and metaphorically and who has the least control over whether the issue arrives before the court or in the way it does. The child may also be the person with whom the court is least able to empathise.[11]

A further important advantage of welfare decision-making is that it is flexible in its application to the facts of individual cases, and can adapt easily to social change and developing attitudes. It is also arguably 'one of the most accurately understood legal principles among the general public'[12] and a useful basis for achieving negotiated settlements, since most parents are likely to be able to agree, at least in principle, on a focus on their child's welfare.[13]

Against these advantages, a major criticism of welfare decision-making relates to its indeterminacy. An American family law scholar, Robert Mnookin, has sought to show how indeterminate a rational decision by application of the welfare principle is.[14] He takes as an example a residence dispute between parents. In order to decide whether the child should live with his or her father or mother, it would be necessary to identify the possible outcomes for the child and then ascertain the probability of each happening. To do this requires considerable information. The decision maker must also contend with various competing theories and bodies of knowledge about human behaviour. There is also the question of what values are to inform any choices. Is the court to take a short-term or long-term view of

The WP may perpetuate accepted norms.

[9] J. Herring, 'Farewell Welfare?' (2005) 27(2) *Journal of Social Welfare and Family Law* 159 , at p. 159.
[10] M. King, 'Playing the Symbols – Custody and the Law Commission' (1987) 17 *Family Law* 1986.
[11] J. Herring, 'The Welfare Principle and the Rights of Parents', in A. Bainham, S. Day Sclater and M. Richards (eds) *What is a Parent?* (Hart Publishing, 1999), p. 100.
[12] Herring, 'Farewell Welfare?', p. 168.
[13] Ibid, p. 163.
[14] R. Mnookin, 'Child-custody Adjudication: Judicial Functions in the Face of Indeterminacy' (1975) 39(3) *Law and Contemporary Problems* 226.

the child's welfare? Is the emotional support one parent can give more important than the educational help the other can provide?

It can be argued that this unpredictability of outcome makes achieving a negotiated settlement more difficult than if a rule-based approach were adopted. Furthermore, against the advantage of flexibility of the welfare principle, it can be said that the investigation of children's individual circumstances is expensive and can result in delay in decision-making.[15] It can be argued that introducing a rule or presumption, for example, that a child is to live with the person who was his or her primary carer prior to the breakdown of the parents' relationship, could reduce costs and make negotiation easier. A counterargument is that a rule-based approach can be too rigid, resulting in different cases being treated alike.[16] Furthermore, the problem of indeterminacy should not be overstated: sometimes it can be solved by drawing on a consensus, particularly as to what does not promote children's welfare. If one parent has harmed the child and the other has not, it may be obvious in whose favour a dispute about the child's sole residence should be decided.

A further objection to the welfare principle is that decisions can lack transparency. Other values, or reasons for the decision, can be smuggled in under the guise of the child's welfare. An example given by Helen Reece[17] is the now dated attitude to homosexual parenting which was displayed in case-law in the 1980s, which stated that, all things being equal, it was better for children to be brought up with a father and a mother rather than by same-sex parents.[18] As Reece points out, such rulings do not impact only upon the child before the court; they can stigmatize as living in inferior environments all children who are living perfectly happily with same-sex parents.[19] However, Herring observes that judges appear to be striving not to let their personal views influence their decisions, at least not overtly, avoiding making value judgments about parents' lifestyles, for example, on matters such as religion and sexuality.[20]

Criticisms of the paramountcy of the child's welfare
In several decisions of the House of Lords/Supreme Court section 1(1) of the CA 1989 has been interpreted to mean that the child's welfare 'rules upon or determines the course to be followed'.[21] In other words, the child's welfare is the sole

---

[15] As Herring points out, this may be compounded by evidential difficulties of ascertaining what happened in private and at times of heightened emotion: Herring, 'Farewell Welfare?', 160.

[16] See C. Schneider, 'Discretion and Rules: A Lawyer's View', in K. Hawkins (ed.), *The Uses of Discretion* (Oxford: Clarendon, 1992), on the relative benefits of discretion and rules.

[17] H. Reece, 'The Paramountcy Principle: Consensus or Construct? (1996) 49 *Current Legal Problems* 267.

[18] E.g. *C v C (A Minor) Custody: Appeal)* [1991] 1 FLR 223.

[19] See Reece, 'The Paramountcy Principle: Consensus or Construct?; H. Reece, 'Subverting the Stigmatization Argument' (1996) 23(4) *Journal of Law and Society* 484.

[20] Herring, 'Farewell Welfare?', 162.

[21] See *J v C* [1970] AC 668; *Re KD (A Minor) (Ward: Terminating Access)* [1988] AC 806; *Re G (Children) (Residence: Same-Sex Partner)* [2006] UKHL 43, [2006] 1 WLR 2305. For discussion, see N. Lowe, 'J v C: Placing the Child's Welfare Centre Stage', in S. Gilmore, J. Herring and R. Probert (eds), *Landmark Cases in Family Law* (Hart Publishing, 2011).

consideration and the interests of others are only relevant insofar as they bear upon that question. In *Re G (Children) (Residence: Same-Sex Partner)* the House of Lords indicated that it could not contemplate any change 'which might have the effect of weakening the protection given to children under the present law'.[22] The second strand of criticism of section 1(1) relates to this elevation of child welfare to the sole consideration. Commentators have argued that the paramountcy principle is unjust in treating adults' interests as only relevant insofar as they bear upon the child's welfare, and arguably falls foul of the Kantian ethic that persons are ends in themselves and not merely to be viewed as means to the promotion of others' welfare.[23]

Helen Reece[24] has shown that defences of the paramountcy principle rely heavily on consensus and are weak on rational argument. For example, while it is sometimes said that treating children's welfare as paramount is needed to protect children, Reece observes this is a fallacy: it does not follow that in order to protect a child adequately his or her welfare must be the sole consideration. She illustrates the point with the example of a parent seeking to take three children of different ages safely across a road. The parent's attention will not be directed solely to one child, nor solely to the children, in ensuring that the whole family crosses safely. Furthermore, as Reece points out, any general arguments in favour of treating children's welfare as paramount are undermined by the fact that the paramountcy principle only applies in court decision-making.[25] If there are good general arguments for it, why does it not apply in *all* decisions or actions concerning children?[26]

Compatibility with the requirements of the Human Rights Act 1998?

The academic arguments have acquired greater practical significance with the enactment of the Human Rights Act 1998 (HRA 1998). Several commentators have cogently argued[27] that the ECHR, and now the HRA 1998, requires the court to take into account the interests of parents independently of the child's welfare. It has been observed that there is a qualitative difference between applying the welfare principle and, for example, Article 8 of the ECHR as scheduled to the

---

[22] See [2006] UKHL 43, [2006] 1 WLR 2305, at para [30], per Baroness Hale of Richmond.

[23] See e.g. J. Elster, 'Solomonic Judgments: Against the Best Interest of the Child' (1987) 54(1) *U Chicago L Rev* 1.

[24] Reece, 'The Paramountcy Principle: Consensus or Construct?, pp. 267–304.

[25] See for discussion, J. Herring, 'The Human Rights Act and the Welfare Principle in Family Law: Conflicting or Complementary?' (1999) 11 *Child and Family Law Quarterly* 223.

[26] The United Nations Convention on the Rights of the Child (UNCRC), Article 3 does not make the child's welfare paramount; it is merely the primary consideration.

[27] Herring, 'The Human Rights Act and the Welfare Principle in Family Law: Conflicting or Complementary?'; J. Fortin, 'The HRA's Impact on Litigation Involving Children and their Families' [1999] *Child and Family Law Quarterly* 237, 253; S. Harris-Short, 'Case Commentary: Putting The Child At The Heart Of Adoption? – Re B (Adoption: Natural Parent)' (2002) 14 (3) *Child and Family Law Quarterly* 325; D. Bonner, H. Fenwick, and S. Harris-Short, 'Judicial Approaches To The Human Rights Act' (2003) 52(3) *International and Comparative Law Quarterly* 549.

Act: the former is a determination of *fact*, the latter a matter of *judgement*.[28] The ECHR requires a weighing of respective interests: an outcome (i.e. respect for family life) is prescribed unless overridden by considerations specified in Article 8(2), and interference with a parent's right must be proportionate.

The differences affect both the process by which decisions are reached and, in some cases, potentially the outcome. While in the majority of cases the outcome may not differ, it may nevertheless be important, as the academic arguments underline, that the decision-making process accords respect to the individual interests of those involved.

Contrary to these arguments, the English courts have asserted that any difference between the requirements of Article 8 of the ECHR and section 1 of the CA 1989 is merely semantic[29] and the balancing of interests required in each case is the same, or that the paramountcy principle is recognized in the jurisprudence of the European Court of Human Rights.[30] Yet it can be strongly argued that the Strasbourg authorities relied on for the latter view do not support the English courts' interpretation of paramountcy: the European Court of Human Rights' view is not that the child's welfare is the sole consideration, but that the best interests of the child are of particular importance and, depending upon their nature and seriousness, may override those of the parents.[31] Provided an outcome will not harm the child concerned, there is scope in this formulation for adults' interests to be taken into account independently. It may be that some re-interpretation of the paramountcy principle is required in the light of human rights jurisprudence and of academic argument.

What could replace the welfare principle?

It is interesting that the welfare principle emerged historically, in the courts of Equity and in statute, as a by-product of the process of equalizing the positions of mothers and fathers in custody disputes.[32] As such it was not the result of a considered debate about whether it represents the most appropriate approach to determining disputes in children cases. Jon Elster[33] has argued that if we were starting afresh to formulate a principle, considerations of justice should also be seen as significant. Other commentators have pointed out that there is at the least a

[28] Herring, 'The Human Rights Act and the Welfare Principle in Family Law: Conflicting or Complementary?'.

[29] *Re KD (A Minor) (Ward: Terminating Access)* [1988] AC 806, at 825.

[30] *Payne v Payne* [2001] EWCA Civ 166, [2001] Fam 473, at para [38], citing *Johansen v Norway* (1996) 23 EHRR 33, 72, at para. 78 and *Re S (Contact: Promoting Relationship with Absent Parent)* [2004] EWCA Civ 18, [2004] 1 FLR 1279, at para [15], citing *Yousef v The Netherlands* (App No 33711/96) (2003) 36 EHRR 20, at para. 73.

[31] *Johansen v Norway* (1996) 23 EHRR 33, 72, at para. 78. The passage of *Yousef v Netherlands* (App No 33711/96) (2003) 36 EHRR 20, at para. [73] which was cited by the court in *Re S (Contact: Promoting Relationship with Absent Parent)* [2004] EWCA Civ 18, [2004] 1 FLR 1279, at para [15], footnoted *Elsholz v Germany* (2002) 34 EHRR 58, para. 52 and *TP and KM v United Kingdom* (2002) 34 EHRR 2, para. 72, which adopt the same approach as in *Johansen v Norway*.

[32] See e.g. S. Maidment, *Child Custody and Divorce: The Law in Social Context* (London: Croom Helm, 1984).

[33] Elster, 'Solomonic Judgments: Against the Best Interest of the Child'.

(Hall + Murphy)
case for justice considerations where welfare considerations are evenly balanced.[34] Elster argues that, while we would recognize the child's need for special protection, justice would require that small gains in the child's welfare should not be achieved at the expense of large losses in parental welfare. A similar approach has been advocated more recently, and discussed in some detail, by John Eekelaar.[35] Imagine a residence dispute between a mother and father in which the court's conclusion is that the child will thrive with either parent but would do better with the father, yet denying residence with the mother will plunge her into a clinical depression, and the father will not be so affected if he is denied residence. As Eekelaar points out, the paramountcy principle would dictate residence with the father, yet arguably a fairer approach which does not entirely deny the existence of the parents' independent interests would be to adopt an approach which promotes the child's well-being, albeit with the least detriment to the parents concerned. In the example given, this would mean residence with the child's mother.

Rather than abandon and replace the principle, however, Herring[36] prefers to reconceptualize it in a way that recognizes the child's interest in learning mutual respect and making sacrifices as part of a beneficial relationship. For Herring, therefore, respecting (or not improperly infringing) others' interests is an aspect of the child's welfare. In this way the welfare principle can accommodate interests of others. This is part of a more general, and important, point that Herring makes about the need for decision-making about children to be taken in the context of their relationships. However, as a response to criticisms that the welfare principle fails to take independent account of adults' interests, the difficulty with Herring's approach is that it recognizes adults' interests only insofar as such recognition is a means of promoting children's welfare. As Eekelaar has argued,[37] if the interests of the participants in a dispute are not isolated, there is a risk of defining one person's interests in terms of another's.[38]

In the light of the HRA 1998, Choudhry and Fenwick have argued that the correct approach now requires what has been termed a 'parallel analysis'. They take as an example a case in which the participants' rights under Article 8 of the ECHR are engaged. Choudhry and Fenwick argue that in any dispute the participants start presumptively equal and interference with the (Article 8(1) rights of each must be considered in accordance with the requirements of Article 8(2). The participants' rights are then weighed against each other in an ultimate balancing exercise, in which (following the approach in Strasbourg case-law) the child's

[34] J. C. Hall, 'Custody of Children – Welfare or Justice?' (1977) 36(2) *CLJ* 252; J. Murphy, 'The Welfare Principle Again, An Old Problem under a New Regime' (1991) 21 *Family Law* 535.
[35] J. Eekelaar, 'Beyond the Welfare Principle' (2002) 14(3) *Child and Family Law Quarterly* 237.
[36] Herring, 'Farewell Welfare?'; and Herring 'The Human Rights Act and the Welfare Principle in Family Law: Conflicting or Complementary?'.
[37] Eekelaar, 'Beyond the Welfare Principle', 243.
[38] For a case-law example, see *Re T (Wardship: Medical Treatment)* [1997] 1 FLR 502, where the mother's and child's interests were conflated.

welfare is privileged but not automatically decisive.[39] As other commentators have pointed out, this process may require examination of the various interests which children might claim within Article 8 of the ECHR, not just a focus on the child's welfare.[40]

right to respect for private and family life

CONCLUSION

The welfare principle has several virtues and can be defended against many criticisms. The elevation of child welfare to the sole consideration, however, is less easy to defend. Both academic criticism of this aspect of the principle, and academic interpretations of the requirements of the HRA 1998, appear to be converging on the view that decision-making in children's cases should be a process in which all the participants' interests are considered, and in which the child's interests are privileged, but not automatically decisive of the outcome.

Debate 2

Do we, and should we, have a norm of shared residence?

As noted at the beginning of this chapter, there have been campaigns arguing that when parents separate the norm should be shared residence. To what extent is this, or should this be, reflected in the law? We shall first consider, in outline, the relevant law,[41] and then the various arguments. Section 11(4) of the CA 1989 permits the making of a shared residence order, by providing as follows:

> Where a residence order is made in favour of two or more persons who do not themselves all live together, the order may specify the periods during which the child is to live in the different households concerned.

The usual basis for making a shared residence order will be that it 'provides legal confirmation of the factual reality of a child's life'.[42] The court will consider the favoured division of the child's time and then proceed to consider whether it should be expressed as terms of a shared residence order or of combination of a

---

[39] S. Choudhry and H. Fenwick, 'Taking the Rights of Parents and Children Seriously: Confronting the Welfare Principle under the Human Rights Act' (2005) 25(3) *Oxford Journal of Legal Studies* 453.

[40] See J. Fortin, 'Accommodating Children's Rights in a Post Human Rights Act Era' (2006) 69 *Modern Law Review* 299; and A. Bainham, 'Can We Protect Children and Protect Their Rights?' [2002] *Family Law* 279.

[41] For detailed accounts of the case-law, see S. Gilmore, 'Court Decision-Making in Shared Residence Order Cases – A Critical Examination' [2006] *Child and Family Law Quarterly* 478; S. Gilmore, 'Shared Residence: A Summary of the Courts' Guidance' [2010] *Family Law* 285.

[42] *Re A (Joint Residence: Parental Responsibility)* [2008] EWCA Civ 867, [2008] 2 FLR 1593, at para. [66], per Sir Mark Potter P; and see *Re H (Children)* [2009] EWCA Civ 902, and *Re F (Children)* [2003] EWCA Civ 592, at para. [21]. In rare cases it may also be used as a legitimate means by which to confer parental responsibility on an individual who would otherwise not be able to apply for a freestanding parental responsibility order (*Re A*, ibid, at para. [70], drawing on *Re H (Shared Residence: Parental Responsibility)* [1995] 2 FLR 883).

residence order and a contact order.[43] The Court of Appeal has suggested that one way of approaching the matter is to ask whether, from the child's perspective, the existing, or proposed arrangements mean that the child lives in two homes, or lives with one parent and has contact with the other.[44] Shared residence is not precluded by the fact of a considerable distance between the child's shared homes,[45] nor by the fact that the child does not spend time evenly, or more or less evenly, in the households concerned.[46]

In *Re AR (A Child: Relocation)*[47] Mostyn J said that a shared residence order 'is nowadays the rule rather than the exception'. In one sense this is right; such orders are no longer exceptional. While early case-law once suggested that shared residence was 'prima facie wrong'[48] or that shared residence orders were to be made only in exceptional,[49] or unusual circumstances,[50] that gloss was seemingly removed by *D v D (Shared Residence Order)*,[51] which, it has been said,[52] now represents the better view. Indeed, in *Holmes-Moorhouse v Richmond-Upon-Thames LBC*[53] Lord Hoffmann commented that 'shared residence orders are not nowadays unusual'.[54] In *D v D* the Court of Appeal held that 'if it is either planned or has turned out that the children are spending substantial amounts of their time with each of their parents then ... it may be an entirely appropriate order to make'.[55] Building on *D v D* the Court of Appeal has held that in such cases some justification for not making a shared residence order is required. In *Re P (Children) (Shared Residence Order)*[56] Wall LJ explained that the making of a shared residence order 'involves the exercise of a judicial discretion and does not automatically follow because children divide their time between their parents in proportions

---

[43] *Re K (Shared Residence Order)* [2008] 2 FLR 380, at para. [6].

[44] *Re H (Children)* [2009] EWCA Civ 902. For examples of the courts' approach to distinguishing between shared residence and contact, compare *Re W (Shared Residence Order)* [2009] EWCA Civ 370; [2009] 2 FLR 436, CA and *Re W (Children) (Residence Order)* [2003] EWCA Civ 116.

[45] *Re F (Children) (Shared Residence Order)* [2003] EWCA Civ 592; [2003] 2 FLR 397, at para. [21].

[46] This was recognized in the Law Commission Report which preceded the CA 1989 (Law Commission, *Family Law: Review of Child Law*, Law Com No 172 (HMSO, 1988)), at para. 4.12.

[47] [2010] EWHC 1346 (Fam); [2010] 2 FLR 1577.

[48] *Riley v Riley* [1986] 2 FLR 429.

[49] *Re H (A Minor) (Shared Residence)* [1994] 1 FLR 717: 'it must be an order which would rarely be made and would depend upon exceptional circumstances.'

[50] *A v A (Minors) (Shared Residence Order)* [1994] 1 FLR 669.

[51] [2001] 1 FLR 495.

[52] *Re W (Shared Residence Order)* [2009] EWCA Civ 370; [2009] 2 FLR 436 at para. [13], citing paras [31]–[32] of Hale LJ's judgment in *D v D (Shared Residence Order)* [2001] 1 FLR 495. See Gilmore, 'Court Decision-Making in Shared Residence Order Cases: A Critical Examination' for some of the complexities of the decision in *D v D*.

[53] [2009] UKHL 7.

[54] Ibid, at para [7] – and see the similar statement by Sir Mark Potter P in *Re A Joint Residence: Parental Responsibility)* [2008] EWCA Civ 867, [2008] 2 FLR 1593, CA at para. [66].

[55] [2001] 1 FLR 495, at 501.

[56] [2005] EWCA Civ 1639; [2006] 1 FCR 309. See also *Re A (Children) (Shared Residence)* [2002] EWCA Civ 1343; [2003] 3 FCR 656 (greatest weight should have been given to reflecting the realities, unless there were some counterbalancing welfare consideration that prevented that sensible outcome).

approaching equality', but added that 'where that does happen...good reasons are required if a shared residence order is not to be made'.[57]

However, care must be taken in saying that a shared residence order is the rule. In *T v T (Shared Residence)*[58] the Court of Appeal was clear that Mostyn J's statement in *Re AR* 'is to go too far. Whether or not a joint or shared residence order is granted depends upon a determination of what is in the best interests of the child in the light of all the factors in the individual case.'[59] Indeed, in *Holmes-Moorhouse*,[60] the House of Lords emphasized that the court's focus in shared residence applications is the children, and that the application of the paramountcy principle in section 1(1) of the CA 1989 'means that it must choose from the available options the future which will be best for the children, not the future which will be best for the adults'.[61] Furthermore, the child's wishes and feelings:

> ought to be particularly important in shared residence cases, because it is the children who will have to divide their time between two homes and it is all too easy for the parents' wishes and feelings to predominate.[62]

The House made clear that shared residence orders are practical solutions, not aspirational orders, and that while ideally 'there may be many cases where it would be best for the children to have a home with each of their parents', 'this is not always or even usually practicable'.[63]

As far as particular welfare considerations are concerned, the Court of Appeal has provided some guidance in several decisions. Any proposed arrangements must be clear and not likely to cause the child confusion.[64] A parent's intention to use an order to undermine the other parent (or other malign motivation) may be a reason for declining an order,[65] although equally the sustained marginalization of one parent by the other may amount to a reason for making an order.[66] However, the parents' inability to work in harmony is not necessarily a reason for declining to make an order, nor is it of itself a reason for making an order.[67]

As an exception to the rule that a shared residence order reflects the reality of the child's living arrangements, an order may also be used as a legitimate means

---

[57] [2005] EWCA Civ 1639; [2006] 1 FCR 309, at para. [22].

[58] [2010] EWCA Civ 1366.

[59] Ibid, at para. [26].

[60] [2009] UKHL 7; [2009] 1 FLR 904.

[61] Ibid, at para. [30].

[62] Ibid, at para. [36]. See also *Re R (Residence: Shared Care: Children's Views)* [2005] EWCA Civ 542; [2006] 1 FLR 491.

[63] Ibid, at para. [38].

[64] *A v A (Minors) (Shared Residence Order)* [1994] 1 FLR 669, at 678.

[65] *Re K (Shared Residence Order)*, at para. [21], per Wilson LJ. *Re M (Children) (Residence Order)* [2004] EWCA Civ 1413 (order made unworkable by the father's domestic violence, rigidity and failure to co-operate over arrangements for the children, and manipulation of the children by involving them in inappropriate discussions).

[66] See e.g. *Re G (Residence: Same-Sex Partner)* [2006] UKHL 43; [2006] 2 FLR 629, HL.

[67] *Re W (Shared Residence Order)* [2009] EWCA Civ 370; [2009] 2 FLR 436, at para. [15], explaining Wall J's comments in *A v A (Shared Residence)* [2004] EWHC 142 (Fam); [2004] 1 FLR 1195, at para. [124].

by which to confer parental responsibility on an individual who would otherwise not be able to apply for a freestanding parental responsibility.[68] The occasions on which shared residence order will be needed to confer parental responsibility, however, have been reduced by the increased freestanding methods by which parental responsibility can be acquired.[69]

While a shared residence order may additionally and incidentally carry the message that both parents are equal,[70] the view expressed in *Re A (Joint Residence: Parental Responsibility)*[71] – that a distinct basis for making a shared residence order also exists 'in a case where one party has the primary care of a child, it may be psychologically beneficial to the *parents* in emphasising the equality of their position and responsibilities' – is not consistent with the child focus required by section 1(1) of the CA 1989 as emphasized by the House of Lords in *Holmes-Moorhouse*, nor with earlier authority.[72]

The combined effect of the opinions in the House of Lords in *Holmes-Moorhouse* is that, while shared residence orders are not to be regarded as unusual orders, neither are they to be regarded as routinely of benefit to children. There is no reason to adopt a negative approach to shared residence, but its appropriateness in the individual case must be carefully considered, applying the child's welfare as the paramount consideration. The courts have not, therefore, introduced a norm of shared residence; indeed, Sir Nicholas Wall P has commented extra-judicially, 'if shared parenting orders as a concept are to become the norm, the initiative, in my view, must come from Parliament.'[73] This leads neatly to the question whether the law *should* adopt a norm of shared residence.

Should there be a norm of shared residence?

The debates surrounding shared residence are complex, and interpreting the research evidence on the well-being of children in such arrangements is not straightforward.[74] In a chapter such as this, it is only possible to draw attention to the main features of the debate.

---

[68] *Re A (Joint Residence: Parental Responsibility)* [2008] 2 FLR 1593, at para. [66], at para. [70], drawing on *Re H (Shared Residence: Parental Responsibility)* [1995] 2 FLR 883).

[69] e.g. CA 1989, sections 4ZA and 4A.

[70] *Re P (Shared Residence Order)* [2005] EWCA Civ 1639; [2006] 2 FLR 347, at para. [22].

[71] [2008] 2 FLR 1593 at para. [66].

[72] See Gilmore, 'Shared Residence: A Summary of the Courts' Guidance', arguing this was a misreading of *Re H (Shared Residence: Parental Responsibility)* [1995] 2 FLR 883, at p. 889 where the making of a SRO was firmly rooted in the psychological benefit to the child not the parent. It is also not consistent with parliamentary intention when enacting the residence order: see P. G. Harris and R. H. George, 'Parental Responsibility and Shared Residence Orders: Parliamentary Intentions And Judicial Interpretations' [2010] *Child and Family Law Quarterly* 151. See also A. Grand, 'In Practice: Disputes between Parents: Time for a New Order?' [2011] *Family Law* 74 (arguing that residence orders are becoming the new custody orders and that it is time a newly worded order: a 'parental time order' which would deal only with time and avoid any references to parental status).

[73] In an address to Families Need Fathers in September 2010, reported in Elizabeth Walsh, 'Newsline Extra: The Shape of Things to Come' [2010] *Family Law* 1232.

[74] B. Fehlberg, B. Smyth, M. Maclean and C. Roberts, 'Legislating for Shared Time Parenting After Separation: A Research Review' (2011) 25(3) *International Journal of Law, Policy and the Family* 318, 319.

First, there is 'no empirical evidence showing a clear linear relationship between shared time and improving children's outcomes'.[75] Of course quantity of contact is not entirely irrelevant to the quality of parent/child interactions since a certain amount of time will be needed to enable a quality relationship to be developed or maintained, but, as Liz Trinder points out, 'it is what parents do with that time that is critical'.[76] Research does show that children benefit from authoritative parenting,[77] and since shared residence can facilitate the opportunity for good, active (authoritative) parenting, this can provide an argument for shared residence as the arrangement most likely to facilitate such a parental role in both parents.[78] However, well-being is most strongly connected to the quality of parenting rather than the particular form of post-separation parenting arrangement.

It is clear that shared residence will not be suitable for all families; the arrangement may be impracticable given the parents' circumstances (such as work patterns), or, in many cases, the provision of two suitably sized homes may simply be financially unattainable. Not surprisingly, therefore, research shows that parents who put in place successful arrangements tend to be well educated and well resourced, perhaps with flexible work arrangements, and involvement in childcare prior to their separation.[79] Some studies of families who self-select into shared residence arrangements have reported positive outcomes for the children concerned, and some studies comparing shared residence with other arrangements show modest comparative benefits of shared residence in some areas of child adjustment.[80] Research shows that shared parenting works well and children feel positive about it 'when arrangements are child-focused, flexible, and cooperative'[81] and successful arrangements tend to reflect such parenting styles. However, when thinking about whether a norm of shared residence should be introduced into court decision-making, it is important to appreciate that the flexible, co-operative attitudes mentioned above are not features typically exemplified by parents who are fighting over shared residence in the courts.

Furthermore, research shows that some children do not fare well in shared care arrangements.[82] There are three main findings which suggest caution in introduc-

---

[75] Ibid, 321.

[76] L. Trinder, 'Shared Residence: A Review of Recent Research Evidence' (2010) 22(4) *Child and Family Law Quarterly* 475, 488.

[77] P. R. Amato and J. G. Gilbreth, 'Non-resident Fathers and Children's Well-Being: A Meta-Analysis' (1999) 61 *Journal of Marriage and the Family* 557.

[78] J. Hunt with C. Roberts, *Child Contact with Non-resident Parents*, University of Oxford, Family Policy Briefing 3, 2004.

[79] See Fehlberg, Smyth, Maclean and Roberts, 'Legislating for Shared Time Parenting After Separation: A Research Review', 322, and references cited therein.

[80] S. Gilmore, 'Contact/Shared Residence and Child Well-Being – Research Evidence and Its Implications for Legal Decision Making' (2006) 20 *International Journal of Law, Policy and the Family* 344.

[81] Fehlberg, Smyth, Maclean and Roberts, 'Legislating for Shared Time Parenting After Separation: A Research Review', pp. 321–22.

[82] For recent reviews and discussion of the research, see Trinder, 'Shared Residence: A Review of Recent Research Evidence'; L. Trinder, 'Shared Residence: A Review of Recent Research Evidence' [2010] *Family Law* 1192; S. Gilmore, 'Shared parenting: the law and the evidence (Part 2)' (2010) 20 *Seen and Heard* 21–35.

ing a norm of shared residence. First, there is evidence from some studies that in cases of high conflict between parents shared residence may be more damaging for children as the arrangements mean that they are more exposed to their parents' conflict.[83] Secondly, some evidence has emerged from Australia that overnight 'shared care of children under four years of age had an independent and deleterious impact'[84] in terms of developmental problems, such as problem behaviours. The researchers suggest that repeated disruption of the child's relationship with his or her primary carer may be stressful and beyond the child's ability to comprehend. Thirdly, there is evidence that some children can find shared residence burdensome,[85] particularly when the arrangements are rigid,[86] for example having to carry their belongings to and fro between different homes and accommodating different rules/practices in each home. As Fehlberg et al. conclude: 'While shared-time parenting is one of many possibilities, empirical support for legislating to prioritise shared time over other parenting arrangements is lacking'.[87]

Evaluations of the recent experience of legislating to encourage shared time parenting in Australia also shed some light on this debate. In 2006 the law there was changed so that judges were enjoined to consider whether it would be in the best interests of a child and reasonably practicable to order equal time or substantial and significant time with both parents. It has been suggested that reforms led to a marked increase in court-ordered shared residence. The provisions were misunderstood as introducing a starting point of equal time, and discouraged mothers from disclosing family violence because they believed that this starting point meant there was no point in doing so.[88] As Liz Trinder has observed:

> The recent Australian experience provides a clear warning against a statutory presumption based on any timeshare arrangement, and particularly

---

[83] See J. McIntosh, B. Smyth, M. Kelaher, Y. Wells and C. Long, *Post-Separation Parenting Arrangements and Developmental Outcomes For Infants And Children* (Attorney-General's Department, 2010). For discussion, see J. McIntosh and R. Chisholm, 'Cautionary notes on the shared care of children in conflicted parental separation' (2008) 14(1) *Journal of Family Studies* 37; J. McIntosh and R. Chisholm, 'Shared Care and Children's Best Interests in Conflicted Separation – A Cautionary Tale from Current Research' (2008) 20 *Australian Family Lawyer* 1; C. Buchanan, E. Maccoby and S. Dornbusch, 'Caught between Parents: Adolescents' Experience in Divorced Homes', (1991) 62 *Child Development* 1008; C. M. Buchanan, E. E. Maccoby and S. M. Dornbusch, *Adolescents After Divorce* (Harvard University Press, 1996).

[84] McIntosh, Smyth, Kelaher, Wells and Long, *Post-Separation Parenting Arrangements and Developmental Outcomes for Infants And Children*, p. 9.

[85] See e.g. the interviews with children reported in C. Smart, 'From Children's Shoes to Children's Voices' (2002) 40(3) *Family Court Review* 307, and the research in C. Smart, B. Neale and A. Wade, *The Changing Experience of Childhood: Families and Divorce*, (Cambridge: Polity Press, 2001); G. Haugen, 'Children's Perspectives on Everyday Experiences of Shared Residence' (2010) 24 *Children and Society* 112; J. Cashmore, P. Parkinson, R. Weston, R. Patulny, G. Redmond, L. Qu, J. Baxter, M. Rajkovic, T. Sitek, and I. Katz, *Shared Care Parenting Arrangements since the 2006 Family Law Reforms: Report to the Australian Government Attorney-General's Department* (Social Policy Research Centre, University of New South Wales, 2010).

[86] See e.g. the findings of McIntosh, Smyth, Kelaher, Wells and Long, *Post-Separation Parenting Arrangements and Developmental Outcomes for Infants and Children*, pp. 47–49.

[87] Ibid, at 332.

[88] See Fehlberg, Smyth, Maclean and Roberts, 'Legislating for Shared Time Parenting After Separation: A Research Review', 236–330.

not one based on shared care...by sending policy messages that shared care is the best option, what has occurred is a shared care paradox where the greatest expansion of shared care has been in precisely those families where shared care is least likely to work and most likely to cause most problems for children.[89]

Sonia Harris-Short highlights a concern that 'the trend towards a greater use of shared residence has more to do with trying to secure a sense of fairness, justice and equality for the parents, and particularly disaffected fathers, than the welfare and interests of the children'.[90] In support of an approach based on justice, it is sometimes said that society has changed and men now play an equal hands-on role in children's upbringing and consequently men are entitled to equal care in the context of post-separation parenting. However, against this view, as Harris-Short observes, the empirical evidence on father involvement 'points very clearly to the wide gulf that exists between the rhetoric and the reality of parenting practices within the UK'.[91] Harris-Short argues powerfully that decisions about the child's future interests should be firmly grounded in the realities of family life, since the pre-separation pattern of care is likely to be an important factor in the child's ability to adjust successfully within a post-separation shared care arrangement.[92] As Harris-Short has pointed out, the debates are 'notably quiet as to whether the child's welfare similarly demands that he or "she spends a substantial and significant amount of time with both parents" when living within the intact family'. [93]

Debate 3

The courts' approach to contact disputes

Academic debate surrounding child contact with a non-resident parent has focused on how the courts' general approach is properly characterized. Some commentators suggest that the law recognizes a right, or a presumption of contact, while others do not accept that view. A connected debate is whether a presumption (or assumption) in favour of contact (or that contact is beneficial) *should* be the courts' approach to such cases. Before examining the debates, it is necessary first

89 Trinder, 'Shared Residence: A Review of Recent Research Evidence', 495.

90 S. Harris-Short, 'Resisting the March Towards 50/50 Shared Residence: Rights, Welfare and Equality In Post-Separation Families' (2010) 32(3) *Journal of Social Welfare and Family Law* 257, 266.

91 Ibid, 268. See the analysis of the research at 267–68. See also K. Skørten and R. Barlindhaug, 'The Involvement of Children in Decisions about Shared Residence' (2007) 21 *International Journal of Law, Policy and the Family* 373, 382, who argue that well-educated fathers, who may be engaged in child care as well as being breadwinners, may see their shared physical care of the child in terms of their right, which can undermine the child's involvement in decision-making.

92 Ibid, 270–71.

93 S. Harris-Short, 'Building A House Upon Sand: Post-Separation Parenting, Shared Residence and Equality – Lessons From Sweden' [2011] *Child and Family Law Quarterly* 344, at 369, drawing on the experience in Sweden, on which see also A. Newnham, 'Shared Residence: Lessons From Sweden' [2011] *Child and Family Law Quarterly* 251.

to set out a brief summary of the law, which will suffice for the purpose of examining the arguments.

THE LAW

In *Re C (Direct Contact: Suspension)*[94] the Court of Appeal explained that our 'domestic jurisprudence, if somewhat differently expressed, is to the same effect'[95] as that set out by the European Court of Human Rights (ECtHR). The starting point[96] is the recognition by the ECtHR that: 'The mutual enjoyment by parent and child of each other's company constitutes a fundamental element of family life'[97] within Article 8 of the ECHR.[98] Article 8 includes in private law contact cases 'a right for parents to have measures taken with a view to their being reunited with their children, and an obligation for the national authorities to take such measures'.[99] However, 'the national authorities' obligation to take measures to facilitate reunion is not absolute'.[100] 'The key consideration is whether those authorities have taken all necessary steps to facilitate contact as can reasonably be demanded in the special circumstances of each case.'[101] There is strict scrutiny of a state's margin of appreciation in relation to contact because the effect of denial of contact is to curtail the parent/child relationship.[102] The ECtHR has stated that:

> the interests as well as the rights and freedoms of all concerned must be taken into account, and more particularly the best interests of the child and his or her rights under Art 8 of the Convention. Where contact with the parent might appear to threaten those interests or interfere with those rights, it is for the national authorities to strike a fair balance between them.[103]

However, a parent 'cannot be entitled under Article 8...to have such measures taken as would harm the child's health and development.'[104] Drawing on the

---

[94] [2011] EWCA Civ 521; [2011] 2 FLR 912.

[95] Ibid, at para. [43].

[96] *Gnahoré v France* (Application No 40031/98) (2002) 34 EHRR 38, at para 50.

[97] Repeated in several cases. See e.g. *Elsholz v Germany* (Application No 25735/94) (2002) 34 EHRR 58, [2000] 2 FLR 486, at para. 43.

[98] See also Article 9(3) of the UNCRC, which enjoins States Parties to 'respect the right of the child who is separated from one or both parents to maintain personal relations and direct contact with both parents on a regular basis, except if it is contrary to the child's best interests; and see also UNCRC, Arts 7, 8, 9 and 18(1), which are usefully identified and discussed in A. Bainham, 'Contact as a Right and Obligation', in A. Bainham, B. Lindley, M. Richards and L. Trinder (eds), *Children and Their Families: Contact, Rights and Welfare* (Hart Publishing, 2003), p. 62.

[99] *Kosmopoulou v Greece* (Application No 60457/00) [2004] 1 FLR 800, para. 44.

[100] *Glaser v United Kingdom* (Case No 32346/96) (2001) 33 EHRR 1, [2001] 1 FLR 153, at para. 65.

[101] Ibid, at para. 66.

[102] See *C v Finland* (Application No 18249/02) (2008) 46 EHRR 485, [2006] 2 FLR 597, at para. 60, and see *Re C (Direct Contact: Suspension)* [2011] EWCA Civ 521 [2011] 2 FLR 912, at para. [41].

[103] *Glaser v United Kingdom* (Case No 32346/96) (2001) 33 EHRR 1, [2001] 1 FLR 153, at para. 65.

[104] E.g. *Scozzari and Giunta v Italy* (Application Nos 39221/98 and 41963/98) (2002) 35 EHRR 12, sub nom *S and G v Italy* (Cases 39221/98 and 41963/98) [2000] 2 FLR 771, ECHR, at para. 169.

above jurisprudence and examining the leading domestic authorities, the Court of Appeal in *Re C (Direct Contact: Suspension)* helpfully summarized the overall position in a series of bullet points as follows:[105]

- Contact between parent and child is a fundamental element of family life and is almost always in the interests of the child.[106]
- Contact between parent and child is to be terminated only in exceptional circumstances, where there are cogent reasons for doing so[107] and when there is no alternative. Contact is to be terminated only if it will be detrimental to the child's welfare.
- There is a positive obligation on the State, and therefore on the judge, to take measures to maintain and to reconstitute the relationship between parent and child, in short, to maintain or restore contact. The judge has a positive duty to attempt to promote contact. The judge must grapple with all the available alternatives before abandoning hope of achieving some contact.[108] He must be careful not to come to a premature decision, for contact is to be stopped only as a last resort and only once it has become clear that the child will not benefit from continuing the attempt.[109]
- The court should take both a medium-term and long-term view and not accord excessive weight to what appear likely to be short-term or transient problems.[110]
- The key question, which requires 'stricter scrutiny', is whether the judge has taken all necessary steps to facilitate contact as can reasonably be demanded in the circumstances of the particular case.
- All that said, at the end of the day the welfare of the child is paramount: 'the child's interest must have precedence over any other consideration.'[111]

One further authority should be added to the Court of Appeal's anthology in *Re C*, namely *In re L (A Child) (Contact: Domestic Violence) In re V (A Child) In re*

---

[105] We have added in footnoted authorities for the various propositions, which are discussed earlier in Munby LJ's judgment, preceding his summary.

[106] See e.g. *Re O (Contact: Imposition of Conditions)* [1995] 2 FLR 124 at 128, drawing upon Balcombe LJ's judgment in *Re H (Minors) (Access)* [1992] 1 FLR 148, at 152; Latey J's judgment in *M v M (Child: Access)*, [1973] 2 All ER 81; *Re S (Contact: Promoting Relationship with Absent Parent)* [2004] EWCA Civ 18, [2004] 1 FLR 1279, Dame Elizabeth Butler-Sloss P, para. [19]; *Re T (A Minor) (Parental Responsibility: Contact)* [1993] 2 FLR 450 at 459; *Görgülü v Germany* (Application No 74969/01) [2004] ECHR 89, [2004] 1 FLR 894, at para. 48: 'it is in a child's interest for its family ties to be maintained, as severing such ties means cutting a child off from its roots, which can only be justified in very exceptional circumstances.' Where 'direct contact cannot for the time being be ordered, it is ordinarily highly desirable that there should be indirect contact'.

[107] *Re M (Contact: Supervision)* [1998] 1 FLR 727, Ward LJ (at 730); *Re O (Contact: Withdrawal of Application)* [2003] EWHC 3031 (Fam), [2004] 1 FLR 1258, para. [6].

[108] *Re P (Children)* [2008] EWCA Civ 1431, [2009] 1 FLR 1056, at para. [38].

[109] *Re S (Contact: Promoting Relationship with Absent Parent)* [2004] EWCA Civ 18, [2004] 1 FLR 1279 (para. [32]).

[110] *Re O (Contact: Imposition of Conditions)* [1995] 2 FLR 124, at 129.

[111] *Re C (Direct Contact: Suspension)* [2011] EWCA Civ 521, [2011] 2 FLR 912, at paras [37]–[47].

M (A Child) In re H (Children).[112] In that case Thorpe LJ made some important observations about the courts' general approach to contact, with which Waller LJ expressly agreed, and which are not uncontroversial. Thorpe LJ observed that the language of the judges in explaining the basis of decision-making in relation to contact has shifted over the years,[113] in judgments sometimes reflective of social attitudes and assumptions of their time.[114] He noted that contact had been described as a parental right[115] and as the child's right,[116] and that judicial statements about how applications for contact should be determined have also used the term 'presumption'[117] or 'principle'.

Thorpe LJ saw difficulty with the language of rights in this context:[118] his Lordship appreciated that the word 'right' can be used loosely, and that seeing contact as giving rise to a claim-right, automatically imposing duties on others, is difficult given that contact is determined applying section 1(1) of the Children Act 1989. Thorpe LJ was also wary of the use of presumptions in the context of deciding contact applications, highlighting that a presumption alters the burden of proof and the consequent danger 'that the identification of a presumption will inhibit or distort the rigorous search for the welfare solution' or 'be used as an aid to determination when the individual advocate or judge feels either undecided or overwhelmed'.[119] While acknowledging that the distinction may be fine, Thorpe LJ preferred the term 'assumption', commenting that 'it perhaps more accurately reflects the base of knowledge and experience from which the court embarks upon its application of the welfare principle in each disputed contact application'.[120]

Is there a right of contact or a presumption of contact?
One leading child law commentator, Andrew Bainham, has argued that provisions in international conventions mentioned above (e.g. Article 8 of the ECHR) establish a parental right of contact.[121] Bainham acknowledges that the protection to which he refers is not absolute and 'liable to be displaced by other considerations, most obviously the welfare of the child'[122] and characterizes it as a fundamental presumption 'which may be rebutted – but only for good reason'.[123]

---

[112] [2001] Fam 260 (CA), hereafter *Re LVMH*.

[113] Ibid, at 291.

[114] Ibid, at 294.

[115] See e.g. *S v S* [1962] 1 WLR 445, 448, per Willmer LJ.

[116] See e.g. *M v M (Child: Access)* [1973] 2 All ER 81, 85, per Wrangham J; *A v L (Contact)* [1998] 1 FLR 361, 365, Holman J describing contact as 'a fundamental right of a child'.

[117] See S. Gilmore, 'Disputing Contact: Challenging Some Assumptions' [2008] *Child and Family Law Quarterly* 285 for an account of judicial use of the term 'presumption' in the context of contact applications.

[118] Referring to the observations of Ormrod LJ in *A v C* [1985] FLR 445, at 455, and of Lord Oliver of Aylmerton *In re KD (Minor) (Ward: Termination of Access)* [1988] AC 806 that there is a danger of loose language in this context.

[119] *Re LVMH* [2001] Fam 260, at 295.

[120] *Re LVMH* at 295.

[121] Bainham, 'Contact as a Right and Obligation', in Bainham, Lindley, Richards and Trinder (eds), *Children and Their Families: Contact, Rights and Welfare*.

[122] Ibid, p. 62.

[123] Ibid, p. 75.

By contrast, one of the authors has questioned whether it is correct to say that the international provisions recognize protection which can be characterized as a 'right of *contact*'.[124] He argues that Article 8 of the ECHR gives substantive protection to the parent/child relationship *through* the right to respect for 'family life'. Contact is one fundamental element of such respect, but the respect for family life guaranteed by the Convention does not protect just one particular form of that relationship (i.e. contact). There are other aspects of family life which may require respect, such as remaining free from a risk of domestic violence. Therefore, it may be more accurate to say: there must be a good reason for denying contact because there is a right to *respect for* the mutual enjoyment by parent and child of each other's company as *one* fundamental *element* of family life. Indeed, the European Court of Human Rights expressly acknowledged in *Gnahoré v France* that 'there is of course a double aspect' to the child's welfare interest in this context:

> On the one hand, there is no doubt that ensuring that the child grows up in a healthy environment falls within this interest and that Article 8 cannot in any way entitle a parent to have such measures taken as would harm the child's health and development. On the other hand, it is clear that it is nevertheless in the child's interest that the links between him and his family should be maintained except where the family is shown to be especially unworthy for that purpose; to break that link amounts to cutting the child off from his roots. It follows that the child's interest necessitates that only wholly exceptional circumstances may lead to a breaking of the family bond and that everything should be done to maintain personal relations and, where possible and when the occasion arises, to 'reconstitute' the family.[125]

It can also be argued that Bainham's equation of the terms 'right' and 'presumption' is problematic in that they are very different jurisprudential terms, and Bainham's descriptive use of the term presumption only serves to underline the fact that what Bainham is referring to is merely a parental interest which may be protected depending on the interests of others. It is very difficult to argue that there is a parental claim-right to contact in English law. English law does not impose any duty on the child or non-resident parent to have contact, and an enforceable duty upon the resident parent arises only upon the making of a contact order.[126] Furthermore, the domestic case-law rejects the use of the term 'right' in this context.[127]

It may, of course, be correct to say that the process of reasoning adopted by the European Court of Human Rights reflects a presumption of parental contact with a child. When a father alleges that his Article 8 right to respect for family life has been violated by a denial of contact, the European Court of Human Rights will consider whether the denial represents a proportionate response to a legitimate

---

[124] Gilmore, 'Disputing Contact: Challenging Some Assumptions'.
[125] Ibid, at para. 59.
[126] In the case of direct contact, even then the duty is merely to 'allow' contact which, as *Re L* makes clear, does not require any active facilitation/encouragement of contact.
[127] See Thorpe LJ's judgment in *Re LVMH*, at pp. 291–92, and the authorities cited therein.

aim in Article 8(2). As we have seen the focus (or starting point) is respect for family life in the sense of mutual enjoyment of contact, and some interference must be justified. However, as we have also seen, domestic case-law has rejected the use of a presumption of contact in the process of deciding whether contact should be ordered or not (or put another way, whether interference with the father's right to respect for family life, in the sense of contact, is justified). To adopt a presumption would be incompatible with the approach currently adopted, namely a focus on the child's welfare as the paramount – that is, sole – consideration.

Should there be an assumption that parent/child contact is beneficial?

In *Re LVMH*[128] the Court of Appeal put in place an assumption that contact is beneficial when deciding contact cases. As Andrew Bainham has argued, such recognition of the value of contact could play an educative or hortatory role in creating an expectation of responsible ongoing relationships.[129] Furthermore, as Hunt and Roberts observe, there are several general points that can be put in favour of contact, such as that it can preserve links with a child's extended family, providing additional sources of support.[130]

However, the issue of whether the courts should assume contact to be beneficial in disputed contact cases is a matter of some debate. In reaching the conclusion that the benefits of contact should be assumed, Thorpe LJ relied on a general psychiatric report produced by Drs Sturge and Glaser, consultant child psychiatrists, which Thorpe LJ saw as fully identifying 'the benefits which children derive from continuing contact with the absent parent'.[131] However, this appears to be a misinterpretation of the Sturge/Glaser report, which emphasizes that cases are fact-sensitive and identifies a range of benefits and detriments of contact which may or may not apply depending on the facts. As Dr Sturge herself has commented, the true position is that the report fully identifies the benefits which children derive from continuing contact with the absent parent *when certain conditions are met*.[132] Thus in the view of its author, the report does not support a general assumption that contact is beneficial.

Reviews of the research evidence on the connection between contact arrangements and child well-being show that it is not contact per se but the quality of contact that is important to children's well-being.[133] Research highlights a range of factors potentially impacting on the relationship between child well-being and post-separation parenting arrangements, such as the quality of the parents'

[128] [2001] Fam 260 (CA).

[129] Bainham, 'Contact as a Right and Obligation', in Bainham, Lindley, Richards and Trinder (eds), *Children and Their Families: Contact, Rights and Welfare*.

[130] Hunt with Roberts, *Child Contact with Non-Resident Parents*, p. 3.

[131] *Re LVMH* [2001] Fam 260, at 365.

[132] Correspondence with S. Gilmore, as discussed in Gilmore, 'Disputing Contact: Challenging Some Assumptions'.

[133] Gilmore, 'Contact/Shared Residence and Child Well-being: Research Evidence and its Implications for Legal Decision-Making', 358.

relationship and the personalities of those involved.[134] As Stephen Gilmore has argued, the complexity revealed by the research 'does not advocate a form of legal decision-making which relies on generalisations'.[135] Indeed, as he has pointed out, given the deleterious effects of conflict on child well-being,[136] the adoption of a presumption (or indeed an assumption) in favour of contact seems particularly contraindicated in disputed contact cases, with their profile of high conflict demonstrated in recent research.[137]

Should there be a presumption against contact in cases of domestic violence?

The courts' general approach to contact means that the cases in which there is a complete denial of contact are rare. So, even in the case of parental abuse of a child, there is no general principle that direct contact will be denied, however serious the abuse.[138]

A parent's opposition to contact is viewed of itself as an unattractive argument, and in cases in which a parent is implacably opposed to contact 'the court will be very slow indeed to reach the conclusion that contact will be harmful to the child' and 'will want to be satisfied that there is indeed a serious risk of major emotional harm before doing so'.[139] Such cases must be distinguished from cases in which a parent has genuine fears relating to proposed contact, whether rationally held or not,[140] such as a fear of domestic violence. How the courts should respond to contact cases where there are allegations of domestic violence has proved a controversial issue.

---

[134] See e.g. J. Dunn, 'Annotation: Children's relationships with their non-resident fathers' (2004) 45(4) *Journal of Child Psychology and Psychiatry* 659; Gilmore, 'Contact/Shared Residence and Child Well-being: Research Evidence and Its Implications for Legal Decision-Making'; J. Hunt, *Researching Contact* (National Council for One Parent Families, 2003).

[135] Gilmore, 'Contact/Shared Residence and Child Well-being: Research Evidence and Its Implications for Legal Decision-Making', at pp. 358–59. See also Hunt with Roberts, *Child Contact with Non-Resident Parents*.

[136] See G. T. Harold and M. Murch, 'Inter-Parental Conflict and Children's Adaptation to Separation and Divorce: Theory, Research And Implications For Family Law, Practice And Policy' [2005] *Child and Family Law Quarterly* 185.

[137] Gilmore, 'Contact/Shared Residence and Child Well-being: Research Evidence and its Implications for Legal Decision-Making', at p. 359. See, for example, A. Buchanan, J. Hunt, H. Bretherton and V. Bream, *Families in Conflict: Perspectives of Children and Parents on the Family Court Welfare Service* (Policy Press, 2001); L. Trinder, J. Connolly, J. Kellett and C. Notley, *A Profile of Applicants and Respondents in Contact Cases in Essex* (DCA Research Series 1/05, 2004); A. Perry and B. Rainey, 'Supervised, Supported and Indirect Contact Orders: Research Findings' (2007) 21 *International Journal of Law, Policy and the Family* 21, at p. 29.

[138] *H v H (Child Abuse: Access)* [1989] 1 FLR 212 (CA); *L v L (Child Abuse: Access)* [1989] 2 FLR 16 (CA); *Re E-L (A Child) (Contact)* [2003] EWCA Civ 1947 [8]: 'There is simply no principle or practice that would justify an inevitable conclusion for the termination of direct contact from the bare finding of past inappropriate sexual conduct.'

[139] *Re D (Contact: Reasons for Refusal)* [1997] 2 FLR 48, at 53, drawing on *Re D (A Minor) (Contact: Mother's Hostility)* [1993] 2 FLR 1.

[140] See e.g., *Re K (Contact: Mother's Anxiety)* [1999] 2 FLR 703. *Re L (Contact: Genuine Fear)*. See also *Re H (Contact Order) (No 2)* (mother's health threatened by fear that father would harm children during contact). The child's feelings about contact may also be a powerful factor in the outcome of a particular case. See e.g. *Re C (Contact: No Order for Contact)* [2000] 2 FLR 723 (Fam).

In the 1990s concern was expressed that the courts' general approach to order-ing contact was obscuring a proper consideration of the issue of domestic violence. Research found that in practice a strong presumption in favour of contact which had achieved such force that it virtually amounted 'to a rule yielding to a different outcome only in very exceptional circumstances',[141] the effect of which was to downplay the genuine and rationally based concerns of resident parents, and erro-neously to characterize such parents as unjustifiably hostile to contact.[142] In 1999 a Lord Chancellor's Department consultation on contact and domestic violence confirmed a widespread problem.[143] A subsequent report of the Children Act Sub-Committee of the Lord Chancellor's Advisory Board on Family Law (CASC) [144] recommended 'Good Practice Guidelines', heightening judicial awareness of the impact of domestic violence and the need for fact-finding in such cases. Shortly before the report was published, the issue of contact and domestic violence came before the Court of Appeal in the *Re LVMH* case discussed earlier.[145] The Court of Appeal was given advance sight of the CASC report and took the opportunity to incorporate a summary of the CASC guidelines into its judgment.[146] Similar guidance has now been incorporated into a Practice Direction. The court also had the benefit of an expert general psychiatric report on the subject of contact and domestic violence, the Sturge/Glaser report, mentioned earlier.[147] The report recommended that there should be a presumption against contact in cases of proven domestic violence.

Contrary to the advice given in the Sturge/Glaser report, however, the Court of Appeal confirmed the view expressed in earlier case-law that there is 'no presumption that, on proof of domestic violence, the offending parent has to surmount a prima facie barrier of no contact'.[148] Thorpe LJ, agreeing with Dame Elizabeth Butler-Sloss P's judgment, said that this would risk creating 'an exces-sive concentration on past history and an over-reflection of physical abuse within

---

[141] Ibid 126.

[142] J. Wallbank, 'Castigating Mothers: The Judicial Response to "Wilful" Women in Disputes Over Paternal Contact in English Law' (1998) 20(4) *Journal of Social Welfare and Family Law* 357; C. Smart and B. Neale, 'Arguments Against Virtue – Must Contact Be Enforced?' (1997) 27 *Family Law* 332.

[143] Although there had been some signs of a changing judicial attitude within case-law; R. Bailey-Harris. 'Contact – Challenging Conventional Wisdom?' (2001) 13 *Child and Family Law Quarterly* 361; F Kaganas and S. Day Sclater, 'Contact and Domestic Violence – The Winds of Change' (2000) 30 *Family Law* 630.

[144] Advisory Board on Family Law Children Act Sub-Committee, *A Report to the Lord Chancellor on the Question of Parental Contact in Cases Where There Is Domestic Violence* (Lord Chancellor's Department, 2000).

[145] [2001] Fam 260 (CA). For comment see F. Kaganas 'Re L (Contact: Domestic Violence); Re V (Contact: Domestic Violence); Re M (Contact: Domestic Violence); Re H (Contact: Domestic Violence): Contact and Domestic Violence' (2000) 12 *Child and Family Law Quarterly* 311.

[146] [2001] Fam 260, at 272–73.

[147] C. Sturge and D. Glaser, 'Contact and Domestic Violence – The Experts' Court Report' (2000) 30 *Family Law* 615.

[148] *Re LVMH* [2001] Fam 260, at 273.

the determination of individual cases.'[149] He agreed with Waller LJ's succinct summary that:

> domestic violence is not to be elevated to some special category; it is one highly material factor amongst many which may offset the assumption in favour of contact when the difficult balancing exercise is carried out by the judge applying the welfare principle and the welfare checklist, s 1(1) and (3) of the Children Act 1989'[150]

The English law's response to concerns about contact in cases of domestic violence has been a procedural one, rather than altering the court's substantive approach by placing an onus on the perpetrator. This is probably the correct approach, given the requirements of section 1 of the CA 1989. However, the reasoning in *Re LVMH* can also be criticized.

It can be argued that the court's considering only a presumption in which the basic facts include any type of domestic violence meant that the conclusion against use of a presumption became almost inevitable. The approach fails to distinguish between, for example, levels of seriousness of the domestic violence or whether the violence is likely to be repeated or not.[151]

Re LVMH may also be attacked for alleged inconsistency. The court rejected an assumption against contact in domestic violence cases because of the inability to generalize about such cases. Yet the inability to generalize about cases as a whole did not prevent the court from putting in place an assumption that contact is beneficial.[152] Furthermore, the court's assumption that contact is beneficial in all cases flies directly in the face of Sturge/Glaser's opinion that in cases of domestic violence there should certainly not be such an assumption.

Further Reading

A. Bainham, 'Contact as a Right and Obligation', in A. Bainham, B. Lindley, M. Richards and L. Trinder (eds), *Children and Their Families: Contact, Rights and Welfare* (Hart Publishing, 2003).

S. Choudhry and H. Fenwick, 'Taking the Rights of Parents and Children Seriously: Confronting the Welfare Principle under the Human Rights Act' (2005) 25(3) *OJLS* 453.

J. Eekelaar, 'Beyond the Welfare Principle' (2002) 14(3) *Child and Family Law Quarterly* 237.

B. Fehlberg, B. Smyth, M. Maclean and C. Roberts, 'Legislating for Shared Time Parenting After Separation: A Research Review' (2011) 25(3) *International Journal of Law, Policy and the Family* 318.

---

[149] Ibid, at 300.
[150] Ibid, at 301.
[151] J. Herring 'Connecting Contact: Contact in a Private Law Context' in Bainham, Lindley, Richards and Trinder (eds), *Children and Their Families: Contact, Rights and Welfare*, p. 105.
[152] S. Gilmore, 'The Assumption that Contact is Beneficial: Challenging the 'Secure Foundation' [2008] *Family Law* 1226, 1228.

J. Fortin, 'The HRA's Impact on Litigation Involving Children and their Families' [1999] *Child and Family Law Quarterly* 237.

S. Gilmore, 'Court Decision-Making in Shared Residence Order Cases – A Critical Examination' [2006] *Child and Family Law Quarterly* 478.

S. Gilmore, 'Disputing Contact: Challenging Some Assumptions' [2008] *Child and Family Law Quarterly* 285.

S. Gilmore, 'Shared Residence: A Summary of the Courts' Guidance' [2010] *Family Law* 285.

P. G. Harris and R.H. George, 'Parental Responsibility and Shared Residence Orders: Parliamentary Intentions And Judicial Interpretations' [2010] *Child and Family Law Quarterly* 151.

S. Harris-Short, 'Building A House Upon Sand: Post-Separation Parenting, Shared Residence and Equality – Lessons From Sweden' [2011] *Child and Family Law Quarterly* 344.

J. Herring, 'Farewell Welfare?' (2005) 27(2) *Journal of Social Welfare and Family Law* 159.

J. Herring 'The Human Rights Act and the Welfare Principle in Family Law: Conflicting or Complementary?' (1999) 11 *Child and Family Law Quarterly* 223.

H. Reece, 'The Paramountcy Principle: Consensus or Construct?' (1996) 49 *Current Legal Problems* 267.

L. Trinder, 'Shared Residence: A Review of Recent Research Evidence' (2010) 22(4) *Child and Family Law Quarterly* 475.

5

CHILD PROTECTION

INTRODUCTION

A matter which stimulates several strands of debate within family law surrounds the question of how an appropriate balance is to be struck between protecting children from abuse, and avoiding inappropriate interference by the state in the private lives of individuals. This chapter explores some of the arguments surrounding various approaches which could be taken to child protection within a society. English law adopts what is termed a 'liberal standard', whereby children are initially placed in the care of their parent(s) and the state only has power to intervene compulsorily to take over a child's care on passing a threshold for intervention. Such an approach raises difficult questions as to the point at which the threshold is to be set, and how it is expressed and interpreted. In English law, the threshold criteria, as they are known, are contained in section 31(2) of the Children Act 1989, a provision which has thrown up many complex, controversial issues and stimulated much difficult case-law. The chapter examines in detail the difficulties and debates this version of the liberal standard and its interpretation in the case-law has provoked.

Debate 1

How should a society protect children?

The moral duty to protect and care for children is arguably one which falls not only on a child's parents (who in most cases will have a natural instinct to do so) but also on members of society as a whole, as part of a wider duty to promote human flourishing;[1] and it follows that while many societies will recognize the special place that parents have in the care of children,[2] quite how the care and protection of children is dealt with in a society is a matter of political choice.

---

[1] J. Eekelaar, 'Are Parents Morally Obliged to Care for Their Children?' (1991) 11(3) *OJLS* 340.
[2] For discussion of philosophical perspectives on the rights and duties of parenthood, see C. Barton and G. Douglas, *Law and Parenthood* (Butterworths, 1995), ch. 2.

The various methods that might be employed to protect children are matters of philosophical debate.

One suggestion for ensuring a very public monitoring of children's well-being is to adopt a collectivist approach[3] to child rearing, with the state directly concerned in the upbringing of all children. The principal argument in a favour of such an approach is the securing of societal unity. However, there are several strong counterarguments. Collectivism 'requires unanimity concerning the purpose and ends of parenting' and it is not at all clear that this is achievable unless people are forced 'to live as others choose'.[4] It thus runs counter to liberal views of liberty as recognizing diversity, and carries the danger of indoctrination. In addition, it can be argued that collectivist upbringings may deny children the benefits of intimate family relationships; the state as parent is unlikely to have the same close emotional relationship with the child as the parent/child relationship within a family.

Another suggested approach to child protection is to adopt a form of licensed parenthood,[5] checking on parenting abilities prior to allowing parents to bear or rear children. Hugh LaFollette[6] has argued that activities that are potentially harmful to others and require demonstrated competence (such as driving a car or dispensing drugs) are usually subject to regulation, and there is thus no reason why parenting should not be so treated.[7] In addition, he points out that some parenting is already 'licensed', such as adoption. LaFollette argues that licensing 'seems to be the best way to prevent children from being reared by incompetent parents'.[8] Further arguments have been advanced by James Dwyer, based on children's relationship rights.[9] Dwyer is concerned that the parent/child relationship is usually founded simply on the biological connection between an adult and a child, without any prior scrutiny of the appropriateness of that relationship. Dwyer points out that adults' rights to choose their relationships are founded in their right to exercise autonomy and also in a utilitarian argument that competent adults are likely to be the best judges of their own *welfare* in such matters. In the case of an incompetent adult, decisions about appropriate relationships are similarly made on the basis of that person's welfare, although they will usually be made by another (e.g. a court-appointed 'guardian' of the person's welfare).

---

[3] See generally D. Archard, *Children: Rights and Childhood*, 2nd edn (Routledge, 2004), ch. 13.

[4] Ibid, p. 182.

[5] See e.g. H. LaFollette, 'Licensing Parents' (1980) 9 *Philosophy and Public Affairs* 182; C. P. Mangel, 'Licensing Parents: How Feasible?' (1988) 22 *Family Law Quarterly* 17; J. C. Westman, *Licensing Parents: Can We Prevent Child Abuse and Neglect?* (Cambridge, MA: Perseus Books, 1994); M. Freeman, 'The Right to Responsible Parents', in J. Bridgeman, H. Keating, and C. Lind (eds), *Responsibility, Law and the Family* (Ashgate, 2008).

[6] LaFollette, 'Licensing Parents'.

[7] Ibid, 183–85.

[8] Ibid, 195.

[9] J. G. Dwyer, *The Relationship Rights of Children* (Cambridge University Press, 2006). For an overview and criticism, see S. Gilmore, 'The Relationship Rights of Children' (2008) 22(2) *International Journal of Law, Policy and the Family* 273; see also C. Sawyer, 'Review Article: A Brave New World Order' [2007] *Child and Family Law Quarterly* 518.

Dwyer argues that the same theoretical underpinning should apply in the case of children. Thus in the case of incompetent children, welfare should be the basis for regulating children's relationships, with scrutiny of the appropriateness of legal parenthood in each case.

Dwyer's philosophical position is tightly argued, and the theoretical arguments in favour of licensed parenthood are not without merit. However, several practical objections to licensed parenthood can be mounted. First there is the difficulty of finding some reliable way of predicting parenting abilities.[10] Secondly, there is arguably a disproportionate cost and administrative burden to license all parents in order to exclude the minority of parents who would potentially present a risk to children. Thirdly, there is the problem of enforcement, and dealing with children who are born to unlicensed parents. Licensed parenthood runs the risk of giving the message, particularly to the unlicensed, that they can have children without the need to take any responsibility for them. Alternatively, such parents who wish to keep a child may avoid medical or other services to avoid detection, and the consequent harm to children may outweigh the benefits of licensing.[11] Like collectivism, licensed parenthood also carries the danger of imposing a state view about appropriate lifestyles and who is suitable to parent a child.

A third approach, and one which is adopted in many liberal democracies, including England and Wales, is to presume that the upbringing of children within families is desirable and that the state should not intrude unless there is consent or stated conditions for state intervention are fulfilled. This liberal standard acknowledges that as a general proposition a child's parents are likely to have a strong interest in the child's well-being and be best suited to caring for the child. It is mindful of the benefits that children's upbringing within individual families brings in terms of promoting diversity within society, whilst also recognizing that in a minority of cases there may be a need for the state to intervene in family life[12] to protect a child or to provide alternative care for the child.

The difficulty which any legislature faces in enacting a threshold for state intervention is the tension between specificity and generality: the need, on the one hand, to ensure that specific harms to children trigger state intervention, whilst, on the other hand, trying to ensure that the criteria are adequately generally expressed so as to ensure that other (perhaps as yet unforeseen) appropriate situations for intervention can also be addressed. The solution adopted in English

---

10 See M. J. Sandmire and M. S. Wald, 'Licensing Parents – A Response to Claudia Mangel's Proposal' (1990) 24(1) *Family Law Quarterly* 53.

11 Ibid, 71.

12 On one view, the notion that there is a private sphere of family life into which the state intervenes is a myth: see F. E. Olsen, 'The Myth of State Intervention in the Family' (1984–85) 18 *University of Michigan Journal of Law Reform*, 835–864, 837: 'Because the state is deeply implicated in the formation and functioning of families, it is nonsense to talk about whether the state does or does not intervene in the family', criticized by L. D. Houlgate, 'What Is Legal Intervention in the Family? Family Law and Family Privacy' (1998) 17 *Law and Philosophy* 141–58 (because nothing can count as non-intervention the conclusion that there is no such thing as non-intervention is logically empty).

law is to be found in section 31(2) of the Children Act 1989, which we examine in some detail below.

Debate 2

The 'liberal standard' in English law: arguments surrounding the interpretation of section 31(2) of the Children Act 1989

Prior to the Children Act 1989 the law on child protection had emerged piece-meal.[13] There were several ways in which a child might be placed into local author-ity care, and the criteria which Parliament had set down[14] could be by-passed by use of the inherent jurisdiction of the High Court to place a child in care, when the criterion would be simply the paramountcy of the child's welfare. One of the aims of the Children Act 1989, following review of the previous law,[15] was to address these problems by putting in place a single entry point and threshold for compulsory state intervention in family life to protect children. Section 31(2) of the Children Act 1989 now provides:

A court may only make a care order or a supervision order if it is satisfied –

(a) that the child is suffering, or is likely to suffer, significant harm; and
(b) that the harm, or likelihood of harm, is attributable to –
    (i) the care given to the child, or likely to be given to him if the order were not made, not being what it would be reasonable to expect a parent to give to him; or
    (ii) the child's being beyond parental control.

'Harm' is widely defined in section 31(9) to mean:

ill-treatment or the impairment of health or development including, for exam-ple, impairment suffered from seeing or hearing the ill-treatment of another; 'development' means physical, intellectual, emotional, social or behavioural development; 'health' means physical or mental health; and 'ill-treatment' includes sexual abuse and forms of ill-treatment which are not physical.

Section 31(10) provides a little further guidance, stating that:

Where the question of whether harm suffered by a child is significant turns on the child's health or development, his health or development shall be compared with that which could reasonably be expected of a similar child.[16]

---

[13] See J. Eekelaar, R. Dingwall and T. Murray 'Victims Or Threats? Children in Care Proceedings' (1982) 4(2) *Journal of Social Welfare and Family Law* 68–82, for discussion of the various strands of development.
[14] E.g. in the Children and Young Persons Act 1969, s. 1.
[15] DHSS, *Review of Child Care Law: Report to Ministers of an Inter-Departmental Working Party* (HMSO, 1985).
[16] For criticism of the similar child concept, see M. D. A. Freeman *Care After 1991* in D. Freestone (ed.) *Children and the Law* (Hull University Press, 1990), and A. Bainham, 'Care after 1991– A Reply' (1993) 3 *Journal of Child Law* 99.

As can be seen, rather than listing specific situations in which intervention would be justified, English law adopted a more general 'catch-all' provision. This places responsibility on the judges to interpret the application of the general provision to specific cases. In such an approach, as we shall see, there is potential for tensions to occur between the interpretations arising in different cases. Although in *Newham London Borough v AG*,[17] Sir Stephen Brown P hoped 'that in approaching cases under the Children Act courts will not be invited to perform in every case a strict legalistic analysis of the statutory meaning of s 31',[18] the wording of section 31(2) has generated much case-law, including several House of Lords/Supreme Court decisions. The emerging body of case-law is complex and has stimulated much debate, not only on the reasoning in individual cases, but also on whether the case-law fits together as a coherent whole.

THE MEANING OF 'SIGNIFICANT HARM'

The point at which state intervention is authorized is regulated by the concept of 'significant harm'. The word 'significant' has provoked debate, particularly as to the extent to which, if at all, the law should take account of different approaches to parenting within different cultures in ascertaining what is significant: to what extent is a finding of 'significant' to take account of cultural pluralism?

There is no definition of 'significant' in the Children Act 1989 and the courts have eschewed, as unwise, any attempt at an all-embracing definition of significant harm,[19] beyond acceptance in *Humberside County Council v B*[20] of the dictionary definition of 'significant' as meaning 'considerable or noteworthy or important'.[21] This is because significant harm is 'fact specific and must retain the breadth of meaning that human fallibility may require of it'.[22] For example, in *Humberside County Council v B* Booth J cited an example of a child who suffers from brittle bones, in whose case 'a push or a slap might be of great significance, whereas in the case of a child who does not so suffer it may be a minimal incident'.[23] Section 31(10) suggests that 'significant harm' is judged relative to other children, by reference to an objective test of what could reasonably be expected. The meaning of 'similar' in this context needs to take account of environmental, social and cultural characteristics of the child. It seems that a similar child is a child with similar attributes, that is, a child of the same age, sex and ethnic origin. Where a child has learning difficulties he should be compared with a child with similar learning difficulties. Where the child was born prematurely the child's achievement of developmental milestones should be compared with those achieved by other premature babies. More contentious is the question of how far a disadvantaged child should be compared with a similar disadvantaged child, or how far he

---

[17] [1992] 2 FCR 119.
[18] Ibid, at 128.
[19] *Re L (Care: Threshold Criteria)* [2007] 1 FLR 2050, at para. [51], per Hedley J.
[20] [1993] 1 FLR 257.
[21] Ibid, at 265.
[22] [2007] 1 FLR 2050, at para. [51].
[23] [1993] 1 FLR 257, at 263.

should be compared with a child who has benefited from greater material, social and intellectual advantages. An example might be of children living in deprived circumstances in an inner-city area. In *Re O (A Minor) (Care Order: Education: Procedure)*[24] in the case of a 15-year-old girl who had been truanting from school for three years Ewbank J, making a care order,[25] held that in that context 'similar child' meant 'a child of equivalent intellectual and social development, who has gone to school, and not merely an average child who may or may not be at school'.[26] The girl was to be taken to school from a children's home until a satisfactory pattern of attendance had been achieved.

In *Re MA (Care Threshold)*,[27] Ward LJ referred to the underlying philosophy of the Children Act 1989 and observed that 'the harm must...be significant enough to justify the intervention of the State and disturb the autonomy of the parents to bring up their children by themselves in the way they choose'.[28] These references to parental autonomy and choice in children's upbringing suggest that 'significance' for the purpose of state intervention cannot be entirely detached from acceptance of pluralism. Indeed Ward LJ endorsed observations of Hedley J and Munby J in *Re L (Care: Threshold Criteria)*[29] and *Re K; A Local Authority v N and Others*[30] respectively. Hedley J had stated that:

> society must be willing to tolerate very diverse standards of parenting, including the eccentric, the barely adequate and the inconsistent. It follows too that children will inevitably have both very different experiences of parenting and very unequal consequences flowing from it. It means that some children will experience disadvantage and harm, while others flourish in atmospheres of loving security and emotional stability. These are the consequences of our fallible humanity and it is not the provenance of the state to spare children all the consequences of defective parenting. In any event, it simply could not be done.[31]

And Munby J commented[32] that:

> the court must always be sensitive to the cultural, social and religious circumstances of the particular child and family. And the court should, I

---

[24] [1992] 2 FLR 7.

[25] See J. Fortin, 'Significant Harm Revisited' (1993) 5 *Journal of Child Law* 151, who argues that the facts did not justify removing a child from her parents, that it was wrong to use removal into state care to deal with a child's lack of self-esteem and self-confidence, and that an application for an education supervision order would have been the appropriate response.

[26] [1992] 2 FLR 7, at p. 12.

[27] [2009] EWCA Civ 853; [2010] 1 FLR 431, at para. [51]. For commentary on this case, see H. Keating, 'Re MA: The Significance of Harm' [2011] CFLQ 115 and J. Hayes, M. Hayes and J. Williams, '"Shocking" Abuse Followed by a "Staggering Ruling": Re MA (Care Threshold)' [2010] *Family Law* 166.

[28] [2009] EWCA Civ 853; [2010] 1 FLR 431 at para [54].

[29] [2007] 1 FLR 2050, at para. [51].

[30] [2005] EWHC 2956 (Fam); [2007] 1 FLR 399.

[31] [2007] 1 FLR 2050, at para. [50].

[32] In the context of considering the threshold for making a care order pursuant to section 31 of the Children Act 1989.

think, be slow to find that parents only recently or comparatively recently arrived from a foreign country – particularly a country where standards and expectations may be more or less different, sometimes very different indeed, from those with which [we] are familiar – have fallen short of an acceptable standard of parenting if in truth they have done nothing wrong by the standards of their own community.[33]

These are deep waters indeed, upon which commentators are likely to disagree.

Re MA was a case in which there was no suggestion that the parents were claiming any cultural justification for the alleged ill-treatment of their children and Hayes et al. are critical of Ward LJ's use of the passages quoted above in that case, commenting:

> any reference to the value placed by society on 'diversity and individuality' cannot be used to justify child cruelty or exposing young children to the risk of significant harm. Our developed laws of child protection are rooted in the protection of the rights and freedoms of all children within our society.[34]

Research does not suggest that the threshold criteria need to be changed because of an inability to accommodate to cultural practices in parenting. Rather, it shows that applications in care proceedings tend to involve allegations of multiple deficiencies in parenting (for example, substance abuse, chaotic lifestyles), and research on cases of ill-treatment in ethnic-minority households has found 'no "single issue" cases where allegations of significant harm to a child rested unequivocally on behaviours/ attitudes defended as culturally acceptable by a parent but that professionals argued were unacceptable within western European assessments of ill-treatment'.[35]

THE TEMPORAL DIMENSION OF THE THRESHOLD AND THE DANGER OF SOCIAL ENGINEERING

A second debate which the threshold criteria have thrown up relates to the point in time at which the 'questions' in section 31(2) are asked. Section 31(2) avoids the use of the term 'has suffered' and therefore excludes the possibility that a child could be taken into care merely on the basis of historic events.[36] Otherwise,

---

[33] [2007] 1 FLR 399, at para. [26].

[34] J. Hayes, M. Hayes and J. Williams, ' "Shocking" Abuse Followed by a "Staggering Ruling": *Re MA (Care Threshold)*' [2010] *Family Law* 166.

[35] J. Brophy, J. Jhutti-Johal, C. Owen, 'Assessing And Documenting Child Ill-Treatment In Ethnic Minority Households' [2003] *Family Law* 756. See also J. Brophy, J. Jhutti-Johal and C. Owen, *Significant Harm: Child Protection Litigation in a Multi-Cultural Setting* (Department of Constitutional Affairs, 2003) (examining cultural context in care proceedings and not recommending any change to the threshold criteria).

[36] See e.g. *Re L (Care: Threshold Criteria)* [2007] 1 FLR 2050 at paras [34] and [35]. (Hedley J). The case had been remitted by the Court of Appeal for rehearing: see *Re L (Children) (Care Proceedings: Significant Harm)* [2006] EWCA Civ 1282; [2007] 1 FLR 1068. The child was sexually assaulted by a man whom the father knew to be a sex offender and allowed to stay in the family home. After working with the family on preventing such risks in the future, the local authority closed its file on the matter: 'cannot, as a matter of law, close its mind to matters that have happened in the past it would be impermissible

a child's parents would always be at risk, at least in principle, of having their child taken into care, no matter how much they improved their parenting following earlier concerns. However, fundamental issues of policy arise where a child has recently been the subject of harm by a parent, but where one of the child's relatives, such as an aunt or a grandparent, steps forward to care for the child. Should the state still have *power* to intervene compulsorily in such cases? Does this run the risk of unnecessary social engineering?

These issues have arisen in the case-law because the words of the threshold test relating to the child's suffering significant harm are expressed in the present tense. The words 'is suffering' have caused difficulties of interpretation, since of course in many cases by the time of the final hearing, steps will already have been taken to protect the child. These issues arose on the striking facts of *Re M (A Minor) (Care Order: Threshold Conditions)*.[37] When M was four months old, his father brutally murdered his mother[38] with a meat cleaver in the presence of M and M's three older half-siblings. The older children were placed with Mrs W, the mother's cousin. Initially M was accommodated with local authority foster parents, and the local authority sought a care order in respect of him. Before the disposal hearing, however, he too went to live with Mrs W, and the local authority, who supported Mrs W's desire to look after M, were no longer pursuing the care order. However, M's guardian still recommended a care order with a view to his adoption outside the family. The question therefore arose whether a care order could be made and whether such an order should be made.

Bracewell J found that the threshold conditions were established and made a care order. Mrs W's appeal was successful in the Court of Appeal, which held that the words 'is suffering or is likely to suffer' in the present tense were not fulfilled at the date of disposal. The court drew an analogy with a case in which a child's parents have been killed in a road traffic accident and relatives offer to care for the child. The Court of Appeal held that to interpret the threshold criteria in a way which would allow the making of a care order in such a case (and in the instant case) would amount to a form of 'social engineering'.[39] However, the House of Lords reversed the Court of Appeal's decision and restored the care order because it would apparently allow the local authority to control the child's father's exercise of parental responsibility for the child[40] and allow Mrs W to obtain help and advice from the local authority. On the temporal dimension of the threshold criteria, Lord Mackay LC held that:

> Where, at the time the application is to be disposed of, there are in place arrangements for the protection of the child by the local authority on an

---

to rely on the historic matter of the sexual assault to address the question in the present whether the children are suffering significant harm'. (Wilson LJ, at [13]).

[37] [1994] 3 All ER 298.

[38] For guidance on dealing with cases where one parent has unlawfully killed the other, see *Re A and B (One Parent Killed by the Other)* [2011] 1 FLR 783. The perpetrator's family should not necessarily be discounted as future carers of the child. The view at para. [1] of the guidance that the threshold will always been met where one parent has killed the other is probably too broadly expressed.

[39] [1994] 1 All ER 424, at 432.

[40] Under s. 33(3)(b).

interim basis which protection has been continuously in place for some time, the relevant date with respect to which the court must be satisfied is the date at which the local authority initiated the procedure for protection under the Act from which these arrangements followed. If after a local authority had initiated protective arrangements the need for these had terminated, because the child's welfare had been satisfactorily provided for otherwise, in any subsequent proceedings it would not be possible to found jurisdiction on the situation at the time of the initiation of these arrangements. It is permissible only to look back from the date of disposal to the date of initiation of protection as a result of which local authority arrangements had been continuously in place thereafter to the date of disposal.[41]

Thus where there has been a continuum of protective measures between the first initiation of proceedings and the final hearing, the fact that the child is currently well cared for does not preclude the making of a care order.

Most commentators have endorsed this ruling on the temporal dimension of the threshold as in line with the policy of the legislation.[42] As Hayes and Williams argue, however, it was regrettable that there was no attempt to address the social policy issues raised by the case, nor Balcombe LJ's telling analogy. As they point out, the ruling has implications in other situations. For example, imagine a child is harmed by one parent when the other parent is absent from the home. It seems that, even where the other parent takes over the child's care, the threshold could be fulfilled, since that parent would be in the same position as Mrs W.

The temporal dimension of the threshold criteria is very loosely expressed in the quotation from Lord Mackay's judgment. The difficulties which that fact, together with the court's failure to explore the social policy issues raised by the case,[43] present are illustrated by *Re SH (Care Order: Orphan)*.[44] An 11-year-old boy was accommodated by the local authority following allegations of sexual abuse by his father, in which the mother and a half-sister were also implicated. During that time, his mother and father died in quick succession, and the local authority sought a care order. On counsel's concession that *Re M (A Minor) (Care Order: Threshold Conditions)*[45] applied, Hollis J made a care order. For the House of Lords' approach to make sense, however, surely the protective measures which must be continuously in place must be not merely accommodation per se, but accommodation

---

[41] [1994] 3 All ER 298, at 305. This approach applies to both limbs of section 31(2)(a) of the Children Act 1989 (i.e. also to 'is likely to suffer significant harm'): see *Southwark London Borough Council v B* [1999] 1 FCR 550, FD, Charles J. See *Re G (children) (care order: evidence)* [2001] EWCA Civ 968; [2001] 2 FCR 757 (information acquired after the relevant date as to the state of affairs at the relevant date can be taken into account but later events cannot be relied upon unless they are capable of showing what the position was at the relevant time).

[42] M. Hayes (1995) 58 *MLR* 878; A. Bainham (1994) 53 *CLJ* 458; J.Whybrow (1994) 6 *JCL* 177. For a contrary view, see J. Masson (1994) 6 *JCL* 170.

[43] This criticism is highlighted by M. Hayes and C. Williams, *Family Law, Principles Policy and Practice* (London: Butterworths, 1999), p. 203.

[44] [1995] 1 FLR 746.

[45] [1994] 2AC 424, which approved *Northamptonshire County Council v S* [1993] Fam 136; [1992] 3 WLR 1010.

which avoids the harm which is relied upon at the hearing to fulfil the threshold. Once the boy's parents were dead, the need to protect the children from sexual abuse attributable to lack of reasonable parental care ceased. From that point, the boy was accommodated for a different reason, because he was orphaned.

THE RISK OF FUTURE HARM

Another lively debate which the threshold criteria have stimulated relates to the basis upon which a future risk of harm to a child can be established. Some argue that the standard set in case-law is too high and risks leaving some children unprotected, while others claim that the law appropriately protects parents from unwarranted state intervention by preventing intervention merely on the basis of suspicion of future harm. The issue was addressed by the House of Lords in *In re H and Others (Minors) Sexual Abuse: Standard of Proof)*[46] in which the House was called upon to determine the meaning of 'likely' and when an inference of likelihood of harm may be drawn. Four girls aged 15, 13, 8 and 2 were living with their mother and Mr R, who was the father of the younger two children and stepfather of the others. The elder stepdaughter, D, alleged that Mr R had sexually abused her since she was about seven years old. He was acquitted on several counts of rape, but the local authority nevertheless brought care proceedings in respect of the younger children, based solely on the alleged sexual abuse of D. The trial judge concluded that the allegation of abuse of D had not been made out to the requisite standard of proof and therefore he could not draw an inference that the younger children were at risk of harm. The local authority's appeal, ultimately to the House of Lords, was dismissed by Lord Nicholls of Birkenhead with the concurrence of Lords Goff and Mustill; Lords Lloyd and Browne-Wilkinson dissented.

Their Lordships were unanimous that 'likely' in the context of the threshold test did not mean more likely than not,[47] rather 'a real possibility, a possibility that cannot sensibly be ignored having regard to the nature and gravity of the feared harm in the particular case'.[48]

The House also held that there must be facts, proved on the balance of probabilities, from which the court can properly conclude that there is a real possibility that the child will suffer harm in the future.[49] An alleged but non-proven fact is not a fact for this purpose. Applying that approach to the facts of this case, Lord Nicholls (for the majority) held that the judge had been right in his conclusion

---

[46] [1996] AC 563. For further comment, see M. Hayes, 'Reconciling Protection for Children with Justice for Parents' (1997) 17 *Legal Studies* 1; I. Hemingway and C. Williams, *Re M and R: Re H and R* [1997] Fam Law 740; C. Keenan, 'Finding That a Child Is at Risk from Sexual Abuse: *Re H (Minors)(Sexual Abuse: Standard of Proof*' (1997) 60 MLR 857; H. Keating, 'Shifting Standards in the House Of Lords – *Re H and Others (Minors)(Sexual Abuse: Standard of Proof)*' [1996] 8 *Child and Family Law Quarterly* 157.

[47] See Lord Browne-Wilkinson at [1996] AC 563, at 572; Lord Lloyd of Berwick at 576.

[48] [1996] AC 563, at 565, per Lord Nicholls, approving *Newham London Borough Council v AG* [1993] 1 FLR 281. Lord Nicholls said that by parity of reasoning the word likely also bore the same meaning in sections 43, 44, 46 and 31(2)(b) ('care given to the child or "likely" to be given him'). In *Re H (A Minor) (Section 37 Direction)* [1993] 2 FLR 541 Scott Baker J ventured the opinion that when looking at the likelihood of significant harm the court is not limited to looking at the present and the immediate future.

[49] [1996] AC 563, at p. 590, per Lord Nicholls.

that an inference of likely harm could not be drawn. By contrast, the dissenting judges took the view that there were a number of 'micro facts'[50] which fell short of proving that D had been abused, but which were nevertheless established as facts and from which it might be inferred that there was a real possibility of harm to the younger children. Lord Browne-Wilkinson illustrated the point by way of a striking example of a possible air raid during World War II (which of course was quite likely at that time):[51]

> Say that in 1940 those responsible for giving air-raid warnings had received five unconfirmed sightings of approaching aircraft which might be enemy bombers. They could not, on balance of probabilities, have reached a conclusion that any one of those sightings was of an enemy aircraft: nor could they logically have put together five non-proven sightings so as to be satisfied that enemy aircraft were in fact approaching. But their task was not simply to decide whether enemy aircraft were approaching but whether there was a risk of an air-raid. The facts relevant to the assessment of such risk were the reports that unconfirmed sightings had been made, not the truth of such reports. They could well, on the basis of those unconfirmed reports, have been satisfied that there was a real possibility of an air-raid and given warning accordingly.

Although academic commentary has emphasized the differences in the majority and minority approaches in this case, there is in fact very little difference in principle between them. Lord Nicholls was at pains to emphasize that the 'range of facts which may properly be taken into account is infinite',[52] and also to stress that it is 'open to a court to conclude there is a real possibility that the child will suffer harm in the future although harm in the past has not been established', for example, where the evidence disclosed a set of worrying features. The difference lies in a rather narrow point about the relevance of the so-called micro facts in the unusual circumstances of this case. The majority took the view that in this case there was only one relevant fact, namely whether Mr R had sexually abused D, and thus the micro facts 'lead nowhere relevant in this case if they do not lead to the conclusion that [D] was abused'.[53] This is undoubtedly correct; the court is only concerned with facts relevant to a fact in issue.

The approach in *In re H* was affirmed in *In re B (Children) (Care Proceedings: Standard of Proof) (Cafcass intervening)*,[54] the House of Lords unhesitatingly declining

---

[50] D had been consistent in her story from the time of her first complaint; that her statement was full and detailed; that there were opportunities for such abuse by Mr R and that he had been lying in denying that he had ever been alone either with D or with any of the other children; that one of the younger children had made statements which indicated that she had witnessed 'inappropriate' behaviour between Mr R and D; that the mother suspected that something had been going on between Mr R and D.

[51] [1996] AC 563, at 572–73.

[52] Ibid, at 591.

[53] Ibid, at 592.

[54] [2008] UKHL 35, [2009] AC 11. For commentary, see John Hayes, 'Farewell to the Cogent Evidence Test: Re B' [2008] *Family Law* 859; H. Keating, 'Suspicions, Sitting on the Fence and Standards of Proof' [2009] *Child and Family Law Quarterly* 230.

an invitation to depart from it, and stating that Lord Nicholls' reasons 'remain thoroughly convincing'.[55] Baroness Hale explained that:

> The threshold is there to protect both the children and their parents from unjustified intervention in their lives. It would provide no protection at all if it could be established on the basis of unsubstantiated suspicions: that is, where a judge cannot say that there is no real possibility that abuse took place, so concludes that there is a real possibility that it did. In other words, the alleged perpetrator would have to prove that it did not.[56]

THE STANDARD OF PROOF IN CARE PROCEEDINGS

Another issue which has caused difficulty is the standard of proof in care proceedings. Here again the debate has centred on a tension between the rights of parents and children, and balancing the need for protection of the child against the fact that an allegation of abuse of a child by a parent is a very serious one. In *In re H and Others (Minors) (Sexual Abuse: Standard of Proof)*,[57] the House of Lords held unanimously that the standard of proof which applies to the threshold test is the balance of probability.[58] However, debate has surrounded the question of whether the seriousness of the issues in care proceedings should be reflected in the approach to proof and how, if at all, that should be expressed. Lord Nicholls for the majority in *Re H* added that 'the court will have in mind as a factor, to whatever extent is appropriate in the particular case, that the more serious the allegation the less likely it is that the event occurred and, hence, the stronger should be the evidence before the court concludes that the allegation is established on the balance of probability'.[59] He emphasized that this does not mean that the standard of proof is higher than the balance of probabilities;[60] rather 'it means only that the inherent probability or improbability of an event is itself a matter to be taken into account when weighing the probabilities and deciding whether, on balance, the event occurred. The more improbable the event, the stronger must be the evidence that it did occur before, on the balance of probability, its occurrence will be established.'[61] In other words: 'The more serious the allegation the more cogent is the evidence required to overcome the unlikelihood of what is alleged and thus to prove it.'[62]

---

[55] [2008] UKHL 35; [2009] AC 11, at para. 54.
[56] Ibid.
[57] [1996] AC 563. For comment, see references at n. 49.
[58] [1996] AC 563, at 586 and 587, per Lord Nicholls.
[59] Ibid, at 586.
[60] Indeed, he expressly rejected a so-called third standard of proof, somewhere between the criminal standard and simple balance of probabilities: see [1996] AC 563, at 587.
[61] Ibid, at 586.
[62] Citing *In re Dellow's Will Trusts* [1964] 1 WLR 451, 455, adding that this substantially accords with the approach adopted by Morris LJ in *Hornal v. Neuberger Products Ltd* [1957] 1 QB 247, 266. On this test, see J. R. Spencer (1994) 'Evidence in Child Abuse Cases – Too High a Price for Too High a Standard? Re M (A Minor) (Appeal) No 2' *6 Journal of Child Law* 160.

The arguments against such gloss are made by Lord Lloyd, dissenting, who expressed the opinion that the standard of proof under section 31(2) ought to be the simple balance of probability, however serious the allegations involved, commenting that it would be 'a bizarre result if the more serious the anticipated injury, whether physical or sexual, the more difficult it became for the local authority to satisfy the initial burden of proof, and thereby ultimately, if the welfare test is satisfied, secure protection for the child.'[63]

Lord Lloyd was also concerned that 'there is a danger that the repeated use of the words will harden into a formula, which, like other formulas (especially those based on a metaphor) may lead to misunderstanding'.[64] Baroness Hale of Richmond later observed in *In re B (Children) (Care Proceedings: Standard of Proof) (Cafcass intervening)*[65] that 'Lord Lloyd's prediction proved only too correct'.[66] She explained that, despite the care with which Lord Nicholls sought to explain that the standard of proof is the balance of probabilities, his 'nuanced explanation left room for the nostrum, "the more serious the allegation, the more cogent the evidence needed to prove it", to take hold', and for later cases to misinterpret it as giving rise to a heightened civil standard.[67]

The House of Lords agreed that, in the light of this difficulty, it should announce 'loud and clear' that the standard of proof in care proceedings 'is the simple balance of probabilities, neither more nor less'.[68] Baroness Hale explained that the consequences of care proceedings are serious either way and:

> Neither the seriousness of the allegation nor the seriousness of the consequences should make any difference to the standard of proof to be applied in determining the facts. The inherent probabilities are simply something to be taken into account, where relevant, in deciding where the truth lies.[69]

As to the seriousness of any allegation, her Ladyship pointed out that:

> there is no logical or necessary connection between seriousness and probability. Some seriously harmful behaviour, such as murder, is sufficiently rare to be inherently improbable in most circumstances. Even then there are circumstances, such as a body with its throat cut and no weapon to hand, where it is not at all improbable. Other seriously harmful behaviour, such as alcohol or drug abuse, is regrettably all too common and not at all improbable.[70]

---

[63] [1996] AC 563, at 577.
[64] Ibid, at 578.
[65] [2008] UKHL 35; [2009] AC 11.
[66] Ibid, at para. 64.
[67] In addition, more confusion was created when in *R (McCann) v Crown Court at Manchester* Lord Steyn cited Lord Nicholls' approach in *Re H (Minors) (Sexual Abuse: Standard of Proof)* in support of there being in some cases a 'heightened civil standard' of proof.
[68] [2008] UKHL 35; [2009] AC 11, at para. 70.
[69] Ibid. Lord Hoffmann stated that having regard to the inherent probabilities was a matter required by common sense, not law (see para. 15).
[70] Ibid, at para. 72.

Baroness Hale also emphasized that the context in which allegations are made is important, commenting:

> Nor are serious allegations made in a vacuum. Consider the famous example of the animal seen in Regent's Park. If it is seen outside the zoo on a stretch of greensward regularly used for walking dogs, then of course it is more likely to be a dog than a lion. If it is seen in the zoo next to the lions' enclosure when the door is open, then it may well be more likely to be a lion than a dog.[71]

While this provides welcome clarification of misinterpretation of Lord Nicholls' gloss, it does not remove the gloss itself. As indicated above, the inherent probabilities are still something to be taken into account, where relevant, in deciding where the truth lies. The difficulty may be in knowing when such probabilities are relevant. In some cases, as Baroness Hale makes clear, the issue of relevance will be clear-cut: if there is evidence that a baby has suffered a non-accidental injury in unknown circumstances, the fact that such non-accidental injuries are relatively rare in the general population is clearly neither here nor there. However, other examples may prove more difficult. For example, when an allegation of sexual abuse has been made against a stepfather, as in *Re H*, is the relevant sample regarding improbability the general population or stepdaughter/stepfather relationships in which allegations are made? The former has a bearing on the likelihood (in general) of a parent being wrongly accused, yet once an allegation is made, the latter, more pertinent probability, relates to the likelihood of a child making a false allegation.

UNKNOWN PERPETRATOR CASES AND THE COHERENCE OF THE CASE LAW

A particular difficulty for the courts has arisen in so-called unknown perpetrator cases in which the child is cared for by more than one person, perhaps in different households, and has suffered non-accidental injuries, yet it remains unclear quite when, and by whom, the child suffered injury. Again, the debate thrown up relates to balancing the child's need for protection against justice for the parent who *may* be entirely innocent. Should the state be able to intervene to take a child from a parent in such cases? The answer in law requires an examination of the second limb of section 31(2)(b), which requires proof that:

the harm, or likelihood of harm, is attributable to –

(i) the care given to the child, or likely to be given to him if the order were not made, not being what it would be reasonable to expect a parent to give to him.

The phrase 'attributable to' connotes a causal connection between the harm or likelihood of harm and the care given or likely to be given, but the connection 'need not be that of a sole or dominant or direct cause and effect: a contributory causal connection suffices'.[72] The care given or likely to be given 'must fall

---

[71] Ibid.

[72] *Lancashire County Council v B* [2002] 2 AC 147, at 162, echoing Donaldson J in *Walsh v Rother District Council* [1978] ICR 1216, 1220.

below an objectively acceptable level'[73] and it has been held that the mere fact of the child's injury is not a basis for intervention.[74] So, for example, if a parent entrusts a child to the care of another without checking that person's suitability and the third party injures the child, the harm may be regarded as attributable to the inadequate care of the parent as well as to the actions of the third party.[75] By contrast, section 31(2)(b) would not be fulfilled where a child is harmed in the circumstances of a 'one-off temporary entrustment of the child to a person reasonably believed by the parents to be suitable'.[76]

The particularly difficult issue of unknown perpetrators came before the House of Lords in *Lancashire County Council v B*.[77] A paid childminder, who had a child of her own (child B) looked after a baby girl, child A, while A's parents were at work. Otherwise, A's parents looked after her. After this arrangement had been in place for two months, A, who was then seven months old, was found to have sustained serious non-accidental head injuries. The local authority applied for care orders in respect of A and B (who was only a month older than A), relying exclusively on the injury sustained to A. The judge found that the injuries to A had been inflicted by a member of household A or household B[78] but not both, but was unable to say which of A's mother, A's father, or B's mother was the perpetrator. The judge was of the view that, having so found, the threshold criteria could not be fulfilled and he dismissed the care applications.[79] On the local authority's appeal, the Court of Appeal dismissed the appeal in respect of B, applying the approach to the standard of proof required by *In re H and Others (Minors) Sexual Abuse: Standard of Proof)*.[80] The Court explained that since it had not been established as a matter of fact that B's mother had harmed A, there was no factual basis (as opposed to suspicion) from which the inference could be drawn that B was at risk in his household.[81] There was no appeal in respect of B. However, the Court of Appeal allowed the appeal in respect of A, and A's case subsequently came before the House of Lords on A's parents' appeal. The House of Lords dismissed the appeal, holding that the threshold was fulfilled. The House could not believe that Parliament intended the threshold criteria to operate so as to preclude protection of a child injured in the circumstances of A's case.[82] Lord Nicholls of Birkenhead, delivering an opinion with which there was unanimous agreement, held that the phrase 'care given to

---

[73] *Lancashire County Council v B* [2002] 2 AC 147, at 162.

[74] *CL v East Riding Yorkshire Council, MB and BL (A Child)*: 'translated into everyday language and experience' this means that a local authority 'must prove that an injury is non-accidental' (at para. [52]). See also *Re J (Care Proceedings: Injuries)* [2009] 2 FLR 99, FD (Hogg J).

[75] The example was given by Lord Nicholls of Birkenhead in *Lancashire County Council v B* [2002] 2 AC 147, at 162.

[76] *Lancashire County Council v B* [2002] 2 AC 147, at 165.

[77] [2002] 2 AC 147.

[78] The judge excluded B's father as a possible perpetrator.

[79] The judge applied a dictum of Wall J in *In re G (A Minor (Care Order: Threshold Conditions)* [1995] Fam 16, at 20, which suggested that the lack of care must be shown to be attributable to the As.

[80] [1996] AC 563.

[81] For criticism of the Court of Appeal's approach, see J. Hayes, 'The Threshold Test and the Unknown Perpetrator' [2000] *Family Law* 260.

[82] Ibid, at 165.

the child' normally refers primarily to the care given to the child by a parent or parents or other primary carers. However, the matter stands differently in a case in which the child's care is shared between primary carers and other carers and the court is unable to distinguish between the care given by those respective carers. Lord Nicholls said that in such a case 'the phrase "care given to the child" is apt to embrace not merely the care given by the parents or other primary carers; it is apt to embrace the care given by any of the carers'.[83] The House recognized that this interpretation meant that parents who were wholly innocent will face the possibility of losing their child but the factor outweighing all others is 'the prospect that an unidentified, and unidentifiable, carer may inflict further injury on a child he or she has already severely damaged'.[84] In a subsequent House of Lords decision, *In re O and another (Minors) (Care: Preliminary Hearing); In re B (A Minor)*,[85] it was held that at the welfare stage of proceedings when deciding whether a care order is dictated by the child's welfare, anyone who was potentially involved in harming the child should be treated as possible perpetrator (and not as innocent).

The outcome in the *Lancashire* cases, that child A could be protected, but B could not, because of the requirements for proof of future harm laid down in *Re H and R*, has proved controversial. In *Re CB and JB (Care Proceedings: Guidelines)*[86] Wall J had adopted the same approach as the House of Lords in the *Lancashire* case in a case in which one of two children was harmed by either of the parents living in the same household, but it was unclear which was the perpetrator. However, in contrast to the Court of Appeal's approach in the *Lancashire* case, Wall J had ruled that the threshold was fulfilled in respect of both children. As to the non-injured child, he held that a finding that the other child's injuries must have been caused by either the mother or the father gave rise to a real possibility that the unharmed sibling would also suffer significant harm were he to be left in the care of both or either of his parents.

It is not easy to reconcile the two decisions, as illustrated by John Hayes,[87] who points to the difficulty the *Lancashire* case creates on facts somewhere between the two cases. Imagine, he says, a case in which Child A in the *Lancashire* case had a twin, Child C, living in the same household, but who had suffered no harm. On the Court of Appeal's reasoning in the *Lancashire* case, A (who has been harmed) can be protected on the basis of suspicion that the parents were responsible for the harm, but the twin cannot. Hayes argues that the Court of Appeal's tortuous reasoning could be avoided if the court focused on the question whether, even without identifying a perpetrator, there was a 'real possibility' of harm.

The consternation of practitioners and commentators has been further stimulated by the subsequent Supreme Court decision in *In re S-B (Children) (Care*

---

[83] Ibid, at 166.

[84] Ibid, at 167. Similar reasoning applies in the case of unknown perpetrators, such as parents living in the same household: see *Re CB and JB (Care Proceedings: Guidelines)* 1998] 2 FLR 211.

[85] [2003] UKHL 18; [2004] 1 AC 523.

[86] [1998] 2 FLR 211.

[87] Hayes, 'The Threshold Test and the Unknown Perpetrator'.

Proceedings: Standard of Proof),[88] which applied the same approach as the Court of Appeal in the *Lancashire* case, this time to siblings. In *In re S-B* a child, Jason, suffered non-accidental bruising when aged 4 weeks. The parents separated and the mother subsequently gave birth to another child, William. Care proceedings were brought in respect of William because of what had happened to Jason. The trial judge was unable to decide which of Jason's parents was responsible for the injuries, but found the threshold crossed in respect of William on the basis that there was a real possibility that the mother had injured Jason. The Supreme Court held[89] that the judge's approach was not permissible. At paragraph [49] of the judgment, Baroness Hale explained that 'It was established in *Re H* and confirmed in *Re O*, that a prediction of future harm has to be based upon findings of actual fact made on the balance of probabilities'.

In Re S-B was cited by the Court of Appeal in *Re F (Interim Care Order)*,[90] in which a father who had been found to be a possible perpetrator set up home with another woman and had another child, C. In care proceedings alleging a risk of harm to C from his father, the trial judge held that the threshold criteria could not be fulfilled. The Court of Appeal endorsed the judge's approach and refused leave to appeal to the Supreme Court. Wilson LJ commented: 'No doubt there are hard and worrying cases. But the requirement of proven factual foundation is a bulwark against the state's removal of a child from his family, which I consider very precious.'[91] Mary Hayes has criticized this approach, observing that *In re H* did not 'make any observations or rulings on whether the threshold test can be crossed where a court finds it impossible to determine who in a pool of possible perpetrators has caused the proven harm'.[92] It does not therefore provide a reason for not applying to a case like this the more liberal approach to section 31(2)(b) in cases of unknown perpetrators as set out by the House of Lords in the *Lancashire* case. Hayes argues that the approach in *Re F*, relying on paragraph [49] of *In Re S-B*, conflates the tests in section 31(2)(a) and (b) respectively and there is no reason to do so.[93] She argues that in *Re F* there was no doubt that harm had been perpetrated, and the harm was attributable to either the mother or the father, and the conclusion must surely be that there is a real possibility that C is at risk. The difficulty that para. [49] of *In re S-B* presents can be shown by way of an example: imagine that the parents, each of whom is a possible perpetrator, separate, and each has a child with a new partner. It is clear that one of those children is at risk, but neither can be protected.

---

[88] [2009] UKSC 178; [2010] 1 AC 678. See I. Goldrein QC, 'There is Only So Much Juice in an Orange: *Re SB*' [2010] *Family Law* 196; J. Hayes, 'Ensuring Equal Protection for Siblings' [2010] *Family Law* 505. *Re CB and JB* was cited to the Supreme Court but was not referred to in the judgment.

[89] [2009] UKSC 178; [2010] 1 AC 678, at para. [49].

[90] [2011] EWCA Civ 258; [2011] 2 FLR 856. For comment, see M. Hayes, 'Why Didn't the Courts Protect this Child? *Re SB and Re F*' [2012] *Family Law* 169.

[91] [2011] EWCA Civ 258; [2011] 2 FLR 856, at para. [15].

[92] Hayes, 'Why Didn't the Courts Protect this Child? *Re SB and Re F*'.

[93] Ibid.

The issue came before the Court of Appeal again in *Re J (Children)*,[94] on facts similar to those in *Re F*, and in which a trial judge had similarly found that the threshold criteria could not be fulfilled. The Court of Appeal dismissed the local authority's appeal, holding that the judgments in *Re F* and *Re S-B* had rendered fanciful any contemplation of departure from the Court of Appeal's approach in the *Lancashire* case.[95] However, McFarlane LJ, following a detailed examination of the relevant authorities, also suggested that the approach in paragraph 49 of *Re S-B* may not be compatible with Lord Nicholls's opinions in earlier decisions. In McFarlane LJ's view the authorities indicated a different approach 'between cases where absolutely no past harm has been proved, and those where past harm is established but the identity of the actual perpetrator cannot be proved'.[96] They did not indicate that the approach to section 31(2)(b) should be materially different if two potential perpetrators were to separate.[97] McFarlane LJ concluded therefore that there was 'a pressing need for the issue to be determined by the Supreme Court so that a clear and full statement of the applicable law is achieved.'[98]

Further Reading

D. Archard, *Children: Rights and Childhood*, 2nd edn (Routledge, 2004), Part III.

J. Bettle and J. Herring, 'Shaken Babies and Care Proceedings' [2011] *Family Law* 1370.

S. Cretney, *Family Law in the Twentieth Century–A History* (Oxford University Press, 2003), ch. 20.

J. Eekelaar, 'Are Parents Morally Obliged to Care for Their Children?' (1991) 11(3) *OJLS* 340.

A. Gillespie, 'Establishing a Third Order in Care Proceedings' [2000] *Child and Family Law Quarterly* 239.

J. Hayes, 'Ensuring Equal Protection for Siblings' [2010] *Family Law* 505.

M. Hayes, 'Why Didn't the Courts Protect this Child? *Re SB* and *Re F*' [2012] *Family Law* 169.

J. Hayes, M. Hayes and J. Williams, ' "Shocking" Abuse Followed by a "Staggering Ruling": *Re MA (Care Threshold)*' [2010] *Family Law* 166.

M. Hayes, 'Removing Children from their Families – Law and Policy Before the Children Act 1989', in G. Douglas and N. Lowe (eds), *The Continuing Evolution of Family Law* (Jordan Publishing, 2009).

H. Keating, 'Suspicions, Sitting on the Fence and Standards of Proof' [2009] *Child and Family Law Quarterly* 230.

H. Keating, '*Re MA*: The Significance of Harm' [2011] *Child and Family Law Quarterly* 115.

B. Lonne, N. Parton, J. Thomson, and M. Harries, *Reforming Child Protection* (Routledge, 2009)

J. Masson, 'From Curtis to Waterhouse: State Care and Child Protection in the UK 1945–2000', in S. Katz, J. Eekelaar, and M. Maclean (eds), *Cross-Currents: Family Law Policy in the US and England* (Oxford University Press, 2000).

---

[94] [2012] EWCA Civ 380.
[95] Ibid, at paras 129 and 146.
[96] Ibid, at para 128.
[97] Ibid, at para 95.
[98] Ibid, at para 131.

6
ADOPTION AND SPECIAL GUARDIANSHIP

Debate 1

Should adoption be abolished?

INTRODUCTION

When a child's birth parents are unable to look after their child or the child has become an orphan a number of options are available to a local authority or others seeking long-term carers for the child. These include finding a relative who will be able to look after the child; placing the child with long-term foster carers; special guardianship; and adoption. It is this last option, adoption, which is the subject of the first debate.

Adoption has become a hugely political issue in recent years. It is generally accepted that it should not be assumed that adoption is the inevitable consequence for children who have been taken into care. As the Children's Minister, Tim Loughton, explained in 2011:

> Most children in care will return to their families when it is safe to do so. Others will need a period in foster care or in a children's home. But for some there will be no realistic prospect of growing up with their birth parents or other family members. In these circumstances, adoption can be a lifeline, and offer the hope of a better future and a second chance at a loving, stable family – something that every child deserves.[1]

However, recently the government has become convinced that adoption is not being used enough, or quickly enough for children in care. Urgent reform, it is said, is needed. To quote Tim Loughton again:

> I am determined to see more children considered for adoption – those who may have been overlooked in the past, such as older and disabled children, and children in sibling groups – and, where adoption is right for a child, I want it to happen without delay. I want more people from all walks of

---

[1] T. Loughton, *The Adopter's Charter* (The Stationery Office, 2012).

life to come forward to adopt these children. When they do, I want them welcomed with open arms and to receive all the help and support they need from the initial point of contact right through the adoption process and, very importantly, as and when needed throughout the adoption journey and beyond.[2]

The government has started a Give a Child a Home campaign and has appointed an 'Adoption Tsar', Martin Narey, charged with improving the rates and speed of adoption.

Despite the popularity of adoption among politicians, academic views are more mixed, as we shall see. To some, rather than being pushed more strongly, adoption needs to be completely rethought.

THE LEGAL STRUCTURE

What distinguishes adoption from other forms of substitute care is its dramatic effect on the legal parenthood of the child. On the making of an adoption order an adopted child is to be treated as the 'legitimate child of the adopter or adopters'.[3] Not only that, but the birth parents of an adopted child cease to be the legal parents of the child and lose parental responsibility.[4] The adoptive parents, therefore, become fully the parents of the child, including having parental responsibility, and can make all decisions about a child. The birth parents lose any status in relation to the child. There are a few ways in which the position of the adopted parent is slightly different from a birth parent, but these tend to be on rather technical issues such as the prohibited degrees of relations for the purposes of marriage or the succession to peerages. Indeed, any departure from parity of treatment needs to be justified, as the European Convention on Human Rights, under Article 14, prohibits improper discrimination between adopted children and birth children.[5]

BACKGROUND TO THE DEBATE

Legal adoption started with the passing of the Adoption of Children Act 1926.[6] Before then informal adoption had taken place under the guise of wet-nursing, apprenticeship and informal arrangements for the care of a child.[7] However, its use has undergone significant changes even during its relatively short history. Originally it was seen as a convenient way of handing children born to an unmarried mother to a married infertile couple. At the time this was seen as optimal for all concerned: the couple would receive a longed-for child; the mother would

---

[2] Loughton, *The Adopter's Charter.*
[3] Adoption and Children Act 2002 (hereafter ACA 2002), s. 67(1)–(3).
[4] There is an exception where the child is adopted by the step-parent: ACA 2002, ss. 51(2), 67(3)(d).
[5] *Pla and Puncernau v Andorra* [2004] 2 FCR 630.
[6] S. Cretney, *Family Law in the Twentieth Century – A History* (Oxford University Press, 2003), ch. 12 provides an excellent history of adoption.
[7] J. Goody, *The Development of the Family and Marriage in Europe* (Cambridge University Press, 1983).

not have the embarrassment of everyone knowing she had had a child out of wedlock; and the child would be better off in a 'good' household. Things are very different today. There is no shame attached to lone parenthood, nor is there any assumption that a child raised by a lone parent will suffer. Infertile couples are more likely to turn to an assisted reproductive clinic than an adoption agency. Adoption is now seen as a service for children, rather than provision for infertile couples.[8]

Another major difference between modern adoption and adoption in the past is that it is now relatively rare for a child to be adopted shortly after birth. Indeed, in England and Wales only about 50 mothers a year place their babies for adoption on birth and this is usually because of the child's disability or their mother's personal circumstances.[9] Statistics from the British Association for Adoption and Fostering indicate that the average age at adoption is now 3 years and 10 months, with only 2 per cent of children adopted during the year ending 31 March 2011 being under 1 year old, and 27 per cent being over the age of 5.[10] A child is very likely to know that they have been adopted and that they are not genetically the child of the adopted family. Indeed they may well remember, and even be in contact with, their birth family.

While most children are now adopted from care,[11] only a small proportion of children in the care system are adopted. There were 65,520 looked-after children at 31 March 2011, while in the preceding year only 3,050 looked-after children were adopted.[12] This represented a fall of 5 per cent from 2010, or 8 per cent since 2007, despite the attempts of successive governments to increase the number of adoption orders. In 2011 Martin Narey, the newly appointed 'Adoption Tsar', published a report describing the current system as slow, failing and in need of a complete overhaul.[13] He recommends moving to a national adoption system, rather than the current one based on local adoption agencies. More controversially, the report calls for a radical increase in the number of adoptions and insists that adoption is the best option for finding children a permanent home.[14]

Not everyone has responded positively to this pro-adoption call, with the Fostering Network commenting:

> Adoption is only the best option for a small minority of children in care. For the vast majority, rehabilitating them with their parents and providing them with the support they need, finding relatives who can meet their needs, or the right foster home or residential care placement, where they

8 J. Lewis, 'Adoption: The Nature of Policy Shifts in England and Wales' (2004) 18 *International Journal of Law, Policy and the Family* 235.
9 R. Parker, *Adoption Now* (Blackwell, 1999), p. 4.
10 BAAF, *Statistics* (BAAF, 2011).
11 A significant proportion of adoptions involve adoption by a step-parent: Lord Chancellor's Department, *Judicial Statistics* (Lord Chancellor's Department, 2000).
12 Department for Education, *Children Looked After by Local Authorities in England including Adoption and Care Leavers) – Year ending 31 March 2011* (DfE, 2012).
13 M. Narey, *Adoption Report* (The Times, 2011).
14 Ibid.

can have security and stability and keep in touch with their birth family, has to be the priority.[15]

There have also been claims, rejected by the government, that local authorities have been inappropriately placing children for adoption in order to meet targets.[16]

The case in favour of adoption

The case in favour of adoption is straightforward: it is good for children.[17] As stated at the start of this chapter, the government is convinced that adoption benefits children. This could be supported on the basis of psychological evidence that children in care permanently placed with a family suffer less than children living in institutional children's homes.[18] Research on adopted children even indicates that there is no difference between the well-being of adopted children and children living with their biological parents.[19] Indeed, the majority of adopted children fare better on various indicators than children with comparable starts in life who live with their birth parents.[20] Tony Blair, when Prime Minister, put it this way:

> It is hard to overstate the importance of a stable and loving family life for children. That is why I want more children to benefit from adoption.
>
> We know that adoption works for children. Over the years, many thousands of children in the care of Local Authorities have benefited from the generosity and commitment of adoptive families, prepared to offer them the security and well-being that comes from being accepted as members of new families.[21]

Castle, Beckett and Groothues, in their study of 52 adopted children, found the child having favourable outcomes in terms of cognitive and social progress. They added:

> Baby adoptions are viewed as a group from whom successful outcomes are usual. In general, studies of children placed as babies have shown favourable levels of psychological function, high parental satisfaction and low levels of adoption disruption. Data from the National Child Development Study (NCDS) indicated that adopted children outperformed birth comparisons

---

[15] The Fostering Network, *Response to the Narey Report and Martin Narey's Appointment* (The Fostering Network, 2012).

[16] BBC News Online, 'Forced Adoption Claims Dismissed', 2 February 2008.

[17] A. Rushton, 'Outcomes of Adoption from Public Care: Research and Practice Issues' (2007) 13 *Advances in Psychiatric Treatment* 305.

[18] D. Quinton and J. Selwyn, 'Adoption: Research, Policy and Practice' (2006) 19 *Child and Family Law Quarterly* 459.

[19] M. Bohman and S. Sigvardsson, 'Outcomes in Adoption: Lessons from Longitudinal Studies', in D. Brodzinsky and M. Schechter (eds) *The Psychology of Adoption* (Oxford University Press, 1990).

[20] P. Rushton, *Adoption as a Placement Choice* (King's College London, 2002).

[21] Cabinet Office, *The Prime Minister's Review of Adoption* (The Stationery Office, 2000), p. 3.

on maths and reading tests at age seven, and on a measure of general ability at age eleven.[22]

It is true that the outcomes for older adopted children are mixed, but they still do much better when compared to children in care.[23] Certainly, more research could be done to establish the benefits of adoption. However, we do know that foster care does not provide the stability that is sought. David Quinton and Julie Selwyn,[24] in their comparison of adoption and long-term foster care, argue that adoption comes out better in terms of disruption rates and attachment of children to their carers.

The central benefit of adoption is stability. Smith and Logan, having interviewed adoptive parents, argue that:

> it was clear from our interviews that adoption achieves far more than legal security – it constructs parenthood. It was the experience and meaning of parenthood – legally, socially and emotionally – that was of enormous significance to the adopters in our sample. For many adoptive parents the phenomenology of parenthood is intrinsically characterized by a sense of ownership and control ... [25]

These, they argue, would be lost if adoption was reconceptualized away from the 'transplant' model.

Those who would seek an alternative to adoption might rely on the model of special guardianship (discussed later in this chapter). However, it should not be assumed that this is a panacea. Any attempt to retain a role for both the parents and the adopters is a recipe for ongoing litigation and dispute. Relations between adults and children require extensive investment of emotion and time. It is not reasonable to expect the children or adults to do this if there is the constant threat of removal hanging over the relationship.

One objection to adoption focuses on the fact that it can lead to trans-racial adoption and this is said to be harmful to the child. However, Hayes rejects the objections to trans-racial placement as based on ideology rather than facts:

> Three mistaken assumptions underlie precise ethnic matching: first, it is assumed that ethnic culture is a natural inheritance rather than a conventional construct; secondly, a minority child's culture is invariably assumed to be exclusive and particular to one ethnic group rather than being universally accessible; and thirdly, ethnic cultures are conceived of in essential, rather than nominal terms.[26]

---

22 J. Castle, C. Beckett and C. Groothues, 'Infant Adoption in England' (2000) 24 *Adoption and Fostering* 26.
23 M. Ijzendoorn and F. Juffer, 'Adoption Is a Successful Natural Intervention Enhancing Adopted Children's iq and School Performance' (2005) 14 *Current Directions in Psychological Science* 326.
24 Quinton and Selwyn, 'Adoption: Research, Policy and Practice'.
25 C. Smith and J. Logan, 'Adoptive Parenthood as a "Legal Fiction" – Its Consequences for Direct Post-Adoption Contact' (2002) 14 *Child and Family Law Quarterly* 281.
26 P. Hayes, 'Giving Due Consideration to Ethnicity in Adoption Placements – A Principled Approach' [2003] *Child and Family Law Quarterly* 255.

Indeed empirical studies have shown that there is no harm caused by transracial placements.[27] In their analysis of the data Quinton and Selwyn argue:

> No differences have been found between breakdown rates or various measures of psycho-social functioning or self-esteem, when same-ethnicity placements are compared with placements of children from minority ethnic backgrounds in 'white' families. The quality of parenting appears to be the principal influence on outcomes in both same-ethnicity and cross-ethnicity placements.[28]

The case against adoption

The current law is based on the 'transplant' model of adoption. This is that children are transplanted from one family and inserted into a new family. The child ceases to be a member of his or her 'old family' and becomes a full member of the new family. Baroness Hale has explained the current law in these terms:

> an adoption order does far more than deprive the birth parents of their parental responsibility for bringing up the child and confer it upon her adoptive parents.... It severs, irrevocably and for all time, the legal relationship between a child and her family of birth. It creates, irrevocably and for all time (unless the child is later adopted again into another family), a new legal relationship, not only between the child and her adoptive parents, but between the child and each of her adoptive parent's families.[29]

This is an outdated and misconceived model for our current age. It would not be difficult to imagine a system of long-term care that does not rely on the transplant model. In this section we outline some of the particular reasons why the transplant model of adoption can be seen as outdated.

First, the transplant model is based on a fiction. As Andrew Bainham writes:

> Much of the case for adoption seems to rest on meeting the insecurities of long-term carers, but it is questionable whether the only or best means of addressing these understandable insecurities is through what has been called a 'constructed affiliation'.[30]

We should prioritize truth. The truth is that adoptive carers are not the 'parents' of the child. They lack the crucial blood tie. They are the long-term carers of the child and we should acknowledge that by giving them the rights and responsibilities to carry out their role. But having the special status of parenthood is not needed. We could, for example, give them parental responsibility, without giving them

---

[27] P. Moffatt and J. Thoburn, 'Outcomes of Permanent Family Placement for Children of Minority Ethnic Origin' (2001) 6 *Child and Family Social Work* 13

[28] Quinton and Selwyn, 'Adoption: Research, Policy and Practice'.

[29] *Re P* [2008] UKHL 38, para. 85.

[30] A. Bainham, 'Arguments about Parentage' (2008) 67 *CLJ* 322, 349.

the name 'parent'. Or we could create a new status, such as the notion of special guardianship (discussed later in this chapter) which would acknowledge the special place the carers play in the child's life, without claiming they are parents. Andrew Bainham, discussing a case in which the aunt of a child was intending to adopt that child, points out the absurd consequences of the transplant model:

> Is it really in the best interests of a child, or consistent with the human rights of that child and his parents, that the law should pretend that his aunt is his mother and his mother is his aunt? This distortion of family relationships can and should be avoided.[31]

Second, supporters of adoption fail to realize the fact that adoption involves a massive interference in the right to respect for the family life of the child and birth family, protected by Article 8 of the European Convention on Human Rights.[32] As Sonia Harris-Short argues:

> The imperative of non-intervention into the private family life of both the birth family and the child underscores the essential responsibility of the state to respect the autonomy and integrity of the family. Thus adoption as an extreme measure of state intervention into the birth family will only be capable of justification on overriding welfare grounds, the responsibility for establishing such grounds resting firmly with the state.[33]

While overriding welfare grounds might justify the removal of a child from the care of her parents, the termination of all legal ties is hard to justify, except in the most extreme cases. This has been recognized by the ECtHR[33] which has used the language of exceptionality to describe the kinds of circumstances in which a severance of legal ties could be justified.[34]

Third, the transplant model is not just a fiction and an interference in human rights, it causes devastating grief.[35] While for the adoptive parent adoption usually brings joy, as Harris-Short and Miles point out:

> A price must be paid for the creation of this new adoptive family – and that price is paid by the birth family. For them, adoption represents the termination of their legal relationship with the child. Put simply, in legal terms, the child is lost to them forever. Often young, vulnerable and marginalized it is usually the birth mother who pays the greatest price, many facing a lifetime of unresolved grief.[36]

---

31 A. Bainham, 'Permanence for Children: Special Guardianship or Adoption?' (2007) 66 *CLJ* 520.

32 Bainham, 'Arguments about Parentage', 349.

33 *Neulinger and Shuruk v Switzerland* (App No 41615/07); [2011] 1 FLR 122.

34 *R and H v UK* (App No 35348/06); [2011] ECHR 844.

35 J. Smeeton and K. Boxall, 'Birth Parents' Perceptions of Professional Practice in Child Care and Adoption Proceedings: Implications for Practice' (2011) 16 *Child and Family Social Work* 444.

36 S. Harris Short and J. Miles, *Family Law* (Oxford University Press, 2011), p. 889.

Given that we could produce a system of long-term care for children which does not involve the termination of parental links, it must be questioned whether the causing of such anguish can be justified.

Fourth, it is not only the tie with the birth parents which is lost on adoption, but the ties with grandparents, uncles, aunts, even siblings, also go. The child also commonly loses the links with the community into which they are born. For many people, their cultural and religious identity is a central aspect of their self-understanding,[37] yet a child's can be lost on adoption. There are particular concerns with trans-racial adoption where the child is placed with a couple from a different racial background from the child's birth family. There is evidence that a child can face serious difficulties in developing a strong positive identity when placed in a family from a different ethnic background. Further, they may lack the skills to deal with the racism they may face in the future.[38]

Fifth, the current law fails to reflect the fact that the average age of children being adopted has risen.[39] Even if one accepts that the transplant model might be appropriate in relation to babies who are handed over at birth, there is little to justify it for older children.[40] The argument that the transplant model of adoption gives children the security of being fully integrated into a new family carries little weight when the child knows that is a fiction. A child being placed for adoption these days is likely to know full well who their real parents are. They may well want to keep in contact with them or at least acknowledge the natural link between parent and child. Pretending that their birth parents are no longer their parents does not necessarily represent children's own understanding of their position or their identity.

Sixth, the children being made available for adoption typically come from very troubled backgrounds and require highly skilled care.[41] In adoption these days we are not, therefore, looking for just a 'replacement parent' but for individuals to take on a complex and demanding caring job. They will require support, advice and respite care. As Nigel Lowe has argued, adoption is moving from a gift/donation model to a contract/services model.[42] To treat those providing caring services as parents may be a convenient way for the local authority to 'wash their hands' of a child (as well as being cheaper for the state), but it is not the most appropriate response to some of our most vulnerable children. Moreover, the transplant model, whereby the adoptive parents become simply replacement parents, may obscure the demands that are placed on adoptive parents. It is a common criticism that the standards required of adoptive parents are far higher than those expected

---

[37] J. Eekelaar, 'Children between Cultures' (2004) 18 *International Journal of Law, Policy and the Family* 178.

[38] B. Goldstein, 'Ethnicity and Placement' (2000) 24 *Adoption and Fostering* 9.

[39] N. Lowe, 'The Changing Face of Adoption – The Gift/Donation Model versus the Contract/Services Model' (1997) 9 *Child and Family Law Quarterly* 371.

[40] M. Ryburn, 'In Whose Best Interests? Post Adoption Contact with the Birth Family' (1998) 10 *Child and Family Law Quarterly* 53.

[41] *Re P* [2008] UKHL 38, para. 91.

[42] Lowe, 'The Changing Face of Adoption – The Gift/Donation Model versus the Contract/Services Model'.

of birth parents, but as we are seeking highly specialized carers, it is wrong to assume that a 'normal' parent will necessary be adequate for the job.[43]

Seventh, the transplant model with its drastic termination of the birth parent's status is largely to blame for the delays that have come to characterize finding long-term solutions for children in care. Jill Kirby has written that:

> social work has been captured by an adult-centred approach: regarding adoption as last resort, giving drug-addicted mothers endless second chances, making children shuttle between foster parents and birth mothers for so long that they are either too old for adoption or too damaged to settle.[44]

But it may well be that social workers are acting in an entirely appropriate way. Until we are sure that there is no hope of returning children to their birth parents we would not want to end their link with the birth parents. The drastic nature of adoption requires the giving of a second chance and thorough investigation until we are sure such a draconian order is appropriate. If only adoption were rethought of as, or replaced with, a long-term care scheme, these could be organized much more quickly and the delay problems could be resolved.

Eighth, despite the widespread assumption that adoption benefits children, in fact there has been remarkably little evidence of the benefits of adoption. Those studies that have been carried out tend to suggest that adoption is beneficial, but the picture is not straightforward and much more research needs to be done before we can confidently assert that adoption is superior to long-term fostering.[45] Most of the research relied upon by the pro-adoption lobby involves children who are adopted at birth. John Eekelaar, one of the country's leading family lawyers, concluded after a thorough survey of the evidence:

> So we find that the research evidence is unable to detect any significant advantages to adoption over long-term fostering. There is evidence that some children prefer it, but against that should be placed the clear statement of risks, notably to the child, but also to the adoptive family.[46]

Finally, the dark side of adoption is inadequately acknowledged.[47] That is, the worrying number of adoptions which are disrupted or break down. It is remarkable that statistics on this are not officially collected. A cynic might suggest that this is because the pro-adoption lobby want to maintain the 'rosy picture' of

43 B. Luckock, 'Adoption Support and the Negotiation of Ambivalence in Family Policy and Children's Services' (2008) 35 *Journal of Law and Society Law* 3.

44 Jill Kirby, 'Martin Narey – Dangerous Anti-Family Ideologue Or Inspired Reformer?' <http://conservativehome.blogs.com/platform/2011/07/martin-narey-dangerous-anti-family-ideologue-or-inspired-reformer.html>

45 J. Eekelaar, 'Contact and Adoption Reform', in A. Bainham, B. Lindley, M. Richards and L. Trinder (eds), *Children and their Families* (Hart Publishing, 2003).

46 Eekelaar, 'Contact and Adoption Reform', in Bainham, Lindley, Richards and Trinder (eds), *Children and their Families* (Hart Publishing, 2003).

47 C. Pemberton, 'Experts Tell Narey to Order Study into Adoption Breakdowns' At <http://www.communitycare.co.uk/Articles/07/07/2011/117137/experts-tell-narey-to-order-study-into-adoption-breakdowns.htm>

adoption. Where an adoption breaks down this is a tragedy for the child, who may feel doubly rejected. It is also a disaster for the adoptive family who will, no doubt, have gone through considerable heartache and distress before deciding to return the child. A small-scale study found that 20 per cent of adoptions break down.[48] If this is correct (and it is such a small-scale and somewhat dated study that this cannot be assumed), then we need to be very concerned about taking a pro-adoption agenda. Indeed the picture may be even worse than the 20 per cent suggested. In one American study, 23 per cent of the sample were found to be disrupted; of the remaining 77 per cent, substantial difficulties were recorded in 28 per cent of cases and only half of adoptions were reported by the adopters as being positive.[49] In another British study[50] 17 per cent of placements had been disrupted and in only two-fifths were there no ongoing behavioural problems remaining after seven years. There is good evidence that adoptions involving older children and children with severe problems are more likely to break down.[51]

CONCLUSION

All parties to this debate can agree that we need a structure to provide secure parenting for those children whose birth parents are unable to look after them. The debate centres on the extent to which the transplant model of adoption is best suited to achieve this. The kind of adoptive parents we are seeking these days need considerable assistance for the complex and demanding job they are under-taking. The 'ordinary parent' model may no longer adequately provide the correct analogy for the kind of support these long-term carers need from the state, nor the reality of the complex family backgrounds from which the children emerge.

Debate 2

Does the law adequately protect the rights of birth parents?

There are a number of ways in which it is claimed that the current law fails to adequately protect the rights of birth parents. We shall set out the law on each first, before looking at the arguments over whether or not the current law fails to protect the rights of birth parents.

SECRET BIRTHS

Sometimes a mother has not wanted the wider family (including her parents) to be informed about the birth of a child[52] and wishes for the child to be adopted

---

[48] Rushton, 'Outcomes of Adoption from Public Care: Research and Practice Issues'.
[49] A. Rushton and C. Dance, 'The Adoption of Children from Public Care: A Prospective Study of Outcome in Adolescence' (2006) 45 *Journal of the American Academy of Child and Adolescent Psychiatry* 877.
[50] J. Selwyn, W. Sturgess, and D. Quinton, *Costs and Outcomes of Non-infant Adoptions* (British Agencies for Adoption and Fostering, 2006).
[51] Rushton, 'Outcomes of Adoption From Public Care: Research and Practice Issues'.
[52] *Re R (A Child) (Adoption: Disclosure)* [2001] 1 FCR 238.

outside the family. In such a case there is a clash between the interests of the different parties. There has not been a consistent judicial approach to such cases.

Some judges have been very sympathetic to the mothers in such cases. Holman J in *Z CC v R* says:[53]

> There is, in my judgment, a strong social need, if it is lawful, to continue to enable some mothers, such as this mother, to make discreet, dignified and humane arrangements for the birth and subsequent adoption of their babies, without their families knowing anything about it, if the mother, for good reason, so wishes.

Few, however, see it in such a straightforward way. Most seek to put the interests of the child as the main consideration. This means that a key question will be whether the wider family members are potential adopters or long-term carers. Where they are, it is much less likely that the court will approve of keeping the birth secret. In *Birmingham CC v S, R and A*[54] a father did not want his parents to be told about the birth or to be considered as adopters. However, the Court of Appeal held that the father's objections could not carry weight because it could not be assumed that his parents would not be interested in caring for the child. They explained:

> Adoption is a last resort for any child. It is only to be considered when neither of the parents nor the wider family and friends can reasonably be considered as potential carers for the child. To deprive a significant member of the wider family of the information that the child exists who might otherwise be adopted, is a fundamental step that can only be justified on cogent and compelling grounds.[55]

The courts have not been persuaded by claims that the father or wider family have strong rights-based claims, preferring to focus on the welfare of the child. In *C v XYZ CC*[56] the Court of Appeal confirmed that there was nothing in the Adoption and Children Act 2002 which compelled a local authority to disclose the identity of a child to the extended family against the mother's wishes. The Act focused on the welfare of the child, which included the potential relationship the child might have with the wider family,[57] but that did not mean they had rights. As to human rights claims, it was held that the father had no family right with the child and so he could not claim any right to be informed of the birth. Interestingly, it was held that the grandparents did have a right to be informed of the birth under Article 8(1), but that interference in their rights was justified. Brief mention was made of the argument that the child may have a right to respect for family life, but any

53 [2001] Fam Law 8.
54 [2006] EWHC 3065 (Fam).
55 Para. 75.
56 [2007] EWCA Civ 1206, discussed in B. Sloan, 'Re C (A Child) (Adoption: Duty of Local Authority) – Welfare and the Rights of The Birth Family In "Fast Track" Adoption Cases' (2009) 21 *Child and Family Law Quarterly* 87.
57 S. 1(4)(f).

interference in that could be justified if the adoption was approved under Article 8(2). It is surprising that the grandparents, but not the father, were found to have a right to be informed of the birth. This is not fully explained in the judgment, but it may have been because the father had indicated that he had no interest in the child and wanted to play no role in the child's life, while the grandparents had not had an opportunity to develop family life with the child. What seemed determinative in this case was the finding that it was in the child's best interests to be adopted as soon as possible and that considering the possibility of care with the grandparents would delay this. There is, perhaps, an implied assumption here that the central right of the child was to be raised by a family (here an adoptive one) and that trumped any links with the wider family.

The most recent discussion of the issue is in *M v F and H*.[58] Here a married woman did not want the father to know of the birth. The mother claimed the father had mental health problems and behaved in an unpredictable, and some-times violent, way. The court treated this case as different from previous ones because there was an established relationship between the mother and father. In the other cases the relationships between the mother and father had been trivial. The risks the mother referred to were speculative and the case was very weak. If the couple had an established family life together it would almost never be justifi-able not to inform the father. Thorpe LJ spoke strongly in favour of truth:

> To grant the declarations sought would be to endorse and formalise a great lie. The family would live in a tangled web of deceit with the female members knowing all about this episode and pretending it never happened, while the male members were oblivious to it. It would have to be a very strong case before the court endorsed dishonesty of this type and scale. In almost every case truth is better than falsehood.[59]

As the couple were married the father had parental responsibility and so his consent would be required before an adoption. Black LJ, looking at the issue more generally, rejected an argument that there would need to be significant physical risk before a father would not be informed, but confirmed that there needed to be 'strong countervailing factors'.

Discussion

As can be seen from the summary of the approach of the courts above a consistent approach has not been taken.[60] The arguments in favour of allowing the birth to be kept secret tend to focus on the interests of the mother. In *Re C (A Child) (Adoption: Duty of Local Authority)* Thorpe LJ held that 'there are valid social policy considerations for permitting the mother to treat the experience of pregnancy and birth as a private experience, even if engaging maternity services and duly

---

[58] [2011] EWCA Civ 27.
[59] Para. 45.
[60] Sloan, *'Re C (A Child) (Adoption: Duty of Local Authority)* – Welfare and the Rights of the Birth Family in "Fast Track" Adoption Cases'.

registering the birth'. He referred to the right under French law for a woman to give an anonymous birth and thereby avoid being even recognized as legally the mother of the child.[61] This can be justified as a way of providing an alternative to abortion or abandoning the baby. It might also be seen as equalizing the position of mothers with that of fathers, who have long had the ability to walk away from paternity and its obligations.

The debate here is whether too much weight is given to the birth mother as opposed to the birth father or wider family. The argument that it is appropriate to prioritize the interests of the mother could be based on the enormous contribution that she has made to the creation of the child. That argument may be bolstered if there is a weak link between the child and other relations.

The arguments the other way are likely to reflect the rights of the birth family to be involved in the child's life; or more importantly, the child's rights to be raised by her birth family. But, does a child not have a right to be raised by his or her birth family? Seen in terms of Article 8 of the ECHR this argument is not strong, as the ECtHR has generally been reluctant to find family life in the absence of an actual relationship between the parties. The blood tie on its own is insufficient.[62] However, the argument may be made that in these cases we are discussing some kind of inchoate right to have the possibility of developing a relationship with a child to whom one is related. Indeed Arden LJ in *Re C (A Child) (Adoption: Duty of Local Authority)* did seem willing to accept the grandparents and child had family life for the purposes of Article 8.

Critics of the approach taken by the courts might argue that it gives too much power to the mother. She should not have the power to determine whether or not the child and wider family can develop a relationship or whether or not family life exists. This goes back to the question of the extent to which the special contribution of the mother to the child justifies her interests being elevated above that of other adults, and how far the welfare of the child is tied up with the wishes of the mother. In short, this question raises issues which are all too familiar to family lawyers: how important are blood ties in family life; are mothers in a different position to fathers; and does the welfare of the child trump the rights of adults?

THE PLACING PROCEDURE

There is not space to go through in full detail here the procedures that are used to lead to an adoption. These are the key features:

1 *Planning for adoption.* The local authority is expected to consider adoption as an option for every child in its care. If it decides that the birth family are unable to meet a child's needs in the foreseeable future and that adoption is likely to provide the best means of doing so, then a plan for adoption should be

---

61 *Odièvre v France*, Application No. 42326/98.
62 *Lebbink v The Netherlands* (App. No. 45582/99).

drawn up.[63] The birth family should be involved sufficiently to protect their interests.[64] A key issue is often whether to keep alive the hope of returning the child to the birth family to seek care for the child within the wider family, or to seek to move to adoption. The correct course of action is often only apparent in retrospect.

2 *Assessment of would-be adopters.* If a couple or person approaches an adoption agency, willing to be considered as adopters, they will be assessed by the agency to determine whether they are appropriate, as well as assessing which children they would be suitable for. The assessment will also involve helping the adopter decide whether they truly do want to be adopters. A report on the potential adopters should be prepared for the adoption panel, who then need to make a decision on the applicants' suitability.[65]

3 *Matching the child and adopter.* Once an adopter has been approved the local authority can seek to match them with the children available for adoption. Details will be exchanged and reports prepared for the adoption agency panel. The focus will be on the child's welfare. The agency will have to pay due regard to the child's religious persuasion, racial origin and cultural and linguistic background.[66] At this point the potential adopters are provided with a full report on the child.[67]

4 *Placement of the child with the would-be adopters.* The next stage will be the placement of the child with the adopters for what is, in effect, a trial period. To place a child, the agency must either have the consent of each parent with parental responsibility[68] or must have obtained a placement order from the court.[69] The court can make a placement order only if all of the following are satisfied:

a. Either a care order has already been made in respect of the child or the court is satisfied that the significant harm test in s. 31 of the Children Act 1989 (see Chapter 9) is satisfied.

b. Parental consent has been given or been dispensed with.[70] Consent will be dispensed with if it will promote the child's welfare.

c. The court is persuaded that it is better to make the placement order than not to do so.[71]

---

[63] ACA 2002, s. 1.

[64] *Scott* v *UK* [2000] 1 FLR 958.

[65] If an applicant could demonstrate that he or she was denied an adoption in a way which discriminated against him or her in a way prohibited by Article 14 (e.g. on the grounds of race) then arguably that would infringe his or her rights: *EB v France* [2008] 1 FCR 236.

[66] See the discussion in *Re C (Adoption: Religious Observance)* [2002] 1 FLR 1119 and *Haringey v Mr and Mrs E* [2006] EWHC 1620 (Fam).

[67] A local authority may be liable in tort if it fails to provide relevant information which, if disclosed, would have persuaded the adopters not to go ahead with the adoption: *A and B v Essex CC* [2002] EWHC 2709 (Fam).

[68] ACA 2002, s. 19(1), unless care proceedings are pending (s. 19(3)).

[69] ACA 2002, ss. 21(3), 52.

[70] If consent has been given the local authority is likely to go down the route of placement by consent.

[71] ACA 2002, s. 1(6).

5 *The agency applies for an adoption order.* If the placement has worked well, the final stage will be for the adoption agency to apply for an adoption order. It is not possible to apply for an adoption order unless (i) there has been a placement order and the child has lived with the applicants for ten weeks (ii) or the parents are consenting to the adoption, with one exception: that is, foster carers who have looked after the child for at least 12 months, who can apply without satisfying any further requirements.[72] The court must consider the two key requirements for an adoption order:

(i) that the making of the adoption order is in the child's best interests; and
(ii) that the birth parents (those with parental responsibility) consent to the adoption or that consent has been dispensed with.

In deciding whether or not an adoption order promotes the welfare of the child the court must consider the checklist in s. 1(4) of the Adoption and Children Act 2002. This is as follows:

(a) the child's ascertainable wishes and feelings regarding the decisions (considered in the light of the child's age and understanding);
(b) the child's particular needs;
(c) the likely effect on the child (throughout his life) of having ceased to be a member of the original family and become an adopted person;
(d) the child's age, sex, background and any of the child's characteristics which the court or agency considers relevant;
(e) any harm (within the meaning of the Children Act 1989) which the child has suffered or is at risk of suffering;
(f) the relationship which the child has with relatives, and with any other person in relation to whom the court or agency considers the relationship to be relevant, including–

(i)   the likelihood of any such relationship continuing and the value to the child of its doing so;
(ii) the ability and willingness of any of the child's relatives, or of any such person, to provide the child with a secure environment in which the child can develop, and otherwise to meet the child's needs;
(iii) the wishes and feelings of the child's relatives, or of any such person, regarding the child.

Discussion

One of the central features of the Adoption and Children Act 2002 was to separate out the making of the placement order and the final adoption order. The issue of parents' lack of consent should be primarily dealt with at the placement stage, rather than the point at which the adoption order is made. The idea behind this

---

[72] Ibid, s. 47.

seems uncontroversial. It is best to deal with the parental consent issue early on so that a child can be placed with the would-be adopters and all concerned can have increased security that, providing the placement goes well, an adoption can go ahead. Otherwise there is the risk of a successful placement, only for the parents then successfully to object to the making of an order. However, there is a tension here. Resolving the objection of a parent early on will assist in more effective and speedy placement, but it might make the law less protective of the rights of the parents. The law's way of resolving the issue works against the interests of the birth parent.

Another concern from the parent's point of view is that the court will often assess their objections in the abstract: is it in the child's interests for the parent's consent to be dispensed with in the hope that there may, 'somewhere out there', be adopters who will be willing to look after the child? The court is not considering whether the children are better placed with the natural parents or the would-be adopters. This makes it far harder for the parents to object because they are objecting to an unknown entity.

A placement order can be made even if it is foreseen that there may be difficulties in placing the child or that adoption may not be able to take place.[73] True, the courts have said that where the children are not even suitable for placement (e.g. due to their emotional state), a placement order would not be appropriate.[74] In *NS-H v Kingston Upon Hull City Council and MC*[75] the Court of Appeal explained that placement was only suitable where 'the child is presently in a *condition* to be adopted and is *ready* to be adopted'. If that was not true, then a placement order was not appropriate, and if necessary could be revoked.

Another major objection from the point of view of birth parents' rights is that a court can dispense with the consent of the birth parents where to do so will be in the interests of the child's welfare. This is far too low a hurdle. Is there a parent in the land who can be confident that it could not be shown that their child would be better off raised by someone else? Under the Adoption Act 1976, parents' objections to adoption could only be overridden if they were unreasonably withholding their consent to the adoption. Section 1 of the Adoption and Children Act 2002 makes clear that now the sole consideration for the court in dispensing with consent is the child's welfare. So the rights of the parents and questions about whether or not the parents were reasonable in their objections are irrelevant. This has led to heavy criticism by some who fear that to permit the adoption of children against the wishes of parents simply on the basis that it would be better for the child rides roughshod over the importance attached to parental rights.[76]

---

[73] *Re T (Children: Placement Order)* [2008] 1 FCR 633.
[74] Ibid.
[75] [2008] 2 FLR 918.
[76] S. Choudhry and J. Herring, *European Human Rights and Family Law* (Hart Publishing, 2010), ch. 10.

Further, it may well be argued that dispensing with the parent's consent fails to adequately respect the parents' rights under the Human Rights Act 1998.[77] The approach of the European Court of Human Rights towards adoption is rather ambiguous. In *Johansen v Norway*[78] the European Court considered the placement of the applicant's daughter in a foster home with a view to adoption. The court stated:

> These measures were particularly far-reaching in that they totally deprived the applicant of the family life with the child and were inconsistent with the aim of reuniting them. Such measures should only be applied in exceptional circumstances and could only be justified if they were motivated by an overriding requirement pertaining to the child's best interests.[79]

This statement appears to suggest that adoption is only permissible in exceptional cases and only if there is a very strong case for it based on the child's interests.[80] However, some later cases suggested a more positive attitude towards adoption. In *Görgülü v Germany*[81] a child was placed by his mother with foster parents for adoption, shortly after birth. When the father sought custody and contact these were refused by the German courts. The European Court found that the father's Article 8 rights had been interfered with. Too much weight had been put on the child's bond with the foster parents and the hope that adoption offered, and insufficient weight had been given to the possibility of reuniting the father and son. This emphasizes the requirement that adoption should be used only when there is no realistic chance of the birth parents providing appropriate care.

It is arguable that these complaints about the ease with which parental consent can be dispensed with are overblown. A careful reading of the Act shows that the hurdle for dispensing with parental consent is not as low as opponents of the current law imply. The Act requires the court specifically to consider the child's relationships with his or her birth family: not just his or her birth parents.[82] In particular, the court must consider whether the child's blood relatives are in a position to care for the child. In *Re C (Family Placement)*[83] the Court of Appeal preferred to make a residence order to a five-year-old's grandmother, rather than place the child for adoption with strangers, as the local authority wished to do. They referred to the law's preference that children be raised within their family. The grandmother's age was noted (she was 70), but the court believed other family members would rally round if the grandmother became unable to care for the child. This shows that the courts are able, even under the welfare test, to attach weight to the birth family's interests.

---

[77] *Re P (Children)(Adoption: Parental Consent)* [2008] 2 FCR 185.

[78] (1996) 23 EHRR 33.

[79] At para. 78.

[80] *R v United Kingdom* (Application 35348/06) 31 May 2011.

[81] [2004] 1 FCR 410.

[82] P. Parkinson, 'Child Protection, Permanency Planning and Children's Right to Family Life', (2003) 17 *International Journal of Law, Policy and the Family* 147.

[83] [2009] 1 FLR 1425.

Further, when considering an application for an adoption order the court must recall the alternative orders that it can make.[84] These include: (i) a residence order in favour of the applicants; (ii) a special guardianship; and (iii) no order. A court will not make an adoption order if one of these orders will protect the interests of the child as effectively as an adoption order.

It should also be noted that subsection 52(1)(b) states that parental consent can only be dispensed with where the welfare of the child so 'requires'. This might suggest that, if it is shown that adoption is only slightly in the interests of the child, this will be insufficient to *require* the consent to be dispensed with.[85] In *Re P (Placement Orders: Parental Consent)*[86] the Court of Appeal held that the word 'requires' carries a connotation of being imperative: that dispensing with the consent is not just reasonable or desirable but required in the interests of the child. Such a reading can be reinforced by the argument that under the Human Rights Act 1998 this subsection must be read in a way which is compatible with the European Convention if at all possible.[87] As we have seen, the European Court of Human Rights has suggested that adoption is only appropriate in exceptional cases. However, all of these discussions must be read in the light of the recent case of *Re Q (A Child)*,[88] where it was held that there was no 'enhanced' welfare test before dispensing with consent to adoption.

OPEN ADOPTION

An open adoption is an adoption where the child retains contact with the birth family. As already mentioned, given the age at which children tend to be adopted, they often know of their birth family. Even in the case of children adopted when very young, adoptive parents nearly always tell their adopted children about their birth family. What is controversial is the extent to which there should be ongoing contact with the birth family.

Generally the courts have been very reluctant to compel the adopting family to allow contact.[89] Contact orders made in favour of birth family members against adoptive parents will be 'extremely unusual'.[90] It is not that the courts are opposed to contact, it is rather that the courts feel that the decision should be left to the adoptive family. If the adopters are willing for contact to take place then there is no need for a court order compelling it,[91] while if adopters do not want there to be contact, it would be wrong to force them to have contact.[92]

---

[84] *Re P (Children)(Adoption: Parental Consent)* [2008] 2 FCR 185.
[85] L. Davis, 'Adoption and Children Act 2002 – Some Concerns' (2005) 35 *Family Law* 294.
[86] [2008] EWCA Civ 535.
[87] S. Choudhry, 'The Adoption and Children Act 2002, the Welfare Principle and the Human Rights Act 1998 – A Missed Opportunity' [2003] *Child and Family Law Quarterly* 119.
[88] *Re Q (A Child)* [2011] EWCA Civ 1610.
[89] *Re R (Adoption: Contact)* [2005] EWCA Civ 1128.
[90] *Re R (A Child)(Adoption: Contact)* [2007] 1 FCR 149; *Oxfordshire County Council v X* [2010] 2 FCR 355, para 6. Although see *X and Y v A Local Authority (Adoption: Procedure)* [2009] 2 FLR 984.
[91] *Re T (Adoption: Contact)* [1995] 2 FLR 251.
[92] Ibid.

Section 46(6) of the 2002 Act requires the court to consider, when making an adoption order, whether to make a contact order in respect of the child. However, it is generally thought that this is unlikely to lead to a dramatic increase in the number of orders made. If the adopted parents refuse to permit contact as expected, it would be possible for the birth parents to apply for a s. 8 contact order. However, they will need the leave of the court before the court will hear their application. The courts are likely to grant leave only where the maintenance of contact with the birth family is of such benefit to the child as to justify overriding the privacy of the adoptive family.

The courts seem slightly more likely to make orders requiring the adoptive family to provide documents or photographs of the child.[93] However, in *Oxfordshire County Council v X*[94] the adoptive parents objected to providing the birth parents with a photograph of the child, for fear they would use it on the internet to find out where the child was. The Court of Appeal held that the adoptive parents should not be required to supply the photographs. The question was not whether or not the parents' fears were correct, but whether the views of the adoptive parents were unreasonable. It was emphasized that the welfare of the child depended on the parents feeling secure and this would be challenged if it was ordered that they supply photographs. The parents were not acting unreasonably. Perhaps at the heart of this case is the blunt message: 'The adoptive parents are J's parents; the natural parents are not.'[95]

This reflects a broader principle of the law, namely that adoptive parents should be given the kind of discretion that birth parents have over how to raise their children. It was held in *Re S (A Minor)(Adoption: Blood Transfusion)*:[96]

> If one were to look over the whole field of imposing conditions on adoptive parents against their will, it might become very common indeed. To my mind this should be a very rare course...The best thing for the child in the ordinary way is that he or she should become as near as possible the lawful child of the adoptive parents. This is what the child's welfare requires. I would not, in this case, regard it as in any way appropriate to impose a condition which derogated from that, and which made very little difference as to what would in fact happen, in circumstances which were in any event unlikely to arise.

Discussion

At present at least 70 per cent of children who have been adopted retain some kind of contact with their birth families.[97] However, there is consider-

---

[93] *Re T Minors (Adopted Children: Contact* [1995] 2 FLR 792.
[94] [2010] 2 FCR 355.
[95] Para 36.
[96] [1995] 2 FR 177, p. 182.
[97] Department of Health, *Adoption and Permanence Taskforce Second Report* (Department of Health, 2002), p. 15.

able debate over whether or not open adoption should be encouraged. As we have already seen, originally adoption was thought best done in secret. Birth parents were not told who had adopted the child, adoptive parents were not told who the birth parents were, and the child was not told that he or she had been adopted. Even if the child did find out, this was a secret to be kept from the rest of the world.[98] Few would support that nowadays. It is widely accepted that some adopted children need detailed information about their birth background to establish a secure sense of who they are, and birth parents needed to know that their child had been successfully and happily adopted.[99] However, more controversial is whether adopted children should have face-to-face contact with the birth family. As mentioned earlier, the courts have taken the view that adopted families should only exceptionally be forced to allow contact and that in general, it should be left to their discretion. Open adoptions, it seems, are encouraged where there is trust between birth families and adopters.[100]

The opposition to open adoption is typically based on the fact that the child needs to bond with the new adoptive family.[101] The obvious concern is that the child may treat their adoptive parents as not their 'real parents' and therefore not form a close relationship with them. Bridget Lindley has questioned this:

> Subsequent studies of children moving to new families suggest that, rather than preventing children from settling, openness can help the child settle in the new family, providing the adults are not hostile to each other, or the idea. [One study] found that contact helped to provide continuity, a positive identity and an understanding for the child of the circumstances of the adoption. It enabled the child to feel free to attach to the new family whilst retaining a link with their birth family.[102]

Ryburn[103] argues that:

> Children also appear to gain a sense of reassurance as a consequence of contact, particularly, direct contact with their birth relatives. In particular, it gives them a clear message that the placement is supported by their original family since otherwise they would not be visiting, and it is a visible symbol that their adoptive parents feel positively about their original family or contact would not be permitted.

Not surprisingly there is evidence that contact provides a significant benefit to the birth parents, enabling them to come to terms with their loss and move on.[104]

---

[98] Cretney, *Family Law in the Twentieth Century – A History*, ch. 17.

[99] D. Howe and J. Feast, (2000) *Adoption, Search and Reunion* (The Children's Society, 2000).

[100] C. Smith, 'Trust v Law: Promoting and Safeguarding Post-adoption Contact' (2005) 27 *Journal of Social Welfare and Family Law* 315.

[101] B. Lindley, 'Open-Adoption – Is the Door Ajar?' [1997] *Child and Family Law Quarterly* 115.

[102] P. 121.

[103] Ryburn, 'In Whose Best Interests? Post-Adoption Contact with the Birth Family'.

[104] Ryburn, 'In Whose Best Interests? Post-Adoption Contact with the Birth Family'.

Ryburn even argues that adopters can benefit and there is evidence that where it takes place adopters are comfortable with it,[105] although it may be that open adoption is only encouraged by adoptive parents who feel comfortable.

Against open adoption it must be recalled that some cases of adoption are those where the child has suffered or been at risk of significant harm because of the parenting they have received. Particularly where the birth family have abused the child, the benefits of contact may be questioned. Further, there are concerns that contact with the birth family might undermine the position of the adopters.[106] It may also deter some would-be adopters from going through with the adoption.[107] Quinton and Selwyn conclude their study:

> There is no evidence that lack of contact causes inevitable long-term harm, and no evidence that contact has ill-effects or affects placement stability in early adoptions. We know little about the consequences of contact for adult adjustment, especially for children with the experiences and profiles of those currently being placed. Moreover, the extent of difficulties many of the children face may militate against finding substantial differences in outcome related to contact, since many improvements in emotional and behavioural adjustment may be hard won, whatever the circumstances. Since information and contact is important to many in the adoption triangle, it is right that this possibility remains open and is facilitated if those involved wish it, but this argument need not rely on research concerning effects.[108]

REVOKING ADOPTION ORDERS

An adoptive parent, like a birth parent, will continue to be a parent unless another adoption order is made. Indeed it is precisely that permanence that gives adoption its appeal. If adoption could be brought to an end in a straightforward way, that would be said by some to undermine the security which provides its main benefit.[109]

The courts have been very reluctant to allow any attempts to set aside an adoption order. Unless there are exceptional circumstances leave to appeal out of time will not be granted.[110] The case-law provides two examples of exceptional circumstances.

---

105 M. MacDonald and D. McSherry, 'Open Adoption: Adoptive Parents' Experiences of Birth Family Contact and Talking to Their Child About Adoption' (2011) 4 *Adoption and Fostering* 35.

106 N. Lowe, 'English Adoption Law', in S. Katz, J. Eekelaar and M. Maclean (eds) *Cross Currents*, (Oxford University Press, 2000).

107 N. Lowe and M. Murch, *The Plan for the Child* (BAAF, 2002), p. 62.

108 Quinton and Selwyn, 'Adoption: Research, Policy and Practice'.

109 *Re B (Adoption: Setting Aside)* [1995] 1 FLR 1 at p. 7.

110 *Re W* [2010] EWCA Civ 1535.

- Consent to the adoption was given on the basis of a fundamental mistake. In *Re M (A Minor) (Adoption)*[111] a father agreed to the adoption of his children by his former wife and her new husband. Unknown to him, his ex-wife was terminally ill and she died shortly afterwards. The court allowed the appeal in what they regarded as a 'very exceptional case' on the basis that ignorance of the wife's condition negated his consent, which was based on a fundamental mistake.
- Where the adoption procedures involved a fundamental defect in natural justice. In *Re K (Adoption and Wardship)*[112] an English woman had adopted a Muslim baby, who had been found under a pile of bodies in the former Yugoslavia. Unfortunately, the adoption process had been deeply flawed. The adoption order was set aside due to the lack of protection for the birth family and the breach of natural justice caused by the faulty procedure.

A dramatic example of the strict adherence of the courts to these issues was *Webster v Norfolk CC*.[113] Mr and Mrs Webster had three children, one of whom was taken to hospital with multiple fractures. The hospital and local authority assessed that the child had been injured by the parents. All three children were adopted in late 2005. Two years later, after a fresh investigation, it was discovered that the injured child had in fact suffered scurvy, a disease virtually unknown in the West. The parents sought to set aside the adoption order. However, by the time of the court case in 2009 the children were settled into life with their new adoptive family. Wall LJ confirmed that 'only in highly exceptional and very particular circumstances' can adoption be set aside. He referred to the dicta of Swinton Thomas LJ in *Re B (Adoption: Jurisdiction to Set Aside)*[114]:

> An adoption order has a quite different standing to almost every other order made by a court. It provides the status of the adopted child and of the adoptive parents. The effect of an adoption order is to extinguish any parental responsibility of the natural parents. Once an adoption order has been made, the adoptive parents stand to one another and the child in precisely the same relationship as if they were his legitimate parents, and the child stands in the same relationship to them as to legitimate parents. Once an adoption order has been made the adopted child ceases to be the child of his previous parents and becomes the child for all purposes of the adopters as though he were their legitimate child.

In the Websters' case there was nothing in the procedure that led to the making of the order which rendered the procedure flawed and hence the adoption order could not be set aside. Wilson LJ emphasized that the children had been with the adopters for four years in an arrangement they had been told was permanent.

---

[111] [1991] 1 FLR 458; [1990] FCR 993.
[112] [1997] 2 FLR 221; [1997] 2 FLR 230.
[113] [2009] EWCA 59.
[114] [1995] Fam 239, at 245C.

Discussion

The debate here is whether the current refusal to revoke an adoption – save where there has been some fundamental procedural error – is too stark. The decision in *Webster v Norfolk CC*[115] highlights the issues well. In that case the children may, by the time of the hearing, have forgotten their life with the birth parents. At best it would be a hazy memory. Removing them from their stable and happy home to return them to people who would to the children be strangers, would be cruel.

But what sense is there in being willing to overturn an adoption order based on failure to serve the correct papers, but not based on a fundamental failure of expert evidence? As the Court of Appeal accepted, this case may well have involved a monstrous miscarriage of justice for Mr and Mrs Webster. They were found in court to be child abusers and had their children removed. That is far graver a breach of justice than if the procedure for the order had been flawed.

What is clearly behind the Court of Appeal's judgement is what Wilson LJ referred to as the 'vast social importance' of making adoption orders irrevocable. But why is this so important? Given the small number of adoption orders made in England and Wales – and around one in six of these are to step parents – it is not clear adoption orders are of huge social importance. Would potential adoptive parents really be put off applying for adoption if there was a slight change to irrevocability? That seems unlikely. But there is a bigger question here. Adoptive parents should feel protected from having their adoption orders set aside due to an injustice, but should not parents be entitled not to have their parenthood set aside based on false evidence? In this case security for adoptive parents is purchased at the cost of insecurity for birth parents.

At the end of the day the question which should have been at the heart of this case was the welfare of the children and the rights of the children. The unfairness to the adopters and the importance of the structure of the adoption order should come second to those. It may well be that a full examination of the facts and a consideration of the rights and welfare of the children would conclude they should remain with the adopters. But at least that would give us a better justification for why such a possible miscarriage of justice cannot be remedied. Children's interests should come first and the principle of the irrevocability of adoption second.

Andrew Bainham has argued that the decision requires a reconsideration of whether adoption should be a preferred model for children in care.[116] His argument that a looser form for long-term care is appropriate would have made a transition of the children back to the parents in this case easier. It was the finality of adoption that made this such a difficult case.

CONCLUSION

Throughout the adoption process there is a need to balance the interests of the birth parents and the would-be adopters. It is likely that your response to the first

---

[115] [2009] EWCA 59.
[116] A. Bainham, 'The Peculiar Finality of Adoption' (2009) *CLJ* 238.

debate on whether adoption is a desirable institution will affect your response to this second debate. Those concerned that adoption inappropriately undermines the position of the birth parents are very likely to feel that the procedure used will fail to protect their interests. However, for those who think that adoption is a useful tool to arrange long-term care of children, adoption should be 'fast tracked' to ensure that we get in place adoptions as quickly and efficiently as possible.

Debate 3

What is the role of special guardianship?

As we have seen in the debates so far, one of the concerns with adoption is the fact that it entails the permanent termination of parental status. Those who share this concern might seek to replace adoption with an institution which will provide security and an appropriate status for the new carer of the child, without ending completely the status of the birth parents. One model would be special guardianship, which was introduced in the Adoption and Children Act 2002.[117]

THE LAW

Currently, special guardianship is not a replacement for adoption, but is an alternative to it. The White Paper mentioned the kind of cases where special guardianship may be appropriate:

> Some older children do not wish to be legally separated from their birth families. Adoption may not be best for some children being cared for on a permanent basis by members of their wider birth family. Some minority ethnic communities have religious and cultural difficulties with adoption as it is set out in law. Unaccompanied asylum seeking children may also need secure, permanent homes, but have strong attachments to their families abroad.[118]

Special guardianship does not terminate the parental status of the birth parents, and Special Guardians are not treated as the parents of the child.[119] However, they are given many of the rights of a parent. They are able to make almost every decision about a child's upbringing. They can even change the child's name, although only with the consent of those with parental responsibility.[120] As Andrew Bainham puts it, in terms of taking decisions over the child the Special Guardians are 'in the driving seat'.[121] They cannot change the child's surname or remove the child

---

[117] See also Special Guardianship Regulations 2005 (SI 2005/1109) and Department for Education and Skills, *Special Guardianship Guidance* (DfES, 2005).
[118] Department of Health, *Protecting Children, Supporting Parents* (The Stationery Office, 2000), para 5.9.
[119] Even where a special guardian has been appointed the birth parents will retain their rights in respect of adoption.
[120] CA 1989, s. 14C(3).
[121] A. Bainham, *Children: The Modern Law* (Jordans, 2005) p. 253.

from the jurisdiction for longer than three months without the written consent of all those with parental responsibility. The status of special guardianship remains until revoked by an order of the court. It is, in a sense, a halfway house between a residence order and an adoption order.

The *Special Guardianship Guidance*[122] lists some of the things special guardianship will do.

- Give the carer clear responsibility for all aspects of caring for the child and for taking the decisions to do with their upbringing. The child will no longer be looked after by a local authority.
- Provide a firm foundation on which to build a lifelong permanent relationship between the child and their carer.
- Be legally secure.
- Preserve the basic link between the child and their birth family.
- Be accompanied by access to a full range of support services including, where appropriate, financial support.[123]

Most people using special guardianship are relatives, especially grandparents.[124] Typically orders have been made in favour of relatives with whom the child had been living for some time.[125] The children involved tend to be young, with 52 per cent under the age of five. Most children had come from troubled backgrounds marked by maltreatment or parental difficulties.[126]

Special guardianship does have a degree of security. Any application to revoke special guardianship must obtain the leave of the court.[127] Unless the application is by the local authority, the child or the Special Guardian him- or herself, it needs to be shown that there has been a significant change in the circumstances from when the special guardianship order was made. This makes special guardianship a little more secure than a residence order.[128]

Discussion

Special guardianship is, therefore, a middle road between an adoption order and a residence order. It has more security than a residence order, but does not remove the status of the birth family. This middle road is, however, both its strength and weakness. Courts have expressed concern that it does not have the security that adoption would provide, especially in cases where children come from troubled backgrounds.[129]

---

[122] Department for Education and Skills, *Special Guardianship Guidance*; Special Guardianship Regulations 2005, SI 2005/1109.

[123] A local authority scheme which paid special guardians at a reduced rate was found to be unlawful in *B v Lewisham BC* [2008] EWHC 738 (Admin).

[124] J. Wade, J. Dixon, and A. Richards, *Implementing Special Guardianship* (Department for Children, Schools and Families, 2009).

[125] Ibid.

[126] Ibid.

[127] One exception is where the child is applying (CA 1989, s. 14D(5)).

[128] Department for Education and Skills, *Special Guardianship Guidance*.

[129] *A Local Authority v Y, Z and Others* [2006] EWHC 1620 (Fam).

Special guardianship is most likely to appeal in cases where there are good reasons why the child should retain links with the birth family, even though they cannot be the full-time carers of the child. For example, in *Re M (Adoption or Residence Order)*[130] the child was strongly of the opinion that she did not want her links with her mother and siblings to be destroyed, even though she wished to live with the applicants in a permanent relationship. This is the kind of case where special guardianship will now be considered. It may also be appropriate for some children from ethnic minorities. For example, the concept of adoption also sits unhappily with Islamic law, which does not recognize the notion of the extinguishment of parental rights.[131] Special guardianship may therefore be more acceptable than adoption to some Muslim parents.

Special guardianship might receive support from a human rights perspective. Under the Human Rights Act 1998, the court must ensure that the intervention in family life was necessary and proportionate. As a special guardianship order was a less fundamental intervention than an adoption order, it should be preferred if it protects the welfare of the child to the same extent as an adoption order.[132] Perhaps not too much should be made of that argument. In *Re S (A Child) (Adoption Order or Special Guardianship Order)* it was held that:

> In choosing between adoption and special guardianship, in most cases Art 8 is unlikely to add anything to the considerations contained in the respective welfare checklists. Under both statutes the welfare of the child is the court's paramount consideration, and the balancing exercise required by the statutes will be no different to that required by Art 8. However, in some cases, the fact that the welfare objective can be achieved with less disruption of existing family relationships can properly be regarded as helping to tip the balance.[133]

Special guardianship is unlikely to be appropriate where there is a real risk of tension between the Special Guardian and the birth family. The dangers are well illustrated by *Re L (A Child) (Special Guardianship Order and Ancillary Orders)*.[134] The parents of child L were in a volatile relationship and were drug addicts. At just 3 months, L was placed with her grandparents, initially under a residence order. Several years later they applied for an adoption order, but a special guardianship order was made. In making the order the Court of Appeal upheld an order that contact take place six times a year and upheld a refusal to allow the grandparents to change the surname of the child.

The decision demonstrates the weaker position of Special Guardians, as compared with adopters. Adopters are typically permitted to give the child their surname and contact is left to their discretion. The Court of Appeal in this

---

[130] [1998] 1 FLR 570.

[131] D. Pearl and W. Menski, *Muslim Family Law*, (Jordans, 1998), p. 410.

[132] *Re S (A Child) (Adoption Order or Special Guardianship Order)* [2007] 1 FCR 271.

[133] [2007] 1 FCR 271, para. 49.

[134] [2007] EWCA Civ 196.

case thought the court could restrict the way the parents raised the child. They explained:

> [Special Guardianship] is intended to promote and secure stability for the child cemented into this new family relationship. Links with the natural family are not severed as in adoption but the purpose undoubtedly is to give freedom to the special guardians to exercise parental responsibility in the best interests of the child. That, however, does not mean that the special guardians are free from the exercise of judicial oversight.[135]

This meant on the surname issue it was important the child knew of her biological background and realized she was being raised by her grandparents. That seems a weak point given that the child was having regular contact with her birth parents. As the court admitted:[136] 'In the scale of things in this child's life, her surname is a fact of little real significance.' With that in mind one might have thought that allowing the Special Guardians, who had undertaken, somewhat reluctantly, the enormous task of raising this troubled child, the liberty to change the name would be a minor concession. The court accepted that 'the care offered by the grandparents was exemplary' but the litigation and surrounding dispute had left them 'not far short from breaking point'.[137]

It is noticeable that special guardianship has not been used much. There were 2,071 special guardianship orders made in 2008.[138] This fell to 410 in 2010.[139] The decision in *Re L (A Child)* perhaps shows why. As mentioned in our discussion of adoption breakdown rates, the job of taking on a troubled abused child is an enormously difficult one. With a long-term commitment expected, but restrictions imposed on how one lives one's family life, it is understandable it will not have widespread appeal to would-be long-term carers of children. Clearly it can work well, especially in cases where the relationship between the Special Guardians and birth family is strong.[140] Where it is not, it seems a recipe for ongoing tensions.

CONCLUSION

At the heart of special guardianship is a tension between the position of the Special Guardians and the birth parents. The aim of the law is to provide a status which allows the birth parents some very limited role in the child's life, while allowing the Special Guardians the day-to-day care of the child and a degree of privacy and security. The difficulty is that the exact striking of this balance is likely to vary from case to case, depending on the particular child and the circumstances of the family situation. The danger is that if special guardianship is seen as too pro-birth

---

[135] Para. 33.
[136] Para. 40.
[137] Para. 22.
[138] Ministry of Justice, *Judicial and Court Statistics* (Ministry of Justice, 2009).
[139] Ministry of Justice, *Judicial and Court Statistics* (Ministry of Justice, 2011).
[140] Wade, Dixon and Richards, *Implementing Special Guardianship*.

families it will not be acceptable to long-term carers of children, while it if it is too pro-Special Guardians, it will become indistinguishable from adoption.

Further Reading

A. Bainham, 'Arguments about Parentage' (2008) 67 *CLJ* 322.

J. Eekelaar, 'Contact and Adoption Reform', in A. Bainham, B. Lindley M. Richards and L. Trinder (eds), *Children and their Families* (Hart Publishing, 2003).

S. Harris-Short 'Making and Breaking Family Life: Adoption, the State and Human Rights' (2008) 28 *Journal of Law and Society* 28.

J. Lewis, 'Adoption: The Nature of Policy Shifts in England and Wales' (2004) 18 *International Journal of Law, Policy and the Family* 235.

B. Luckock, 'Adoption Support and the Negotiation of Ambivalence in Family Policy and Children's Services' (2008) 35 *Journal of Law and Society Law* 3.

D. Quinton and J. Selwyn, 'Adoption: Research, Policy and Practice' (2006) 19 *Child and Family Law Quarterly* 459.

J. Smeeton and K. Boxall, 'Birth Parents' Perceptions of Professional Practice in Child Care and Adoption Proceedings: Implications for Practice' (2011) 16 *Child and Family Social Work* 444.

7

MARRIAGE, CIVIL PARTNERSHIP AND COHABITATION

INTRODUCTION

In this chapter we consider some of the key contemporary debates relating to marriage, civil partnerships and cohabitation. The institution of marriage is, of course, so freighted with history that a longer historical perspective is needed to put contemporary debates in context. It would be wrong, however, to see marriage as merely a historical curiosity that already has, or soon will be, overtaken by other family forms: marriage remains the most popular family form, with married couples accounting for 12.2 million families (out of a total of 17.9 million) in 2010.[1]

It is true that there has been a decline in the numbers marrying since 1972, in which year 426,241 couples tied the knot. But the official statistics – according to which 231,490 marriages were celebrated in England and Wales in 2009,[2] the 'lowest since 1895', as all the newspapers trumpeted – do not give a full picture. Estimates based on the International Passenger Survey suggest that, in 2009, over 90,000 UK residents travelled abroad to marry.[3] Since such couples do not need to register their marriage upon their return to this jurisdiction, the popularity of overseas marriages is clearly having a significant impact on the official statistics.

It is still the case that most couples who share a home are married, and litigation over the 'right to marry' as set out in Article 12 of the European Convention on Human Rights indicates that individuals continue to attach considerable value to marriage as an institution.

Such litigation underpins the first two debates considered in this chapter. We will consider first whether marriage should be described as a status or a contract, and the extent of choice accorded to couples in how and whom to marry. This leads on to the second debate, as to whether marriage should be opened up to same-sex couples, which requires an examination of civil partnerships as well as the literature on same-sex marriage.

---

1 Office for National Statistics, 'Families and Households in the UK, 2001 to 2010' (ONS, 2011).
2 Office for National Statistics, 'Marriages in England and Wales, 2009' (ONS, 30 March 2011).
3 Office for National Statistics, 'Population Estimates by Marital Status: Methodology Paper' (ONS, 2010).

Whether marriage *deserves* the value that is placed on it – and whether it merits its current privileged legal position – is of course a different matter. Rosemary Auchmuty, for example, has argued that seeking access to marriage is the wrong tactic:

> formal equality claims are not always progressive…. [W]hether you see marriage as an oppressive bastion of male power, as the second-wave feminists did, or simply as outmoded and irrelevant, as many contemporaries do, the goal should surely be to get rid of it, or at least to let it die out of its own accord – not to try to share in its privileges, leaving the ineligible out in the cold.[4]

Whether marriage remains 'an oppressive bastion of male power' is in itself disputed. Over the course of the twentieth century marriage became more like cohabitation in a number of different ways. The legal disabilities which applied to married women were swept away,[5] and the social roles of husbands and wives became increasingly interchangeable.[6] As Baroness Hale tartly pointed out in *Re P (Adoption: Unmarried Couple)*: 'These are not the olden days when the husband and wife were one person in law and that person was the husband. A desire to reject legal patriarchy is no longer a rational reason to reject marriage.'[7]

Whatever the reasons for rejecting marriage, it is clear that since the late 1970s there has been a significant rise in the number of couples who are cohabiting outside marriage.[8] By 2011 there were 2.9 million such couples, and 1.8 million children were living in families headed by a cohabiting couple. Cohabiting couples do of course enjoy *some* legal rights, but not the full package seemingly promised by the common but misleading term 'common-law marriage'.[9] In some contexts they are, as Auchmuty noted, simply left 'out in the cold'. The third debate explored in this chapter accordingly shifts the focus to those who have not formalized their relationship, and asks whether cohabitants should be treated like married couples.

Debate

Is marriage a status or a contract?

Whether marriage should be regarded as a status or a contract has been much debated ever since Henry Maine postulated his thesis that 'movement of the

---

4 R. Auchmuty, 'What's So Special about Marriage? The Impact of *Wilkinson v Kitzinger*' [2008] 20 *Child and Family Law Quarterly* 475, 497.

5 B. Hale, 'The Future of Marriage', in G. Douglas and N. Lowe (eds) *The Continuing Evolution of Family Law* (Jordans Publishing, 2009).

6 See e.g. J. Lewis, *The End of Marriage?* (Edward Elgar, 2001); M. Collins, *Modern Love: An Intimate History of Men and Women in Twentieth-Century Britain* (Atlantic Books, 2003).

7 [2008] UKHL 38.

8 On the historical rarity of cohabitation, see R. Probert, *The Legal Regulation of Cohabitation, 1600–2010: From Fornicators to Family* (Cambridge University Press, 2009).

9 On the origins and evolution of the term, see R. Probert, 'Common-law Marriage: Myths and Misunderstandings' [2008] 20 *Child and Family Law Quarterly* 1.

progressive societies has hitherto been a movement from Status to Contract'.[10] Central to this argument was the contention that there had been a move away from relationships determined by kinship – 'derived from...the powers and privileges anciently residing in the Family' – to ones based on the free agreement of individuals. Against this background, Maine defined marriage as a contract, in that it rested on the free choice of the parties, even if the consequences of entering into such a contract were set. More recent work on marriage has, by contrast, seen the inability of couples to alter the terms of the marriage contract as an indication that it should be regarded as a status.[11]

Whether a marriage should be categorized as a contract or a status is a question that has implications for many issues within family law. If it is a contract, should the parties to it be able to vary the terms relating to entry, exit, and the rights and responsibilities to which it gives rise? If marriage is a status, is it one that should be regarded as life-long, at least in terms of the obligations of the parties, if not the personal relationship?

Of course, the existence of these two categories should not oblige us to fit marriage within one or the other: marriage could, for example, be regarded as a contract that confers a status,[12] or as Barret and McIntosh have pointed out, a contract that is regulated by the state rather than by the parties to it.[13] The intertwining of contract and status was well explained by Thorpe LJ in *Bellinger v Bellinger*, describing marriage as:

> a contract for which the parties elect but which is regulated by the state, both in its formation and in its termination by divorce, because it affects status upon which depend a variety of entitlements, benefits and obligations.[14]

To avoid the debate spilling into areas of family law covered elsewhere in this book, this section will focus on the issue of entry into marriage, and how this is regulated by the state, highlighting the key debates in each area. Such regulation is not, of course, necessarily inimical to the idea of marriage as a contract, as becomes apparent if we consider the rules designed to ensure that the marriage is based on the free and full consent of both parties.

MARRIAGE AS A CONTRACT: ENSURING THAT CONSENT IS FREELY GIVEN

Consent has long been regarded as being at the heart of marriage in English law. As the philosopher John Locke put it in the late seventeenth century, a marriage should be contracted 'between two free, equal, consenting adults'.[15] While parents

---

10 Henry Maine, *Ancient Law* (John Murray, 1861), ch. 2.

11 See e.g. S. Cretney, 'The Family and the Law – Status or Contract?' [2003] 15 *Child and Family Law Quarterly* 403, which focuses on the possibility of opting out of the standard contract.

12 See e.g. J. Dewar and S. Parker, 'English Family Law since World War II: From Status to Chaos', in S. Katz, J. Eekelaar and M. Maclean (eds) *Cross-Currents* (Oxford University Press, 2000), p. 125.

13 M. Barret and M. McIntosh, *The Anti-Social Family* (NBI, 1982), p. 55.

14 [2001] EWCA Civ 1140. See also the comments of Baroness Hale in *Re P* [2008] UKHL 38, para. 107.

15 *Two Treatises of Government* (1689).

had[16] the power to veto the marriages of their minor children, they did not have the power to make marriages for their children without their consent. While examples of forced marriages can be found from this period – and indeed from later decades – it is clear that the law did not sanction such abuses of parental power. Nor, indeed, would the courts recognize a marriage if one of the parties did not have the ability to consent to it.[17]

It is thus clear that ensuring that consent is freely given involves ensuring that the parties are both able to consent and that they do consent to the marriage. Ideas of contract and status have been integral to the debates over both capacity and duress. In relation to the former, for example, we find that the courts have set the level of capacity required to enter into a marriage at a relatively low level on the basis that 'the contract of marriage is a very simple one, which does not require a high degree of intelligence to comprehend'.[18] Similarly, in *Sheffield City Council v E and S*, Munby J identified marriage as a contract that conferred a status:

> Marriage, whether civil or religious, is a contract, formally entered into. It confers on the parties the status of husband and wife, the essence of the contract being an agreement between a man and a woman to live together, and to love one another as husband and wife, to the exclusion of all others. It creates a relationship of mutual and reciprocal obligations, typically involving the sharing of a common home and a common domestic life and the right to enjoy each other's society, comfort and assistance.[19]

Thus those intending to marry need to understand that they are thereby taking on certain obligations, but need not have any knowledge or understanding of what those obligations are. In addition, the discussion of what is 'typical' neatly sidesteps the issue of what is legally required.[20] Status and contract are, however, inextricably intertwined here: the idea is that the level of capacity to enter into the contract of marriage has to be set at a certain level because marriage is a status from which certain obligations flow. Marriage, in other words, is more than the relationship (as is indicated by the fact that the level of capacity deemed necessary for a person to engage in a sexual relationship is set at a significantly lower level).[21]

Turning to the issue of duress, the key debates have been (i) what level of duress should be regarded as sufficient to invalidate the contract, and (ii) what the effect of this should be. The centrality of consent to marriage was reflected in Lord

---

[16] And still have: see R. Probert, 'Parental Responsibility and Children's Partnership Choices', in R. Probert, J. Herring and S. Gilmore (eds) *Responsible Parents and Parental Responsibility* (Hart Publishing, 2009).

[17] See C. W. Brooks, *Law, Politics and Society in Early Modern England* (Cambridge University Press, 2009), p. 382, for an early example.

[18] *Durham v Durham* (1885) 10 PD 80, at 81, per Sir James Hannen P.

[19] [2004] EWHC 2808 (Fam), para. 132.

[20] See further R. Gaffney-Rhys, '*Sheffield City Council v E and Another* – Capacity to Marry and the Rights and Responsibilities of Married Couples' [2006] 18 *Child and Family Law Quarterly* 139.

[21] See e.g. *Local Authority X v MM (by her litigation friend, the Official Solicitor), KM* [2007] EWHC 2003 (Fam).

Penzance's description of marriage in *Hyde v Hyde and Woodmansee*[22] as a *voluntary* union and the fact that a marriage entered into as a result of duress was void. It has been questioned, however, whether the test for duress gives adequate weight to the requirement that the marriage be 'voluntary'. While those wishing to annul their marriage no longer need to show that there has been 'a threat of immediate danger...to life, limb, or liberty',[23] but simply that their will was overborne by the pressure applied,[24] it would seem that there must still be some indication of dissent at the time of the marriage. The case of *Singh v Singh*[25] illustrates the limits of the law in this respect. The case involved a Sikh girl who was perfectly happy to have an arranged marriage and did not meet her proposed husband before the wedding. However, when she met him, she decided that he was neither as handsome nor as well-educated as had been represented to her. She went through the ceremony but refused to have anything to do with him afterwards and petitioned for a decree of nullity. The court refused to grant such a decree. It was stated that while the girl had obeyed the wishes of her parents – 'no doubt having a proper respect for them and for the traditions of her people'[26] – there was nothing to indicate that she had not consented to the marriage. *Singh* in fact shows how the concept of consent is subject to the importance of marriage as a status: the challenge for the law is how best to balance the need to ensure that consent is real and freely given with the desire to ensure that marriages cannot be challenged too easily.

In recent years it has been emphasized that forcing another individual into a marriage is an abuse of their human rights and a form of domestic violence.[27] Various initiatives have been implemented in order to attempt to prevent forced marriages: in particular the new provisions of the Family Law Act 1996 allow a court to make an order preventing a person from being forced into a marriage, or protecting those who have been forced into marriage.[28] Regulation is here being used to *protect* the idea of marriage as a contract.

Yet, for all the emphasis laid upon the centrality of consent to marriage, it remains the fact that a formal ceremony of marriage to which one or both of the parties do not or cannot consent is merely voidable,[29] rather than void, while an exchange of consent not given in the correct form might not create a marriage at all.[30] Whether lack of consent should render a marriage void or voidable is a matter on which there has been considerable debate: in the light of the increased

---

[22] (1866) LR 1 P & D 130.

[23] *Szechter v Szechter* [1971] P 286.

[24] *Hirani v Hirani* (1983) 4 FLR 232.

[25] [1971] P 226.

[26] At 231.

[27] Foreign and Commonwealth Office and Home Office, *Forced Marriage: A Wrong Not a Right* (September 2005).

[28] Family Law Act 1996, s. 63A(1), as inserted by s. 1 of the Forced Marriage (Civil Protection) Act 2007.

[29] Matrimonial Causes Act 1973, s. 12(c).

[30] See e.g. R. Probert, 'When are we Married? Void, Non-Existent And Presumed Marriages' (2002) 22 *Legal Studies* 398.

awareness of forced marriage there is clearly increasing disquiet with the implications of this, and the courts have been creative in side-stepping statutory provisions that might prevent relief being granted to the victims.[31]

MARRIAGE AS A CONTRACT REQUIRING COMPLIANCE WITH CERTAIN FORMALITIES

The fact that certain formalities are necessary for the creation of a valid marriage does not mean that a marriage is not a species of contract: after all, the law does specify that other types of contracts must be made in a certain way.[32] Moreover, the formal requirements can also be seen as a means of ensuring that consent is freely given: after all, the international Convention on Consent to Marriage, which was ratified by the UK in 1970, states that 'No marriage shall be legally entered into without the full and free consent of both parties, such consent to be expressed by them in person after due publicity and in the presence of the authority competent to solemnize the marriage and of witnesses, as prescribed by law.' Or, as Poulter put it, there is 'a public interest in providing adequate publicity, checking that the basic requirements for a valid marriage are complied with in terms of capacity and consent, and preventing fraud and abuse.'[33] Again, however, it is the fact that marriage gives rise to a status and particular obligations that justifies the stipulation that the contract should be made in a certain form. And in the debates as to how much choice the parties should have over the form of the ceremony – and as to the consequences of a failure to comply with the stipulated form – we see just how much importance is attached to clarity rather than choice.

Accepting that some formalities are necessary, how much choice do couples have as to the form in which they express their consent to marriage? Historically, of course, the ways in which couples could marry were rather limited. Setting aside a brief period under the Commonwealth, when a civil ceremony was required, the presence of an Anglican minister was necessary in order to create a legally recognized marriage. The claims that have been made by historians about various esoteric ceremonies such as 'handfasting' and 'jumping the broomstick' have, perhaps disappointingly, turned out to be based on misunderstandings of contemporary phrases rather than actual practice.[34] When the law of marriage (previously regulated by the church courts) was put on a statutory basis in 1753, the only specified form was that of the Church of England. While Jews and Quakers were

---

[31] See, for example, *B v I* [2010] 1 FLR 1721: declaration that there had never been a marriage capable of recognition within the jurisdiction; *SH v NB (Marriage: Consent)* [2009] EWHC 3274 (Fam); and *Re P (Forced Marriage)* [2011] EWHC 3467 (Fam), all involving the court issuing a declaration that there had never been a marriage capable of recognition within the jurisdiction (a decree of nullity being time-barred in each case).

[32] For example those relating to the sale of land: Law of Property (Miscellaneous Provisions) Act 1989, s. 2.

[33] S. Poulter, *English Law and Ethnic Minority Customs* (Butterworth, 1986), p. 33.

[34] See R. Probert, *Marriage Law and Practice in the Long Eighteenth Century: A Reassessment* (Cambridge University Press, 2009), ch. 3.

exempted from this legislation, it did not state what status their ceremonies would have, and this remained ambiguous until the Marriage Act 1836 made provision for a wider range of ceremonies. From 1837 it was accordingly possible to marry in a civil ceremony or a non-Anglican religious ceremony, as long as the preconditions laid down in the legislation were observed. In 1994 further legislation was passed allowing civil ceremonies to take place on 'approved premises'; this has proved a popular option, with the range of approved venues including hotels, stores and even the London Eye (although not, notoriously, Windsor Castle).[35]

So couples have considerable choice as to where to enter into the contract of marriage. Nonetheless, the fact that the expansion of the possible range of venues for marriage was influenced by ideas of choice does not mean that couples have a right to marry in *any* form they choose. In *Muñdoz Díaz v Spain*[36] the fact that no civil effects were attached to a Roma marriage was held not to constitute discrimination, since the option of civil marriage had been open to the couple.

A further aspect of the idea of marriage as a contract requiring compliance with certain formalities is the issue of how the law should deal with ceremonies that do not comply with the stipulated formalities. The relevant legislation states that a marriage will be void if the parties *knowingly and wilfully* fail to comply with certain stipulated requirements. In the case of an innocent failure to comply, the task for the courts is to determine how far the ceremony was from the prescribed form. One that is deemed 'close enough' will give rise to a valid marriage,[37] whereas one that was too far removed from the formal requirements will be relegated to the non-status of non-marriage and the parties will have no rights as all, not even those available where a marriage is declared void.[38]

At present, however, there is concern that an increasing number of marriages are being celebrated in this country without official sanction, generally although not exclusively among ethnic minorities. Those who go through a religious ceremony of marriage do not always appreciate the need to ensure that the necessary legal formalities are completed. The potential for confusion is exacerbated by the fact that some mosques and temples are licensed for marriage, and couples who marry there after complying with the preliminaries laid down by statute do not need to go through a civil ceremony as well. Others, however, are not: around one-quarter of Sikh temples, and more than three-quarters of mosques, are not licensed for marriages despite being certified places of worship.[39] The evidence suggests that some Muslim couples have both a religious and a civil ceremony; some consider a civil marriage the equivalent of the *nikah* and do not feel the need

---

[35] See further R. Probert, *The Rights and Wrongs of Royal Marriage: How the Law Has Led to Heartbreak, Farce and Confusion, and Why it Must be Changed* (Takeaway, 2011).

[36] [2010] 1 FLR 1421.

[37] As discussed in *Gereis v Yagoub* [1997] 1 FLR 854.

[38] *Gandhi v Patel* [2001] 2 FLR 603; *Hudson v Leigh* [2009] EWHC 1306 (Fam); [2009] EWCA Civ 1442.

[39] Office for National Statistics (2009).

for an additional religious ceremony,[40] while others marry solely in a religious ceremony.[41] The legal categorization of the latter is complex, since the governing legislation states that a marriage will only be void for non-compliance with the relevant formalities where the parties 'knowingly and wilfully' failed to observe them. This leaves the courts a choice between upholding a marriage entered into in good faith as legally valid, or consigning it to the non-status of a non-marriage with no legal consequences.[42] The latter course has been adopted in a number of cases where the ceremony was thought to depart too radically from that laid down by the statute. While it is difficult to see what alternative the courts have under the law as currently drafted – there would clearly be problems in accepting each and every self-defined ceremony as a marriage – the fact that an unknown number of ceremonies are vulnerable to legal challenge must be a cause for concern. The issue is rendered all the more difficult by the fact that some men are choosing to marry in this way in order to take a second or third wife, as they are allowed to under Islamic (but not English) law. It appears that consideration is being given to the issue within official circles,[43] but any reform that gave recognition to polygamous marriages would be highly controversial.

This brings us on to the next issue for discussion, namely the limitations on who can marry whom.

MARRIAGE AS A CONTRACT THAT ONLY CERTAIN INDIVIDUALS CAN ENTER INTO?

As many commentators have noted, if marriage is a contract it is one that is distinct from all other types of contracts, 'not only in that to make the agreement peculiar formalities must be carried out, but also in that the law relating to "capacity" is special'.[44]

As a reminder, here are the grounds on which a marriage is void:[45]

(i) the parties are within the prohibited degrees;
(ii) either party is under the age of 16;
(iii) the parties have knowingly and wilfully failed to comply with the requisite formalities;
(iv) one or both is already in an existing formal relationship (marriage or civil partnership);

---

[40] U. Khaliq, 'The Accommodation and Regulation of Islam and Muslim Practices in English Law' (2001) 6 *Ecclesiastical Law Journal* 332.

[41] S.N. Shah-Kazemi, *Untying the Knot: Muslim Women, Divorce and the Shariah* (Nuffield Foundation, 2001).

[42] Probert, 'When Are We Married? Void, Non-Existent and Presumed Marriages'.

[43] C. Barker and T. Ross, 'Government Rules Out Legalising Multiple Islamic Marriages After Whitehall Leak', *Daily Telegraph*, 21 July 2011.

[44] D. Leonard Barker, 'The Regulation of Marriage: Repressive Benevolence', in G. Littlejohn, B. Smart, J. Wakeford and N. Yuval-Davis (eds) *Power and the State* (Croom Helm, 1978), p. 248.

[45] Matrimonial Causes Act 1973, s. 11. A similar provision – with obvious variations – is contained in the Civil Partnership Act s. 49.

(v) the parties are of the same sex;

(vi) the marriage was polygamous and contracted overseas while either party was domiciled in England and Wales.

Alternatively, the existence of such rules could also be seen as supporting the idea of marriage as a status: while the general law of contract limits the contractual capacity of minors, it does not otherwise impose restrictions on who can contract with whom.

While the debate as to whether marriage is a contract or a status provides a useful framework for some of the key debates about capacity and the regulation of entry into marriage, it does not tell us much about the actual relationship of marriage. It is the contract that confers the status, not the level of love and commitment within marriage. It matters not, indeed, whether the marriage is one of convenience, a sham entered into for the purposes of obtaining certain benefits: the law does not enquire into the parties' reasons for marrying, and it is 'the marriage itself that determines whether the parties to it are husband and wife'.[46] It is only in the debates over whether marriage should be opened up to same-sex couples that we tend to find any real discussion of what marriage is for – which brings us on to our second topic of debate.

Debate ❨2❩

Should same-sex couples be allowed to marry?

ARE CIVIL PARTNERSHIPS NOT MARRIAGE?

Reading the 264 sections and 30 Schedules of the Civil Partnership Act 2004, one cannot but be struck by the extent to which the rules applicable to spouses have been replicated for civil partners. It would have saved a considerable amount of time, effort and trees had the legislature adopted the same approach as the Danish Registered Partnership Act and simply stipulated that, with certain exceptions, 'the registration of a partnership shall have the same legal effects as the contract-ing of a marriage.'[47]

For the most part, indeed, the Civil Partnerships Act slavishly incorporates all of the provisions relating to marriage, even where those provisions are abolishing rights that no one would ever have imagined applying to civil partners. Much of the Act cannot be understood without an understanding of the correspond-ing provisions relating to marriage. Thus section 73 of the Act precludes civil partners from bringing an action for breach of promise (echoing the Law Reform (Miscellaneous Provisions) Act 1970, s. 1), and section 69 is the equivalent of section 1 of the Law Reform (Husband and Wife) Act 1962, which abolished the last vestiges of the doctrine of unity in English law.

---

[46] *Adetola v First Tier Tribunal and SSHD* [2010] EWHC 3197 (Admin).

[47] Registered Partnership Act, s. 3.

Moreover, even in the short space of time since the Act was passed, civil part-nerships have become more like marriage. The Equality Act 2010 removed the bar to civil partnerships being celebrated on religious premises (although not the bar on any religious service being used)[48], and the modernization of language effected by the Family Procedure Rules 2010 brings proceedings relating to marriage into line with those involving civil partnerships.

Much, however, has been made of the minor differences that do remain: that it is not possible to annul a civil partnership on the basis of non-consummation or because one partner was suffering from a communicable venereal disease; and that adultery is not specified as a fact from which the irretrievable breakdown of the civil partnership can be inferred. The Women and Equality Unit originally explained these omissions on the basis that both 'consummation' and 'adultery' had a specifically heterosexual meaning and it was not 'appropriate in present day circumstances to include [transmission of a venereal disease] as a ground to nullify a civil partnership'. It was, however, suggested that infidelity, the absence of any sexual activity and the deliberate transmission of a sexually transmitted disease could be 'evidence of unreasonable behaviour leading to the irretrievable breakdown of a civil partnership'. In practice, therefore, these omissions make little difference.[49]

Nonetheless, there are a number of practical issues to be considered. One advantage of marriage, it has been said, is that it travels well: it is a more or less universal legal concept. The enactment of civil partnership regimes in individual countries raises questions as to whether such unions will be recognized elsewhere, and, if so, on what basis? Toner has noted the problems raised by the 'mobile registered partnership',[50] pointing out that such unions would probably not be recognized as marriages and could only be recognized as registered partnerships if the state to which the couple were migrating had its own registered partnership. Even if this were the case, complex issues could arise if the new state had a form of registered partnership that differed markedly from marriage (or indeed from the rights the couple would have been entitled to in their home country).

Furthermore, many same-sex couples seem to feel that there is a difference between marriage and civil partnerships. Once same-sex marriage had been introduced in the Netherlands, which already had the option of registered partnerships, the number of new partnerships plummeted. While some same-sex couples continued to prefer a more neutral alternative to marriage, the majority of those formalizing their relationship wanted marriage itself rather than an institution that was marriage-like. Similarly, research carried out among *pacsés* couples in France showed that many same-sex couples hoped that PaCS (pacte civil de solidarité – a system which allows a couple to

---

[48] See further R. Probert, 'Civil Rites', in R. Probert and C. Barton (eds), *Fifty Years in Family Law: Essays for Stephen Cretney* (Intersentia, 2012).

[49] Note also Auchmuty's suggestion that adultery was omitted at the behest of gay men: Auchmuty, 'What's So Special about Marriage? The Impact of *Wilkinson v Kitzinger*'.

[50] H. Toner, *Partnership Rights, Free Movement and EU Law* (Hart Publishing, 2004), p. 45.

register their relationship and thereby acquire some rights) – hailed by some as a radical alternative to marriage – would evolve into a more marriage-like institution.[51] However, whether these views are shared by same-sex couples in the UK is perhaps a moot point. As Rosemary Auchmuty has pointed out, in contrast to the US, '[t]here is no comparable body of pro-same-sex marriage literature originating in the UK' and Stonewall refused to support Wilkinson and Kitzinger in their claim for their Canadian marriage to be recognized in this jurisdiction.[52]

IS THERE ANYTHING IN THE LEGAL DEFINITION OF MARRIAGE THAT PRECLUDES RECOGNITION OF SAME-SEX MARRIAGE?

The immediate answer to this is yes: section 11 of the Matrimonial Causes Act provides that a marriage is void where the parties 'are not respectively male and female' and the authority of Lord Penzance in *Hyde v Hyde and Woodmansee*[53] that '[m]arriage as understood in Christendom, may...be defined as the union for life of one man and one woman to the exclusion of all others'. In *S-T (Formerly J) v J* Ward LJ quoted *Hyde* and noted that 'although some elements of that may have been eroded, bigamy and single-sex unions remain proscribed as fundamentally abhorrent to this notion of marriage'.[54] Indeed, in that case the marriage was not only declared to be void, but in addition the court refused to grant ancillary relief to the 'husband', who was a female-to-male transsexual.

But, of course, definitions of marriage are not set in stone. *Hyde* was relied upon in a number of cases involving transsexuals to justify the courts in their refusal to recognize the reassigned sex for the purpose of marriage,[55] while in Canada it was held in *EGALE v Canada* that Penzance's definition of marriage became part of the constitution when the federal Parliament was given constitutional jurisdiction over marriage by the Constitution Act in 1867.[56] But *Hyde* did not ultimately prevent the reform of marriage law, with the Gender Recognition Act 2004 allowing transsexuals to marry in their reassigned sex in England and Wales,[57] and the Canadian courts and legislature accepting same-sex marriage.[58] Nor would it prevent the legislature here accepting same-sex marriage.

The definition in *Hyde v Hyde* has been seen as authoritative simply because successive judges have agreed with the ideas it articulated, not because it bears any independent authority. As a definition of marriage it was always deficient; it was, rather, a *defence* of marriage, articulated against the background of Victorian

---

51 Gérard Ignasse, *Les Pacsé-E-S: Enquête sur les Signataires d'un Pacte Civil de Solidarité* (L'Hamilton, 2002).
52 Auchmuty, 'What's So Special about Marriage? The Impact of *Wilkinson v Kitzinger*'.
53 (1866) LR 1 P & D 130.
54 *S-T (Formerly J) v J* [1998] Fam 103, at 108.
55 *The Rees Case* [1987] FLR 111; *The Cossey Case* [1991] 2 FLR 492; *J v S-T (Formerly J)* [1998] Fam 103; *Bellinger v Bellinger* [2001] EWCA Civ 1140; [2003] UKHL 21.
56 N. Bala, 'Controversy over Couples in Canada: The Evolution of Marriage and Other Adult Interdependent Relationships (2003) 29 *Queen's LJ 41*.
57 See e.g. S. Gilmore, '*Corbett v Corbett*: Once a Man, Always a Man?' in S. Gilmore, J. Herring and R. Probert (eds) *Landmark Cases in Family Law* (Hart Publishing, 2011).
58 *Halpern v Canada* (2002) 60 OR (3d) 321.

concerns about Britain's place in the hierarchy of civilizations.[59] Today, its role seems to be to allow modern policy decisions to be masked in the name of precedent.

This, of course, does not mean that those policy decisions are not valid, nor does the fact that other jurisdictions have moved in a particular direction inevitably mean that this is the correct course to follow. A deeper objection might be that marriage has a meaning independent of law and policy. Girgis, George and Anderson have recently argued against the 'constructivist' view that marriage is 'just whatever we say it is', arguing that marriage has an independent reality rooted in biological union. Pointing to the fact that coitus consummates or completes the marriage between the parties, they argue that marriage is by its very nature the union of one man and one woman, describing it as 'a comprehensive union of two sexually complementary persons who seal (consummate or complete) their relationship by the generative act – by the type of activity that is by its nature fulfilled by the conception of a child.'[60]

By contrast, they argue that 'two men or two women cannot achieve organic bodily union since there is no bodily good or function toward which their bodies can co-ordinate'.[61] Pleasure, in their view, cannot be an appropriate 'good' for this purpose. The law, however, has long taken a different view: in 1948 the then Lord Chancellor, Viscount Jowitt, quoted with approval the words of a seventeenth-century Scottish jurist, Lord Stair:

> ... it is not the consent of marriage as it relateth to the procreation of children that is requisite; for it may consist, though the woman be far beyond that date; but it is the consent, whereby ariseth that conjugal society, which may have the conjunction of bodies as well as of minds, as the general end of the institution of marriage, is the solace and satisfaction of man.[62]

This brings us to a second potential bar to a same-sex union being regarded as a marriage, i.e. the requirement that a marriage be consummated. Of course, an inability or wilful refusal to consummate a marriage only renders it voidable, and, unless and until steps are taken to annul it, such a union is still regarded as a marriage for all legal purposes. Moreover, given the very minimal activity needed in order for the law to regard a marriage as consummated – only one act of 'ordinary and complete intercourse' is required, and mutual or even individual satisfaction is not deemed necessary[63] – one way forward might be to abolish the

---

[59] See R. Probert, '*Hyde v Hyde*: Defining Or Defending Marriage?' (2007) 19 *Child and Family Law Quarterly* 322.

[60] S. Girgis, R. P. George and R. T. Anderson, 'What Is Marriage?' (2010) 34 *Harvard Journal of Law & Public Policy* 245, 256.

[61] Ibid, 255.

[62] *Baxter v Baxter* [1948] AC 274, at 289.

[63] It was suggested in *Grimes v Grimes* [1948] P 323 that an insistence by the husband upon practising coitus interruptus amounted to a wilful refusal to consummate as this was 'no intercourse designed to give the proper satisfaction to the woman'; however a different result was reached in *White v White* [1948] P 330 and *Cackett v Cackett* [1950] P 253.

consummation grounds altogether,[64] or to substitute an expanded definition of consummation. This would also assist transsexuals: while their reassigned sex is now accepted for the purpose of marriage, the Gender Recognition Act 2004 makes no mention of consummation, so their marriages are still vulnerable to being annulled.[65]

DOES HUMAN RIGHTS LAW REQUIRE THE RECOGNITION OF SAME-SEX MARRIAGE?

In 2010 the European Court of Human Rights held that Article 12 of the European Convention on Human Rights – which guarantees 'men and women' the right 'to marry and found a family' – 'does not impose an obligation on the respondent Government to grant a same-sex couple…access to marriage'.[66] The key reason was that there was as yet 'no European consensus regarding same-sex marriage'.[67] Although same-sex couples may now marry in a number of European countries, including the Netherlands, Belgium, Spain, Portugal, Norway and Sweden, it is still far more common for such couples to be offered an alternative opt-in regime. Indeed, Andorra, Austria, the Czech Republic, Denmark, Finland, France, Germany, Hungary, Iceland, Ireland, Luxembourg, Slovenia and Switzerland have all enacted forms of registered partnerships.

One reason given in *Schalk* for the refusal to read the Convention as requiring member states to open up marriage to same-sex couples was the fact that Article 12 refers to 'men and women'. By contrast, Article 9 of the Charter of Fundamental Rights of the European Union, which entered into force on 1 December 2009, provides simply that '[t]he right to marry and to found a family shall be guaranteed in accordance with the national laws governing the exercise of these rights'. However, as the accompanying Commentary noted, this was intended to reflect the 'diversity of domestic regulations on marriage': on the one hand there would be 'no obstacle to recognize same-sex relationships in the context of marriage' but on the other there was 'no explicit requirement that domestic laws should facilitate such marriages'.

That the European Court has not yet held that the denial of the right to marry is a violation of the Convention does not mean that it will not do so in the future.[68] Its judges are well aware of the speed with which public attitudes can change. As late as 1998 the Court refused to find that the UK was in breach of the Convention for refusing to recognize transsexuals in their reassigned gender for the purposes of marriage (or indeed any other legal rights); a mere four years on the Court held that UK law did indeed breach Article 12. What was particularly significant about this reversal was that no more member states recognized transsexuals in 2002 than

---

[64] As advocated by e.g. L. Green, 'Sex-Neutral Marriage' (2011) 64 *Current Legal Problems* 1.

[65] See e.g. R. Probert, 'How Would *Corbett v Corbett* Be Decided Today?' [2005] *Family Law* 382.

[66] *Schalk and Kopf v Austria* (2011) 53 EHRR 20, [63].

[67] Ibid, [58].

[68] N. Bamforth, 'Families But Not (Yet) Marriages? Same-sex Partners and the Developing European Convention "Margin of Appreciation"' [2011] 23 *Child and Family Law Quarterly* 128.

had done so in 1998; rather, weight was attached to international developments in this area. It is therefore pertinent to note that an increasing number of states within the US, as well as Canada and South Africa, now allow same-sex marriage.

In other respects, however, the precedent of allowing transsexuals to marry in their reassigned sex is a somewhat ambiguous one. On the one hand, it marked the separation between marriage and procreation: while the European Court of Human Rights had previously asserted that Article 12 of the Convention was 'mainly concerned to protect marriage as the basis of the family',[69] it subsequently held that the inability of a couple to conceive did not remove their right to marry. Yet at the same time the recognition of transsexuals confirmed the idea of marriage as a union between a man and a woman: the individuals in question were claiming the right to be recognized in their reassigned gender, not simply the right to marry the person of their choosing, and the subsequent reforms required those who were married at the time they underwent gender reassignment to dissolve that marriage before their change of gender could be legally accepted.

WOULD ALLOWING SAME-SEX MARRIAGE MAKE ANY DIFFERENCE?

At a very basic level, opening up marriage to a new constituency might be seen as one way of boosting its popularity. Yet given that the number of civil partnerships is small by comparison with the number of marriages celebrated each year, and that – judging from trends elsewhere – the number of same-sex couples who choose to marry is likely to be slightly lower than the number who register a civil partnership[70] – any such increase would be minimal.

A different argument has been advanced by Girgis, George and Anderson, who contend that opening up marriage to same-sex couples would 'weaken the social institution of marriage, obscure the value of opposite-sex parenting as an ideal, and threaten moral and religious freedom'.[71] If, they argue, marriage is reconceptualized as being about adult emotions rather than bodily union or children, it becomes increasingly difficult to distinguish it from other forms of friendship, and more vulnerable to breakdown if emotions change. But the conjunction of bodies within same-sex unions would seem to offer sufficient reason to distinguish them – and therefore marriage – from friendship, and it could also be argued that the parties are unlikely to continue doggedly engaging in coitus once their emotions have changed, whereas affection may well keep a couple together after all sexual relations have ceased.

Another way of posing the question is to ask whether marriage would make a difference to same-sex couples. The issue of social recognition is clearly an important one to many couples. Whether being married, as opposed to being in a civil

---

[69] *Rees v UK* [1993] 2 FCR 49, [49].

[70] The data from the Netherlands suggests that where both options are available, more same-sex couples will marry than will register a partnership, but the numbers choosing to marry were lower than those originally choosing to register a partnership.

[71] Girgis, George and Anderson, 'What Is Marriage?', 160.

partnership, would change the nature of the parties' relationship is perhaps more open to question. Auchmuty suggests that marriage 'is associated with a whole range of conservative issues (settling down, investing in a home, raising a family, getting involved in the community and so on)',[72] but whether this is a matter of correlation or cause is difficult to ascertain.

Finally, would opening up marriage to same-sex couples transform marriage for the better for heterosexual couples? If marriage can involve two partners of the same sex, then it can no longer be seen as imposing a particular division of responsibilities within the home.

WHAT'S IN A NAME?

The term 'marriage' has a resonance that goes beyond the bare legal consequences that flow from it. The point has been made forcefully by one American commentator:

> Denying gays and lesbians access to marriage, despite giving them a grab bag of marriage like rights, is to deny them full citizenship and is a form of government-endorsed stigmatization.[73]

Similarly, in *Halpern v Canada*, La Forme J argued that any alternative to marriage would simply offer 'the insult of formal equivalency without the Charter promise of substantive equality'.[74]

Equally, the passion with which some commentators defend the traditional concept of marriage is perhaps misguided in that it merely serves to raise the stakes. The more that the unique status of marriage is highlighted, the more desirable it becomes as an institution to those who are excluded from it. Rosemary Auchmuty, no fan of marriage, has noted that civil partnerships 'will always be seen as second-best if marriage is unattainable'.[75]

THE FUTURE

It is perhaps significant that the media regularly refer to civil partnerships as 'marriage', even if it is sometimes prefixed with the adjective 'gay'. The degree of social acceptance of same-sex civil partnerships is a step towards social and legal acceptance of same-sex marriage.[76]

Civil partnerships are *almost* marriage in all but name, but when a word is so freighted with history as 'marriage', marriage 'in all but name' is, effectively, not marriage. The Coalition government has recently announced strong support for

---

[72] R. Auchmuty, 'Same-sex Marriage Revived: Feminist Critique and Legal Strategy' (2004) *Feminism and Psychology* 101, 117.
[73] E. Gerstmann, *Same-Sex Marriage and the Constitution* (Cambridge University Press, 2004), p. 200.
[74] (2002) 60 OR (3d) 321, at 450.
[75] Auchmuty, 'Same-sex Marriage Revived: Feminist Critique and Legal Strategy', 105.
[76] B. Shipman and C. Smart, '"It's Made a Huge Difference": Recognition, Rights and the Personal Significance of Civil Partnership' (2007) 12 *Sociological Research Online* 1.

legalization of same-sex marriage and has embarked on a consultation exercise to consider such a reform. Should this occur, it seems likely that the option of civil partnership would remain available to same-sex couples: the option of converting civil partnerships into marriages would doubtless be resisted by many same-sex couples who do not want the label of marriage to be attached to their relationship.[77]

One concern expressed by Auchmuty was that the campaign for same-sex marriage 'may impede a natural extra-legal movement towards substantively equal treatment for all family forms'[78] – which leads us on to the next debate.

Debate 3

Should cohabitants be treated like married couples?

HAVE COHABITANTS EVER BEEN TREATED LIKE MARRIED COUPLES?

Contrary to popular belief, English law has never recognized the concept of 'common-law marriage'. The idea that prior to 1753 it was possible to enter into a marriage by a simple exchange of consent derives from the mistaken interpretation of English authorities by a New York court in 1809. In fact, the presence of an Anglican clergyman was necessary in order to create a valid marriage, even if exact compliance with all of the prescribed formalities was not. Nor would the law infer that a couple who were living together were married: indeed, such a couple might be brought before the church courts and punished for fornication or the more specific offence of 'living scandalously and suspiciously together without lawful marriage'.[79]

The idea that cohabitants have a 'common-law marriage' can be traced back no further than the 1960s. In the wake of debates on immigration – in which the issue of the 'common-law wives' of West Indian men was raised – the term began to be applied to cohabitation. The myth itself emerged still later. Misunderstandings were fostered in the early 1970s when opponents of the 'cohabitation rule' argued that the aggregation of resources for the purpose of determining entitlement to means-tested benefits should not apply to all cohabitants but only those living in 'common-law marriages' and individuals began to ask what rights they had as a result of their 'common-law marriage'. As a result, when the courts and the legislature began to confer new rights on cohabiting couples between 1974 and 1979, it was understandable that the media should present them in terms of the entitlements of the 'common-law wife'. By 1979 individual misunderstandings

---

[77] K. McK. Norrie, 'Marriage is for Heterosexuals – May the Rest of Us Be Saved From It' [2000] 12 *Child and Family Law Quarterly* 363.

[78] Auchmuty, 'What's So Special About Marriage? The Impact of *Wilkinson v Kitzinger*', 497.

[79] See Probert, *Marriage Law and Practice in the Long Eighteenth Century: A Reassessment* and *The Legal Regulation of Cohabitation, 1600–2010: From Fornicators to Family* (Cambridge University Press, 2012).

had crystallized into a myth that the common-law wife enjoyed the same rights as a legal wife.[80]

Research has shown that a large proportion of the population – and an even larger proportion of cohabiting couples – does now believe that living together gives rise to a common-law marriage. Attempts to dispel this misunderstanding by means of a public information campaign have had only a limited effect.[81] This forms an essential background to evaluating possible avenues for reform. But it must be remembered that any reform would not be 'reviving' common-law marriage, but rather inventing it.

DO COHABITANTS WANT TO BE TREATED LIKE MARRIED COUPLES?

One argument frequently advanced against conferring rights on cohabiting couples is that this would run counter to their choice to opt out of marriage. Back in 1980, Deech argued that women 'do not need and ought not to require to be kept by men after the conjugal relationship between them has come to an end';[82] returning to the topic thirty years on, she remained equally convinced that there 'should be a corner of freedom where couples may escape family law with all its difficulties'.[83] Freeman similarly argued that the choice of cohabitants to opt out of marriage should be respected, linking protection to the perpetuation of a patriarchal system.[84] Yet in one recent nationally representative survey only one-tenth of cohabitants could be classified as 'ideologues' who had deliberately turned their backs on marriage, and few perceived legal rights as oppressive.[85] Nor does respect for freedom necessarily require that no rights are conferred on cohabiting couples; rather, the law could give such couples the option of opting out (as the Law Commission in fact proposed when advancing its scheme for enhancing the rights of cohabiting couples).

Moreover, the findings on the prevalence of the common-law marriage myth[86] raise questions about what expectations cohabiting couples actually have. The picture is complicated still further by the ubiquity of misunderstandings about the rights enjoyed by married couples: thus, even if some cohabitants do believe that they have a 'common-law marriage', this does not mean that they have any

---

[80] R. Probert, 'The Evolution of The Common-Law Marriage Myth' (2011) *Family Law* 283.

[81] A. Barlow, C. Burgoyne and J. Smithson, *The Living Together Campaign: An Investigation of Its Impact on Legally Aware Cohabitants* (Ministry of Justice Research Series 5/07), p. 35; A. Barlow, C. Burgoyne, E. Clery and J. Smithson, 'Cohabitation and the Law: Myths, Money and the Media', in A. Park, J. Curtice, K. Thomson, M. Phillips, M. Johnson and E. Clery (eds) *British Social Attitudes: The 24th Report* (Sage, 2008).

[82] R. Deech, 'The Case Against Legal Recognition of Cohabitation' in J. Eekelaar and S. Katz (eds) *Marriage and Cohabitation in Contemporary Societies* (Butterworths, 1980), p. 300.

[83] R. Deech, 'Cohabitation' [2010] *Family Law* 39, p. 43.

[84] M. Freeman, 'Legal Ideologies, Patriarchal Precedents and Domestic Violence', in M. Freeman (ed.) *The State, the Law and the Family: Critical Perspectives* (Sweet & Maxwell, 1994).

[85] A. Barlow and J. Smithson, 'Legal Assumptions, Cohabitants' Talk and the Rocky Road to Reform' [2010] 22 *Child and Family Law Quarterly* 328.

[86] Barlow, Burgoyne, Clery and Smithson, 'Cohabitation and the Law: Myths, Money and the Media', in Park, Curtice, Thomson, Phillips, Johnson and Clery (eds) *British Social Attitudes: The 24th Report*.

specific expectations in relation to the rights that the law accords to married couples.

Research indicates that most cohabitants intend to marry at some point, which again raises questions about whether they can be seen as rejecting marriage;[87] indeed, in some cases delaying marriage reflects the value that is placed on it by those who wish to marry only 'when everything is exactly right'.[88] Cohabitants themselves seem disinclined to argue for any advantages to not being married: a mere 10 per cent of cohabitants thought that cohabiting was better than being married, as opposed to the 16 per cent of them who thought that being married would be better, and the 59 per cent of married couples who preferred marriage.[89]

However, not all cohabitants will go on to marry. One recent longitudinal study found that 39 per cent of those who were cohabiting in 1991 had separated ten years later, while 39 per cent had married their partner, and the remaining 22 per cent were still cohabiting.[90] The indications are that fewer cohabiting unions are converting into marriages[91] and that the decision whether or not to marry is heavily influenced by socio-economic factors, religion and ethnic background.[92] This raises a further question: are cohabiting couples the same as married couples?

ARE COHABITANTS THE SAME AS MARRIED COUPLES?

Some studies suggest that cohabiting couples regard themselves as just as 'committed' as married couples,[93] while others have identified a spectrum of commitment within cohabiting relationships, from 'mutual' to 'contingent' commitment, or, in some cases, no commitment at all.[94] Much, of course, depends on the way in which questions are phrased in different studies.[95] While two-thirds of the public agree that 'there is little difference socially between being married and living together', it is still significant that fewer than half – 48 per cent – agreed that

---

[87] A. Barlow, S. Duncan, G. James and A. Park, *Cohabitation, Marriage and the Law – Social Change and Legal Reform in the 21st Century* (Hart Publishing, 2005); A. de Waal, *Second Thoughts on the Family* (Civitas, 2008).

[88] Barlow and Smithson, 'Legal Assumptions, Cohabitants' Talk and the Rocky Road to Reform'.

[89] S. Duncan and M. Phillips, 'New Families? Tradition and Change in Partnering and Relationships' in Park, Curtice, Thomson, Phillips, Johnson and Clery (eds) *British Social Attitudes: The 24th Report*.

[90] B. Wilson and R. Stuchbury, 'Do Partnerships Last? Comparing Marriage and Cohabitation using Longitudinal Census Data' (2010) 139 *Population Trends* 37.

[91] Barlow, Burgoyne, Clery and Smithson, 'Cohabitation and the Law: Myths, Money and the Media', in Park, Curtice, Thomson, Phillips, Johnson and Clery (eds) *British Social Attitudes: The 24th Report*.

[92] J. Eekelaar and M. Maclean, 'Marriage and the Moral Bases of Personal Relationships' (2004) 31 *Journal of Law and Society* 510; J. Miles, P. Pleasence and N. Balmer, 'The Experience of Relationship Breakdown and Civil Law Problems by People in Different Forms of Relationship' [2009] 21 *Child and Family Law Quarterly* 47; Goodman and Greaves 2010; C. Crawford, A. Goodman, E. Greaves and R. Joyce, *Cohabitation, Marriage, Relationship Stability and Child Outcomes: An Update* (Institute for Fiscal Studies, 2011).

[93] A. Barlow and G. James, 'Regulating Marriage and Cohabitation in 21st Century Britain' (2004) 67 *MLR* 143.

[94] C. Smart and P. Stevens, *Cohabitation Breakdown* (Family Policy Studies Centre, 2000).

[95] C. Marsh, 'Informants, Respondents and Citizens' in M. Bulmer (ed.), *Essays on the History of British Sociological Research* (Cambridge University Press, 1985).

'living with a partner shows just as much commitment as getting married'.[96] Cohabitation is not celebrated in the same way: there is no 'big day' or reception for family and friends, no 'moving in' list comparable to the wedding list, and the nearest equivalent – the housewarming present – tends to be 'fewer in number' and 'have less material and symbolic weight'.[97]

Certainly if one examines the available data on the ways in which couples deal with their assets, differences do begin to emerge. Cohabiting couples are less likely than are spouses to hold the family home and indeed other assets in joint names[98] or to have made a will.[99] In one study of the practices adopted by couples under the age of 35, it was found that cohabitants were more likely to opt for independent financial management than married couples, although overall the 'joint pool' was the most popular option for all couples.[100] The positive 'spin' on the data would be that cohabiting couples are keeping money separate in order to resist the inequality and dependency associated with marriage; a more negative interpretation is, however, suggested by the finding that those earning similar amounts of money were more likely to use the joint pool system, whereas partly or totally separate money management systems tended to be adopted where one earned more than the other. The separation of assets thus worked to the disadvantage of the economically weaker partner (usually the woman). As Vogler pointed out, 'in the context of a gendered labour market...individualised systems of money management tend to have highly unequal outcomes'.[101]

The evidence that cohabiting mothers are less likely to give up paid work than their married counterparts is also significant. While 34 per cent of married couples had adopted role specialization – with the husband taking the role of breadwinner and the wife being a full-time carer – this was the case for only 1 per cent of cohabitants. While one interpretation of this is that the married couples subscribe to more conservative ideas about family life (which raises a further question of whether this is the result of marriage or a reflection of the types of couples who marry), another is that cohabiting mothers do not feel secure enough to abandon paid work entirely in reliance on a partner. A third, of course, is that the overall household income does not allow them the luxury of choice.

In addition to the values and expectations of the individuals themselves, policy-makers are also concerned with the consequences of different types of relationships. A third issue in the literature is whether cohabiting unions do perform

---

96 Duncan and Phillips, 'New Families? Tradition and Change in Partnering and Relationships', in Park, Curtice, Thomson, Phillips, Johnson and Clery (eds) *British Social Attitudes: The 24th Report*.

97 L. Purbrick, *The Wedding Present: Domestic Life Beyond Consumption* (Aldershot, 2007), p. 176.

98 J. Haskey, 'Cohabiting Couples in Great Britain: Accommodation Sharing, Tenure and Property Ownership' (2001) 103 *Population Trends* 26; C. Vogler, 'Managing Money in Intimate Relationships: Similarities and Differences Between Cohabiting and Married Couples' in J. Miles and R. Probert (eds), *Sharing Lives, Dividing Assets* (Hart Publishing, 2009).

99 A. Humphrey, L. Mills, G. Morrell, G. Douglas and H. Woodward, *Inheritance and the Family: Attitudes to Will-Making And Intestacy* (NatCen, 2010).

100 Vogler, 'Managing Money in Intimate Relationships: Similarities and Differences Between Cohabiting and Married Couples' in Miles and Probert (eds), *Sharing Lives, Dividing Assets*.

101 Ibid, p. 80.

the same functions as marriage, and as well. If marriage is still the institution that provides the best outcomes for the children and for the parties themselves, then there might be good reasons to privilege it above other family forms.[102] There is ample evidence that the children of married couples do better on a range of measures than those whose parents are unmarried, and that marriages tend to last longer than cohabiting unions, but the extent to which these benefits are caused by marriage, as opposed to reflecting the types of couples who marry, is a matter of debate.

New research is constantly refining our understanding of cohabiting relationships and the questions that need to be posed. Research carried out by the Institute of Fiscal Studies, for example, has demonstrated that the lower cognitive development of children of cohabiting parents 'is largely accounted for by the fact that cohabiting parents have lower education qualifications than married parents'; the majority of the gap in their socio-emotional development could also be explained by factors such as education and income. The role of selection in determining who marries was confirmed by drawing on longitudinal data: evidence from the British Cohort Study identified differences between parents who were currently either married or cohabiting 'that were present during those parents' childhoods'; in summary, 'married parents are more likely to have scored better on cognitive and behavioural measures as children, to have grown up in privileged socio-economic circumstances, and with parents who stayed together and took an interest in their education'.[103]

Yet questions still remain about the influence of relationship quality, and whether this is something that is itself influenced by marriage. This is perhaps more pertinent to the issue of relationship stability than to the development of those in ongoing relationships. At first sight the differences are stark: children born to married parents are twice as likely as the offspring of cohabitants to continue living with both parents throughout their childhood.[104] Such differences are reduced but do not disappear completely once one controls for socio-economic characteristics. This then raises further questions about the direction of influence. One study found that marriage remained more stable than cohabitation even after controlling for such factors as education, employment and class, but noted that those social factors 'which are known to be associated with marital stability … are also associated with cohabitation stability' and hypothesized that there might be a potential selection effect if those with more stable relationships chose to marry.[105] The researchers at the Institute for Fiscal Studies similarly concluded that 'the majority of the difference in the likelihood of separation between cohabiting and

---

[102] See e.g. R. Probert, 'Cohabitation: Current Legal Solutions' (2010) 62 *Current Legal Problems* 316.

[103] Crawford, Goodman, Greaves and Joyce, *Cohabitation, Marriage, Relationship Stability and Child Outcomes: An Update.*

[104] J. Ermisch and M. Francesconi, 'Cohabitation in Great Britain: Not for Long But Here to Stay' (ISER, 1999). See also J. Holmes and K. Kiernan, *Fragile Families in the UK: Evidence from the Millennium Cohort Study* (2010).

[105] Wilson and Stuchbury, 'Do Partnerships Last? Comparing Marriage and Cohabitation using Longitudinal Census Data'.

married couples is driven by the types of people who choose to get married, rather than that marriage plays a large role in promoting relationship stability'.[106] But selection is clearly not the whole story, and other researchers have found evidence that marriage has a beneficial effect on the physical and psychological health of the parties that cannot be explained by selection alone.[107]

Standing back from such debates, what is perhaps most striking is the difficulty in divining how the law should treat cohabiting couples from the accumulated evidence. The greater stability of married relationships could be seen as a reason for promoting marriage, but the fact that cohabiting relationships are more likely to break down could equally be interpreted as indicating a greater need for some legal regulation. Similarly, the data that suggest that cohabitants are less likely to share their assets during their relationship might on the one hand be taken as indicating that they should not be required to do so when it comes to an end, but on the other that the financially weaker partner has a greater need for assets to be reallocated if the relationship comes to an end.[108] The problem in attempting to determine policy according to the characteristics of different family relationships, then, is that the evidence is not always clear-cut and could be used to justify a variety of different policy approaches.

This is not to decry the value of such work. The research carried out by the Institute for Fiscal Studies, for example, was designed to test the advisability of Conservative proposals to encourage marriage through the tax system, and it showed very clearly that such incentives were unlikely to yield dividends in terms of child development. But it will not be so easy to draw conclusions from more general studies about the direction that policy should (or should not) take. Underlying this indeterminacy is the basic fact that it is very difficult to design studies to test whether cohabitants should be accorded the same rights as married couples when the justification for according rights to spouses remains opaque.

SHOULD COHABITANTS BE EXPECTED TO MAKE USE OF EXISTING LEGAL REMEDIES?

There are a number of steps that cohabiting couples can take to safeguard their position under the existing law. The problem is that many do not. Even after a government-funded campaign intended to alert cohabitants to their lack of legal rights, only 12 per cent of such couples in a nationally representative sample had made wills and only 15 per cent had a declaration as to the beneficial interest in their shared home.[109] This renders them extremely vulnerable should the relationship break down. If a cohabiting couple split up, the law dictates that their assets

---

[106] Crawford, Goodman, Greaves and Joyce, *Cohabitation, Marriage, Relationship Stability and Child Outcomes: An Update.*

[107] C. M. Wilson and A. J. Oswald, 'How Does Marriage Affect Physical and Psychological Health? A Survey of the Longitudinal Evidence' (IZA Discussion Paper No. 1619, 2005).

[108] Vogler, 'Managing Money in Intimate Relationships: Similarities and Differences Between Cohabiting and Married Couples', in Miles and Probert (eds), *Sharing Lives, Dividing Assets.*

[109] Barlow and Smithson, 'Legal Assumptions, Cohabitants' Talk and the Rocky Road to Reform', 346.

should be divided strictly in accordance with their property rights rather than being reallocated on the basis of needs or principles of sharing. The way in which this operates to the disadvantage of the cohabitant whose name does not appear on the legal title has been well documented over the past few decades[110] and the law has been extensively criticized.[111]

Same rights or some rights?

Williams, Potter and Douglas in a survey examining rights on intestacy, noted how '[g]iven that the respondents were told that the surviving spouse would have taken the entire estate in each scenario, the fact that fewer than half thought that the surviving cohabitant should do so does suggest that being married was felt to give her a greater entitlement'.[112] Even more significantly, in one recent study of attitudes towards intestacy, cohabiting couples were less likely than were married couples to state that a surviving cohabitant should have priority over grown-up children.[113]

One suggestion is that different policies are needed to address the differing attitudes and needs of different types of cohabiting couples. Thus the law could make civil partnerships available to those who are ideologically opposed to marriage and put more resources into dispelling the common-law marriage myth for those 'pragmatists' who would marry if necessary to secure legal rights; for the rest 'a presumptive approach which provided a legal safety net for the vulnerable partner might be the most appropriate legal response'.[114] This, of course, is easier said than done.

Form or function?

It is important not to overstate the extent to which the current system focuses on form when dealing with assets on divorce. It has been claimed, for example, that 'it is the initial public commitment to the institution of marriage, rather than to the relationship that is rewarded within our redistribution of assets on divorce'.[115] It would, however, be fairer to say that it is the initial public commitment that gives the court jurisdiction to consider how the assets of the now ex-spouses should be redistributed. Fault may no longer play a role, but the duration of the relationship certainly does.

---

[110] S. Arthur, J. Lewis, M. Maclean, S. Finch and R. Fitzgerald, *Settling Up: Making Financial Arrangements After Separation* (NatCen, 2002); G. Douglas, J. Pearce and H. Woodward, *A Failure of Trust: Resolving Property Disputes on Cohabitation Breakdown* (Cardiff Law School Research Papers No. 1, 2007); J. Lewis, R. Tennant and J. Taylor, 'Financial Arrangements on the Breakdown of Cohabitation', in Miles and Probert, *Sharing Lives, Dividing Assets*.

[111] Law Commission, *Cohabitation: The Financial Consequences of Relationship Breakdown* (TSO, 2007).

[112] C. Williams, G. Potter and G. Douglas, 'Cohabitation and Intestacy: Public Opinion and Law Reform' [2008] 20 *Child and Family Law Quarterly* 499, 517.

[113] Humphrey, Mills, Morrell, Douglas and Woodward, *Inheritance and the Family: Attitudes to Will-Making And Intestacy.*

[114] Barlow and Smithson, 'Legal Assumptions, Cohabitants' Talk and the Rocky Road to Reform'.

[115] Ibid, 342.

The contrast between 'form' and 'function' in family law also implies that the one is a matter of appearance and the other an issue of substance, but we need to think about what the formal commitment actually signifies. Some couples are cohabiting precisely because they – or at least one of them – wishes to avoid the obligations associated with marriage; entering into a marriage, by contrast, is an indication of one's willingness to assume such obligations. And function may follow form where the mutual agreement to marry creates a sense of commitment security for the parties (or, conversely, where the refusal of one to marry engenders feelings of insecurity in the other).

WOULD EXTENDING RIGHTS TO COHABITANTS UNDERMINE MARRIAGE?

Another way of posing the question might be to ask whether there are any clear reasons for *not* extending rights to cohabiting couples. One concern that has been expressed is that this might have the effect of undermining marriage. This raises the difficult question of the relationship between legal reform and social behaviour. Scholars have analysed rates of marriage in Australia before and after the introduction of legislation conferring rights on cohabitants, and concluded that there was 'no statistical evidence of a relationship between the introduction of the legislation giving rights to cohabiting couples and the falls in the propensity to marry'.[116]

There are, however, some difficulties with this conclusion. The process of conferring rights on cohabitants tends to be a gradual process, with limited legal recognition being later followed by more extensive rights. Moreover, beliefs about the law, even if mistaken, may be of more significance in shaping behaviour than what the law actually is. This can, for example, be seen in the context of England and Wales, in which the most significant increase in cohabitation occurred after the emergence of the common-law marriage myth in the late 1970s.

Secondly, given the optimism bias that affects couples embarking on any form of relationship,[117] one would not expect the availability or otherwise of rights on *separation* to encourage couples to choose one form over another. More immediately available rights may, however, have an effect on behaviour. This can be seen particularly starkly in the context of tax law, with the evidence that many couples marrying in the 1960s timed their wedding to maximize the fiscal benefits, while in the 1980s home-buyers rushed to take advantage of beneficial mortgage interest relief before the law was changed.[118]

Of course, this latter argument cuts both ways. If the availability of rights on separation does not encourage couples to cohabit, then the introduction of such rights would not necessarily lead to any further move away from marriage.

---

116 K. Kiernan, A. Barlow and R. Merlo, 'Cohabitation Law Reform and Its Impact on Marriage' [2006] *Family Law* 1074, 1075.
117 A. Baker and R. E. Emery, 'When Every Relationship Is Above Average: Perceptions and Expectations of Divorce at the Time of Marriage' (1993) 17 *Law and Human Behavior* 439.
118 See Probert, *The Legal Regulation of Cohabitation, 1600–2010: From Fornicators to Family*, chs 5 and 8.

THE FUTURE

Nor are England and Wales alone within Europe in its tentative approach to this issue. Even in Sweden, where cohabitation is socially much more similar to marriage, legal distinctions remain.[119] Yet the fact that both Scotland and Ireland have enacted legislation,giving respectively, economically disadvantaged (Family Law (Scotland) Act, s. 28) or dependent (Civil Partnership and Certain Rights and Obligations of Cohabitants Act 2010, s. 173) partners a claim in the event of separation does raise questions as to whether England and Wales can continue to justify the lack of any protection for such couples.

However, the indications of support for same-sex marriage may bring one option a step closer. The Equal Love campaign was not just about claiming the right of same-sex couples to marry, but also the right of heterosexual couples to enter into a civil partnership. It would be difficult to justify extending marriage to same-sex couples without also giving heterosexual couples the choice of an alternative such as a civil partnership. While the need for this may not be obvious – as we have seen, a civil partnership has virtually the same consequences as a marriage, and one assumes that the requirement to consummate the marriage is not the reason for some heterosexual couples' wanting to enter into a civil partnership – the very reasons that make a civil partnership an unacceptable substitute for some same-sex couples also make it a more attractive option for those couples who are ideologically opposed to marriage.

Further Reading

R. Auchmuty, 'Same-sex Marriage Revived: Feminist Critique and Legal Strategy' (2004) *Feminism and Psychology* 101.

R. Auchmuty, 'What's So Special about Marriage? The Impact of *Wilkinson V Kitzinger*' [2008] 20 *Child and Family Law Quarterly* 475.

N. Bamforth, 'Families But Not (Yet) Marriages? Same-Sex Partners and the Developing European Convention "Margin of Appreciation"' [2011] 23 Child and Family Law Quarterly 128.

A. Barlow, C. Burgoyne, E. Clery and J. Smithson, 'Cohabitation and the Law: Myths, Money and the Media', in A. Park, J. Curtice, K. Thomson, M. Phillips, M. Johnson and E. Clery (eds) *British Social Attitudes: The 24th report* (Sage, 2008).

A. Barlow and J. Smithson, 'Legal Assumptions, Cohabitants' Talk and the Rocky Road to Reform' [2010] 22 *Child and Family Law Quarterly* 328.

J. Eekelaar and S. Katz (eds) *Marriage and Cohabitation in Contemporary Societies* (Butterworths, 1980).

R. Gaffney-Rhys, '*Sheffield City Council v E and Another* – capacity to marry and the rights and responsibilities of married couples' [2006] 18 *Child and Family Law Quarterly* 139.

---

[119] A. Björklund, D. Ginther and M. Sundström, 'Does Marriage Matter for Children? Assessing the Impact of Legal Marriage in Sweden', Working Paper Series 3/2010, Swedish Institute for Social Research.

S. Girgis, R. P. George and R. T. Anderson, 'What is Marriage?' (2010) 34 *Harvard Journal of Law & Public Policy* 245.

K. Kiernan, A. Barlow and R. Merlo, 'Cohabitation Law Reform and Its Impact on Marriage' [2006] *Family Law* 1074.

J. Miles and R. Probert (eds), *Sharing Lives, Dividing Assets* (Hart Publishing, 2009).

R. Probert, 'When Are We Married? Void, Non-Existent and Presumed Marriages' (2002) 22 *Legal Studies* 398.

R. Probert, '*Hyde v Hyde*: Defining or Defending Marriage?' (2007) 19 *Child and Family Law Quarterly* 322.

R. Probert, *The Legal Regulation of Cohabitation, 1600–2010: From Fornicators to Family* (Cambridge University Press, 2012).

B. Shipman and C. Smart, ' "It's Made a Huge Difference": Recognition, Rights and the Personal Significance of Civil Partnership' (2007) 12 *Sociological Research Online* 1.

C. Williams, G. Potter and G. Douglas, 'Cohabitation and Intestacy: Public Opinion and Law Reform' [2008] 20 *Child and Family Law Quarterly* 499.

8

DIVORCE

INTRODUCTION

In recent years the actual basis for divorce – as opposed to the consequences of relationship breakdown – has attracted relatively little academic debate. Yet in numerical terms the granting of a divorce is probably the aspect of family law that affects more couples than any other – save only marriage itself, and few couples think of seeking legal advice when entering into marriage. While both the number of divorces and the divorce rate[1] have fallen in recent years (both having peaked in 1993, when there were over 165,000 divorces in England and Wales, a rate of 14.3 divorces per thousand married persons[2]), there were still 113,949 divorces in 2009, the most recent year for which statistics are available.[3] And divorce is very much perceived as a legal act: indeed, in one survey of access to justice it was found that those affected by divorce were more likely to seek legal advice than in the case of any other problem.[4] Moreover, the current law has been widely criticized for many years, and its problems have not lessened over time. There is thus good reason for revisiting the debates about what the law of divorce should be.

The current law, despite a number of recommendations for, and attempts at, reform (the most significant being the Family Law Act 1996), remains substantially the same as that enacted in the Divorce Reform Act 1969 and consolidated in the Matrimonial Causes Act 1973. The sole ground for divorce is that the marriage has

---

[1] It is important to bear in mind the distinction between the number of divorces and the divorce rate: while the former is an absolute number, the latter is calculated according to the number of divorces per 1,000 married persons in the overall population. A fall in the number of divorces may, therefore, simply reflect a fall in the number of married persons in the population; a fall in the divorce *rate*, by contrast, indicates that fewer married persons are getting divorced.

[2] Office for National Statistics, *Marriage, divorce and adoption statistics*, Series FM2, No 27 (Office for National Statistics, 2001), table 4.1.

[3] Office for National Statistics, 'Divorces in England and Wales – 2009' (Office for National Statistics, 2011). This was, as the ONS noted, the lowest number of divorces since 1974, when 113,500 were granted. The divorce rate also fell, to 10.5 divorces per thousand married persons.

[4] H. Genn, *Paths to Justice* (Hart Publishing, 1999), p. 89.

broken down irretrievably;[5] breakdown, however, is not regarded as a justiciable issue in itself and has to be proved by one or more of the five facts listed in the legislation.[6] Since their terms are the basis for some debate, they are presented in full here:

(a) that the respondent has committed adultery and the petitioner finds it intolerable to live with the respondent;
(b) that the respondent has behaved in such a way that the petitioner cannot reasonably be expected to live with the respondent;
(c) that the respondent has deserted the petitioner for a continuous period of at least two years immediately preceding the presentation of the petition;
(d) that the parties to the marriage have lived apart for a continuous period of at least two years immediately preceding the presentation of the petition...and the respondent consents to a decree being granted;
(e) that the parties to the marriage have lived apart for a continuous period of at least five years immediately preceding the presentation of the petition.>

Virtually the same rules govern the dissolution of civil partnerships,[7] with the only distinction being that adultery is not listed as a specific fact from which breakdown can be inferred (having, as it does, a specific legal meaning that relates only to sex between a man and a woman, one of whom is married[8]). However, it was specifically envisaged at the time the legislation was formulated that infidelity within a same-sex partnership would be capable of constituting behaviour with which the other person could not be expected to live.

The three debates considered in this chapter examine both what the law is and what it should be. Of course, to discuss how the law should and could develop we need to know what the current law is, and what factors have shaped it. We begin by looking at the role of the state on divorce, and then go on to consider the lessons to be learned from the failure to implement the key provisions of the Family Law Act 1996. We conclude by considering whether English law already has a system of 'no-fault' divorce – and, if it does not, whether we should move to such a system.

Before we start, however, a brief note on terminology is necessary. The traditional language of divorce, as the statute quoted above makes clear, involved one spouse *petitioning* for a divorce from the *respondent*. When civil partnerships were made available, a more modern language was used, with civil partners *applying* for *dissolution* of the partnership. Procedural reforms have now extended the language of applications to divorces and this will be used when referring to the modern

---

[5] Matrimonial Causes Act 1973, s. 1(1).
[6] Ibid, s. 1(2).
[7] Civil Partnership Act 2004, s. 44(5).
[8] Women and Equality Unit, *Response to Civil Partnership: A Framework for the Legal Regulation of Same-Sex Couples* (November 2003), p. 35, noting that adultery 'has a specific meaning within the context of heterosexual relationships and it would not be possible nor desirable to read this across to same-sex civil partnerships'.

law; however, when earlier precedents are discussed, the terms used will be those used in the actual judgment.

Debate **1**

What is the role of the state on divorce?

For many centuries, the role of the state on divorce did not arise, for the simple fact that divorce was not an option. The Catholic church taught that a valid marriage was indissoluble save by death, and the state did not challenge this.[9] Reform was discussed at the time of the Reformation in the sixteenth century, with the *Reformatio Legum Ecclesiasticorum* of 1552 proposing that divorce be available in England and Wales on the basis of adultery, cruelty, desertion or 'mortal enmity'.[10] This, however, was never implemented, and the seventeenth-century poet Milton mused bitterly that 'the misinterpreting of some scriptures ... hath changed the blessing of matrimony ... into a drooping and disconsolate household captivity, without refuge or redemption'.[11]

Indeed, the first divorce – in the modern sense of ending an existing marriage and allowing the parties to remarry[12] – only took place in the 1660s, when Parliament passed a private Act allowing Lord Roos to remarry after his separation from his adulterous wife.[13] A trickle of aristocrats and other wealthy men followed his example, but the number of divorces by private Act of Parliament barely exceeded three hundred over the subsequent two hundred years.[14] Even so, by the mid-nineteenth century such legislation was proving increasingly burdensome to a Parliament that was progressively more concerned with general legislation, and under the Matrimonial Causes Act 1857 a new court was founded with the task of granting divorces. The sole ground for divorce remained that of a spouse's adultery, and a wife had in addition to show that her husband was guilty of cruelty, two years' desertion, incest, bestiality, bigamy, sodomy or rape. Not until 1923 was a wife able to petition for divorce simply on the ground of her husband's adultery, while the addition of extra grounds – cruelty, desertion and incurable insanity – did not occur until 1937.

In short, the state has had a long history of limiting the availability of divorce, and this, as we discuss in the next section, has been linked to the first of its suggested roles in this area.

---

[9] See e.g. J. Eekelaar, *Regulating Divorce* (Clarendon Press, 1991), ch. 2.
[10] L. Stone, *Road to Divorce* (Oxford University Press, 1995), p. 302.
[11] J. Milton, *The Doctrine and Discipline of Divorce* (Westley and Davis, 1835; original edn 1643), p. 124.
[12] Somewhat confusingly, an annulment was referred to as a divorce *a vinculo matrimonii* – from the bonds of matrimony – giving rise to the popular if misconceived idea that Henry VIII broke with Rome in order to 'divorce' his first wife.
[13] See e.g. R. Probert, 'The Roos Case and Modern Family Law', in S. Gilmore, J. Herring and R. Probert (eds) *Landmarks in Family Law* (Hart Publishing, 2011).
[14] See e.g. S. Wolfram, 'Divorce in England 1700–1857' (1985) 5 *OJLS* 155.

ENSURING THE STABILITY OF THE FAMILY UNIT

While opposition to divorce had its roots in religion, it could also be seen as having a justification independent of religious belief. As Cretney has noted:

> the view that marriage should in principle be indissoluble was not necessarily explicitly founded on religious dogma: this view could be based simply on utilitarian notions of the function of social institutions. The stability of the family unit was seen as the basis of stability in society; and this could best be promoted by insisting that marriage, the basis of the family, should remain intact.[15]

Given our modern awareness of a distinction between the fact of breakdown and the legal mechanism of divorce – and that the first may well occur without the latter – it is important to note the conviction on the part of commentators in earlier centuries that barring the exit from marriage would guard against the union breaking down in the first place. As Sir William Scott famously (if somewhat idealistically) put it in *Evans v Evans*:

> When people understand that they must live together, except for a very few reasons known to the law, they learn to soften by mutual accommodation that yoke which they know they cannot shake off; they become good husbands and good wives from the necessity of remaining husbands and wives; for necessity is a powerful master in teaching the duties which it imposes. If it were once understood that upon mutual disgust married persons might be legally separated, many couples who now pass through the world with mutual comfort, with attention to their common offspring and to the moral order of civil society, might have been at this moment living in a state of mutual unkindness, in a state of estrangement from their common offspring, and in a state of the most licentious and unreserved immorality. In this case, as in many others, the happiness of some individuals must be sacrificed to the greater and more general good.[16]

Of course, even at the time that Scott was writing not all unhappily yoked couples were willing to live together: contemporary records provide examples of informal separation, outright desertion, and even 'wife-sale'.[17] Even so, it would be implausible to claim that the levels of marital breakdown were on the same scale as today: the vast majority of couples lived together until death divided them.

But it was this belief that the state *could* ensure the stability of the family unit by restricting the availability of divorce which increasingly began to be questioned over the course of the twentieth century. Many commentators pointed out that

15 S. Cretney, 'Breaking the Shackles of Culture and Religion in the Field of Divorce?' in K. Boele-Woelki (ed.) *Common Core and Better Law in European Family Law* (Intersentia, 2005), p. 3.

16 *Evans v Evans* (1790) 1 Hag Con 35; 161 ER 466.

17 For discussion see R. Phillips, *Putting Asunder: A History of Divorce in Western Society* (Cambridge University Press, 1988); J. Bailey, *Unquiet Lives: Marriage and Marriage Breakdown in England, 1660–1800* (Cambridge University Press, 2003).

preventing a divorce was not the same as preventing a marriage from breaking down. Reformers noted the number of married couples living apart, either as a result of a formal separation or because one had simply left the other. Such marriages 'in name only' began to be seen as more problematic than divorce itself, and there was much critical commentary focusing on the 'vindictive' spouse who refused to take proceedings for divorce despite having grounds to do so. As Lord Walker put it in 1956, 'each empty tie...adds increasing harm to the community and injury to the ideal of marriage'.[18]

In addition, there was increasing evidence that separated couples were forming new ties that could not be formalized: in 1966 the newly-created Law Commission argued that to allow long-broken marriages to be ended would enable the regularization of existing 'illicit unions', and that if divorce were more widely available 'about 180,000 living illegitimate children could be legitimated'.[19] The Commission therefore suggested that a good divorce law should seek '(i) to buttress, rather than to undermine, the stability of marriage; and (ii) when, regrettably, a marriage has irretrievably broken down, to enable the empty legal shell to be destroyed with the maximum fairness, and the minimum bitterness, distress and humiliation'.[20] In essence, ensuring the stability of family life was to be ensured not by limiting divorce but by allowing new 'stable illicit unions' to be regularized by marriage.

To some extent this was achieved. The number of divorces increased considerably when the Divorce Reform Act 1969 came into force in 1971, but a large part of that increase was generated by petitions citing separation as the fact from which breakdown was to be inferred. Of those petitions filed on or after 1 January, half relied on either two or five years' separation, as did 46,274 petitioners – 41 per cent of the total – in 1972.[21] The stories behind the bare statistics were movingly summarized by Stephen Cretney, recalling his youthful observations of a courtroom:

> A succession of elderly persons of eminently respectable appearance came to the witness box to give the oral testimony then required in support of divorce petitions. All had lived apart from their lawful spouse for more – usually much more – than the stipulated five years. In almost every case the story was essentially the same: the youthful wartime marriage, the long separation in service of 'King and Country', the drift apart, the formation of a new relationship...In each case, the decree was granted; in each case the elderly couple's faces reflected happiness and quiet domestic content.[22]

---

[18] *Royal Commission on Marriage and Divorce* (1956), Cmd 9678, p. 341 (dissenting opinion).
[19] Law Commission, *Reform of the Grounds of Divorce: The Field of Choice* (1966), Cmnd 3123, p. 36.
[20] Ibid.
[21] OPCS, *The Registrar General's Statistical Review of England and Wales for the Year 1972* (HMSO, 1974), table P1(c)(i).
[22] S. Cretney, 'Divorce Reform in England: Humbug and Hypocrisy or a Smooth Transition?' in M. Freeman (ed.) *Divorce – Where Next?* (Dartmouth, 1996), p. 41.

In 1972 there were more marriages than ever, with just over a quarter of them involving at least one partner who had previously been married.[23]

However, not all of those in 'illicit unions' took the opportunity of regularizing their relationship, and by the end of the 1970s there were more children being born to cohabiting couples than there had been when the Commission had made its recommendations.[24] As Ruth Deech noted some years later, '[p]eople...simply do not seem to be as interested in formalised relationships as the Law Commission had thought'.[25] The strategy of trying to ensure the stability of family life by facilitating divorce thus had only limited success.

Yet at the same time the evidence of the previously unmet demand for divorce effectively precluded any arguments that the reforms should be reversed. Whether the reforms actually *contributed* to the subsequent rise in divorce has since generated much debate. At one level reform of this kind will always generate an increase in the number of divorces, because by its very nature it is responding to a demand for divorce that was not met by the previous law. But it has also been suggested that any increase, even if generated by the backlog of marriages that have long since broken down, contributes to the increasing acceptability of divorce as a solution to an unhappy marriage. As Deech noted, 'The increased divorce rate results in greater familiarity with divorce as a solution to marital problems [and] more willingness to use it'.[26]

Insofar as individuals may previously have stayed in unhappy marriages because of the stigma associated with divorce, this is no doubt true. Yet, as Andrew Bainham has pointed out, this does not mean that divorce law affects the quality of marital relationships – 'surely the factor most likely to determine whether those relationships end or survive'.[27] And Martin Richards' comments about the limits of the law in this context reflect the prevailing scepticism:

> Those who argue for harder divorce seem to have an exaggerated view of the power of the law to control people's domestic living arrangements. Their model seems to be that of a sluice gate which stands between the married and the divorced. The wider this sluice is opened, the more of the married that will become divorced. Such a view suggests that it is only the difficulty of getting out that keeps people married.[28]

In the light of this, what other roles remain for the state on divorce?

---

[23] OPCS, *Marriage and Divorce Statistics: Review of the Registrar General on marriages and divorces in England and Wales: Series FM2 No 1* (HMSO, 1977), table 2.1; OPCS, *The Registrar General's Statistical Review of England and Wales for the Year 1972*, table H2.

[24] See R. Probert, *The Legal Regulation of Cohabitation, 1600–2010: From Fornicators to Family* (Cambridge University Press, 2012), ch. 6.

[25] R. Deech, 'Divorce Law and Empirical Studies' (1990) 106 *LQR* 229, 231.

[26] Ibid, 242.

[27] A. Bainham, 'Divorce and the Lord Chancellor: Looking to the Future or Getting Back to Basics' (1994) 53 *CLJ* 253.

[28] M. Richards, 'Private Worlds and Public Intentions – The Role of the State at Divorce', ch. 1 in A. Bainham and D. Pearl (eds) *Frontiers of Family Law* (Chancery Law Publishing, 1993), p. 15.

ENCOURAGING COUPLES TO TAKE STEPS TO SAVE THEIR MARRIAGE

A second but distinct role for the state is to encourage couples to take steps to save their marriage while allowing them the option of divorce should such steps prove unsuccessful, in line with the Law Commission's 1966 conception of a 'good divorce law'. When the Family Law Act was passed in 1996, its opening provisions declared that the institution of marriage was to be supported and that couples were to be encouraged to take 'all practicable steps' to save a marriage that might have broken down.[29] Indeed, the hope that marriages could be saved played an important role in the reform process. In his foreword to the White Paper, Lord Mackay had expressed the hope that during the period of reflection and consideration 'some will change their minds about going through with divorce', and that the reforms would give 'the best opportunity of saving saveable marriages'.[30] As Dewar noted, the attempt to use divorce legislation as an opportunity to encourage couples to save their marriage represented:

> a significant departure from the previous model in that it seeks explicitly to use the divorce process itself as a means of affecting divorcing behaviour. Gone is the idea that the role of law is to facilitate and implement private decisions: it now seeks to influence the decisions themselves.[31]

But, aside from exhortations and expressions of hope, is there anything that the state can (or should) do to encourage couples to take steps to save their marriages?

One possible role for the state in this regard is to provide more public funding to bodies that provide counselling for couples experiencing difficulties in their relationship. Such funding may well save the state money in the long run, whether it staves off the breakdown of the relationship or simply makes the parties better able to co-operate when considering the practical implications of breakdown. And it has a long history: state funding for bodies such as the National Marriage Guidance Council has been provided since the late 1940s. However, it is important to recognize what such counselling entails. As Jane Lewis explains, the emphasis of such agencies soon shifted away from 'marriage saving' and guidance to 'non-directive counselling', with the result that 'since the 1960s counsellors have kept an open mind in the counselling room and, if appropriate, couples have been "enabled to part"'.[32]

Moreover, research by Walker questions what is meant by 'saving' a marriage. While a follow-up study of those who had attended information meetings in the late 1990s found that, two years on, '19 per cent of people who were seriously contemplating divorce had managed to save their marriage', interviews revealed

---

[29] Family Law Act 1996, s. 1.
[30] Lord Chancellor's Department, *Looking to the Future: Mediation and the Ground for Divorce* (HMSO, 1995), pp. iii–iv.
[31] J. Dewar, 'The Normal Chaos of Family Law' (1998) 61 *MLR* 467.
[32] J. Lewis, 'Marriage Saving Revisited' [1996] *Family Law* 423, p. 424.

that 'continuation of co-residence is not necessarily an indicator of the marriage being happy'.[33] Thus the success of such counselling cannot be gauged simply by the number of marriages 'saved', although the state is certainly performing a valuable role by providing financial support for organizations that try to help couples to understand and address their difficulties. As Walker also found:

> counselling did help some people to improve their relationship, enabled others to manage their relationship difficulties, assisted other people to bring their marriage to an end, and supported some through the process of getting on with a life beyond marriage.[34]

Even harsher verdicts have been delivered on the provisions, initially introduced in the 1969 legislation, requiring a solicitor to 'certify whether he has discussed with the petitioner the possibility of a reconciliation' and allowing the court to adjourn proceedings '[i]f at any stage of proceedings for divorce it appears to the court that there is a reasonable possibility of a reconciliation between the parties to the marriage'.[35] Eekelaar describes the 1969 Act as paying only 'lip service' to the possibility of reconciliation,[36] while in practice the provisions are regarded as a 'dead letter' or, more bluntly still, a 'sham'.[37] The fact that most divorce petitions are no longer heard in open court means that there is scant opportunity for judges to evaluate the possibility of reconciliation between the parties; more fundamentally, perhaps, by the time proceedings have reached this stage the possibilities of reconciliation are likely to be slim. Those who have reached the stage of petitioning for divorce are likely to have contemplated the possibility of reconciliation already, probably on numerous occasions.

A different twist on the debate is provided by the American scholar Elizabeth Scott, who suggests that 'easy termination policies can undermine the freedom of individuals to pursue their life goals'.[38] In other words, some couples may want the sense of security and commitment that comes from knowing that the marriage cannot be ended without good reason, and if this encourages them to invest more in their marriage then its quality, and stability, is likely to improve. Her suggestion – made against a background of no-fault divorce – is that couples should be able to choose an alternative marital regime in which divorce is more restricted, and that providing such a choice is rooted in modern ideas of autonomy and privacy. Thus, '[t]he state can play a role in promoting marital stability, but that

[33] J. Walker, *Picking Up the Pieces: Marriage and Divorce Two Years After Information Provision*, p. 33.
[34] Ibid, p. 103.
[35] Matrimonial Causes Act 1973, s. 6.
[36] Eekelaar, *Regulating Divorce*, p. 26.
[37] M. Freeman, 'Divorce without Legal Aid' [1976] 6 *Family Law* 255. The empirical evidence from J. Eekelaar, M. Maclean and S. Beinart, *Family Lawyers: The Divorce Work of Solicitors* (Hart Publishing, 2000), ch. 8, does however indicate that solicitors will counsel reflection if the client seems uncertain about whether to proceed with a divorce.
[38] E. Scott, 'Marital Commitment and the Legal Regulation of Divorce', in A. Dnes and R. Rowthorn (eds) *The Law and Economics of Marriage & Divorce* (Cambridge University Press, 2002), p. 35.

role should be to assist couples to achieve their goal of a lasting relationship, not to impose the values and preferences of one group in society on another'.[39]

While the background in England and Wales is different to that in the USA, the arguments that limitations on divorce play a role in underpinning commitment during the marriage is equally applicable. Scott makes a powerful argument that the commitment of marriage is fundamentally altered when it is as easy to exit as to enter. Yet, given the evidence that couples embarking on marriage rarely believe that they are likely to divorce – even when they are fully aware of the statistics on marital breakdown[40] – one might question whether individuals' investment in marriage is dependent upon them being aware that there are formal barriers to ending it.

It should also be borne in mind that divorce may have a positive role to play – in other words, there are some marriages that should not be saved. There are all too many appalling cases of domestic violence, and in such cases the law of divorce provides a lifeline for the victim. It is thus worth noting that, alongside the emphasis on supporting the institution of marriage, the opening provision of the Family Law Act 1996 also set out the general principle 'that any risk to one of the parties to a marriage, and to any children, of violence from the other party should, so far as reasonably practicable, be removed or diminished'.[41] In some cases this can only be achieved by ensuring that a divorce is granted as swiftly as possible.

As Walker has pointed out, 'if the divorce law cannot save marriages, it must concentrate on its other objectives, to dissolve marriages as painlessly and with as few negative consequences as possible'.[42] Can the state play any role in this context?

MINIMIZING THE BITTERNESS, HUMILIATION AND DISTRESS

At the time that the Law Commission suggested that a good divorce law should seek to ensure that marriages could be ended with the 'minimum bitterness, distress and humiliation', it was still necessary for at least the petitioner to attend court and give evidence in public about the other spouse's adultery, cruelty or desertion. The humiliating aspects of the process thus affected the legally inno-cent spouse more than the one deemed to be at fault. However, when the legal system was faced with an increase in the number of divorces in the wake of the 1969 reforms, a 'special procedure' that allowed divorces to be dealt with on the basis of written evidence, rather than the parties attending court, was introduced in 1973.[43] Initially this was limited to childless couples who were divorcing on

---

[39] Ibid.

[40] See L.A. Baker and R. E. Emery, 'When Every Relationship Is Above Average: Perceptions and Expectations of Divorce at the Time of Marriage' (1993) 17 *Law and Human Behavior* 439.

[41] Family Law Act 1996, s. 1(d).

[42] J. Walker, 'Divorce – Whose Fault? Is the Law Commission Getting It Right?' [1991] *Family Law* 234.

[43] See e.g. Freeman, 'Divorce without Legal Aid'; G. Davis and M. Murch, 'The Implications of the Special Procedure in Divorce' [1977] 7 *Family Law* 71.

the basis of two years' separation plus consent, but it was quickly extended to all undefended divorces and the 'special' procedure now accounts for all but a tiny proportion of divorces. Today, therefore, in 99 per cent of cases the forms are simply scrutinized by a district judge in private. The element of public 'humiliation' has therefore vanished in the vast majority of cases.[44]

Of course, the law can do little to address the feelings of *private* humiliation and distress that an individual may experience upon divorce – particularly where he or she has been rejected in favour of a new partner. As Richards has pointed out:

> for most couples the difficulty or ease of divorce lies not in negotiating the legal procedures but in the inevitably painful process of reaching a decision to end a relationship and the enormous emotional, social and economic upheavals that are involved in uncoupling.[45]

We shall return to the question of whether the law is doing as much as it might to minimize the bitterness, humiliation and distress of divorce when we consider the possibility of moving to a system of no-fault divorce, but before doing so there are two final aspects of the state's role that need to be considered.

ENCOURAGING COUPLES TO ACT RESPONSIBLY

In one of the most sophisticated evaluations of the Family Law Act 1996, Helen Reece argued that the legislation enshrined a 'post-liberal conception of autonomy', in that divorce was to be made available not on the basis of fault, nor yet that of simple individual choice, but rather after *thought*.[46] Central to the Act, as discussed below, was the provision of information, coupled with mandatory periods of delay for 'reflection and consideration'. Divorcing responsibly meant engaging with the process, absorbing the message that divorce was undesirable, reflecting on whether there was any prospect of reconciliation and learning moral lessons from the process.[47] Of course, as Reece went on to discuss, any such reflections would be private, and so beyond the ken of the law: it is one thing to stipulate a waiting period, it is quite another to ensure that it is used in the manner intended. Stephen Cretney rather teasingly suggested that at least some might spend the period for reflection and consideration 'in the far more pleasurable activity of conceiving – necessarily illegitimate – babies'.[48]

There was another element to 'divorcing responsibly' under the 1996 Act. Included in the 'general principles' underpinning the legislation was the idea that if a marriage was brought to an end, any issues should be 'dealt with in a manner designed to promote as good a continuing relationship between the parties and

---

44 On the feelings of petitioners under the old system, see e.g. E. Elston, J. Fuller and M. Murch, 'Judicial Hearings of Undefended Divorce Petitions' (1975) 38 *MLR* 609.
45 M. Richards, 'Divorce Numbers and Divorce Legislation' [1996] *Family Law* 151, 152.
46 H. Reece, *Divorcing Responsibly* (Hart Publishing, 2003), ch. 2.
47 Ibid, ch 4.
48 S. Cretney, 'The Divorce White Paper – Some Reflections' 1995] *Family Law* 302, 303.

any children affected as is possible in the circumstances'.[49] This is a principle that has assumed even more importance in the intervening years, and the way in which the law has sought to ensure that children have a continuing relationship with both parents was considered in detail in Chapter 4. For now it simply suffices to note once again that although the law can take steps to ensure the existence of a relationship between a non-resident parent and the child (at least where the former is eager for that relationship), it has little influence over the quality of that relationship.

PROVIDING A MECHANISM FOR THE LEGAL DISSOLUTION OF A MARRIAGE

All the debates about the role of the state have so far come to the rather pessimistic conclusion that there may not be much that the state *can* do today to ensure the stability of marriages or encourage couples to take steps to save their marriages. After all, the most important aspect of a divorce, from a legal point of view, is not that it allows the parties to separate (there are other legal mechanisms to ensure this) but that it allows them to remarry. The greater incidence and acceptability of cohabitation has meant that restricting divorce no longer acts as any real brake on the formation of new relationships.[50] And, as Stephen Cretney has noted, while:

> we have come to accept a hugely increased role for the state in our everyday lives…at the same time we are confronted by the increasing belief that the courts – the state's enforcement agencies – are often not appropriate bodies to deal with family relationships and these are not apt for submission to judicial monitoring.[51]

But, as cynics are fond of commenting, divorce was invented almost immediately after marriage, and as long as a formal procedure for entry into marriage exists, it will be necessary for the state to provide some formal mechanism for exit from marriage as well.

Just how formal it should be remains a matter of debate. When judicial divorce was first introduced, it was thought necessary that three High Court judges should preside over the new Court for Divorce and Matrimonial Causes, to emphasize the serious nature of the step being taken. Even when the task of granting divorces was delegated to more junior members of the judiciary, it was still suggested that they should wear the robes of their more senior brethren when so doing.

Today, by contrast, the emphasis is on making the procedure as simple as possible, driven by the need to save costs. As Katherine O'Donovan commented, the debate 'has shifted from idealised standards and a confident morality, to consumer-led opinions and efficiency as the standard of justice'.[52] When the Family Law Act

---

[49] Family Law Act, s. 1(1)(c)(ii).
[50] On these trends see further Probert, *The Legal Regulation of Cohabitation, 1600–2010: From Fornicators to Family*, in particular ch. 7.
[51] S. Cretney, 'Private Ordering and Divorce – How Far Can we Go?' [2003] *Family Law* 399, 400.
[52] K. O'Donovan, *Family Law Matters* (Pluto Press, 1993), p. 110.

was passed in 1996, one of the key principles expressed in its opening provision was that the process of divorce should be managed 'without costs being unreasonably incurred in connection with the procedures to be followed in bringing the marriage to an end'.[53] The recent Family Justice Review has proposed a new and potentially less costly procedure for bringing a marriage to an end:

> Where a person seeks a divorce they should go first to the information hub, where they will be able to access an online divorce portal. This would explain the process and possible grounds [sic] for divorce and give access to the necessary application forms.... The online form would then be submitted to a centralised court processing centre.... The application would be received by a court officer who would check that the application had been filled out correctly, acknowledge receipt and serve the application on the other party.... Where the ground for divorce is uncontested the court officer would issue both parties with a decree nisi.... As now, after six weeks the applicant would be able to apply for the decree to be made absolute.[54]

Given that 99 per cent of applications are already dealt with by post, is this any more than a sensible use of new technology? The crucial change lies in the shift of responsibility from a judge to a court officer. Under these proposals – which could, as the Review noted, potentially release 'perhaps 10,000 judicial hours'[55] – divorce would finally become an administrative, rather than judicial, decision. It also becomes a process shorn of any pretence of solemnity, which risks trivializing the loss that divorce represents for the couple.[56]

This step would raise questions about the need to retain any ground for divorce at all – a point to which we will return. But, since repeated allusion has been made to the Family Law Act 1996, some explanation is needed as to why its substantive provisions were never brought into force, as well as what lessons can be learned for the future from its failure.

Debate 2

What are the lessons to be learned from the failure of the reforms of divorce from the 1996 Act?

Here we need to start with a brief overview of the genesis, enactment and provisions of the ultimately ill-fated Family Law Act 1996. In the wake of the increase in divorce that had followed the enactment of the 1969 legislation, concern had grown that saveable marriages were being terminated by divorce. At the same

---

53 Family Law Act 1996, s. 1(1)(c)(iii).
54 Family Justice Review, *Family Justice Review: Final Report* (November 2011), p. 225.
55 Ibid, p. 180.
56 See further J. Herring, 'Divorce, Internet Hubs and Stephen Cretney', in R. Probert and C. Barton (eds), *Fifty Years in Family Law: Essays for Stephen Cretney* (Intersentia, 2012).

time, the law was criticized for its continued reliance on fault, and the way in which this had the potential to exacerbate hostilities between divorcing parties.

Thus in 1990, after a process of consultation, the Law Commission put forward proposals for reform that tried to address both sets of concerns.[57] It suggested that while irretrievable breakdown should remain the sole ground for divorce, it should be established by the passage of time rather than the need to demonstrate specific facts. After a statement of marital breakdown there was to be an eleven-month period of 'reflection and consideration', during which parties would be encouraged to use mediation and to finalize any issues relating to the division of assets or care of the children. This would eliminate allegations of fault from the process while ensuring that couples had adequate time to reflect on whether their marriage was really over before bringing about its legal termination.

The then Conservative government, after further consultation, accepted the idea of 'divorce after a period for the consideration of future arrangements and for reflection', although (as was evident from the titles of the 1993 consultation paper and 1995 report) it envisaged a greater role for mediation,[58] and took the view that a divorce should not be granted if the parties had not made arrangements for the future. It also suggested that information meetings should form part of the process. Thus the terms of the Bill that was introduced into Parliament had already departed in a number of respects from the Law Commission's recommendations. As tensions between the different aims that it was intended to fulfil emerged during the course of the debates in Parliament,[59] further changes were made and the final version of what became the Family Law Act 1996 bore little resemblance to the Commission's simple scheme.

In brief, the Act would first have required a person contemplating divorce to attend an 'information meeting', either alone or with his or her spouse. A minimum period of three months would then have to elapse before either could file a statement that the marriage had broken down, and only then would time start to run for the purposes of the prescribed period of reflection and consideration. The length of this was to vary according to the circumstances and wishes of the parties: a minimum of nine months for those without children; an automatic extension to 15 months for those with children under 16 (unless delay would be detrimental to the welfare of any child or there was an occupation order or non-molestation order in force); and a possible further extension to 21 months if either party applied (with the same exceptions). In addition, it was made compulsory for anyone in receipt of public funding to attend a meeting with a mediator in order to assess whether the case was suitable for mediation.[60]

---

[57] Law Commission, *The Ground for Divorce*, Law Com. No. 192 (HMSO, 1990).

[58] Lord Chancellor's Department, *Looking to the Future: Mediation and the Ground for Divorce* (HMSO, 1993); Lord Chancellor's Department, *Looking to the Future: Mediation and the Ground for Divorce* (1995). For comment see e.g. G. Davis, 'Divorce Reform – Peering Anxiously into the Future' [1995] *Family Law* 564.

[59] See e.g. E. Hasson, 'Setting a Standard or Reflecting Reality? The "Role" of Divorce Law and the Case of the Family Law Act 1996' (2003) 17 *International Journal of Law, Policy and the Family* 338.

[60] Family Law Act 1996, s. 29, continued as part of the Legal Services Commission Funding Code.

Implementation of the main provisions was delayed to allow pilot schemes to test the most effective way of delivering information meetings and the use of mediation. The results were not deemed to be satisfactory, and it was accordingly announced that the main provisions of the Act would not be implemented because they did 'not meet Government objectives of saving marriages or helping divorcing couples to resolve problems with a minimum of acrimony'.[61]

LESSONS TO BE LEARNED FROM THE FINAL FORM OF THE ACT

One lesson to be learned from the fate of the 1996 Act is that simple ideas do not always translate into straightforward legislation. The scheme proposed by the Law Commission was clear and simple; by contrast, the final version of the 1996 Act, after its passage through Parliament, was memorably described as 'a dog's breakfast'.[62] As Stephen Cretney has commented, this complexity was due in part to the role of pressure groups and 'the opportunity which the British law-making process gives to those concerned to promote a particular interest'.[63] Also evident was the desire to guide and influence those involved in the divorce process: the Advisory Board on Family Law later noted somewhat acerbically that 'the lesson for future legislation in this area is that Parliament should exercise greater restraint over detailed prescription and leave greater scope for the incorporation of experience gained during the implementation process'.[64]

LESSONS TO BE LEARNED FROM THE PILOT SCHEMES TESTING INFORMATION MEETINGS

Judging from the fact that 7,863 men and women voluntarily attended information meetings, one lesson to be learned from the pilot schemes is that there was a great unmet need for information about divorce. This, however, is much less likely to be true today than it was in the late 1990s, given the amount of information that is available on the internet. There are government sites that provide a step-by-step guide to the procedure,[65] as well as commercial operations promising quick and cheap divorces.[66]

The second practical lesson was the difficulty of devising a standard form for these meetings. Different ways of presenting information were tested – including individual face-to-face meetings, group presentations or CD-ROMs – but attendees, while valuing the information given, wanted it to be tailored to their specific needs and situation, in the way that it would be if they consulted a solicitor.

---

[61] Statement issued by Lord Chancellor's Department, 16 January 2001.

[62] See *The Lawyer*, 8 April 2001.

[63] S. Cretney, 'Breaking the Shackles of Culture and Religion in the Field of Divorce?' in Boele-Woelki (ed.) *Common Core and Better Law in European Family Law*, p. 11.

[64] Advisory Board on Family Law, *Fourth Annual Report, 2000/01*, para. 4.3.

[65] At, for example, www.direct.gov.uk, which provides sections on 'Divorce, Separation and Relationship Breakdown', 'Ending a Marriage Or Civil Partnership' and 'Getting a Divorce'.

[66] See sites such as www.fasttrack-divorce.co.uk and www.quickie-divorce.com/divorce.

The third and perhaps most crucial lesson was that most of those who attended the information meetings had already made the decision to end their marriage. Fifty-five per cent of those attending the meetings were already separated. This inevitably meant that encouragement of counselling and reconciliation as part of the divorce process would have a somewhat limited application.

The fourth and final lesson – and one unlikely to be welcomed by a government that is again placing considerable faith in mediation – is that individuals still want the expertise and advice that a lawyer can provide in this context. The proportion of those who went on to consult a solicitor – 73 per cent – was far higher than the 23 per cent who went on to try counselling or the 10 per cent who tried mediation. In fact, an unexpected finding of the pilot schemes was that individuals were *more* likely to go to a lawyer after attending an information meeting. Moreover, since attendance at the information meetings was voluntary, those attending may well have been those more willing to try other options before divorcing, and these results may therefore over-estimate the true proportion willing to contemplate mediation or counselling.

Helen Reece has noted that the reason given for non-implementation of the 1996 Act – the 'disappointing' results of the pilot schemes – was untenable, pointing out that since the purpose of providing information is to inform, the success of such schemes should be assessed by the extent to which attendees found the information useful rather than what they did after the meeting. The weight placed by the government on the subsequent resort to solicitors 'tells us that for the Government, the purpose of providing information was not to inform but to direct decision-making'.[67] This evaluation echoed that of the Advisory Board on Family Law, which noted that one lesson for policy-makers was to clarify what any pilot scheme was intended to achieve and how it should be evaluated.[68]

LESSONS TO BE LEARNED FROM THE RESEARCH INTO MEDIATION

One lesson that was swiftly learned was that many cases were simply not suitable for mediation. The most obvious of such cases was where one spouse was publicly funded and was therefore required to attend a meeting with a mediator as a condition of such funding, while the other spouse was not.[69] Only 30 per cent of those required to attend this 'intake meeting' went on to engage in the mediation process.[70] Changes were therefore implemented to remove the need for an intake meeting in such cases.

A second lesson from the research – reinforcing the lessons learned from the information meetings pilots – was that the role played by solicitors was valued. As Gwynn Davis noted, 'solicitors scored rather higher than mediators' in the

---

[67] Reece, *Divorcing Responsibly*, p. 169.

[68] Advisory Board on Family Law, *Fourth Annual Report, 2000/01*, para. 4.8.

[69] Advisory Board on Family Law, *Fourth Annual Report, 2000/01*, para. 2.23.

[70] G. Davis, *Monitoring Publicly Funded Mediation: Summary Report to the Legal Services Commission*, Annex D to the Advisory Board on Family Law's *Fourth Annual Report, 2000/01*, para. 7.1.

approval ratings.[71] Indeed, much research both before and since the Family Law Act has emphasized how the image of solicitors as fomenting conflict between their clients is misconceived. John Eekelaar, Mavis Maclean and Sarah Beinart noted the varied work of family law solicitors and the emphasis on negotiation and settlement rather than a day in court; indeed, they provided many examples of how the lawyer's role 'is not confined to merely giving legal advice [but] extends to providing reassurance and practical support for many clients during a particularly stressful period'.[72] To the extent that involving lawyers did mean negotiating at arm's length, Katherine Wright concluded that this might actually be a benefit, 'potential conflict over finances and property being able to be contained, leaving the parties and their children free to communicate over other family matters'.[73] Those individuals who feel particularly vulnerable on divorce may well feel that they need an advocate to represent their interests: Eekelaar, Maclean and Beinart go on to point out that while engaging in legal contests may be seen as troublesome and selfish, it may also be necessary to achieve justice in certain cases. They conclude:

> We therefore feel that it is important to reaffirm the importance of the principle that proper respect for individual rights requires recognising that people should have the opportunity to pursue them.[74]

In the wake of these findings a new scheme was devised to put lawyers 'at the centre of a more holistic service'.[75] The pilots of the Family Advice and Information Networks (FAINs), as they were initially termed, were premised on the basis that clients would be consulting solicitors on legal issues and that solicitors could take this opportunity to refer them on to mediation, counselling and other services. However, a pre-pilot indicated that solicitors were not necessarily aware of what other services were available, and the focus of the scheme shifted to the way in which the service provided by solicitors went beyond the mere provision of legal advice (as reflected in the change of name to Family Advice and Information Service, or FAInS). As Walker noted in the final evaluation of the project:

> Family solicitors have had to respond to human and emotional matters well beyond those that could be described as purely legal. If that is what solicitors were already doing prior to the introduction of FAInS, it is hardly surprising that we did not detect much change in solicitors' behaviour as a result of their adopting a FAInS approach: they were almost certainly

---

71 Ibid, para. 10.1.
72 Eekelaar, Maclean and Beinart, *Family Lawyers: The Divorce Work of Solicitors*, p. 184.
73 K. Wright, 'The Divorce Process: A View from the Other Side of the Desk' (2006) 18 *Child and Family Law Quarterly* 93, p. 111.
74 Eekelaar, Maclean and Beinart, *Family Lawyers: The Divorce Work of Solicitors*, p. 185.
75 J. Walker, P. McCarthy, S. Finch, M. Coombes, M. Richards and C. Bridge, with K. Laing, A. Melville, S. Kitchen, N. Wood, S. Raybould, C. Wren, S. Day-Sclater and P. Webber, *The Family Advice and Information Service: A Changing Role for Family Lawyers in England and Wales? Final Evaluation Report* (Newcastle Centre for Family Studies, 2007), p. 14.

offering what they would describe as 'a holistic service' already.[76]

A broader lesson was that 'mediation may be attractive only to a comparatively small proportion of the divorcing population, and that there are unlikely to be significant cost savings in respect of public funding'.[77] None of this is intended to detract from the valuable role that mediators can play in the divorce process. It is, rather, to emphasize that mediation works best when it is undertaken freely.

THE BROADER LESSONS TO BE LEARNED

The Advisory Board on Family Law, reflecting on the reasons for the non-implementation of the 1996 Act, highlighted the limitations of legislation in bringing about social change:

> The move from a confrontational culture implicit in a fault-based approach to divorce to a more consensual focus on the future … represents a profound shift in attitudes. The desirability of such a change is readily apparent to the professionals involved in the process…. However to move the world from where it is to where it should ideally be is an inescapably slow process, which changes in the law can at best only facilitate.[78]

This tension between life as it is, and life as we would like it to be, was a point made by many commentators.[79]

Another lesson to be learned from the failure of the Act is that the compromises struck during the legislative process may create contradictions in the final product. As Dewar noted – even before the decision had been made not to implement the legislation – the 1996 Act was seeking 'to pursue simultaneously the objectives of behaviour modification and of party control or informalisation' – the former being evident in the attempts to influence couples' decisions whether or not to divorce and the latter in the emphasis on mediation and private ordering – which created 'rich possibilities of potentially unworkable contradictions'.[80] In other words, the different objectives of the Act were incompatible with each other, and it could never have achieved them all.

However, one aspect of the Family Law Act emerged relatively unscathed from the critical commentary – the idea that we should move to a system that does not require one spouse to blame the other in order to obtain a divorce. And this brings us on to our third and final debate on the topic.

---

[76] Ibid, p. 254.
[77] Advisory Board on Family Law, *Fourth Annual Report, 2000/01*, para. 2.16.
[78] Ibid, para. 4.2.
[79] See e.g. J. Eekelaar, 'Family Law – Keeping us "On-message"' [1999] 11 *Child and Family Law Quarterly* 387; E. Hasson, 'Wedded to "Fault": The Legal Regulation of Divorce and Relationship Breakdown' (2006) *Legal Studies* 267, 269.
[80] Dewar, 'The Normal Chaos of Family Law'.

Debate 3

Do we have no-fault divorce? Should we?

It has been noted that since the 1969 reforms 'divorce has been available, effectively, on demand'.[81] But divorce 'on demand' is not quite the same as no-fault divorce, although some might argue that the ability to procure divorce on demand renders the remaining element of fault redundant. Thus in considering how far English law already has 'no-fault' divorce, it is important to think both about the law as it is expressed 'on the books' and the law as it operates in reality.

DIVORCE ON THE BASIS OF BREAKDOWN

At one level it could be said that the 1969 Act introduced the possibility of 'no-fault' divorce in making the breakdown of the marriage the sole ground on which a divorce could be obtained. Moreover, while three of the facts from which such breakdown could be inferred resembled the old matrimonial offences, at least two of the three were subtly rephrased in order to make the shift in emphasis clear.

In the case of adultery, for example, it was no longer the mere fact of adultery that entitled the petitioner to a divorce, but rather the fact that he or she also found it intolerable to live with the other spouse. (By contrast, the assumption underpinning the matrimonial offence had been that a right-thinking individual would and indeed should find it intolerable to live with an adulterous spouse.) However, this attempt to re-package adultery as a symptom of breakdown, rather than an offence against the other spouse, was somewhat undermined by the way in which the new provision was interpreted: the Court of Appeal held that there was no need for the petitioning spouse to show that he or she found it intolerable to live with the other on account of the latter's adultery.[82] Moreover, research into the experiences of clients suggests that adultery is, perhaps understandably, still associated with fault: as Katherine Wright noted, '[a]dultery appeared to generate very clear feelings amongst the clients regarding perceptions of guilt or innocence'.[83]

In a similar way, the old matrimonial offence of 'cruelty' – which could trace its history back to the ecclesiastical courts' practice of granting separations – was in 1969 rephrased as what is usually, and misleadingly, summarized as 'unreasonable behaviour'; misleadingly, because the emphasis of the provision is on the impact that the behaviour is having on the petitioning spouse. As Eekelaar has pointed out, it is not the respondent's behaviour that must be shown to be unreasonable, but rather the expectation that the petitioner will continue to live with such

---

[81] Richards, 'Private Worlds and Public Intentions – The Role of the State at Divorce', in Bainham and Pearl (eds) *Frontiers of Family Law*, p. 9.

[82] *Cleary v Cleary and Hutton* [1974] 1 WLR 73.

[83] Wright, 'The Divorce Process: A View From the Other Side of the Desk', 106.

behaviour. The courts will therefore consider the characteristics of *both* spouses in considering what is reasonable. In the terms of the question posed by the Court of Appeal in *O'Neill v O'Neill*:

> Would any right-thinking person come to the conclusion that this husband has behaved in such a way that his wife cannot reasonably be expected to live with him, taking into account the whole of the circumstances and the characters and personalities of the parties?[84]

The fact that a divorce may be granted even when the behaviour complained of is the result of mental or physical illness – and therefore not the fault of the spouse in question – illustrates the difference between the old matrimonial offence and the new emphasis on breakdown.[85]

Yet in practice spouses who are on the receiving end of a list of their 'unreasonable behaviour' may well feel that they are being blamed for the breakdown of the marriage. The novelist Marian Keyes captures this in *Sushi for Beginners*, depicting a couple in the throes of divorce. Although Lisa and Oliver have agreed that it is he who will petition, upon receiving the formal legal document '[e]ach instance cut through her like a knife'.[86] Katherine Wright, researching the reactions of clients to different stages of the divorce process, similarly found respondents who were upset by the details set out in the petition.[87]

Moreover, the third 'fact' inherited from the old law, that of desertion, was not reshaped to fit with the new concept of breakdown. While it only accounts for a tiny percentage of divorces, its existence on the statute books means that the law cannot be regarded as completely 'no-fault'. In addition, it is clear from cases such as *Buffery v Buffery*[88] that the breakdown of the relationship will not, by itself, be sufficient for the court to grant a divorce. In this case the husband and wife had simply grown apart and, after 20 years of marriage, no longer had anything in common. The Court of Appeal accepted that the marriage had broken down, but was unable to grant a decree since the wife had failed to establish any of the five facts.

DIVORCE ON THE BASIS OF SEPARATION

A second and more convincing way in which English law could be said to have 'no-fault' divorce is that two of the five grounds from which breakdown can be inferred do allow the possibility of a marriage being brought to an end without either spouse blaming the other. A court can find that a marriage has irretrievably broken down on the basis that the couple have lived apart for at least five

---

[84] [1975] 1 WLR 1118. See also *Ash v Ash* [1972] Fam 135 and *Birch v Birch* [1992] 1 FLR 564.
[85] See e.g. *Thurlow v Thurlow* [1976] Fam 32.
[86] Apart, Lisa muses, 'from the owning-too-many-clothes one. She presumed that by example five he'd run out of real complaints.' Marian Keyes, *Sushi for Beginners* (Michael Joseph, 2000), p. 473.
[87] Wright, 'The Divorce Process: A View From the Other Side of the Desk', 101.
[88] [1988] 2 FLR 365.

years, or, if the period of separation is shorter, that the respondent consents to the divorce being granted.

When the law came into force in 1971, many petitioners did indeed rely on five years' separation, with only 'behaviour' being more frequently cited in petitions. However, after the backlog of long-dead marriages was cleared, fewer divorces were based on either of these facts. The majority of petitions are now based on either adultery or behaviour. Thus, while it can be said that no-fault divorce is an option under the current system, it is not the prevailing option.

DIVORCE BY PRETENCE

But does the continued invocation of fault represent the real situation? A third way in which English law could be said to have 'no-fault' divorce involves looking behind the fact cited in the petition. It has been suggested that couples who wish to divorce more quickly than the required separation periods allow may collude – or, in less pejorative language, agree – to present a petition based on manufactured facts.[89] This could be termed 'divorce by pretence': both spouses are agreed that the marriage has broken down and that they want a divorce; neither is willing to wait two years, but either is willing for the other to put together a petition setting out a few facts that will not be unduly hurtful but which will be sufficient to convince a district judge sitting in his chambers.

The number of couples resorting to such subterfuge is, for obvious reasons, difficult to determine, although the available evidence suggests that only a minority do so. Walker found that only 38.3 per cent of respondents in her study wanted a divorce – and in some of these cases no doubt a new relationship was both the fact cited in the petition and the reason for the respondent's desire for a divorce.[90]

Such 'divorce by pretence' is now a possibility because of the way in which applications are processed. Given that the allegations made in the petition are not tested in court, and that extrinsic evidence is not available to them, judges have limited scope to judge the validity of the claims made. But this raises a darker possibility: the consensual nature of divorce by pretence may shade into divorce by repudiation, where one spouse has no means of countering the allegations made.

DIVORCE BY REPUDIATION

As the Law Commission noted in 1988, the incidents relied upon in a divorce petition might be exaggerated, one-sided or even untrue. But there is, in truth, little that a spouse faced with an exaggerated or even untrue petition can do. Public funding is not available to defend a divorce; nor, indeed, would there be much point in doing so: contesting a divorce is hardly likely to save the marriage. Moreover, given that fault no longer has any impact on the division of assets

---

[89] See e.g. G. Davis and M. Murch, *Grounds for Divorce* (Clarendon Press, 1988).
[90] Walker, *Picking Up the Pieces: Marriage and Divorce Two Years after Information Provision.*

or the future care of children – save in the most egregious cases – there is little point in wrangling about who was responsible for the breakdown of the marriage. The darker side of 'no-fault' divorce is therefore that one spouse may be divorced against his or her will without being what the law would regard as 'at fault' in any way, and even without the statutory time periods being satisfied.

Having considered whether English law can be said to have no-fault divorce – and concluded that the answer is 'up to a point' – let us turn to the question of whether it should move to a system in which fault plays no part at all.

THE CASE FOR REFORM

The criticisms of the current law made by the Law Commission back in 1990 have lost none of their force in the intervening years. It pointed out that the law is 'confusing and misleading' in its combination of the idea of irretrievable break-down and its stipulation that there are only five facts from which such breakdown can be inferred; in the lack of any necessary connection between the fact cited and the reasons for the breakdown of the relationship; and in the pretence 'that the court is conducting an inquiry into the facts of the matter, when in the vast majority of cases it can do no such thing'.[91] It also argued that it was 'discrimina-tory', in that the separation grounds assume the viability of setting up two house-holds (which 'can be extremely difficult to achieve without either substantial resources of one's own, or the co-operation of the other spouse at the outset') and 'unjust', in doing little to ensure 'the accurate allocation of blameworthiness for the breakdown of the marriage'.[92] And it asserted that a law 'which is arbitrary or unjust can exacerbate the feelings of bitterness, distress and humiliation so often experienced at the time of separation and divorce'.[93]

Hassan, interviewing key policy-makers, found that 'the vast majority of study participants strongly favoured the introduction of a no-fault framework'.[94] Their reasons for so doing varied: some pointed to the fact that it no longer acted as a deterrent to a divorce but rather provided a quicker way of obtaining one; others noted that it was irrelevant to the resolution of ancillary issues; while yet others saw it as contributing to the damaging nature of the divorce process. There is indeed some evidence to support the idea that the invocation of fault can exacer-bate hostility between the parties: research into the reactions of clients confirmed that 'where the evidence for irretrievable breakdown of the marriage had been supported by facts relating to the respondent's behaviour, this did appear, in some cases, to lead to an increase in hostility'.[95]

Forty years on from the coming into force of the Divorce Reform Act, there has been an increasing emphasis on the importance of agreement and co-operation

---

[91] Law Commission, *The Ground for Divorce*, p. 5.
[92] Ibid, p. 6.
[93] Ibid, p. 7.
[94] Hassan, 'Wedded to "Fault": The Legal Regulation of Divorce and Relationship Breakdown', 272.
[95] Wright, 'The Divorce Process: A View from the Other Side of the Desk', 101.

upon relationship breakdown, both in relation to the division of assets and in the context of the arrangements to be made for the children. Family lawyers are of course alert to the future problems that may be caused by antagonizing the other spouse: co-operation over future arrangements for the children and negotiations on the division of assets will be much more difficult. As one lawyer has put it:

> We lag behind many of our European neighbours and other countries in failing to reform the law to reflect changes in the way society thinks about divorce. Even though in practice the finding of fault has become little more than a paper exercise, by encouraging parties to look back at what has happened in the past rather than focusing on future arrangements and responsibilities, the process itself runs completely counter to the objectives set out so clearly in Part I of the Act.[96]

Readers may have spotted a possible contradiction between the willingness of commentators to argue that restricting divorce has no impact on behaviour and, at the same time, to accept that the need to cite fault may exacerbate the hostility of the divorce process. Is it really the case that the law cannot encourage people to be good, but only to behave worse than they would otherwise have done? The contradiction can, however, be reconciled if one thinks about when these different laws come into play. While there is a valid argument for saying that the law has a role to play in setting standards of behaviour, its influence will be limited if people are unaware of what those standards are. Media reportage inevitably focuses on the number of divorces and hardly gives the impression that there are any barriers to obtaining a divorce. The reality of the law – or rather its fictions – only has an impact on the parties once they have begun to engage in the process of divorce. At that point they may well find that its requirements exacerbate their feelings of bitterness, distress and humiliation.

THE CASE AGAINST REFORM

Yet it should also be recognized that while the removal of fault from the law may reduce one source of tensions, it is not capable of eliminating conflict altogether. As Joanne Brown and Shelley Day Sclater have pointed out, preoccupations with blame, responsibility and culpability 'reflect psychological coping strategies and will not easily be disposed of simply by virtue of a change in the law'.[97] The hope that the divorce process can become more civilized by removing opportunities for argument is just as idealistic, in its way, as Scott's assumption that couples debarred from divorcing will become good husbands and wives. The vast amount of litigation over ancillary matters rather suggests that frustrations will find an outlet somewhere.

---

[96] N. Shepherd, 'Ending the Blame Game: Getting No Fault Divorce Back on the Agenda' [2009] *Family Law* 122.
[97] J. Brown and S. Day Sclater, 'Divorce: a Psychodynamic Perspective', in S. Day Sclater and C. Piper (eds), *Undercurrents of Divorce* (Ashgate, 1999), p. 155.

In addition, the Centre for Social Justice argued in 2009 that there were positive reasons for retaining the current fault-based facts:

> First, we remain concerned about the signal which no-fault divorce, as the sole basis for divorce in a society, gives about marriage, marriage commitments and the ease of opportunity to leave a marriage…. Secondly, there are some cases in which the fault basis does indeed recognise the reality of the breakdown of the marriage…. Whilst undoubtedly in many marriage breakdowns there is fault on both sides, perhaps equal or unequal, there are also some marriage breakdowns where fault lies wholly or very substantially with one spouse alone.[98]

In support of this, it might be added that while many people are perhaps unaware that most divorces are still based on fault, any change to the law would no doubt lead to much publicity and debate about the signal being sent. And we can no doubt all think of examples from our personal experience where the breakdown of the marriage does seem to be very clearly the fault of one spouse alone. To deny the existence of fault would run counter to much of the literature on domestic violence, and would reinforce the feeling of many victims that the abuse is in some way *their* fault.

Equally, of course, there are many cases where there is fault on both sides, and encouraging each to accept this may be important for future negotiations.

POSSIBLE OPTIONS FOR REFORM

The organization Resolution has proposed a simplified version of the Family Law Act 1996, whereby the filing of a statement of marital breakdown would be followed by a waiting period of six months before either or both of the spouses could confirm that the marriage had broken down and a divorce could be granted.[99] The proposal is intriguingly similar to that advanced by Robert Owen in the early nineteenth century. Under his scheme, divorce 'could be declared any time after 12 months of marriage, but then the couple would have to wait six months before the divorce itself, in order to leave open every possibility of reconciliation'.[100] What was once a utopian socialist vision is thus now part of mainstream debate (although modern family lawyers are likely to be less sanguine than Owen about the impact on the children of divorcing couples[101]).

A slightly different scheme has been proposed by the Commission on European Family Law with a view to harmonizing family law across Europe. Working on

---

[98] Centre for Social Justice, *Every Family Matters: An In-Depth Review of Family Law in Britain* (2009), p. 70.
[99] Shepherd, 'Ending the Blame Game: Getting No Fault Divorce Back on the Agenda'.
[100] B. Taylor, *Eve and the New Jerusalem* (Virago, 1983), p. 53.
[101] 'As all the children of the new world will be trained and educated under the superintendence and care of the Society, the separation of the parents will not produce any change in the condition of the rising generation': R. Owen, *A Development of the Principles and Plans on Which to Establish Self-Supporting Home Colonies* (The Home Colonization Society, 1841), Appendix 4, p. 44.

the dual basis of 'common core' (where common ground could be identified) and 'better law' (where it could not), it advocated that the law should permit divorce by mutual consent without any period of separation, and that unilateral divorce should be available after a period of separation, save where delay would cause exceptional hardship to the petitioner.[102]

This proposal would signal an even greater change in allowing immediate divorce by mutual consent. English law was of course traditionally hostile to consent playing *any* role in the divorce process, categorizing it as 'collusion' and as such a bar to a divorce being granted. This policy was modified in the 1960s and reversed in 1969 when it was accepted that a marriage could be held to have broken down irretrievably if the parties had lived apart for two years and the respondent agreed to the divorce being granted. Indeed, it was hoped that this would become the most common basis for a divorce, and that the process would become more civilized as a result. That this has not materialized has been seen as a result of the length of separation required, not the lack of agreement among divorcing couples (although one might point out that it would be just as easy to pretend to have been living apart for two years as to fabricate details of the other's behaviour). There are also indications that there would be public support for such a reform. When the Law Commission carried out a public opinion survey in the late 1980s, 90 per cent of respondents felt that immediate divorce by mutual consent was acceptable.[103]

One counter-argument is that to allow divorce by mutual consent without any delay might facilitate the speedy termination of marriages entered into solely for immigration purposes that have served their function. Yet the current system does little to prevent such strategic use of the law. After all, couples who have conspired to flout the immigration laws are unlikely to be concerned about colluding to present a case for divorce and obtaining a speedy divorce on manufactured fault grounds. The special procedure offers little opportunity for the genuineness of the petitioner's claim to be tested.[104] Moreover, in such cases it is the marriage that is the sham, not the wish to divorce, and it would be preferable for the law to focus on preventing entry rather than denying exit.

NO-FAULT DIVORCE BY DEFAULT?

Most reforms to the basis for divorce have been swiftly followed by reforms to the procedure by which divorces are granted, as the legal system struggles to cope with the unexpected demand. As long ago as 1989 the American academic Mary Ann Glendon commented that judicial divorce had by virtue of the special procedure

---

[102] K. Boele-Woelki et al., *Principles of European Family Law Regarding Divorce and Maintenance Between Former Spouses* (Intersentia, 2004); for evaluation see J. Mair and E. Örücü (eds) *Juxtaposing Legal Systems and The Principles of European Family Law: Divorce and Maintenance* (Intersentia, 2007).

[103] Law Commission, *The Ground for Divorce*, Law Com. No. 192 (HMSO, 1990), para. 3.13.

[104] Although see *Bhaiji v Chauhan* [2003] 2 FLR 48 for an example of such detection.

'been converted unobtrusively into a summary administration procedure, a kind of registration divorce'.[105]

Given that the special procedure was still administered by judges, this was something of an overstatement, but current proposals for reform might finally make it a reality. As noted above, the Family Justice Review has proposed making undefended divorces subject to a purely administrative procedure. This change, should it take place, is likely to increase the pressure for no-fault divorce, since the transfer of responsibility from judges to administrators 'might well lead to concern about the evaluative decisions that need to be made, and thus pave the way for a simpler law of divorce as a result – or, conversely, expose the fact that the decisions being made are already administrative in nature and that the only effect of the current law is to require an extra box or two to be ticked'.[106]

CONCLUSION

As the group appointed by the Archbishop of Canterbury noted as long ago as 1966:

> Since theology lost its dominance legislators have been sceptical of meta-physics, regarding law as concerned only with the empirical – with what can be agreed independently of men's diverse religions and philosophies.[107]

What this chapter has shown is how little can be agreed on account of individuals' 'diverse religions and philosophies'. Disagreements about what the state can do are just as common as debates about what the state should do. Even those who agree that reform is necessary disagree on what form it should take: Nigel Shepherd, discussing the deliberations of Resolution's National Committee, rather wryly noted that 'there were almost as many views about how no fault divorce might work as there were National Committee representatives'.[108] Perhaps the last word should be left to Rheinstein, who has gently mocked the concerns of academic lawyers:

> The conservatives are made happy by the strictness of the law on the books. Those who are liberal to the extent of seeking freedom of remarriage for themselves are satisfied by the ease with which their desire is accommodated in practice…. The only ones who feel troubled are those occasional academics who view with alarm the hypocrisy of the system, the light-hearted way in which perjuries are committed and condoned, and who fear for the integrity of the law and the respect in which the law and its priests should be held by the public.[109]

---

[105] M. A. Glendon, *The Transformation of Family Law* (University of Chicago Press, 1989), p. 156; see also Freeman, 'Divorce without Legal Aid'.

[106] R. Probert, 'Marriage at the Crossroads in England and Wales', in M. Garrison and E. Scott (eds) *Marriage at a Crossroads* (2012, forthcoming).

[107] *Putting Asunder: A Divorce Law for Contemporary Society* (London: SPCK, 1966), para. 15.

[108] Shepherd, 'Ending the Blame Game: Getting No Fault Divorce Back on the Agenda'.

[109] M. Rheinstein, *Marriage Stability, Divorce and the Law* (University of Chicago Press, 1972), ch. 10.

Further Reading

S. Cretney, 'Private Ordering and Divorce – How Far Can We Go?' [2003] *Family Law* 399.

S. Cretney, 'Breaking the Shackles of Culture and Religion in the Field of Divorce?', in K. Boele-Woelki (ed.) *Common Core and Better Law in European Family Law* (Intersentia, 2005).

G. Davis and M. Murch, *Grounds for Divorce* (Clarendon Press, 1988).

S. Day Sclater and C. Piper (eds), *Undercurrents of Divorce* (Ashgate, 1999).

R. Deech, 'Divorce Law and Empirical Studies' (1990) 106 *LQR* 229.

A. Dnes and R. Rowthorn (eds), *The Law and Economics of Marriage & Divorce* (Cambridge University Press, 2002).

J. Eekelaar, M. Maclean and S. Beinart, *Family Lawyers: The Divorce Work of Solicitors* (Hart Publishing, 2000).

M. Freeman (ed.) *Divorce – Where Next?* (Dartmouth, 1996).

E. Hasson, 'Setting a Standard or Reflecting Reality? The "Role" of Divorce Law and the Case of the Family Law Act 1996' (2003) 17 *International Journal of Law, Policy and the Family* 338.

E. Hasson, 'Wedded to "Fault": The Legal Regulation of Divorce and Relationship Breakdown' (2006) *Legal Studies* 267.

J. Herring, 'Divorce, Internet Hubs and Stephen Cretney', in R. Probert and C. Barton (eds), *Fifty Years in Family Law: Essays for Stephen Cretney* (Intersentia, 2012).

J. Mair and E. Örücü (eds) *Juxtaposing Legal Systems and The Principles of European Family Law: Divorce and Maintenance* (Intersentia, 2007).

H. Reece, *Divorcing Responsibly* (Hart Publishing, 2003).

N. Shepherd, 'Ending the Blame Game: Getting No Fault Divorce Back on the Agenda' [2009] *Family Law* 122.

L. Stone, *Road to Divorce* (Oxford University Press, 1995).

J. Walker, *Picking up the Pieces: Marriage and Divorce Two Years After Information Provision* (DCA, 2004).

J. Walker et al., *The Family Advice and Information Service: A Changing Role for Family Lawyers in England and Wales? Final Evaluation Report* (Newcastle Centre for Family Studies, 2007).

S. Wolfram, 'Divorce in England 1700–1857' (1985) 5 *OJLS* 155.

K. Wright, 'The Divorce Process: A View from the Other Side of the Desk' (2006) 18 *Child and Family Law Quarterly* 93.

9

DOMESTIC VIOLENCE

INTRODUCTION

Traditionally the family has been seen as a site of safety in a frightening world: a haven where we lay down our masks and can be ourselves.[1] Domestic violence threatens such a vision of family life. The statistics on domestic violence indicate that for many families domestic violence is a central part of life. According to the British Crime Survey 2009/2010,[2] 29 per cent of women and 16 per cent of men have experienced some kind of domestic abuse since their sixteenth birthday, while 7 per cent of women and 4 per cent of men had experienced domestic abuse in the year prior to the questionnaire. Even these statistics may not capture the whole picture[3] as they do not cover domestic violence during childhood; moreover, some victims do not regard themselves as the victims of crime, even regarding violence as an aspect of 'normal life'.[4] Such disturbing statistics lead Anthony Giddens to claim:

> The home is, in fact, the most dangerous place in modern society. In statistical terms, a person of any age or of either sex is far more likely to be subject to physical attack in the home than on the street at night.[5]

Traditionally, non-intervention was seen as the dominant response to domestic violence.[6] The family, it was thought, could only flourish if the government kept out: it was the role of the state to regulate the streets and public places, but people's homes were not the government's business. Catharine Mackinnon characterized this 'ideology of privacy' as 'a right of men "to be let alone" to oppress

---

[1] C. Lasch, *Haven in a Heartless World* (Basic Books, 1997).

[2] Home Office, *Homicides, Firearm Offences and Intimate Violence 2009/10* (Home Office, 2011).

[3] House of Commons Home Affairs Select Committee, *Domestic Violence, Forced Marriage and 'Honour Based' Violence* (The Stationery Office, 2008).

[4] F. Kaganas and C. Piper, 'Domestic Violence and Divorce Mediation' (1994) 16 *Journal of Social Welfare and Family Law* 1265.

[5] A. Giddens, *Sociology* (Polity Press, 1989).

[6] E. Schneider, 'The Violence of Privacy', in M. Fineman and R. Myktiuk (eds) *The Public Nature of Private Violence* (Routledge, 1994).

women one at a time'.[7] As that comment reminds us, non-intervention cannot be regarded as the state taking a neutral role, because it means any abuse can continue unchecked.[8]

It is now generally accepted that domestic violence *is* the government's business. In 2010 the government produced a report on domestic violence,[9] which opened with the words of the Home Secretary, Theresa May:

> The ambition of this government is to end violence against women and girls. This is not a short-term task, but a long-term goal, the achievement of which will not be easy. But it is essential to make clear that however much progress we make in tackling this problem, no level of violence against women and girls is acceptable in modern Britain or anywhere else in the world...
>
> No woman should have to live in fear of violence. No man should think it acceptable to perpetrate violence against women. No child should grow up in a home where violence is an everyday occurrence. Working together we can make that a reality.[10]

Far from being a private matter, domestic violence is now regarded as an appropriate subject for concerted government action.

The legal response to domestic violence has been two-pronged. First, the criminal law is used to prosecute offences which are part of domestic violence. There is not a crime of domestic violence as such, but assaults which occur in the home can be prosecuted under the criminal law just like any other assaults. It is widely accepted that in the past it was treated as 'just a domestic' and rarely prosecuted. As we shall see there is now considerable effort to ensure that there is a prosecution where appropriate. Most police forces have dedicated officers who focus on ensuring that the force as a whole takes domestic violence seriously.

Second, there are civil remedies that a victim of violence can use to obtain a degree of protection. The two primary remedies are the non-molestation order[11] and the occupation order.[12] The non-molestation order is, as the name suggests, an order which prohibits the respondent from molesting the applicant. The order can specify the particular act which concerns the applicant, such as contacting by text or coming within a certain distance of the applicant's house.[13] Notably, following a reform of the law in the Domestic Violence Crime and Victims Act 2004, breach of a non-molestation order is a criminal offence.[14] An occupation order is a more drastic order and enables the court to regulate the occupation of

---

[7] C. Mackinnon, *Feminism Unmodified* (Harvard University Press, 1987), p. 32.

[8] M. Freeman, 'Legal Ideologies: Patriarchal Precedents and Domestic Violence' in M. Freeman (ed.) *The State, The Law and the Family* (Sweet & Maxwell, 1984).

[9] HM Government, *Call to End Violence Against Women and Girls* (The Stationery Office, 2010).

[10] Ibid, p. 3.

[11] Family Law Act 1996, s. 42.

[12] Ibid, ss. 33–41.

[13] Ibid, s. 42(6).

[14] Ibid, s. 42A.

the family home. This can include requiring one party to leave it or to restrict them to part of the house.

It is noticeable that in recent years there has been a drop in the number of applications for civil orders.[15] This might reflect the more aggressive approach that the police are taking towards domestic violence or reflect a belief that in some cases the civil orders are not effective. Restrictions on access to legal aid may also be a cause.

While those are the primary legal responses to domestic violence, the issue has significance throughout family law. It is a major issue in the law on contact disputes and child protection. It is also a significant aspect of the law on homelessness. Arguably it is significant in financial disputes,[16] although the courts have been slow to recognize that. In recognition of the multi-faceted nature of the legal response, specialist Domestic Violence Courts have been set up in many parts of the country. These seek to ensure there is an integrated legal response to cases of domestic violence.

In this chapter we shall consider three major debates over the nature of domestic violence. The first is over its definition. This debate is of significance for lawyers because the housing legislation uses the term domestic violence. But, more significantly, the debate over its definition helps us understand what are the wrongs at the heart of domestic violence and why, therefore, it is important for the law to address it. The second is over whether we should have a pro-prosecution policy in relation to domestic violence. This debate brings to the fore the balancing between the rights of the victim to protection and her rights to determine what legal intervention, if any, she wishes. The final debate concerns the circumstances in which it is appropriate for the law to constrain an individual's right to occupy the family home in the interests of the safety of other occupants. Have the courts been overly restrictive in their interpretation of the statutory provisions, making it unduly difficult to obtain an occupation order?

Debate

What is domestic violence?

The definition of domestic violence used by the government has varied over time. The one used currently is:

> Any incident of threatening behaviour, violence or abuse (psychological, physical, sexual, financial or emotional) between adults who are or have been intimate partners or family members, regardless of gender or sexuality.[17]

---

[15] M. Burton, 'The Civil Law Remedies for Domestic Violence: Why are Applications for Non-Molestation Orders Declining?' (2009) 31 *Journal of Social Welfare and Family Law* 109.

[16] S. Choudhry and J. Herring, *European Human Rights and Family Law* (Hart Publishing, 2010), ch. 10.

[17] Home Office, *Domestic Violence: A National Report* (Home Office, 2005), para. 10.

There are two things in particular to note about this definition. First, it is not restricted to physical attacks, but is widely drafted to include financial and emotional abuse. Ward LJ has acknowledged the breadth of the term, saying: 'Domestic violence, of course, is a term that covers a multitude of sins. Some of it is hideous, some of it is less serious.'[18] Secondly, the government's definition is not restricted to people living together, but includes violence between family members. This wide definition is not universally supported. As we shall see shortly, some commentators believe it is important to treat physical violence differently from abuse.

THE LAW

Rarely have the courts had to address the definition of domestic violence. Although much discussed by lawyers, sociologists and politicians, for lawyers the term has less relevance. This is because there is a wide range of responses to the issues: non-molestation orders; occupation orders; criminal law; housing law and the like. There is no reason why these different areas of law should only apply in the same set of cases. The law can define who can apply for a non-molestation orders ('associated persons') without having to define domestic violence. Similarly, it could take the view that the group of people who should be able to obtain emergency housing as a result of domestic violence need not be the same who are entitled to apply for a non-molestation order. Of course, the list of who can apply for the different orders provides some indication of who the law regards as being victims of domestic violence. Section 62 provides such a list which includes not only couples who are married, civil partners or cohabitants, but also those who are relatives (broadly defined to include even former cohabitant's half-niece[19]) and those who are in an intimate personal relationship with each other which is or was of a significant duration (which need not involve cohabitation or even sex).

The definition of domestic violence did, however, come before the Supreme Court in *Yemshaw v London Borough of Hounslow*.[20] The case concerned the duties a local housing authority owes towards homeless people under Part 7 of the Housing Act 1996. Under that legislation a person can be treated as homeless even though they have a house if it is no longer 'reasonable' for them to live there.[21] Section 177 of the Housing Act 1996 states:

(1) It is not reasonable for a person to continue to occupy accommodation if it is probable that this will lead to domestic violence or other violence against him, or against –
(a) a person who normally resides with him as a member of his family, or
(b) any other person who might reasonably be expected to reside with him.

---

18 *Re P (Children)* [2009] 1 FLR 1056, para. 12.
19 S. 63.
20 [2011] UKSC 3.
21 Housing Act 1996, s. 175(3).

(1A) For this purpose 'violence' means –
    (a) violence from another person; or
    (b) threats of violence from another person which are likely to be carried out;
       and violence is 'domestic violence' if it is from a person who is associated
       with the victim.

The issue before the court was whether Ms Yemshaw was a victim of domestic violence for the purposes of this provision. She claimed to be facing emotional, psychological and financial abuse at the hands of her husband. She was fearful of him, but accepted that he had never physically assaulted her. She applied to Hounslow Housing Authority for housing, having been forced from the matrimonial home by the abuse. The housing authority held that as there was no violent touching, nor probability of it, there was no domestic violence. That meant it was reasonable for her to occupy the matrimonial home and so the Authority was under no obligation to rehouse her. She sought a judicial review of the approach taken by the Authority to the definition of domestic violence. The court at first instance and the Court of Appeal[22] held that domestic violence was limited to physical assaults. It did not include threats of physical violence, or other forms of abusive behaviour that did not involve physical touching. The issue for the Supreme Court was whether that was the correct interpretation.

Lady Hale gave the leading judgment. She accepted that while physical force was an example of violence, it was not the only form of violence. She cited the Shorter Oxford English Dictionary in support of her approach. It includes the following within the definition of violence: 'strength or intensity of emotion; fervour, passion'.[23]

Lady Hale went through the understanding of violence in documents from a range of national and international bodies showing that they did not restrict the concept of domestic violence to physical attacks. She referred to reports from the United Nations Committee monitoring the Convention on the Elimination of all forms of Discrimination against Women; the General Assembly of the United Nations; the House of Commons Home Affairs Committee; the Law Commission; the National Inter-Agency Working Party; the Association of Chief Police Officers; the Crown Prosecution Service; the Ministry of Justice; the UK Border Agency; and even the London Borough of Hounslow itself.[24] The approach of the Court of Appeal appeared badly out of line with this broad range of opinion.

Perhaps the strongest legal argument against Lady Hale's approach was that, at the time of drafting the housing legislation, Parliament would have had an 'old-fashioned' understanding of domestic violence, which would have restricted it to physical touching. However, Lady Hale[25] argued that Parliament could not fix

---

[22] [2009] EWCA Civ 1543.
[23] [2011] UKSC 3 Para. 19.
[24] Ibid. Para. 24.
[25] Citing *Fitzpatrick v Sterling Housing Association Ltd* [2001] 1 AC 27, at 49.

the meaning of violence and an updated meaning was justified because it served the general broader statutory purpose. That purpose, she explained, was:

> to ensure that a person is not obliged to remain living in a home where she, her children or other members of her household are at risk of harm. A further purpose is that the victim of domestic violence has a real choice between remaining in her home and seeking protection from the criminal or civil law and leaving to begin a new life elsewhere.[26]

Lady Hale acknowledges that domestic violence includes kinds of behaviour which would generally be regarded as domestic violence, but not amount to physical assaults. She gives these examples: '[l]ocking a person (including a child) within the home, or depriving a person of food or of the money to buy food'.[27] Lady Hale held that domestic violence 'includes physical violence, threatening or intimidating behaviour and any other form of abuse which, directly or indirectly, may give rise to the risk of violence'.[28]

Significantly, however, the Supreme Court declined to define domestic violence. In the passages from Lady Hale's speech just quoted we can see what domestic violence includes, but they do not define its parameters. It is perhaps understandable that the Supreme Court was wary about providing too much of a 'bright line' definition where so much can depend on the impact of the behaviour on the particular victim and the nature of the particular relationship. What is notable about Lady Hale's approach, however, is that while she is clear that the phrase 'domestic violence' is not restricted to violent acts, she does keep the definition tied to violence, because non-violent behaviour is only expressly included if it gives rise to a 'risk of violence'.[29] As we shall see shortly, it is a matter of some debate whether domestic violence should be restricted to violent activities.

Of course, it was not for the Supreme Court to rule on the ultimate outcome of the applicant's case for housing. It was remitted to the Authority to approach the question again with the benefit of their Lordships' judgment. Lady Hale helpfully set out what she regarded as the key questions the Authority would need to address:

> Was this, in reality, simply a case of marriage breakdown in which the appellant was not genuinely in fear of her husband; or was it a classic case of domestic abuse, in which one spouse puts the other in fear through the constant denial of freedom and of money for essentials, through the denigration of her personality, such that she genuinely fears that he may take her children away from her however unrealistic this may appear to an objective outsider?[30]

---

[26] Para. 27.

[27] Para. 32.

[28] Para. 38.

[29] It would be wrong to suggest that Baroness Hale is saying that conduct that was not violent nor risked violence was not domestic violence. It just would not clearly be included within her definition.

[30] Para. 36.

Notably, this quotation implies that she is open to recognizing explicitly that behaviour which is not violent, nor likely to cause violence, but is denigrating of the victim's personality, can be domestic violence. Support for that might be found in Lord Rodger's speech, which agreed with Baroness Hale's approach, but emphasized the severity of psychological harm.[31]

Lord Rodger's speech, unlike Lady Hale's, insisted that the conduct must be deliberate if it is to fall within the definition of domestic violence. That is a potentially dangerous requirement. A man who beats his partner when he gets drunk should not escape a claim that he is engaging in domestic violence on the basis that his conduct is not deliberate. What Lord Rodger may have had in mind was more a case where there was simply a personality clash and no deliberately abusive conduct.

Lord Brown did not dissent, but was clearly less than happy with the proposed approach. He placed weight on the legislative history of the Housing Act which indicated that only physical violence would be included within the concept of domestic violence. As to the policy issue, he thought that the imperative to rehouse victims of physical violence was stronger than where there was no physical violence. He explains:

> Tempting though it is to accept this argument – one does not, after all, like to appear old-fashioned – I confess to doubts and hesitation here too. If one considers just why it is that domestic violence (indeed, violence generally), in contradistinction to all other circumstances, has been thought to justify a deeming provision – a provision, that is, which deems it unreasonable that a probable victim of future such violence should continue to occupy his or her present accommodation, the explanation would seem to me to lie partly in the obvious need for the speedy re-housing of those identified as being at risk of violence in order to safeguard their physical safety, and partly in the comparative ease with which this particular class of prospective victims can be identified. With the best will in the world I find it difficult to accept that there is quite the same obvious urgency in re-housing those subject to psychological abuse, let alone that it will be possible to identify this substantially wider class of prospective victims, however precisely they may be defined, with anything like the same ease.[32]

It may well be that in the future the courts will be required to be more precise about the definition of domestic violence. We now know for sure that acts which are not assaults can amount to domestic violence. We do not yet know where the outer boundaries of the definition are.

---

[31] Para. 46.
[32] Para. 38.

MADDEN DEMPSEY'S DEFINITION

A useful starting point for the debate is the writing of Michelle Madden Dempsey. She sets out what she regards as the three elements that make up domestic violence:

- Illegitimate violence
- Domesticity
- Sustaining wrongful structural inequality[33]

Let us explain these terms a little more. Violence is the use of physical force by one person against another. Whether domestic violence should be restricted to violent acts is something that will be discussed shortly. By domesticity Madden Dempsey means 'a relationship characterized by intimacy, familial ties, or a shared household'.[34] That is a fairly broad definition and others might wish to restrict it to only cases where the couple live together or where there is an intimate relationship. Again, more on that shortly. She explains wrongful structural inequalities in this way:

> Structural inequalities are functions of social structures, the 'sets of rules and principles that govern activities in the different domains of social life'. When social structures sustain or perpetuate the uneven distribution of social power, they can be understood as structural inequalities.[35]

It might be useful to separate out structural inequalities within the relationship and structural inequalities within the wider society, although these two are closely linked. Madden Dempsey's point is that domestic violence within the relationship can be a tool used to maintain the dominance of one party in the relationship, usually the man. Domestic violence may also, alongside a range of other social pressures, be seen as working against the interests of women generally. So, domestic violence is linked to inequalities within the relationship and within society more widely.

The benefit of Madden Dempsey's approach is that it enables a careful analysis of an incident in order to bring out the different wrongful elements of what is done. A man who is constantly demeaning to his wife might satisfy the domesticity and structural inequality elements, but would not exhibit violence. Where a woman is raped by a stranger in an alley-way that might exhibit elements of illegitimate violence and structural inequality, but would not have domesticity. A man who beat his partner regularly within an abusive relationship would exhibit characteristics of all three.

---

[33] She calls this 'patriarchy': M. Madden Dempsey, *Prosecuting Domestic Violence* (Oxford University Press, 2009).

[34] Madden Dempsey, *Prosecuting Domestic Violence*, p. 111.

[35] Ibid, p. 112.

For Madden Dempsey domestic violence in a 'strong sense' arises where all three elements are present, while domestic violence in a 'weak sense' only requires proof of domesticity and structural inequality in the relationship. But not everyone will agree with her on that. It is worth exploring how essential the elements should be in a definition of domestic violence.

IS VIOLENCE ESSENTIAL?

A ferocious debate among writers in the field centres on whether violence is an essential element of domestic violence. At first sight it seems obvious that violence should be at the heart of domestic violence. The clue is in the name. A man striking his wife is the archetypal image of domestic violence.

The argument against restricting domestic violence to violent acts could work as follows. The experiences of victims of domestic abuse show that it is best understood not as simply a series of violent or abusive acts, but rather as a programme of 'coercive control' (to use Evan Stake's[36] phrase) or 'patriarchal terrorism' or 'intimate terrorism' (to use Michael Johnson's[37] phrase). Michael Johnson distinguishes intimate terrorism from what he calls 'situational couple violence' or 'mutual violence'. Patriarchal terrorism is 'violence enacted in the service of taking general control over one's partner'.[38] By contrast, in the situational couple violence or mutual violence case, there is violence but there is no attempt to control the relationship. Rather, there is an incident of violence that arises in a moment of conflict during an intimate relationship which is not generally marked with inequality. It involves a lashing out in self-defence, anger or frustration, rather than an attempt to exercise control. As this distinction shows, it is not whether or not there is violence which matters, so much as whether there is a pattern of control.

The 'coercive control' model of domestic violence argues that understanding the impact of domestic abuse requires an appreciation of its controlling intent and impact. This can only be understood by looking at the relationship between the parties as a whole. Psychologist Mary Ann Dutton[39] explains:

> Abusive behaviour does not occur as a series of discrete events. Although a set of discrete abusive incidents can typically be identified within an abusive relationship, an understanding of the dynamic of power and control within an intimate relationship goes beyond these discrete incidents. To negate the impact of the time period between discrete episodes of serious violence – a time period during which the woman may never know when the next incident will occur, and may continue to live with on-going psychological abuse – is to fail to recognize what some battered woman experience as a continuing 'state of siege'.

---

[36] E. Stark, *Coercive Control* (Oxford University Press, 2007).

[37] M. Johnson, 'Apples and Oranges in Child Custody Disputes: Intimate Terrorism Vs. Situational Couple Violence' (2005) 2 *Journal of Child Custody* 43.

[38] Ibid.

[39] M. Dutton, 'Understanding Women's Response to Domestic Violence' (2003) 21 *Hofstra Law Review* 1191, 1204.

The whole aim of the behaviour of the abuser is to dominate the victim and diminish her sense of self-worth. This is done by restricting the victim's access to work; isolating her from friends; manipulating the victim emotionally; and using physical attacks. Physical violence, then, is but one tool used in the relationship to keep one party inferior.[40] From this perspective, it is intimidation, isolation and control which should be the hallmarks of domestic violence rather than the means to achieve them, which may, or may not, involve violence.[41]

Seeing domestic abuse as coercive control has important implications. It means that an assessment of whether there is domestic violence must look at the whole relationship between the parties, rather than assessing the severity of individual attacks. Incidents which might appear trivial can be seen as having a significant impact when appreciated in their broader context. Coercive control abuse may involve physical attacks, and often does, but the abuser may not need to resort to those. The abuser seeks to intimidate, to isolate and to control. These effects, rather than physical violence, should be seen as the hallmarks of domestic violence.

Helen Reece has argued against this view. She makes two points. The first is that the argument 'represents a remarkable downplaying of the physical'.[42] This raises the controversial issue of whether a physical injury should necessarily be regarded as more serious than an emotional or psychological one. Certainly the law has traditionally taken the view that physical injuries are the focus of the criminal law and emotional injuries are not covered.[43] There must be a concern that once the notion of domestic violence moves beyond physical actions it becomes far harder to define. What to one person is 'nagging' may be 'emotional abuse' to another. Restricting domestic violence to physical assaults will make it easier to prove in a particular case. The second is that there is a danger that a focus on 'coercive control' means that 'domestic violence is...defined as what men do to women, not what women do to men'.[44] However, that suggests women never seek to control men, which is not necessarily the case.

IS PATRIARCHY RELEVANT?

Madden Dempsey's emphasis on the role played by structural inequality highlights the way that domestic violence can involve and build on coercive control exercised by one party over the other in a myriad of ways.[45] It recognizes that physical violence is part of a relational inequality that enables, reinforces and is

---

[40] O. Rachmilovitz, 'Bringing Down the Bedroom Walls: Emphasizing Substance Over Form in Personalized Abuse' (2007) 14 *William and Mary Journal of Women & Law* 495.

[41] N. Jacobson and J. Gottman, *When Men Batter Women: New Insights into Ending Abusive Relationships* (Simon & Schuster, 2007).

[42] H. Reece, 'Feminist Anti-Violence Discourse as Regulation', in E. Jackson et al. (eds) *Regulating Autonomy: Sex, Reproduction and Families* (Hart Publishing, 2009), p.46.

[43] M. Burton, 'Commentary: *R v Dhaliwal*', in R. Hunter, C. McGlynn and E. Rackley (eds) *Feminist Judgements* (Hart Publishing, 2010).

[44] Reece, 'Feminist Anti-Violence Discourse as Regulation', in E. Jackson et al. (eds) *Regulating Autonomy: Sex, Reproduction and Families*, p.47.

[45] See also Stark, *Coercive Control*; Johnson, 'Apples and Oranges in Child Custody Disputes: Intimate Terrorism Vs. Situational Couple Violence'.

reinforced by the violence. However, as she explains, there is more to the notion of structural inequality than this. It reflects and is reinforced by sexist structures within society. She explains:

> the patriarchal character of individual relationships cannot subsist without those relationships being situated within a broader patriarchal social structure. Patriarchy is, by its nature, a social structure – and thus any particular instance of patriarchy takes its substance and meaning from that social context. If patriarchy were entirely eliminated from society, then patriarchy would not exist in domestic arrangements and thus domestic violence in its strong sense would not exist…. Moreover, if patriarchy were lessened in society generally then *ceteris paribus* patriarchy would be lessened in domestic relationship as well, thereby directly contributing to the project of ending domestic violence in its strong sense.[46]

Domestic violence not only impacts on the couple themselves. It reinforces and relies upon power exercised by men over women in society more generally. As the Parliamentary Assembly of the Council of Europe's Committee on Equal Opportunities for Women and Men[47] puts it:

> Violence against women is a question of power, of the need to dominate and control. This in turn is rooted in the organization of society, itself based on inequality between the sexes. The meaning of this violence is clear: it is an attempt to maintain the unequal relationship between men and women and to perpetuate the subordination of women.

One example of this point is that domestic violence commonly involves attempts by the male perpetrators of abuse to prevent their female partners entering the workplace or public arena. These are but imitations of broader attempts to restrict women's access to the workplace.

On such a view, domestic violence must be seen in its broader context as part of a set of power relationships which enable men to exercise control over women. The broader context is relevant for several reasons. It explains how domestic violence gets its power: the woman is disadvantaged not only by the abuse in the home, but by the lack of power outside the home. It may also explain why the law has been so reluctant and ineffective in its response to it. According to Currie:

> (A)lthough experienced and more easily recorded as an episode or event, violence is an extreme expression of one moment in on-going processes through which heterosexual relationships are 'negotiated'.[48]

---

[46] M. Madden Dempsey, 'What Counts as Domestic Violence?' (2006) 13 *William and Mary Journal of Women and the Law* 301; M. Madden Dempsey, 'Towards a Feminist State' (2007) 70 *MLR* 908, p. 938.

[47] Parliamentary Assembly, Council of Europe, Committee on Equal Opportunities for Women and Men, *Domestic Violence* (2002), para. 12.

[48] D. Currie, 'Violent Men Or Violent Women? Whose Definition Counts?' in R. Bergen (ed.) *Issues in Intimate Violence* (Sage, 1998).

Taking such a view sees the genders of the parties as crucial to an understanding of domestic violence. It is true that the vast majority of domestic violence takes place against women,[49] although many men are also subject to violence from their partners.[50] It has further been argued that most violence by women against men is quite different from violence by men against women because women's violence is often in self-defence rather than being an aspect of an ongoing oppressive relationship,[51] and that where men are the victims the injuries involved tend to be less serious.

Such an interpretation will be rejected by others. First, there will be some who reject entirely the feminist description of a society in which men exercise power over women in a myriad of ways. They might argue that although that may have been true to some extent in the past, it is no longer true, or at least not to any great extent. Nowadays men and women operate on a roughly equal playing field. Indeed it might be said that the standard feminist presentation risks portraying women as passive and powerless.[52] Perhaps the fact that so many victims of 'domestic violence' do not recognize themselves as victims is not down to the fact they are insufficiently 'enlightened', but rather are accurately reflecting their own experience.

Second, there will be some who are suspicious of an attempt to 'smuggle' a feminist agenda into the definition. Helen Reece warns that:

> when contemporary [Violence Against Women] researchers maintain that violence must be studied in the context of patriarchy, they are not exploring the connection between the concepts of violence and patriarchy but rather are collapsing the concepts of violence and patriarchy.[53]

The point here being that by including patriarchy as an element of domestic violence one is in its very definition excluding most (perhaps all) violence by woman against men as domestic violence.

WHY IS DOMESTICITY IMPORTANT?

A further and related issue is the question of what makes violence, *domestic* violence? And specifically what do we mean by domestic? As we noted earlier, in the past the fact an incident of violence was 'domestic' was seen as a reason for treating it as less serious than an incident of violence between strangers or in

---

[49] For a discussion of violence in lesbian relations see M. Eaton, 'Abuse By Any Other Name: Feminism, Difference and Intralesbian Violence', in Fine and Myktiuk (eds) *The Public Nature of Private Violence: The Discovery of Domestic Abuse*.

[50] C. Mirless-Black, *Home Office Research Study 191: Domestic Violence* (Home Office, 1999). Where men are abused the degree of violence tends to be less: E. Buzawa and C. Buzawa, *Domestic Violence: The Criminal Justice Response*, 3rd edn, (Sage, 2003).

[51] R. Dobash and R. Dobash, 'Women's Violence to Men in Intimate Relationships' (2004) 44 *British Journal of Criminology* 324, p. 343.

[52] D. Patai, *Heterophobia: Sexual Harassment and the Future of Feminism* (Rowman and Littlefield, 1998).

[53] At 44.

public. However, nowadays, domestic violence is considered as serious as other violence, or even more so.[54] Why?

One reason might be that in a case of domestic violence, the ability of the victim to escape from the violence is restricted. This makes it a particular kind of violence. Helen Reece, for example, has argued that isolation of the victims and inequality in the relationships are the factors which signify domestic violence.[55] These are experienced by those female partners suffering domestic violence as part of an ongoing unequal relationship, from which there is no easy exit, but not for those who are not living with their abusers. Reece[56] argues that the wide definition used by the government loses sight of the fact that domestic violence involves the abuse of unequal cohabiting relations. Her survey of the statistics indicates that violence between relatives outside the context of cohabitation is very rare, but she focuses on those under 60. Elder abuse is commonly committed by those not living with the victim.[57] This might suggest it is wrong to assume that domestic violence cannot be coercive if the parties are not living together.

Second, domestic violence can be seen as a breach of trust.[58] Intimate relationships involve becoming physically and emotionally vulnerable. The trust which is central to close relationships creates special obligations not to misuse that vulnerability. Intimate relationships rely on trust so that we can flourish.[59] If domestic abuse is unchecked this could inhibit trust and thereby undermine personal relationships.

Third, and linked to the second point, the harm in an abusive intimate relationship goes particularly deep. It is through our intimate relationships that we form our identity and sense of self.[60] Domestic abuse strikes at the very conception of the self for the victim. Domestic abuse, therefore, turns what should be a tool for self-affirmation and self-identification into a tool for alienation and self-betrayal. The victim almost becomes used as a tool against herself.[61] It is unsurprising that domestic abuse is linked to a broad range of mental health problems.[62]

These arguments seem to point to the 'domesticity' requirement being better understood as a point not so much about the location of the incident as about the nature of the relationship between the parties: in short, is it a close relationship? Whether the parties are living together or whether they are related is much less relevant than whether their relationship is of the kind where there is trust and vulnerability.

---

[54] J. Herring, 'No more Having and Holding: The Abolition of the Marital Rape Exemption', in S. Gilmore, J. Herring and R. Probert (eds), *Landmark Cases in Family Law* (Hart Publishing, 2011).

[55] H. Reece, 'The End of Domestic Violence' (2006) 69 *MLR* 770.

[56] Ibid.

[57] J. Herring, *Older People in Law and Society* (Oxford University Press, 2010), ch. 3.

[58] J. Herring, 'The Serious Wrong of Domestic Abuse and the Loss of Control Defence', in A. Reed and M. Bohlander (eds) *Loss of Control and Diminished Responsibility* (Ashgate, 2011).

[59] J. Eekelaar, *Family Law and Personal Life* (Oxford University Press, 2007), pp. 44–47.

[60] Rachmilovitz, 'Bringing Down the Bedroom Walls: Emphasizing Substance Over Form in Personalized Abuse'.

[61] L. Arnault, 'Cruelty, Horror, and the Will to Redemption' (2003) 18 *Hypatia* 155.

[62] C. Itzen, A. Taket and S. Barter-Godfrey, *Domestic and Sexual Violence and Abuse* (Routledge, 2010).

CONCLUSION

As is apparent, there is no 'right answer' to the definition of domestic violence. The difficulty is that providing too broad an answer can dilute the notion so that the central wrongs of domestic violence are not apparent. However, define it too broadly and the danger is that victims of serious domestic abuse are not covered. It may be the best we can do is isolate the features of domestic violence that make it a particular wrong and then accept that these will be present to a greater or lesser extent in different cases.

Debate 2

Should we have a pro-arrest policy?

The fact that a violent incident occurred in a home does not affect its position in the criminal law.[63] An assault in a home is as much an assault as if it took place in a pub; at least, that is the theory. However, the history of the criminal law in this area shows that the police and courts have often regarded domestic violence as a less serious offence than other crimes.[64] In recent years Parliament, the courts and police have shown an increasing awareness of the problems of molestation, domestic violence and stalking, but there is still much dissatisfaction with the operation of the criminal law.

There has been a long history of the criminal law failing to take domestic violence seriously. A 2004 report by Her Majesty's Inspectorate of Constabulary and Crown Prosecution Service Inspectorate admitted:

> Until relatively recently for example, dominant police culture depicted violence in the home as 'just another domestic' – a nuisance call to familiar addresses that rarely resulted in a satisfactory policing outcome. To the service's credit, tremendous efforts have been made in the last five years or so to overturn this stereotype and ensure that domestic violence is treated as a serious incident, requiring a high standard of professional investigation. The CPS too has raised the profile of domestic violence, issuing revised policy and guidance and setting up a network of Area domestic violence coordinators. But all too often, policies and rhetoric are not matched on the ground by effective responses and solid investigative practice.[65]

As these comments indicate, although at present much work is being done to change attitudes, for too long the attitudes of the police were that 'domestics'

---

[63] S. Cowan and J. Hodgson, 'Violence in the Family Context', in R. Probert (ed.) *Family Life and the Law* (Ashgate, 2007).

[64] C. Cammiss, 'The Management of Domestic Violence Cases in the Mode of Trial Hearing: Prosecutorial Control and Marginalising Victims' (2006) 46 *British Journal of Criminology* 704.

[65] HMIC/CPSI, *A Joint Inspection of the Investigation and Prosecution of Cases Involving Domestic Violence*, (HMIC, 2004).

were not proper crimes which warranted a thorough investigation.[66] Further, the prosecution authorities were reluctant to take such cases to court unless there was a very high chance of success. Indeed the report noted that there was a 50 per cent attrition rate at each stage of process (the police being called; the making by the police of a potential crime report; the making of a full crime report; the making of an arrest; the charging of the defendant; the conviction). As a result only a tiny percentage of domestic assaults were ending up in court. There is a determination within the police to change the attitudes of officers towards domestic violence and within the Crown Prosecution Service (CPS) to pursue, where appropriate, prosecutions for domestic violence.[67] The government has declared it as an aim of its domestic violence policy to increase arrest and prosecution rates.[68]

Early signs are of an improvement: the rate of 'successful' prosecutions for domestic violence has increased from 46 per cent in 2003 to 67 per cent in 2007–8.[69] However, it is not all good news. In one small study only 27 of the 54 respondents who had contacted the police after an incident of domestic violence said they would contact the police if there was another incident.[70] The Home Office has issued guidance[71] on arrest and domestic violence, suggesting that there should be an arrest in all cases of domestic violence unless there are exceptional circumstances. The guidance from the CPS takes this further:

> When considering the public interest stage, one of the factors that Crown Prosecutors should always take into account is: 'the consequences for the victim of the decision whether or not to prosecute, and any views expressed by the victim or the victim's family' (paragraph 5.12 of the Code for Crown Prosecutors). We always think very carefully about the interests of the victim when we decide where the public interest lies. But we prosecute cases on behalf of the public at large and not just based on the interests of any particular individual. There can be difficulties in striking this balance. The views and interests of the victim are important, but they cannot be the final word on the subject of a CPS prosecution. Any future risks to the victim, their children or any other potential victim have to be taken into consideration.[72]

The guidance makes it clear that even if the victim withdraws support for the prosecution it may be appropriate to proceed:

> If the victim withdraws support for the prosecution but we have enough evidence to proceed, we have to decide whether to prosecute. The safety of

---

[66] M. Hester and N. Westmarland, *Tackling Domestic Violence* (Home Office, 2005).

[67] HMIC/CPSI, *A Joint Inspection of the Investigation and Prosecution of Cases Involving Domestic Violence*.

[68] Home Office, *National Domestic Violence Delivery Plan* (Home Office, 2006).

[69] Burton, 'The Civil Law Remedies for Domestic Violence: Why Are Applications For Non-Molestation Orders Declining?'.

[70] A. Musgrove and N. Groves, 'The Domestic Violence, Crime and Victims Act 2004: Relevant or "Removed" Legislation?' (2007) 29 *Journal of Social Welfare and Family* Law 233. Among minoritized cultures only 4 of the 17 women who had reported incidents to the police said they would again.

[71] Home Office, *Domestic Violence: Break the Chain* (Home Office, 2000), ch. 2.

[72] Para 4.6.

the victim and any children and young person will be a key factor for us to consider at this stage. Some examples of what helps us to decide whether it is in the public interest to prosecute are:

- the seriousness of the offence;
- the victim's injuries – whether physical or psychological;
- if the defendant used a weapon;
- if the defendant made any threats before or after the attack;
- if the defendant planned the attack;
- if there are any children living in the household;
- if the offence was committed in the presence of, or near, a child or young person;
- the chances of the defendant offending again;
- breaches of any court orders;
- the continuing threat to the health and safety of the victim or anyone else who is, or may become, involved;
- the history of the relationship, particularly if there has been any violence in the past;
- the defendant's criminal history, particularly any previous violence; and
- any other factors that are relevant to the public interest.[73]

The focus of this debate will be whether there should be a formal pro-arrest and pro-prosecution policy. These policies typically require the police to arrest and prosecution to prosecute any case of domestic violence unless there are particularly good reasons not to. The CPS guidance issued is perhaps best seen as a weak pro-prosecution policy. Most significantly such policies do not accept the victim's wish that there be no prosecution as a good reason not to prosecute.

IN FAVOUR OF PRO-ARREST AND PROSECUTION POLICIES

Some argue for a firm pro-arrest and prosecution policy. That will mean that unless there were very good reasons not to do so there should be a prosecution. Generally, the wishes of the victim not to prosecute should be insufficient. There are a number of arguments that could be advanced in favour of following that approach:

1 Sending a message

The law needs to send a clear message that domestic violence is unacceptable and will be taken very seriously by the state.[74] It is important to remember that prosecutions are brought by the state and not the victim. That is why in criminal law all cases take the form R v Smith, where R stands for Regina, the Queen. It does not lie in the victim's hand to decide whether the state should prosecute. The

---

[73] Para. 6.3
[74] Madden Dempsey, *Prosecuting Domestic Violence* describes how effective prosecution of domestic violence can exhibit the characteristics of a feminist state.

state is entitled to take a strict line against domestic violence, even if the victim is ready to forgive the abuser. The cost to the state caused by domestic violence is considerable. The government states:

> Domestically, the cost of providing public services (including health, legal and social services) to victims and the lost economic output of women affected runs to billions of pounds. An indicative figure for the minimum and overlapping cost of violence against women and girls in the United Kingdom is estimated to be £36.7bn annually. However, this does not take into account the long-term emotional and mental health problems experienced by victims.[75]

As this shows, the argument that domestic violence only affects the victim can be firmly rejected. The state must see it as a social problem which needs to be addressed, whatever the views of the victim.

2 Protection of children

One particular reason why the state should take a strict line against domestic violence is in order to protect children. An issue of particular concern is the impact of domestic violence on children.[76] A UNICEF report suggests that up to 1 million children in the UK are living with domestic violence.[77] There is widespread acceptance that children raised in a household where there is domestic violence suffer in many ways.[78] This includes psychological disturbance and often a feeling that they are to blame for the violence.[79] The impact of the domestic violence on the mother may itself harm the child.[80] Indeed, one study of children who had suffered abuse showed that 39 per cent of them had come from families in which there was domestic violence.[81] Marianne Hester found that found that children were present in 55 per cent of cases of domestic violence.[82] Ten per cent of children who witnessed domestic violence witnessed their mother being sexually assaulted.[83]

3 Protection of the victim

If we do attach weight to the views of the victim in deciding whether or not to prosecute, all we will do is open up victims to further abuse as the defendant seeks

---

[75] HM Government, *Call to End Violence Against Women and Girls*.

[76] M. Hester, C. Pearson, and N. Harwin, *Making an Impact – Children and Domestic Violence: A Reader* (Jessica Kingsley, 2007).

[77] UNICEF, *Behind Closed Doors: The Impact of Domestic Violence on Children* (UNICEF, 2006).

[78] A. Mullender, *Tackling Domestic Violence: Providing Support For Children Who Have Witnessed Domestic Violence* (Home Office, 2005).

[79] Barnardo's, *Bitter Legacy* (Barnardo's, 2004).

[80] L. Radford and M. Hester, *Mothering through Domestic Violence* (Jessica Kingsley, 2006).

[81] E. Farmer and S. Pollock, *Substitute Care for Sexually Abused and Abusing Children* (John Wiley & Sons, 1998).

[82] M. Hester, *Who Does What to Whom? Gender and Domestic Violence Perpetrators* (Northern Rock, 2009).

[83] Mullender, *Tackling Domestic Violence: Providing Support For Children Who Have Witnessed Domestic Violence*.

to pressurize the victim into withdrawing her complaint. The *Opuz v Turkey*[84] case is a good example where, although the victim made complaints to the police, such complaints were then withdrawn in the face of threats from the defendant and the police then dropped the prosecutions. Tragically in that case ultimately the man went on to kill his mother-in-law and seriously injury his wife. The European Court of Human Rights was critical of the Turkish authorities for not investigating whether the withdrawal of the complaints had been genuine. A mandatory prosecution avoids threats and pressures being exerted on the victim in an attempt to persuade her to drop the prosecution.

4 Autonomy

It is too readily assumed that if the victim says she does not want an arrest or prosecution that that this represents her autonomous wish. There are good reasons to question this. First, as already mentioned, her withdrawal of the complaint may, in fact, be a result of fear or pressure, rather than a genuine wish. Second, as Choudhry and Herring argue, in most cases where the victim is withdrawing the complaint she has two contradictory wishes: she wants the violence to stop and she wants the relationship to continue. In fact domestic violence is one of the crimes with the highest recidivist rate. Not intervening by prosecution is very likely to mean the violence will continue. We must therefore decide which of the two wishes to respect: the wish for the violence stop or the wish not to prosecute. It is far from clear that the wish not to prosecute is the stronger desire.

5 Human rights

Shazia Choudhry and Jonathan Herring[85] argue that an analysis of the European Convention on Human Rights not only allows a pro-arrest and prosecution policy, but actually mandates it. Their argument is that domestic violence can interfere with rights under Article 2, 3 and 8. Article 2 will be invoked when there is a risk of death. Article 3 arises where there is torture or inhuman or degrading treatment. Of the three kinds of prohibited conduct torture is seen as worse than inhuman or degrading treatment.[86] The phrase 'inhuman treatment' in Article 3 includes actual bodily harm or intense physical or mental suffering.[87] 'Degrading treatment' includes conduct which humiliates or debases an individual; or shows a lack of respect for, or diminishes, human dignity. It also includes conduct which arouses feelings of fear, anguish or inferiority capable of breaking an individual's moral and physical resistance.[88] Serious domestic abuse, particularly of the kind which involves coercive control, would clearly fall within this category. Crucial to their argument is that Article 3 not only prohibits the state from inflicting torture

---

[84] Application no. 33401/02.
[85] S. Choudhry and J. Herring, 'Righting Domestic Violence', (2006) 20 *International Journal of Law, Policy and the Family* 95.
[86] *Ilascu and others v Moldova and Russia* [GC], no. 48787/99, 08 July 2004, para. 440.
[87] *Ireland v the United Kingdom* 2 EHRR 25.
[88] See *Price v the United Kingdom*, no. 33394/96, para 24–30 and *Valašinas v. Lithuania* [2001] ECHR 479.

or inhuman or degrading treatment on its citizens, but also requires the state to protect one citizen from torture or inhuman or degrading treatment at the hands of another.[89] A state will infringe an individual's right under Article 3 if it is aware that she or he is suffering the necessary degree of abuse at the hands of another and fails to take reasonable[90] or adequate[91] or effective[92] steps to protect that individual.[93] There is a particular obligation on the state to protect the Article 3 rights of vulnerable people.[94] The obligations imposed on the state include ensuring that there is an effective legal deterrent to protect victims from abuse; to ensure that there is proper legal investigation and prosecution of any infringement of the individual rights; and where necessary to intervene and remove a victim from a position where she or he is suffering conduct which is prohibited by Article 3.[95]

The right under Article 3 is an absolute one.[96] Unlike many of the other rights mentioned in the European Convention there are no circumstances in which it is permissible for the state to infringe this right. This makes it clear that the rights of another party cannot justify an infringement of someone's Article 3 rights. So, for example, it cannot be successfully argued that a family's right of privacy justifies non-intervention by the state if that non-intervention is an infringement of one family member's Article 3 rights. Indeed, and perhaps this is more controversial, it is suggested that other rights of the victim cannot justify an infringement of Article 3. In other words, in an elder abuse case the state cannot justify its failure to protect a victim's Article 3 rights by referring to that person's right to respect for private life.[97] Of course, the fact that the older person is 'happy' with the abuse might mean it falls short of amounting to inhuman or degrading treatment in borderline cases. However, where it does not, it is arguable that Article 3 is automatically engaged. Further, it should be emphasized that although Article 3 is drafted in absolute terms the state's obligations towards its citizens in respect of Article 3 are only to take *reasonable* measures to protect an individual's Article 3 rights.[98] Again, where a victim of abuse is 'happy' with being in the abusive relationship that may mean that it is not reasonable to expect the state to intervene. However, that might be very rare where the victim is facing inhuman or degrading treatment.

A similar approach is taken in relation to Article 8, which protects the right to respect for private life. Again not only must the state not show a lack of respect to a person's private and family life, there is a positive obligation to protect where

---

[89] *A v UK* [1998] 3 FCR 597, *E v UK* [2002] 3 FCR 700.
[90] *Z v UK* [2001] 2 FCR 246.
[91] *A v UK* [1998] 3 FCR 597, para. 24.
[92] *Z v UK* [2001] 2 FCR 246, para. 73.
[93] *E v UK* [2002] 3 FCR 700.
[94] A v UK [1998] 3 FCR 597, para. 20.
[95] *MC v Bulgaria* (2005) 40 EHRR 20. *Opuz v Turkey* [2009] ECHR 33401/02. See further, Choudhry and Herring, *European Human Rights and Family Law*, chs 8 and 9.
[96] M. Addo and N. Grief, 'Does Article 3 of the European Convention on Human Rights Enshrine Absolute Rights?' (1998) 9 *European Journal of International Law* 510.
[97] Although the state may argue that the victim's views make it unreasonable for the state to intervene.
[98] *E v UK* [2002] 3 FCR 700.

possible. Included within the right to respect for private life is the right to bodily integrity and this includes 'psychological integrity' and 'a right to personal development, and the right to establish and develop relationships with other human beings and the outside world'.[99]

So, how can these competing rights and interests under Article 8 be balanced? One approach[100] is that in a case of clashing rights the court should look at the values underpinning the right.[101] In the case of Article 8 the underlying value is that of autonomy: the right to pursue your vision of the 'good life'. A judge could then consider the extent to which the proposed order would constitute a blight on each of the party's opportunities to live the good life and make the order which causes the least blight. Applying that in this context, it could be argued that although removing the victim of domestic violence from an abusive partner will infringe the partner's autonomy, it will do so to a much lesser extent than leaving the victim to suffer abuse would do. But what if the victim does not want the assistance?

Here there is a balance between protecting the current autonomous wish of the victim, and the increase in autonomy they may experience if they were removed from the abuse. Many victims in these cases have conflicting wishes. They want to remain in the relationship, but they want the abuse to stop. In such a case it is not easy to determine what outcome will best promote their autonomy. It is not possible to respect these two conflicting desires. Where the abuse is low-level, the infringement of autonomy in remaining in the relationship will be limited. If, however, the relationship consists of persistent emotional abuse, the interference in her autonomy in removing her from the relationship may be less than allowing her to remain in it. It must be remembered that being in an abusive relationship is itself undermining of autonomy. Leaving a person to suffer abuse, who does not want to be protected, is not necessarily justified in the name of autonomy.

6   Discrimination

The human rights argument can be strengthened further by reference to Article 14. That is to argue that a failure to offer effective protection in domestic violence cases is a form of sex discrimination. Article 14 prohibits discrimination in the enjoyment of the rights. The article is not a 'stand- alone' right and can only apply when one of the other rights in the convention is interfered with. In this context the argument can be made that a failure to provide effective protection against domestic violence not only amounts to an interference in a person's Article 3 or 8 rights, it does so in a way which amounts to sex discrimination. The argument would be that failure to have an effective legal response to domestic violence has a

---

[99] Choudhry and Herring, 'Righting Domestic Violence'.

[100] J. Herring and R. Taylor, 'Relocating Relocation' (2006) 18 *Child and Family Law Quarterly* 517; S. Choudhry and H. Fenwick, 'Taking the Rights of Parents and Children Seriously: Confronting tdhe Welfare Principle and the Human Rights Act' (2005) 25 *OJLS* 453.

[101] This seeks to develop a dicta of Lord in *Re S (A Child) (Identification: Restrictions on Publication)* [2005] 1 AC 593 at para. 17, which refers to the need to consider the values underlying the right when considering cases of clashing rights.

particular impact on women and hence discriminates against them on the basis of sex. The rights under Article 14 are not absolute rights and interference with them can be justified if there are reasonable and objective grounds. However, the courts have been very reluctant to find a justification for discrimination.[102]

7 Privacy

It is commonly argued that if society focuses on the victim's privacy rather than the privacy of the 'home', intervention is justified. Schneider[103] maintains that the state needs to promote 'a more affirmative concept of privacy, one that encompasses liberty, equality, freedom of bodily integrity, autonomy and self-determination, which is important to women who have been battered'. Intervention in domestic violence can therefore be justified in order to promote the privacy of the victim. We need to look, as Schneider suggests, at the reasons why we want to respect people's privacy: we do so to enable them to develop as people and have an intimate sphere in which love and trust can grow.[104] Those very reasons militate in favour of intervening in a case of domestic violence. Properly understood, therefore, privacy is a reason in favour of intervention, not against it.

AGAINST PRO-ARREST AND PROSECUTION POLICIES

1 Disempowering the victim

An arrest or prosecution policy which placed no weight on the victim is in danger of disempowering the victim. It assumes that the victim does not know what is best for her. Having had her ability to make decisions for herself removed by her abuser, the state makes things worse by removing from her the decision as to how to respond to the incident.[105] Carolyn Hoyle and Andrew Saunders have argued in favour of the victim choice model (that the victim should be allowed to choose whether there is to be a prosecution):

> The pro-arrest approach assumes a position opposite to that of the victim choice model approach: that victims have little agency and that the police and policy makers know what is best for them. It seems presumptuous that policy makers or the feminist advocates who have influenced them can easily determine what is best for, or in the interests of, a diverse group of battered women. It is as much a conceit as the theory of deterrence in this area, which assumed that violent men are a homogeneous group.[106]

---

[102] For further discussion see Choudhry and Herring, *European Human Rights and Family Law*, ch. 2.

[103] Schneider, 'The Violence of Privacy', in Fineman and Myktiuk (eds) *The Public Nature of Private Violence*, p. 37.

[104] J. Eekelaar, *Family Law and Personal Life* (Oxford University Press, 2007), pp. 44–47.

[105] J. Dayton, 'The Silencing of A Woman's Choice: Mandatory Arrest and No Drop Prosecution Policies in Domestic Violence Cases' (2003) 9 *Cardozo Women's Law Journal* 281.

[106] C. Hoyle and A. Sanders, 'Police Responses to Domestic Violence: From Victim Choice to Victim Empowerment' (2000) 40 *British Journal of Criminology* 14, p.19.

2   Lessons from America

One well-known example of a mandatory arrest policy in practice was the Minneapolis Experiment in the United States. Although this policy led to a reduction in the rate of reported domestic violence, it was unclear whether this was because victims were not reporting violence because of the policy or whether the policy did indeed reduce the level of violence.[107] Further replica studies in Omaha, Nebraska and Charlotte, North Carolina failed to replicate the Minneapolis results.[108] There is therefore no conclusive evidence that such a policy would lead to a reduction in the level of violence.

3   Right to private life

Although human rights arguments have been adduced in favour of an aggressive pro-arrest and prosecution policy, in fact they point the other way. It should be remembered that Article 8 of the ECHR protects the important right to respect for private and family life. Prosecution for an incident between the parties against the victim's consent will interfere in their private life. This is a right which should not be lightly interfered with. Nothing can be a graver interference in family life than separating two people who wish to live together. We must question the public benefit of prosecuting a defendant if the victim is happy with the situation. Who has been harmed? The flaw in the pro-prosecution argument is to assume that the response to every crime is punishment by the state. One of the major movements in criminological studies in recent years has been the move towards restorative justice.[109] This has been defined thus: 'Restorative processes bring those harmed by crime or conflict, and those responsible for the harm, into communication, enabling everyone affected by a particular incident to play a part in repairing the harm and finding a positive way forward.'[110] Where the couple have resolved their differences and are keen to move on the state should not in a ham-fisted way seek to intervene.

4   Practical concerns

There is a further reason to be sceptical of using a strong pro-arrest and prosecution policy. That is because it is simply impractical. If the victim is unwilling to give evidence then what hope does the prosecution have? It is true that Louise Ellison,[111] for example, has done work on victimless prosecutions. She comes up with some sensible suggestions: relying on statements when the police arrive; use of photographic and sound recording; and providing evidence as to why a complainant might withdraw a complaint. However, it should be recalled that in a criminal trial the jury must be persuaded of the defendant's guilt beyond reason-

---

[107] Buzawa and Buzawa, *Domestic Violence: The Criminal Justice Response*.

[108] A further difficulty with the approach is that it might lead to both parties being arrested, if both have been violent. It might be possible to require arrest of the primary aggressor, but it will not always be obvious who this is.

[109] Cowan and Hodgson, 'Violence in the Family Context', in Probert (ed.) *Family Life and the Law*.

[110] Restorative Justice Council, *What is Restorative Justice* (Restorative Justice Council, 2010).

[111] L. Ellison, 'Prosecuting Domestic Violence Without Victim Participation' (2002) 65 *MLR* 834.

able doubt. Relying on statements and recordings might produce a reasonable case, but without the actual words of the victims it is unlikely there will be sufficient evidence.

CONCLUSION

This debate requires a careful balancing of the protection from violence and protection of a victim's autonomy. The issue is all the harder given that in some cases even if the law does intervene to protect the victim, the alternative options open to the victim may be marginally more attractive than the current one. To offer true protection from domestic violence requires not only an effective legal response but a broad range of social and economic provisions for those escaping from abuse.

Debate 3

Are occupation orders too hard to get?

THE LAW

The law on occupation orders is complex and can only be briefly summarized here. An occupation order can remove an abuser from the home and can give a right to the victim to enter or remain in the home. Although the occupation order is most commonly used in cases of domestic violence it can also be applied for if there is no violence, but simply a dispute over who should occupy the home.

The complexity of the law is revealed by the fact that there are five different sections which can be used by an applicant. It is only possible for an applicant to obtain an occupation order against a respondent with whom she is associated. If the applicant is married to the respondent or is entitled to occupy the property, she should use s. 33.[112] However, if the applicant is not entitled to occupy the property, the key question is whether the applicant is the ex-spouse of the respondent or is the cohabitant or former cohabitant of the respondent. If she is the ex-spouse, s. 35 is appropriate; if she is the cohabitant or ex-cohabitant then an application should be made under s. 36. In the very unlikely event that neither the applicant nor the respondent are entitled to occupy the dwelling-house then s. 37 or s. 38 should be used. It seems unlikely that a child could seek an occupation order against a parent as they would not fall within any of these categories.[113] We will not go into the precise differences between these sections, but they essentially relate to two areas. The first is the way that the 'significant harm test', which is discussed below, operates. In essence, satisfaction of the significant harm

---

[112] Except in the very unusual situation where neither spouse is entitled to occupy their home (e.g. if they are squatters).
[113] *Re Alwyn (Non-Molestation Proceedings By A Child)* [2010] 1 FLR 1363.

test means that an occupation order must be made if the claim is brought under section 33, while the same is not true under the other sections. The second is the length of time the order can last. Under section 33 an occupation order can last indefinitely, while under the other sections the length is restricted. As will be seen, applicants will much prefer to use section 33: the order is easier to obtain and will last longer.

As most cases will fall under section 33, we will explore that a little more. The starting point for the court's deliberations is the significant harm test set out in s. 33(7):

> If it appears to the court that the applicant or any relevant child is likely to suffer significant harm attributable to conduct of the respondent if an order under this section containing one or more of the provisions mentioned in subsection (3) is not made, the court shall make the order unless it appears to it that –
>
> (a) the respondent or any relevant child is likely to suffer significant harm if the order is made; and
> (b) the harm likely to be suffered by the respondent or child in that event is as great as, or greater than, the harm attributable to conduct of the respondent which is likely to be suffered by the applicant or child if the order is not made.

This requires the court to first consider what will happen if no order is made: is it likely that the applicant or relevant child will suffer significant harm attributable to the conduct of the respondent? If the answer to that question is 'no' then the significant harm test is not satisfied and the court does not have to make an order, although it may. If the answer to the first question is 'yes', then the court must consider what will happen if the court does make an order: will the respondent or any relevant child suffer significant harm? If the answer to that question is 'no', then the court must make an occupation order. If the answer is 'yes', then the court must consider whose risk of harm is greater. If it is the applicant's or child's then the court must make an order but if it is the respondent's or child's then the court does not have to make an order.

If the significant harm test is satisfied then the court must make an order. If, however, it is not, the court must then consider the general factors. These are set out in s. 33(6):

> (a) the housing needs and housing resources of each of the parties and of any relevant child;
> (b) the financial resources of each of the parties;
> (c) the likely effect of any order, or of any decision by the court not to exercise its powers…, on the health, safety or well-being of the parties and of any relevant child; and
> (d) the conduct of the parties in relation to each other and otherwise.

If the court does make an order there are a range of orders that can be made and these are set out in s. 33(3). They range from removing a party from their house, to regulating how the parties occupy the house.

So are occupation orders too difficult, or too easy to make? That is the question in this third debate. We mentioned earlier that there has been a notable drop in the number of occupation orders being made.[114] There was an 8 per cent drop in the number of these orders from 2008 to 2009. This is part of a general downward trend. In 2005 10, 042 occupation applications were made, but by 2009 this figure was 7,124. Even more dramatic was the decrease in the number of orders made from 8,805 in 2005 to 4,423 in 2009. That suggests the success rate of applications has fallen from 88 per cent to 62 per cent. This raises the issue of whether the law has made it too hard to apply for an occupation order, in particular, whether the courts have interpreted the statutory provisions too restrictively.

View 1: the courts have been too restrictive

One view is that the courts have been too restrictive in their interpretation of the requirements of an occupation order. The 1996 Family Law Act was passed with the avowed intent of clarifying the law and making sure that the courts were not unduly deterred from making an occupation order. What we have in fact seen is a series of decisions in which the courts have interpreted the provisions of the Family Law Act 1996 in a unduly narrow way. Those supporting this argument might make two general points.

First, the courts have read into the statute a need for there to be exceptional circumstances before an order can be made. Thorpe LJ in *Chalmers v Johns*[115] held that when considering the general factors a judge should bear in mind that an occupation order 'overrides proprietary rights and … is only justified in exceptional circumstances'.[116] In his view, occupation orders should be seen as 'draconian'.[117] In *G v G (Occupation Order: Conduct)* it was stressed that to succeed, an applicant must show that more tensions exist than normally surround a family during a divorce,[118] while in *Re Y (Children) (Occupation Order)*[119] Sedley LJ suggested occupation orders should be seen 'as a last resort in an intolerable situation'.[120] What is remarkable about these decisions is that had Parliament wished to include a statement that occupation order should only be made in exceptional circumstances it could easily have done so.

Second, the courts' interpretation of 'significant harm' also stresses the need for harm to be exceptional. In the statute, harm is simply defined as including 'ill-treatment and the impairment of health' (which includes emotional health).[121]

---

[114] Ministry of Justice, *Judicial and Court Statistics 2009* (Ministry of Justice, 2011).

[115] [1999] 1 FLR 392 CA.

[116] [1999] 1 FLR 392 at p. 397; see also *Re Y (Children) (Occupation Order)* [2000] 2 FCR 470, at p. 477.

[117] See also *G v G (Occupation Order: Conduct)* [2000] 2 FLR 36.

[118] [2000] 2 FLR 36.

[119] [2000] 2 FCR 470.

[120] [2000] 2 FCR 470, at 480.

[121] FLA 1996, s. 63(1).

For a child, harm also involves impairment of development. Ill-treatment 'includes forms of ill-treatment which are not physical and, in relation to a child, includes sexual abuse'.[122] There is no definition of 'significant' in the Family Law Act 1996. In *Chalmers v Johns* the Court of Appeal rejected an argument that a one-and-a-half-mile walk to school for the mother and child was 'significant harm'. The court stressed that in order to be 'significant harm' some kind of exceptional harm needed to be shown. Again there seems no reason why the word significant should be treated as 'exceptional'. The trouble with this interpretation is that statistics on domestic violence show that such violence is far from exceptional. Booth J, considering the phrase 'significant harm' in the context of child protection, suggested it was harm that was 'considerable, noteworthy or important'.[123] That seems a far more suitable approach than that provided by the Court of Appeal.

The following two cases could be used by those seeking to show that the courts have taken an inappropriately restrictive interpretation of the requirements for an occupation order. *B v B*[124] concerned a married couple who had two children living with them: the husband's son from his previous relationship and a baby of their own. The husband was extremely violent and so the wife and baby moved out to temporary accommodation, leaving the husband and his son in the flat. The court considered the significant harm test. They were satisfied that if they made no order the mother and baby who were living in unsatisfactory temporary accommodation would continue to suffer significant harm and that this was attributable to the husband's violence. However, the court also accepted that if the husband and his son were ordered from the flat they would suffer significant harm too. In particular, the local authority would not be under any obligation to house them and so the son's education and general welfare would suffer.[125] The court decided that the harm, especially to the son, if the order was made would be greater than the harm that the mother and baby would suffer if the order was not made, and so the significant harm test was not satisfied.

This decision shows a weakness with the significant harm test. It fails to place weight on who is the abuser. Here there were disadvantages for the wife and her baby if she had to move out and there were disadvantages for the husband and his son if he had to move out. What the court failed to pay attention to was that this was a case where the husband had been extremely violent to his spouse. His disadvantage should have been weighted considerably less than the wife's. Of course, the court placed much weight on the impact of any occupation order on the son. However, it must be asked: is it in a child's welfare to remain with a man who treated his wife with serious violence? We know that there is a strong correlation between domestic violence and child abuse.[126] We also know that children

---

[122] Ibid.
[123] *Humberside CC v B* [1993] 1 FLR 257, at 263.
[124] [1999] 2 FCR 251.
[125] A similar fear was expressed in *Re Y (Children) (Occupation Order)* [2000] 2 FCR 470.
[126] See the discussion in Choudhry and Herring, 'Righting Domestic Violence'.

who witnesses domestic violence are caused serious harm. The court here seems to have lost sight of the significance of domestic violence for children.

In *Re Y (Children) (Occupation Order)* a couple were divorcing. They had two children living with them, aged 16 and 13. Various allegations of violence had been made by the parties. The judge described the situation as 'a family divided among itself and at war with itself, with people taking sides'. The family was described as 'dysfunctional', with the 16-year-old being pregnant and the 13-year-old often staying at home rather than being at school. The relationship between the father and daughter was described as 'appalling' and involving frequent rows and fights.[127] The judge concluded: 'There is hatred in the house; there is dislike; there is constant fighting.'[128] Both spouses were seeking occupation orders against the other.

The Court of Appeal determined that no occupation order should be made. Ward LJ stated: 'the problem about the exercise of discretion under section 33(6) is that the eviction of a co-owner of a matrimonial home is a Draconian remedy. It is a last resort and is not an order lightly to be made.'[129] He held that the undertakings the parties had provided not to molest each other were adequate remedies.

It might be argued that the judgments in this case show a failure to understand the impact of domestic violence and arguments on children. There were ample signs that the 13-year-old was suffering significantly from the atmosphere in the house. There had been violence and fights. The suggestion of the two judges that an occupation order must be a 'last resort' is not found in the statute and fails to account for the impact of domestic violence.

View 2: the courts have struck the correct balance

A viewpoint more sympathetic to the approach taken by the courts might claim that supporters of the previous view have not adequately given weight to the harm caused by removing someone from their house. English law has long jealously guarded property rights. 'An Englishman's house is his castle' is an out-dated and not politically correct statement, but it captures an important truth. English law has historically been very wary of removing someone from their home. It is therefore entirely proper that the judges have described an occupation order as 'draconian' or a 'last resort', and correct too in saying that the word 'significant' in the significant harm test must be treated as showing that a highly unusual event has occurred. The courts' interpretation is justified as a major interference in property rights takes place when an occupation order is made.

The two cases to which supporters of View 1 might refer show that the courts are interpreting the provisions of the Family Law Act 1996 in too narrow a way. Take *B v B*.[130] It can be argued that criticisms of the Court are unfair. First, the Court of Appeal in *B v B* considered the position had the father not had the son

---

127 Para. 9.
128 Para. 10.
129 Para. 31.
130 [1999] 2 FCR 251.

with him. The Court suggested that in that case, even if the significant harm test might not have been satisfied,[131] the court would still be minded to make an order, when looking at the general factors and in particular bearing in mind his violence towards the wife. The Court went out of its way to state:

> The message of this case is emphatically *not* that fathers who treat their partners with domestic violence and cause them to leave the home can expect to remain in occupation of previously share accommodation.

It was the special factors connected with the son that played a crucial role. These comments show the Court was highly critical of the father's conduct and would normally expel someone who used serious violence from the home. Second, the Court of Appeal was quite right to put greatest weight on the interests of the children. Having concluded that the best way to promote the welfare of the children was to allow the son and father to remain in the home, and let the mother and baby be accommodated by the local authority, the Court had little option but to make no order.

The criticism of *Re Y (Children) (Occupation Order)*[132] is likewise unduly harsh. A key point in that decision was that the couple were divorcing and it would not be too long before a financial order was made on divorce, determining the long-term division of property. In such a case it would be foolish to pre-empt the court's decision by requiring one party or the other to move out under an occupation order unless there was a real need to. A further point about this case is that no one party was clearly more to blame than the other: each had been abusive to the other. There was no real basis on which the court could remove one party, as opposed to the other. The father, for example, was blind and alternative accommodation would be hard to find.

More recently, moreover, it would appear that the Court of Appeal has endorsed a broader approach to the making of occupation orders. In *Dolan v Corby* it held that 'exceptional circumstances can take many forms',[133] while in *Grubb v Grubb* an order was made removing the husband 'from what one might almost call his ancestral home'.[134] In neither case was there any issue of significant harm, and in the latter case the order was explicitly seen as a temporary solution to relationship breakdown. This suggests that even if the courts' approach to occupation orders has been unduly strict in the past, this is no longer the case, at least at the appellate level.

All in all, the courts have been right to ensure occupation orders do not become too freely available. The claim of a one-and-a-half-mile walk to school being significant harm in *Chalmers v John*[135] shows the dangers that otherwise

---

131 The husband being rendered homeless would be a greater harm than the mother and baby living in poor accommodation.

132 [2000] 2 FCR 470.

133 *Dolan v Corby* [2011] EWCA Civ 1664, [27].

134 [2009] EWCA Civ 976, [26].

135 [1999] 1 FLR 392 CA.

occupation orders will become used as tools in an ancillary relief battle, rather than being used for what they should be: protection from serious violence in cases where there is no alternative.

CONCLUSION

One point that may emerge from these debates is that there is an important difference between cases where an order is needed for a short-term protection and cases where the order is intended to regulate the long-term occupation of the home. While in the former, concerns over protection must be paramount, in the latter case it is important that property interests are given due protection. The danger is that in the name of immediate protection the courts may end up giving, in effect, long-term property rights; or that concern over the longer-term consequences may deter the court from giving immediate protection.[136]

The government has recently piloted so-called 'go orders', where the police can order a perpetrator of domestic abuse from his home for up to four weeks, even if a prosecution cannot be brought.[137] This short-term protection is important because it enables the victim to find alternative accommodation and reassess her options. The difficulty is that the emotional, psychological and financial consequences of domestic abuse can take much longer than four weeks to resolve.

Further Reading

M. Burton, *Legal Responses to Domestic Violence* (Routledge, 2008).

S. Choudhry, 'Mandatory Prosecution and Arrest as a Form of Compliance with Due Diligence Duties in Domestic Violence – The Gender Implications', in J. Wallbank, S. Choudhry and J. Herring (eds) *Rights, Gender and Family Law* (Routledge, 2010).

S. Choudhry and J. Herring, 'Righting Domestic Violence' (2006) 20 *International Journal of Law, Policy and the Family* 95.

M. Freeman, 'Legal Ideologies: Patriarchal Precedents and Domestic Violence', in M. Freeman (ed.) *The State, The Law and the Family* (Sweet & Maxwell, 1984).

L. Harne and J. Radford, *Tackling Domestic Violence: Theories, Policies and Practice* (Open University Press, 2008).

J. Herring, 'The Meaning of Domestic Violence' (2011) 33 *Journal of Social Welfare and Family Law* 297.

C. Hoyle and A. Sanders, 'Police Responses to Domestic Violence: From Victim Choice to Victim Empowerment', (2000) 40 *British Journal of Criminology* 14.

M. Madden Dempsey, 'What Counts as Domestic Violence? A Conceptual Analysis',12 *William and Mary Journal of Women and the Law* 301.

M. Madden Dempsey, (2009) *Prosecuting Domestic Violence* (Oxford University Press, 2009).

---

[136] See *G v G* [2009] EWCA Civ 976 where the court showed an acute awareness of this issue.
[137] BBC News Online, 'Domestic Violence Suspects Face Being Banned from Home', 25 November 2010.

H. Reece, 'The End of Domestic Violence' (2006) 69 *MLR* 770.

H. Reece, 'Feminist Anti-Violence Discourse as Regulation', in S. Day Sclater, F. Ebtehaj, E. Jackson and M. Richards (eds) *Regulating Autonomy: Sex, Reproduction and Families* (Hart Publishing, 2009).

E. Schneider, *Battered Women and Feminist Law Making* (Yale University Press, 2000).

E. Stark, *Coercive Control: How Men Entrap Women in Personal Life* (Oxford University Press, 2007).

10
DIVISION OF ASSETS ON SEPARATION

INTRODUCTION

One issue that has dominated the family law reports for the last decade is how the assets of divorcing couples should be divided. The short answer is simple: the assets should be divided in a fair way. However, that is only the start of the debate, because fairness is a hotly contested notion in this context. One answer might be that each couple should decide this for themselves, in line with the emphasis on private ordering. However, doing so may lead to a contract which is not regarded generally as fair. Before considering whether individuals should be able to specify and limit the extent of their obligations towards each other, we should consider why the law intervenes in this area at all.

Debate 1

What is the theoretical justification for division of assets on divorce?

On divorce or dissolution a court has authority to redistribute property and make orders for future payments. This is a remarkable power. Every last penny a person has can, in theory at least, be taken from them and handed over to someone else. Not only that, but every last penny they are to earn in the future can be taken too. Of course, a court would never order that. Fairness, as we shall see, is regarded as the touchstone for the law in this area. From one point of view, ordering the transfer of ownership of property from one person to another in the absence of a contract or a tort is a major invasion of property rights. The spouse who has earned the money and 'kept' their partner should not be required to pay any more. But from another point of view, it is just as outrageous that after a lengthy marriage the parties might be left with an enormous difference in their financial positions. The intertwining of lives, the sharing of resources, the whole range of non-financial contributions, also need to be taken into account. The financial

226

orders on divorce, far from being an intrusion into property rights are an essential aspect of fairness.

THE LAW

On divorce the court has a wide range of orders available. These include, among others, periodic payments orders (e.g. that one spouse pay the other a specified sum of money per week); lump sum orders (e.g. that one spouse transfer to the other a certain sum); transfer of property orders (e.g. that one spouse transfer to the other their share in the matrimonial home); and powers to order sale[1] (e.g. that the former matrimonial order be sold).[2]

The factors to be taken into account by a court in deciding which orders to make are listed in s. 25 of the Matrimonial Causes Act 1973 (MCA 1973). However, judges are given a very wide discretion in how to operate these factors: the Act deliberately has no one overall objective[3] and it is permissible for the court to take into account factors not listed in s. 25, if it believes them to be relevant.[4] The House of Lords has accepted that different judges may quite properly reach different conclusions as to what the most appropriate order is in a particular case.[5]

The courts have avoiding setting down firm rules which determine the amount that should be paid on divorce. They have even been rather tentative about stating general principles of application. The closest we have to a judicial interpretation of the overriding purpose of the jurisdiction is the suggestion of Lord Nicholls in the House of Lords in *White v White*[6] that fairness is the overriding purpose of the Act. But he accepted that this guidance was not of enormous assistance: as he put it, 'fairness, like beauty, lies in the eye of the beholder'.[7] In *Miller; McFarlane* he said:

> Fairness is an illusive concept. It is an instinctive response to a given set of facts. Ultimately it is grounded in social and moral values. These values or attitudes, can be stated. But they cannot be justified, or refuted, by any objective process of logical reasoning.[8]

Baroness Hale was perhaps more helpful in suggesting that 'The ultimate objective is to give each party an equal start on the road to independent living'.[9]

It would, however, be wrong to give the impression that every divorce is followed by a court carefully evaluating all the relevant factors and deciding what order to make. As a study by Barton and Bisset-Johnson showed, less than half of

---

[1] Matrimonial Causes Act 1973 (MCA 1973), s. 24A.
[2] MCA 1973, ss. 23, 24, 24A.
[3] [2001] AC 596, at 316–17.
[4] *Co v Co* [2004] EWHC 287 (Fam).
[5] *Piglowska v Piglowski* [1999] 2 FLR 763.
[6] [2000] 3 FCR 555.
[7] *White v White* [2000] 3 FCR 555 at para. 1.
[8] *Miller v Miller; McFarlane v McFarlane* [2006] UKHL 24, para. 4
[9] Para. 144.

cases involve the making of any ancillary relief orders.[10] One reason for this is that there may be very little to divide. One of us[11] well remembers giving a lecture on the law in this area to a group of practitioners and discussing the principle of division of assets. The first questioner at the end of the lecture was a legal aid solicitor who started his comments: 'Assets... I haven't had a case involving assets for years. All my cases involve debts.' Even if there are *some* assets, it is often the case that they are barely sufficient to cover the needs of the two new households. For the vast majority of cases it is the meeting of needs, nearly always inadequately, which is at the heart of the lawyers' task. Any other principle, arguably even fairness itself, goes out of the window when faced with substantial needs, especially those of the children, and negligible assets.

The academic and professional debate, however, focuses on cases involving the very wealthy. For it is really only in these cases that there is any argument to be had about what to do. The law is now dominated by two key decisions: *White v White*[12] and *Miller v Miller; McFarlane v McFarlane*.[13] Following these it has been generally accepted that in 'big-money' cases there are three key principles: needs, sharing and compensation. Meeting the needs is rarely difficult in such cases: more difficult is determining how the remaining assets should be divided.

Sharing

The principle of equality was introduced by the decision of the House of Lords in *White v White*.[14] That case broke new ground. The Whites had assets of roughly £4.5 million when their marriage ended after 33 years together. The trial judge awarded the wife £800,000 which he assessed as meeting the wife's reasonable needs for the rest of her life. That followed the approach which had been adopted by the courts up until this date. A wife (typically) would be restricted to claiming a sufficient amount to meet her needs, while the husband (typically) would be entitled to the remainder. This reflected an assumption that the money-maker was entitled to the money he had made and the non-money-maker needed to show why she should have some of 'his' money. In the House of Lords this approach was rejected. Lord Nicholls argued:

> there is one principle of universal application which can be stated with confidence. In seeking to achieve a fair outcome, there is no place for discrimination between husband and wife and their respective roles. Typically, a husband and wife share the activities of earning money, running their home and caring for their children. Traditionally, the husband earned the money, and the wife looked after the home and the children. This traditional division of labour is no longer the order of the day. Frequently

---

[10] C. Barton and A. Bissett-Johnson, 'The Declining Number of Ancillary Relief Orders' (2000) 30 *Family Law* 94.

[11] JH.

[12] [2000] 3 FCR 555.

[13] [2006] 1 FCR 213.

[14] [2000] 3 FCR 555.

both parents work. Sometimes it is the wife who is the money-earner, and the husband runs the home and cares for the children during the day. But whatever the division of labour chosen by the husband and wife, or forced upon them by circumstances, fairness requires that this should not prejudice or advantage either party.... If, in their different spheres, each contributed equally to the family, then in principle it matters not which of them earned the money and built up the assets. There should be no bias in favour of the money-earner and against the home-maker and the child-carer.[15]

From this approach came the following central principle:

As a general guide equality should only be departed from if, and to the extent that, there is good reason for doing so. The need to consider and articulate reasons for departing from equality would help the parties and the court to focus on the need to ensure the absence of discrimination. This is not to introduce a presumption of equal division under another guise.[16]

The House of Lords was clear that this principle could be departed from where fairness required it. On the facts of the case the wife ended up with less than half because of the significant contribution of the husband's family to the family business. In *Miller; McFarlane*[17] Lord Nicholls emphasized that the yardstick was intended as 'an aid, not a rule'. Indeed, given that in many cases there are insufficient assets to meet the needs of the couple and children, it will, in fact, be rare for there not be a good reason for departing from the starting point of equal division.

Indeed it is notable that among the reported cases it is in fact rare for an equal division to be made. Reasons for departing from an equal division can include the needs of the parties;[18] an extra-ordinary contribution by one of the parties;[19] the fact that a part of the couple's wealth was inherited or donated by one of their parents;[20] that property was brought into the marriage;[21] that property was acquired after the marriage had come to an end; obvious and gross misconduct;[22] or to ensure adequate compensation for losses caused by the marriage; or the way the parties organized their marriage.[23] Given the range of factors that might be taken into account, it is difficult to say more than that the principle of equality will be departed from when it is considered fair to do so.

15 Para. 24.
16 *White v White* [2000] 3 FCR 555, at para. 24.
17 [2006] UKHL 24 at para. 16.
18 *Lambert v Lambert* [2002] 3 FCR 673, at para. 39.
19 *Lambert v Lambert* [2002] 3 FCR 673, at para. 39; see also *Charman v Charman (No 4)* [2007] EWCA Civ 503.
20 *B v B (Ancillary Relief)* [2008] 1 FCR 613; *K v L* [2011] EWCA Civ 550, at para. 15.
21 *Miller; McFarlane* [2006] 2 FCR 213.
22 *K v L* [2010] EWCA Civ 125; *Clark v Clark* [1999] 2 FLR 248.
23 In *J v J* [2009] EWHC 2654.

A different way of approaching the issue might be to take the approach that only certain property is to be shared. The position the courts appear to have reached is that while in principle all of the assets that a couple have at the time of the hearing[24] is available for redistribution, especially where the needs of the parties require it,[25] in a 'big-money' case the court may take into account that some property is non-marital. Given that English law does not have any concept of matrimonial property, this raises further questions about what property should be excluded from equal division. In *Miller;McFarlane* there was a difference between the approach of Lord Nicholls and Baroness Hale. Lord Nicholls in *Miller* understood marital property[26] to be all assets acquired by either party during the marriage, save those acquired by gift or inheritance. He also included the matrimonial home as 'matrimonial property' even if one party had brought it into the marriage. Baroness Hale, by contrast, used a narrower understanding of 'marital assets', preferring the phrase 'family assets'. These were restricted to assets generated by the family: it could include the family home, family savings and income generated by a business organized by both parties. It would not include assets which were produced by the efforts of one party alone. She explained that in relation to non-family assets 'it simply cannot be demonstrated that the domestic contribution, important though it has been to the welfare of the family as a whole, has contributed to their acquisition'.[27] Subsequently, however, the Court of Appeal in *Charman v Charman* – evidently hoping to side-step the increasingly detailed and arid debates about exactly what property could be regarded as matrimonial – simply held that the sharing principle 'applies to all the parties' property but, to the extent that their property is non-matrimonial, there is likely to be a better reason for departure from equality'.[28] Moreover, as both Lord Nicholls and Baroness Hale agreed, in a case of a lengthy marriage whether the assets were family assets or marital assets becomes increasingly irrelevant. So the nature of the property has to be viewed in the context of the property as a whole. Even then, their lordships made it clear they were not setting down a hard and fast rule that in long marriages you divide all the property equally and in short marriages you divide only the marital property. In each case the judge must seek to determine what would be fair in the circumstances at hand.

Compensation

Intimate relationships often create disadvantage. Baroness Hale in *Miller v Miller* explained that the court is concerned with fairness not just at the time of divorce but also in the 'foreseeable (and on occasions more distant) future'.[29] The unfairness of future inequality is particularly acute when one spouse has given up a career

---

[24] *H v H (Financial Provision)* [2009] 2 FLR 795.
[25] *Charman v Charman* [2007] EWCA Civ 503.
[26] He used the phrase 'matrimonial property', but later cases have preferred the terminology 'marital property'.
[27] [2006] 2 FCR 213, at para. 151.
[28] *Charman v Charman* [2007] EWCA Civ 503, para. 66.
[29] [2006] 2 FCR 213, at para. 129.

to pursue child care, leaving the other to generate substantial earning potential.[30] For example, when Mr McFarlane was earning around £1 million per year, while Mrs McFarlane had, early in the marriage, given up her very promising career to care for the children, a simple division of the £3million assets would not ensure equality, even in the near future, nor would it provide adequate compensation for her lost career. The court therefore ordered that the husband pay the wife periodic payments to make up her lost career. Mrs McFarlane returned to the courts several years later (*McFarlane v McFarlane*[31]) and applied for an increase in maintenance payments for herself and the children. Charles J agreed, although he ordered that the payments would stop in 2015, that being the date when the husband was due to retire. Interestingly, the order was made in terms of a percentage of the husband's earnings, rather than a specific sum.

Balancing the principles

What is to be done if the application of the principles of sharing, compensation and needs suggest different sums? Some guidance was supplied in *Charman v Charman*.[32] The Court of Appeal explained that if an assessment of the wife's needs was greater than the sum that she would be granted on the basis of sharing or compensation then she should be awarded that sum. If, however, the sum she would be awarded on the basis of sharing was greater than her needs, she should be awarded the sharing sum. In short, she should receive the sharing amount or the needs amount, whichever was greater. As regards what to do if the sum to be awarded under the principle of compensation was greater than the award based on needs or sharing, the court decided that that question was best left to another case. Despite making these points, it was emphasized that, at the end of the day, the key issue is fairness. None of the Court of Appeal's comments was intended to set down a rule.[33]

Of course, to say that the governing principles underpinning the current law are needs, compensation and sharing does not tell us why this should be so: what are the justifications that underpin these ideas? It is now time to consider the different theories that could be used to justify the redistribution of property on divorce.[34]

To bring out the differences between the theories consider this couple.

Mary and Nigel, both aged 50, have been married for twenty-five years. When they married Nigel had £5million of an inheritance. This money has remained untouched during the marriage. Mary had a successful career as an accountant when they married but has given this up to care for their two children, who have now grown up and left home. Nigel's business has thrived during the marriage

---

[30] See also *Murphy v Murphy* [2009] EWCA Civ 1258.

[31] [2009] 2 FLR 1322.

[32] [2007] EWCA Civ 503, para. 73; *Miller; McFarlane* [2006] 2 FCR 213, paras 11–13.

[33] *C v C* [2007] EWHC 2033 (Fam).

[34] B. Fehlberg, '"With All My Worldly Goods i Thee Endow"? The Partnership Theme In Australian Matrimonial Property Law' (2005) 19 *International Journal of Law, Policy and the Family* 176.

and he has generated assets of £20 million and an income of £5 million per year. Mary has no assets to her name.

Contract: marriage for life
Explanation of the theory
One view is that on marriage or civil partnership the parties enter into a contract for life. The divorce is the breaking of that contract and as a result damages must be paid. The 'damages' therefore payable on divorce should seek to put the financially weaker spouse (typically the wife) in the position that she would have been in had she not got divorced. Indeed this was what courts were directed to do under the original version of the Matrimonial Causes Act. It also seems, in part, to have informed the approach of the courts to the 'big-money' cases prior to *White* . In *Dart v Dart*[35], for example, the wife was given a lump sum to cover her expected reasonable requirements for the rest of her life.

Application of the theory
In Mary's case we would need to calculate the sum of money which would ensure she could continue in the kind of lifestyle that she enjoyed during the marriage for the remainder of her life. Crudely this would involve a calculation of her life expectancy and of the cost of her lifestyle. We might estimate this as 30 years' life expectancy with an average income of £100,000 (£3 million) plus a house of a high standard (£1 million). Possible award: £4 million.

Difficulties with the theory
First, it might be questioned whether marriage does include a promise to remain with the other spouse forever, given the ready availability of divorce. True, the Church of England's Book of Common Prayer describes marriage as being 'til death us do part', but it is by no means clear that such a belief is shared by even a majority of those who get married, and in any case most do not marry in church. For many it may be more of a case of marrying "til unhappiness do us part'. Second, on divorce the law has abandoned trying to work out which party breached the contract, that is, who it is that has caused the marriage breakdown; if we are seeking an analogy with a breach of contract, proving which party is in breach would appear to be central. Not only is no real attempt made to ascertain who breached the contract, even where that is known only in exceptional cases will the court attach significance to it in making financial orders.[36]

Equal contribution to a partnership
Explanation of the theory
According to this view marriage should be regarded as analogous to a business partnership.[37] The husband and wife co-operate together as a couple as part of

---

[35] [1996] 2 FLR 286.

[36] *Miller v Miller; McFarlane v McFarlane* [2006] UKHL 24, para. 4.

[37] See the approach of the Canadian Supreme Court in *Moge v Moge* (1993) 99 DLR (4th) 456, discussed in A. Diduck and H. Orton, 'Equality and Support for Spouses' (1994) 57 *MLR* 681.

a joint economic enterprise.[38] It may be that one spouse is employed and the other works at home, but they work together for their mutual gain. Therefore, on divorce each spouse should be entitled to their share of the profits of their enterprise, normally argued to be half each.[39] There are echoes of this kind of argument in Lord Nicholls's reasoning in *Miller v Miller*:

> [in marriage] the parties commit themselves to sharing their lives. They live and work together. When their partnership ends each is entitled to an equal share of the assets of the partnership, unless there is a good reason to the contrary. Fairness requires no less.[40]

At first sight this argument might justify redistributing assets that have accumulated during the marriage, but would not apply to assets owned by the parties before entering the marriage or assets acquired after the marriage breakdown. However, the approach can be developed to extend to future assets. It is possible to argue that the partnership assets are not limited to tangible assets, but extend to the earning capacity of the parties.[41] So, if the wife had supported the husband at home while he developed his career, she could argue that he has only been able to reach the position where he is able to earn as much money as he does because of the help she provided. This argument would entitle the wife to a share in his future earnings, reflecting the increase in his earning potential acquired during the marriage.

Notably the equal contribution to a partnership approach does not imply that the husband is giving the wife some of 'his' money. Rather it is regarding the matrimonial assets as the produce of both of their labour and fit for division between them.[42] One of the more appealing aspects of this approach is the weight that it attaches to carrying out care giving obligations.[43] So often in the law care work is ignored and not valued.[44]

Application of the theory

Mary should be entitled to a half of the assets generated during the marriage (£25 million). Nigel would retain the £5million he brought into the marriage. Mary may even be able to claim a share in his future earnings in so far as they still can be regarded as fruits of the relationship (say £5 million, a third of his income for the next three years of marriage). Possible total award: £30 million.

---

[38] Fehlberg, '"With All My Worldly Goods i Thee Endow"? The Partnership Theme in Australian Matrimonial Property Law'.

[39] See C. Burch, 'Of Work, Family Wealth and Equality' (1983) 17 *Family Law Quarterly* 99.

[40] [2006] 2 FCR 213, at para. 16.

[41] This argument is developed in C. Frantz and H. Dagan, 'Properties of Marriage' (2004) 104 *Columbia Law Review* 75. It was rejected in *Q v Q* [2005] EWHC 402 (Fam) by Bennett J.

[42] L. Weitzman, (1985) *The Divorce Revolution* (The Free Press, 1985), p. 360.

[43] L. Glennon, 'The Limitations of Equality Discourses on the Contours of Intimate Obligations', in J. Wallbank, S. Choudhry and J. Herring (eds) *Rights, Gender and Family Law* (Routledge, 2010).

[44] J. Herring, 'Where Are the Carers in Healthcare Law and Ethics?' (2007) 27 *Legal Studies* 51.

Problems with the theory

The partnership model is based on an assumption that child care and home-making activities are equal in value, and that the two business partners are contributing jointly. There may be reasons to question that. First, while it is not difficult to imagine a case where, say, a wife's contribution to her husband is extensive and it seems not unreasonable to assume that we have a team (imagine an author whose work is substantially rewritten by his wife, although the books are published in his name), there is no reason why that should always be the case. The spouse's contribution may have been limited and may not have directly benefited him in his work. The husband might argue that he would have earned just the same salary if his wife had not made these contributions. Similarly it is hard to believe that all contributions through child care and home making are equal. Are not some people more gifted in these areas than others? Indeed the partnership approach suggests that the child care given by the wife of a multi-millionaire is equal to millions of pounds, while that provided by the wife of an impoverished academic may be worth just a few thousand. This seems particularly odd as the wife of the millionaire is likely to have a veritable bevy of assistants in terms of cleaners, nannies and the like. Stephen Cretney asks:

> is it far-fetched to suggest that there is something rather simplistic about the notion that home-making contributions are to be equated in terms of economic value with commercially motivated money-making activity? And even if right-thinking people now want to make such an equation, is this not essentially a matter of social judgment for decision by Parliament rather than the courts?[45]

The response to this argument may be twofold. One is to accept that while this is true in theory it is impossible to assess the genuine contributions of the parties. We assume the contributions of the parties are equal because it would be invidious and costly to undertake an assessment of the actual contributions to the marriage.[46] We assume, therefore, an equal contribution, while acknowledging there will be cases where that is untrue.

A second response is to say that during the marriage the couple have, we take it, regarded themselves as equal contributors. Would anyone really remain in a relationship if they regarded themselves as 'doing all the work'? The law should reflect their own attitudes to their marriage. The value of contributions of a non-financial nature is impossible to assess. How can you put a price on love? As we assume nowadays a marriage of equals, we can assume that the parties intended their contributions to be regarded as equal.

As mentioned above, the contribution claim may be made in relation not only to the assets generated directly during the marriage, but also to future earnings, if they can be said to relate to contributions during the marriage. Specifically

---

[45] S. Cretney, 'Black and White' (2001) 31 *Family Law* 3, p. 3.
[46] See e.g. *AR v AR* [2011] EWHC 2717 (Fam).

it might be claimed that a spouse's earning capacity was generated during the marriage. However, if one friend helps another to advance in her career we do not normally think this creates a financial obligation, even if the friend has been instrumental in obtaining the break.[47] In *H v H*[48] the argument was accepted by Charles J, but in restrictive terms. First, a wife would need to show that 'but for' her contribution the husband would not have been earning at the level he was. In many cases this will be hard to do. Second, even where the wife can demonstrate this she will not be entitled to substantial sums because the balance of his income will be earned by his work and endeavours after the marriage, rather than relating back to the help the wife offered during the marriage. In that case the wife was awarded one-third, one-sixth and one-twelfth of his income for the three years after the marriage. To some, however, such claims should not be entertained. On divorce the clean break principle supports each party being free to develop their own careers and earning potential, without fear that doing so will generate new claims. The claim that future earnings are the result of the earlier marriage must be, at best, speculation.

It can be argued that the approach takes insufficient account of the needs of the parties. Particularly where one spouse is raising the child, a one-half share may not adequately meet his or her needs.[49] In other words, dividing the assets equally might leave the spouse with the child effectively in a worse financial position (because of the extra expenses of child care) and not receiving a 'fair' share of the economic benefits of the joint enterprise.

Finally, as Lisa Glennon points out, from a care-friendly perspective the argument is not entirely without difficulty, because it only rewards care work performed within the context of marriage. Also, although it recognizes the value of care work during the relationship it does not recognize post-divorce care of children, unless this is integrated as a separate claim.[50] This is true, but it must be better to acknowledge it somewhere than nowhere and now that the value of care work is acknowledged in this context it should be acknowledged elsewhere.

Equality
Explanation of the theory
It might be argued that on the breakdown of the marriage the parties should be treated equally as a basic aspect of justice.[51] This argument may be put in a number of ways. Perhaps the most convincing is this: on marriage a couple throw all they have into their marriage – their skills, character, personalities, etc. It would be a most peculiar marriage for a spouse to 'hold back' one of their talents: 'I am good

---

[47] J. Eekelaar, *Family Life and Personal Life* (Oxford University Press, 2006), p. 48.
[48] [2008] 2 FCR 714.
[49] C. Forder, 'Might and Right in Matrimonial Property Law: a Comparative Study of England and the German Democratic Republic' (1987) 1 *International Journal of Law and the Family* 47.
[50] P. Laufer-Ukeles, 'Selective Recognition of Gender Difference in the Law: Revaluing the Caretaker Role' (2008) 31 *Harvard Journal of Law and Gender* 1.
[51] P. Parkinson, 'The Yardstick of Equality: Assessing Contributions in Australia and England' (2005) 19 *International Journal of Law, Policy and the Family* 163.

at cooking, but am not going to cook well because that was a skill I developed prior to the marriage'. So why should money be treated differently? Pre-acquired assets should be treated no differently from other things a person has acquired prior to the marriage.

One difficulty with this approach is that the term 'equality' is an ambiguous one. It could refer to equality of outcome or equality of opportunity.[52] Equality of outcome requires that at the point of divorce each spouse has the same total value of assets. Equality of opportunity is that 'each former spouse should be in an equal position to take advantage of the opportunities to enhance her or his economic position in the labour market'.[53] Neither in its most simple form is satisfactory. The difficulty with equality of outcome is that as the needs of the parties (particularly in relation to children) are different, giving the parties equal assets will not truly produce an equal standard of living. The problem with the equality of opportunity approach is that the prevailing social structures (such as discrimination against women in the employment market) are such that perfect equality of economic opportunity would be impossible to achieve.

A more sophisticated version of equality of income for both households post-divorce would have to take carefully into account the costs of raising children. This might involve ensuring that each household has the same amount of spare cash after the payment of essential expenses.[54] That would normally involve giving more money to the household that has children living in it.

Application of the theory

The approach would clearly advocate an equal division of all of the couple's assets (including the assets they entered the marriage with): here £27.5 million each. The approach might also advocate an attempt to ensure that the two households are roughly equal into the future. A sum of say, £10 million could ensure that at least for the next 4 years the households would have an equal income. Possible award: £37.5million.

Difficulties with the theory

It is not obvious that equality is, in and of itself, a sufficient reason for ordering redistribution. Ingleby[55] argues that our society is characterized by inequality, in part due to the abilities of families to pass on wealth to their members. Why is equality in the abstract important or significant? He sees equality as too easy a way of avoiding the difficult question of assessing the contributions of the parties to the marriage. In many areas of life we do not treat people as equals; in everything from sport to exams we seek to rank and assess people. While this is true, if an objective valuation of contributions cannot be made and if, as argued above, the

---

[52] J. Eekelaar, 'Equality and the Purpose of Maintenance' (1988) 15 *Journal of Law and Society* 188.
[53] Ibid, 192.
[54] Weitzman, *The Divorce Revolution*.
[55] R. Ingleby, 'Lambert and Lamposts: The End of Equality in Anglo-Australian Matrimonial Property Law?' (2005) 19 *International Journal of Law, Policy and the Family* 137, p. 147.

couple themselves regard their contributions as equal there is a case for treating them as equal.

The analogy with other talents and skills that parties bring to the marriage may be challenged. There is, it might be said, a difference between sharing your talent at cooking and sharing your wealth. At the end of the marriage the skilful cook leaves the marriage with their talent intact, yet that analogy is being used to justify a sharing of the wealth post-marriage. If the analogy were to work it would suggest that on divorce there should be a life-long obligation to share cooking skills. In response it might be said that this is to misunderstand the argument in support of the sharing principle. That is that on marriage a couple's whole lives become intermingled and interconnected so that the 'mine' and 'yours' breaks down into 'ours'. However, such a response depends on a particular view of marriage and that may not be how many couples see their marriage. Is it right to impose such a perspective on those who do not adopt it?

John Eekelaar[56] has suggested an approach which attaches greater significance to the length of time the parties have lived together than the current law does.[57] He explains that

> duration of marriage is an excellent proxy for measuring a number of factors which are important in achieving a 'fair' outcome. They include: the degree of commitment to a relationship; the value of contributions made to it, which is not susceptible of straight-forward economic measurement; and the extent of disadvantage undergone on separation.[58]

By contrast Thorpe LJ has stated: 'What a party has given to a marriage and what a party has lost on its failure cannot be measured by simply counting the days of its duration.'[59] John Eekelaar accepts that in a lengthy marriage equality is appropriate, but where one party brings to the marriage substantial assets the poorer party should be regarded as gradually earning an increasing share in the other's assets. He suggests 2.5 per cent per annum, leading to an equal share after 20 years. Similarly, in relation to maintenance he suggests that the person who has taken on the majority of child care receive an award of 30 per cent of the income at the time of separation after a 20-year marriage, scaled down if the marriage is shorter. Payments should last for 60 per cent of the duration of the marriage.[60]

Eekelaar's argument is strongest when considering an extreme case: if, for example, a woman marries a multi-millionaire but the marriage lasts only a few weeks she should not be entitled to half the fortune. But if the marriage has lasted 30 years she has a strong claim for an equal share of the fortune. Against

---

[56] J. Eekelaar, 'Asset Distribution On Divorce – The Durational Element' (2001) 117 *LQR* 24; Eekelaar, 'Asset Distribution on Divorce – Time and Property'.

[57] See also I. Ellman, 'Do Americans Play Football?' (2005) 19 *International Journal of Law, Policy and the Family* 257.

[58] J. Eekelaar, 'Property and Financial Settlement on Divorce – Sharing and Compensating', (2006) 36 *Family Law* 754, p.756.

[59] *Miller* [2005] EWCA Civ 984, para. 34.

[60] Eekelaar, 'Property and Financial Settlement on Divorce – Sharing and Compensating', 758.

his argument is the view that it does not accord with how most couples under-stand their marriage and finances. The notion of the child carer/homemaker day by day earning a little more in his or her spouse's assets is not one with which many couples would feel comfortable. Rebecca Bailey-Harris[61] also argues that it is discriminatory that domestic contributions earn equal value only over time, whereas financial ones do not. Eekelaar responds to this comment by suggesting that unlike financial contributions homemaking is linked to duration. His point is that one day's housework cannot be worth more or less than one day's house-work; however, the money-earner's value depends on the amount brought home. So homemaking can be valued only by time, but money-earning need not be.[62] 'Homemaking for one day, however brilliantly done, is in itself of relatively little value,' he says. This, at least if it includes child care (as it appears to), is debatable. Would that be true of the day of birth? Or the day the child was finally helped by the parent to understand multiplication? Or the day the teenager was given comfort for his first broken heart?

Compensation

Explanation of the theory

The extent of disadvantage for women on divorce is closely related to their employ-ment history during marriage.[63] There is convincing evidence that following divorce those who have undertaken primary care of the child (normally the wife) suffer significantly.[64] Child-care responsibilities mean that women are far more likely to have given up employment than men; where they are employed, moth-ers are more often in part-time low status, poorly paid jobs.[65] Even where they have returned to full-time employment, the time taken out to care for children will have set back their earning potential.[66] In part, ex-wives' financial hardships also reflect the wage differences which exist generally between men and women: average earnings of women are 22 per cent lower than those of men.[67] Women face discrimination in finding employment, both on the basis of their sex and on the basis that they are caring for children and therefore in a weaker position to advance their careers.[68] It is not just child care that can restrict a woman's ability to advance her career. Women still carry the primary duty of housework.[69] In one

---

[61] R. Bailey-Harris, 'Lambert v Lambert – Towards the Recognition of Marriage As A Partnership of Equals' (2003) 15 Child and Family Quarterly 417.

[62] The argument is less convincing if one includes as a contribution to the marriage not only money-earning, child care and household tasks, but also emotional support, love, etc.

[63] K. Funder, 'Women, Work and Post-Divorce Economic Self-Sufficiency: An Australian Perspective', in M. Meulders-Klein and J. Eekelaar (eds) Family, State and Individual Economic Security (Kluwer, 1988).

[64] S. Dex, K. Ward and H. Joshi, Changes in Women's Occupations and Occupational Mobility over 25 Years (Centre for Longitudinal Studies, 2006).

[65] J. Scott and S. Dex, 'Paid and Unpaid Work', in J. Miles and R. Probert (eds) Sharing Lives, Dividing Assets (Hart Publishing, 2009).

[66] Scott and Dex, 'Paid and Unpaid Work', in Miles and Probert (eds) Sharing Lives, Dividing Assets.

[67] National Statistics, Gender Pay Gap (ONS, 2009).

[68] M. Maclean, Surviving Divorce (Oxford University Press, 1991).

[69] J. Trew and S. Drobnic (eds), Dividing the Domestic (University of Stanford Press, 2010)

survey 48 per cent of men did no, or only a little, housework.[70] The impact of this becomes particularly apparent on retirement where women suffer particular poverty as compared with men.[71]

In response to facts such as these the compensation theory focuses on the disadvantages that the parties have suffered as a result of the marriage.[72] Typically this will involve one spouse giving up their career to care for the children. However, it could involve a spouse sacrificing career-developing opportunities, so that the other spouse can pursue their career. The compensation principle was accepted in *Miller v Miller*,[73] where Lord Nicholls explained:

> [Compensation] is aimed at redressing any significant prospective economic disparity between the parties arising from the way they conducted their marriage. For instance, the parties may have arranged their affairs in a way which has greatly advantaged the husband in terms of his earning capacity but left the wife severely handicapped so far as her own earning capacity is concerned. Then the wife suffers a double loss: a diminution in her earning capacity and the loss of a share in her husband's enhanced income.

Baroness Hale similarly referred to the need to compensate for 'relationship-generated disadvantage'.

The compensation argument can take two forms (assuming the wife to be the non-earning spouse):

(i) The wife should be compensated for loss of the earnings which she would have earned had she not been at home caring for the children or the home.
(ii) The wife should be paid in retrospect an appropriate wage for her work. A court could assess how much the house-cleaning and child-caring would have cost the husband had he employed people to do it. Mom.salary.com, an American website, suggests a 'stay at home mom' with three children is worth over $150,000 in a year in terms of the economic value of her work. Cheekily some have even suggested prostitution services should be added in too, which would increase the sum. Some who adopt this approach accept that, as the non-earning spouse herself benefits from the housework, the cost should be shared and so the husband should only pay for half of this work.

Whichever way the argument is put the claim shares a benefit with the 'equal contribution to the partnership' approach, in that it puts the wife's claim in terms of an entitlement, rather than classifying her as in especial need.[74] It is, however, notably different from the sharing approach, in that the claim is not tied to the

---

[70] C. Geist, 'Men and Women's Reports about Housework', in Trew and Drobnic (eds) *Dividing the Domestic*, which notes that in surveys men tend to exaggerate the amount of housework they do.
[71] For a useful discussion of compensation claims see A. Murray, 'Guidelines on Compensation' [2008] *Family Law* 756.
[72] In *VB v JP* [2008] 2 FCR 682 the wife refused to take up a promotion because the husband did not want to move. This was regarded as an economic disadvantage due to the marriage.
[73] [2006] 2 FCR 213, at para. 13.
[74] J. Eekelaar, 'Back to Basics and Forward into the Unknown' [2001] 31 *Family Law* 30.

gains made by the husband. So the argument is likely to produce a lower award in cases where the husband has been especially economically productive, but a higher award where he has not.

Application of the theory

This depends on which version of the compensation approach is taken. If we focus on the lost earnings from her career, we would need to ascertain what salary Mary has lost as a result of the marriage. This is, of course, to some extent speculative. We are told that Mary had a successful career as an accountant. Let us say that she would have earned on average £100,000 a year for the 25 years of the marriage; that would produce a figure of £2.5 million. She might also claim that given her age she is unlikely to be able to find highly paid work and so the disadvantage will continue for the next 15 years (until retirement age). That will produce a further £1.5 million. Possible total award: £5 million.

If the retrospective payment is made here then an attempt would be needed to ascertain the market value of her work during the marriage. Let us say this is £100,000 and that would produce £2.5 million total for the twenty-five years of marriage. Possible total award: £2.5 million.

Difficulties with the theory

There may be a questioning of whether there is a 'sacrifice' for which compensation is necessary. The spouse who gives up their career to raise children may have chosen the joys of child-raising over the world of work, just as some people take a lower-paid job due to the pleasure it provides.[75] Therefore, any loss is as a result of her choice and is not a ground for compensation. Two replies may be made to this. The first is that the choice is, presumably, the choice of both spouses. If the husband has agreed that they should share their family responsibilities in this way then it is only fair that the economic disadvantages caused by the decision are shared. Second, it might be argued that the choice of bearing and raising children is one that is essential to society's well-being. It is therefore a choice which society must seek to encourage and support by ensuring that it is paid for if the relationship breaks down.

Some argue that the costs that women who care for children suffer are due to the inequalities of society, rather than being married. It is the state's failure to provide adequate childcare facilities and employment protection for mothers that is the root cause of the disadvantages suffered. The losses women suffer should be compensated for by the state rather than by husbands.[76] However, in the absence of state support, it is surely unfair for mothers alone to have to carry the burden of financial sacrifice for the raising of children. Further, the husband had gained

---

[75] M. Maclean and J. Eekelaar, 'Taking the Plunge: Perceptions of Risk-Taking Associated with Formal and Informal Partner Relationships' [2005] 17 *Child and Family Law Quarterly* 247, find that there is widespread awareness of the financial losses that will often flow from motherhood.

[76] L. Ferguson, 'Family, Social Inequalities and the Persuasive Force of Interpersonal Obligation', (2008) 22 *International Journal of Law, Policy and the Family* 61.

from the care work undertaken as a result of the loss of paid employment and so requiring him to compensate is not without justification.

John Eekelaar sees a different objection to the compensation approach, arguing that even if the wife had not married her husband she would have married someone else, and so it is not realistic to claim that the lack of development in her career is this man's fault.[77] This, however, overlooks the benefit the husband has gained by the wife's sacrifices: the joys of family and home life. That might, however, lead to a preference for a retrospective payment approach rather than one based on lost salary.

A major practical difficulty for the compensation approach is calculating what salary a wife would have earned had she not been engaged in housework or child care. In some cases a calculated guess can be made, for example where the wife's career was well established at the time of the marriage. However, where the couple marry in their teens, as they did in *Charman v Charman*,[78] estimating salary is pure speculation.

The state's interests
Explanation of the theory
Most people who have written on the issue of justifications for redistribution of property on divorce have assumed that the issue is about achieving fairness between the parties themselves.[79] However, it is arguable that financial orders on divorce can be justified by the interests of the state, regardless of what would be fair or just between the parties.[80] So what state interests are there here? The following are suggested:[81]

(i) *Saving public money.* There is a state interest in avoiding, if possible, either spouse or children becoming dependent on welfare payments, either now or in the future. Orders should be made, if at all possible, without the economic cost of the breakdown falling on the state.

(ii) *Childcare issues.* The way the law structures financial orders on divorce could have an impact on whether parents choose to stay at home to care for children or undertake paid employment. The state might take the view that each member of society should be as economically productive as possible, and so it would want to discourage a spouse giving up employment to undertake child care, in which case the state might want to limit financial awards on divorce. If there were no financial orders on divorce then this would discourage a spouse from thinking of giving up employment to care for children;

---

[77] J. Eekelaar, 'Equality and the Purpose of Maintenance' (1988) 15 *Journal of Law and Society* 188.

[78] [2007] EWCA Civ 503.

[79] Many commentators make the assumption that redistribution of property on divorce is a private matter: see, e.g. S. Cretney, 'Private Ordering and Divorce – How Far Can We Go?' [2003] *Family Law* 399.

[80] J. Herring, 'Why Financial Orders on Divorce Should Be Unfair' (2005) 19 *International Journal of Law, Policy and the Family* 218.

[81] Ibid. But see also R. Bailey-Harris, 'Equality or Inequality within the Family? Ideology, Reality and the Law's Response', in J. Eekelaar and T. Nhlapo (eds) *The Changing Family: International Perspectives on the Family and Family Law* (Hart Publishing, 1998).

instead they would be likely to rely on paid child care. However, the state might believe that children's interests are promoted if one spouse gives up work to care for the children, in which case some form of protection from financial disadvantage would be necessary. Hale J in the Court of Appeal in *SRJ v DWJ (Financial Provision)*[82] has stated:

> It is not only in [the child's] interests but in the community's interests that parents, whether mothers or fathers, and spouses, whether husbands or wives, should have a real choice between concentrating on breadwinning and concentrating on home-making and child-rearing, and do not feel forced, for fear of what might happen should their marriage break down much later in life, to abandon looking after the home and the family to other people for the sake of maintaining a career.

(iii) *The symbolic valuing of child care.* The state could decide to reward child care as an important social activity.[83] Financial orders on divorce would be one way of doing that.

(iv) *The interests of children.* The existence and nature of financial orders on divorce can have a significant impact on the welfare of the children. It will affect whether the primary carer will need to undertake work to earn money; their state of emotional and material well-being; and their sense of self-respect. These can be used to justify payments of financial support.

(v) *Stability of marriage.* Some economists have argued that the level of maintenance can act as a deterrent against divorce.[84] Whether this is correct may be debated, as may the question of whether we want to encourage people to remain in unhappy marriages.

(vi) *Post-divorce life.* The level of financial support after divorce will affect the behaviour of the spouses after divorce. Do we want ex-wives to find employment and seek to become financially self-sufficient or is it proper to recognize that the duties owed to a spouse continue after divorce because the disadvantages flowing from the marriage do?[85] Whatever one's view on such questions the kind of orders made on divorce will affect the spouse's behaviour.

(vii) *Sex discrimination.* The state has a particular interest in seeking to promote equality between men and women. As already mentioned, divorce plays a significant role in leading to equality among women. The state can legitimately seek to combat discrimination through state orders. A rather different kind of argument is to see equality as an appropriate aim to deal with the inequalities caused by divorce. There is convincing evidence that following divorce women who are caring for children suffer a detrimental downturn in

---

[82] [1999] 2 FLR 176, at 182.

[83] It might be thought that orders on divorce are not an effective way of getting this message across. Unmarried parents are not rewarded and the level of the award does not reflect the amount or quality of the work done.

[84] A. Dnes, 'The Division of Marital Assets Following Divorce' (1998) 25 *Journal of Law and Society* 336.

[85] See M. Regan, *Alone Together: Law and the Meaning of Marriage* (Oxford University Press, 1999).

their finances, while their ex-husbands do not.[86] The conclusion of a recent study of the impact of divorce on women was blunt:

> The stark conclusion is that men's household income increases by about 23 per cent on divorce once we control for household size, whereas women's household income falls by about 31 per cent. There is partial recovery for women, but this recovery is driven by repartnering: the average effect of repartnering is to restore income to pre-divorce levels after nine years. Those who do not repartner...the long term economic consequences of divorce are serious.[87]

Ensuring an equal division of assets on divorce can be seen, therefore as a way of ensuring equality.

Application of the theory

The arguments made under this head are too diverse to lead to a straightforward result and depend on the public policy which it is sought to pursue. A figure cannot, therefore, be provided.

Difficulties with the theory

Lucinda Ferguson has argued that the state has over-extended the appropriate interpersonal obligations owed between spouses and by parents to children in order to deal with poverty which should be resolved by state support:

> The notion of interpersonal obligation has been distorted in both contexts in an attempt to respond to social inequality. More concerning than this distortion, however, is the fact that neither of these support obligations manages to successfully respond to social inequality anyway. Separated and divorced women and children raised in single-parent families represent a disproportionate percentage of those Canadians[88] living below the low income cut-off. Focus on expanding and strengthening these interpersonal obligations has distracted us from the urgent need to address the root causes of the inequality that these obligations have been adapted to address.[89]

Ferguson's argument is that if we accept these state-based justifications for intervention we should not impose the burden on the other spouse, but recognize them as public claims which the government should meet.

There is much to be said in favour of Ferguson's argument. One of the difficulties with the current law is that the extent to which the claims of the spouse may be met, or the goals of the state furthered, depends on the wealth of the husband. Whether it is in terms of compensation, recognition of contribution, or

---

86 W. Sigle-Rushton, 'Great Britain: 'things can only get better ...', in H-J Andreß, and D. Hummelsheim, (eds) *When Marriage Ends* (Edward Elgar, 2009).
87 H. Fisher and H. Low, 'Who Wins, Who Loses and Who Recovers From Divorce?' in Miles and Probert (eds) *Sharing Lives, Dividing Assets*, p. 254.
88 The point could equally well be made about this in England.
89 Ferguson, 'Family, Social Inequalities and the Persuasive Force of Interpersonal Obligation', 75.

pursuit of state aims, these goals are only met in cases where the husband is very wealthy. For the vast majority of cases they are fine-sounding words of no practical significance. Putting the burden on the state to recognize the value of care work, promote equality and limit disadvantage to employment patterns caused by family responsibilities is more likely to ensure these aims are met.

But – and it's an massive but – the costs of doing this through state funds would be enormous. Especially in the current economic climate it is hard to imagine it being taken on. Further it would not capture the fact that the losses caused to the wife have resulted in the gains to the husband in terms of home and family life.[90]

The state interest could be used to argue in favour of abolishing maintenance payments. The argument is that the existence of maintenance perpetuates the fact that women are dependent upon men.[91] A vicious circle exists in that, because the law tells wives that they will be entitled to financial support if their relationships ends, they are willing to take lower-paid jobs and they thereby do become dependent upon their husbands.[92] If maintenance were abolished and financial independence encouraged, women would have to find jobs that paid adequately.[93] Although there may be a short period during which women would suffer from the lack of maintenance, over time the market would have to provide adequately paid jobs for women, or provide economic rewards for homemaking and child-rearing activities.

Another issue is that the better response to the financial equalities produced by marriage is to improve the extent of child care undertaken by men. Although there is evidence of fathers seeking to play an increased role in child care[94] the vast majority is still undertaken by women.[95] Some commentators take the view that the government should attempt to encourage a more equal division of child-caring roles. However, the trend is for those working to be working for longer and longer hours, making it harder for couples to share child care and work.[96] The alternative is to encourage both parties to work and for ever greater use to be made of day care. However, this raises the debate over whether day care or care at home is preferable for children. This is a heated debate. Although the evidence suggests that there are some advantages and disadvantages to both, there is controversy as to whether, overall, one is preferable.[97]

---

[90] Glennon, 'The Limitations of Equality Discourses on the Contours of Intimate Obligations', in Wallbank, Choudhry and Herring (eds) *Rights, Gender and Family Law*.

[91] In practice it is far more common for a wife to be awarded maintenance than a husband.

[92] R. Deech, 'What's a Woman Worth?' (2009) 39 *Family Law* 1140.

[93] Although the levels of maintenance are low, and it is unlikely that women would choose not to work in the hope of getting maintenance should they divorce. Perhaps more convincing is the argument that maintenance is symbolic of the culture of dependency.

[94] S. Maushart, *Wifework* (Bloomsbury, 2001), esp. see pp. 129–34.

[95] E.g. J. Eekelaar and M. Maclean, *The Parental Obligation* (Hart Publishing, 1997) p. 137.

[96] P. Moen, *It's About Time* (Cornell University Press, 2003).

[97] J. Ermisch and M. Francesconi, *Working Parents: The Impact on Kids* (Institute for Social and Economic Research, 2003) argue that children whose parents both work suffer in a variety of ways. The Daycare Trust, *Towards Universal Child Care* (The Daycare Trust, 2003) paints a much more positive view of day care.

CONCLUSION

The problems identified in this discussion are significant. The difficulties that arise reflect broader problems of gender equality and distribution of child care and housework roles. If there is to be financial fairness between spouses on divorce, some fundamental change in society is required. Diduck and Orton look forward to a better future:

> Along with true equality in employment and pay and affordable good quality child care, an adequate valuation of domestic work would mean it would not be necessary that each partner play exactly the same role in wage earning…. Roles in marriage could be adopted based on the partners' actual interests and skills. Maintenance on divorce would still sometimes be necessary, then, but it would no longer overwhelmingly be women who require it and it would no longer result in economic disadvantage for the recipient. Maintenance would be seen as a right, expected and earned, rather than as a gift, act of benevolence or based on a notion of women's dependency on men.[98]

The real problems are social: a society with gendered inequalities in terms of distribution of child care, housework, wages and access to the employment market; and a society that fails to adequately recognize the value of care work. Given these issues any attempt to produce a 'fair' law on ancillary relief is doomed to failure.

Ruth Deech opens her recent discussion of financial orders on separation by asking her readers to consider three sisters:

> One is very pretty and marries a national footballer; they have no children and it is a short marriage before she leaves him for an international celebrity. The second sister marries a clergyman and has several children; the marriage ends after 30 years as he is moving into retirement. The third sister never marries; she stays at home and nurses first their mother, who has a disability, and then their father, who has Alzheimer's and dies without making a will. Which of the three sisters will get the windfall: an amount sufficient to keep her in luxury for the rest of her days, when her relationship with a man comes to an end? And which one most needs and deserves financial support, even of the bare minimum? The message is that getting married to a well-off man is an alternative career to one in the workforce.[99]

Her implied message is that the current law on financial orders on separation has gone badly wrong. The undeserving footballer's wife ends up with millions, the carer of the demented father ends up with nothing. She is right that this seems unfair. As one commentator put it over a century ago:

---

[98] Diduck and Orton (1994) 'Equality and Support For Spouses', 686–87.
[99] Deech, 'What's a Woman Worth?'.

the monetary reward of wifehood and motherhood depends entirely on the life, good luck and the good nature of another person; the strictest attention to duty on the part of a wife and mother is of no avail without that.[100]

But, of course it does not follow that the problem is the award to the footballer's wife. It may be the real issue is the lack of provision for carers, rather than excessive awards to wives. And the way resources are distributed in the world is generally unfair.

Before setting them out it should be stressed that it may not be appropriate to adopt a single theory. The redistribution of property on divorce is a controversial issue. There is a wide range of competing policies that the law seeks to hold together. There is a desire to ensure that on divorce a fair redistribution of the property takes place so that one party is not unduly disadvantaged by the divorce. On the other hand there is the desire to enable the parties to achieve truly independent lives after the divorce. To do both is often impossible. The truth is that for many couples suitable financial orders cannot be made. Neither party will be able to live at a standard of living they regard as acceptable. Both will feel they have been hard done by. As Symes explains:

> Quite clearly, marriage as it has traditionally been practised is not intended to be ended by divorce. Indeed, traditional housewife marriage has a most potent feature of indissolubility built right into it – dependency.... The accumulation of responsibilities and obligations, the consequences of an unequal partnership based on dependency – all mean that an absolute severance of the bond without massive adjustment would be manifestly unjust, more likely impossible.[101]

Debate 2

Should pre-nuptial contracts be enforced?

INTRODUCTION

A pre-nuptial agreement is a contract entered into by a couple prior to marriage. According to one survey the following were the most commonly listed issues that people would want to find in a 'pre-nup':

1 No cheating
2 Equal share of housework
3 Limit on shopping sprees
4 Not letting your appearance go
5 No contact with ex-partners
6 Control of the remote

---

[100] C. Hamilton, *Marriage as a Trade* (1909; Detroit: Singing Tree Press, 1971), p. 96.
[101] P. Symes, 'Indissolubility and the Clean Break' (1985) 48 *MLR* 44, 57.

7 No snoring
8 No unwanted family visits
9 No breaking wind
10 No leaving the toilet seat up.[102]

In reality few people are likely to put such requirements into a pre-nuptial contract! They would not be enforceable and descending to such detail might be prohibitively expensive if lawyers were employed in the negotiating and drafting of the agreement. Far more realistic is a pre-nuptial agreement which seeks to determine the financial consequences of divorce or dissolution. We will, therefore, focus on those.

A recent study by Emma Hitchings showed that few people currently use pre-nuptial agreements.[103] Of the 39 practitioners interviewed, 24 had never encountered them. The 15 who had had only done so very rarely. The few cases that had occurred tended to involve either couples from an international background or where one had significant assets, typically inherited or in an established business, which they wished to protect.

THE LAW

Historically it was seen as contrary to public policy for a couple to make a contract that determined what should happen to their finances on separation.[104] There were three public policies that were seen to be in play. The first was that rendering such an agreement enforceable might be regarded as amounting to an encouragement to separate,[105] the fear presumably being that more calculating individuals might value the money more than the marriage if they knew exactly what they would receive financially in the event of a divorce. The second was that it was seen as contrary to public policy for a couple to contemplate separation at the very time they were meant to be contemplating what is intended to be a life-long union.[106] The third is that it was seen to deprive the courts of their Parliament-given jurisdiction to determine how property disputes should be resolved on divorce.[107]

Over the last decade, however, the courts have been giving decreasing weight to the second of these arguments and increasing weight to pre-nuptial agreements.[108] They were recognized as having evidential weight[109] and guiding the

---

[102] *Distributed by PR Newswire on behalf of Smile.co.uk*, http://www2.prnewswire.co.uk/cgi/news/release?id=121959.
[103] E. Hitchings, 'From Pre-Nups to Post-Nups: Dealing with Marital Property Agreements' (2009) *Family Law* 1056.
[104] See G. Miller, 'Pre-nuptial Agreements and Financial Provision', in G. Miller (ed.) *Frontiers of Family Law* (Ashgate, 2003) for a general discussion of the issue and the law.
[105] *Cocksedge v Cocksedge* (1844) 14 Sim 244; 13 LJ Ch 384; *H vW* (1857) 3 K & J 382.
[106] Rejected in Connell J in *M v M (Prenuptial Agreement)* [2002] *Family Law* 177.
[107] *Hyman v Hyman*.
[108] Resolution, *A More Certain Future: Recognition of Pre-Marital Agreements in England and Wales* (Resolution, 2011).
[109] *N v N (Jurisdiction: Pre-nuptial agreement)* [1999] 2 FLR 745, at 752.

court;[110] and, if the pre-nuptial agreement was within the range of orders a court might give, then that might sway the court to making an order in those terms. The approach of the courts then fell to be considered by the Supreme Court in *Radmacher v Granatino*.[111]

Katrin Radmacher, a German heiress, married Nicholas Granatino, a French investment banker. While engaged they entered a pre-nuptial agreement under German law, which provided that each was to manage his or her property independently. Both waived any claims for financial provision on divorce or inheritance. Baron J, the judge at first instance, placed negligible weight on the agreement and granted the husband (the less wealthy of the two spouses) over £5 million. The Court of Appeal,[112] however, held that Baron J had erred and that the agreement should have carried more weight in the light of the clear trend in the case-law. The Supreme Court endorsed the outcome of the Court of Appeal decision, but went still further, concluding that courts in future 'should accord respect to the decision of a married couple as to the manner in which their financial affairs should be regulated'.[113] It held that:

> [t]he court should give effect to a nuptial agreement that is freely entered into by each party with a full appreciation of its implications unless in the circumstances prevailing it would not be fair to hold the parties to their agreement.[114]

In effect, once it is shown that the agreement was freely entered into, the onus is on the party who is seeking to avoid the agreement to prove to the court that it would be unfair to give effect to it. In future cases, therefore, two key questions will arise:

▸ Is the agreement valid: was it 'freely entered into by each party with full appreciation of its implications'?[115]
▸ Is the agreement fair?

Looking first at validity, it is clear that an agreement may be found to be invalid using the normal principles of contract law: that there was a misrepresentation; undue influence or duress. However, the Supreme Court held that the agreement can also be challenged if there is evidence of 'unworthy conduct such as exploitation of a dominant position to secure an unfair advantage';[116] or 'a party's emotional state and what pressure he or she was under to agree'.[117] The court may also consider 'whether the marriage would have gone ahead without

---

[110] *M v M (Prenuptial Agreement)* [2002] 1 FLR 654, para. 44.
[111] [2010] UKSC 42.
[112] [2009] EWCA Civ 649.
[113] [2010] UKSC 42, para. 78.
[114] Para. 75.
[115] Para. 75.
[116] Para. 71.
[117] Para. 72.

the agreement or without the terms agreed'[118] and whether there was a material disclosure of 'all the information that is material to his or her decision'.[119]

Even if the agreement is valid, a court may still decide not to give effect to it if 'in the prevailing circumstances it would not be fair to hold the parties to the agreement'.[120] It seems from the judgment that the following factors will be considered in deciding whether the contract is unfair:

1 'A nuptial agreement cannot be allowed to prejudice the reasonable require-ments of any children of the family.'[121]
2 If events occurred which were not foreseen by the parties at the time of the agreement, then these have the potential to render it unfair.
3 The agreement fails to meet the needs of one spouse and leaves the spouse 'in a predicament of real need'.[122] This is a strict interpretation of needs. Contrast the reference to 'need (generously interpreted)' in the earlier case- law regulat-ing property division on divorce).[123] The earlier case-law, and even s. 25(1)(c) of the Matrimonial Causes Act 1973, interpreted needs in the light of the standard of living during the marriage, rather than 'real need'.
4 'If the devotion of one partner to looking after the family and the home has left the other free to accumulate wealth, it is likely to be unfair to hold the parties to an agreement that entitles the latter to retain all that he or she has earned'.[124] Notably this does not require the party who has accumulated wealth to provide the other with anything like an equal share. It will only be unfair if the earning party retains all (or presumably nearly all) of the accumulated wealth.

The court also listed two factors in particular which might indicate that the agree-ment was fair or at least not unfair:

1 The Supreme Court was clear that even though the agreement was not an equal sharing of the product of the marriage, it could still be regarded as fair. In particular it may be fair to ensure that the other spouse does not have a claim on property acquired before the marriage.
2 If the parties had entered the contract in an overseas jurisdiction in which the contract would have been enforceable (as was the case in *Radmacher*) then it is likely to be fair.

There is a strong dissenting judgment in *Radmacher*, written by the only specialist family lawyer in the Supreme Court, Lady Hale. She rejected the view that the

---

[118] Para. 72.
[119] Para. 69.
[120] Para. 75.
[121] Para. 77.
[122] Para. 81.
[123] E.g. *Miller v Miller; McFarlane v McFarlane* [2006] UKHL 24, para. 144.
[124] Para. 81.

starting point should be giving effect to the pre-nup, referring to the principles established in the earlier case-law:

> It seems to me clear that the guiding principle in *White, Miller* and *McFarlane* is indeed fairness: but it is fairness in the light of the actual and foreseeable circumstances at the time when the court comes to make its order. These circumstances include any marital agreement made between the parties, the circumstances in which the agreement was made, and the events which have happened since then. (para 169)

THE VIEW OF A SUPPORTER

There are a number of good arguments in favour of the approach taken by the majority in *Radmacher v Granatino*.[125]

1 Costs
Rather than going through the lengthy and time-consuming process of ancillary relief proceedings, the parties can rely on the pre-nup as setting out their legal rights and obligations. This is especially important given that legal costs can eat up much of a couple's assets

2 Certainty
Under the current law it is impossible for either party to be certain what they would receive on divorce. Allowing the parties to set down in advance what will happen to their finances will provide them with predictability.

3 Autonomy
The majority of their Lordships in *Radmacher* quite rightly emphasized the importance of autonomy:

> The reason why the court should give weight to a nuptial agreement is that there should be respect for individual autonomy. The court should accord respect to the decision of a married couple as to the manner in which their financial affairs should be regulated. It would be paternalistic and patronising to override their agreement simply on the basis that the court knows best. This is particularly true where the parties' agreement addresses existing circumstances and not merely the contingencies of an uncertain future.[126]

We need to acknowledge that marriage means different things to different people. For some, marriage is a profound religious sacrament; for others, no more than a bureaucratic convenience. Given that diversity of views, it is arguably sensible to allow parties to set out what marriage means for them in a marriage contract, with the details of the marital relationships being regarded as a private matter.

---

[125] [2010] UKSC 42.
[126] Para. 78.

Maybe a standard form model for marriage was appropriate when the vast majority of people were members of the Church of England and accepted the Church's understanding of marriage, but those days are now long gone.

Moreover, if reasonable people can disagree (as they do) about the appropriate division of assets on divorce, why not let the parties decide for themselves what is fair, rather than have a judge's view on what is fair or not imposed upon them?

4 Encouraging agreement

The law already encourages couples to decide how their assets should be divided on breakdown. It has also been accepted that post-nuptial agreements (i.e. those entered into after marriage but before separation) are enforceable.[127] If the court can overturn the agreement reached by the parties this would undermine the benefits of negotiation and settlement, to which family law attaches so much importance.

5 Pre-marriage contracts are pro-marriage!

It is commonly claimed by opponents of pre-nups that they are anti-marriage. But the opposite is true. The Law Commission in its consideration of the issue reported:

> Proponents of reform point to couples who will not marry because the law as it stands does not allow them to make conclusive decisions about the eventual ownership of their property in the event of divorce or dissolution. We have heard considerable anecdotal evidence that this is of great concern to individuals who come from countries where marital property regimes, and the ability to contract into a regime of choice, are commonplace and who find that their expectations simply cannot be met here. It is unlikely that such concerns are unique to people from abroad. We have heard evidence of people who have already gone through a divorce and are unwilling to re-marry through fear of having to go through ancillary relief again should the second marriage fail.[128]

In short, people are being deterred from marrying because they cannot choose an appropriate financial regime for their marriage. Allowing people to make pre-nups will make marriage a more attractive option. People say it is unromantic to discuss financial issues before marriage. But a discussion between the couples about their future finances is important to encourage openness in the relationship.

THE VIEW OF AN OPPONENT

There are, however, a number of flaws in the above arguments as well as powerful arguments against pre-nuptial contacts being given any legal effect.[129]

---

[127] *Macleod v Macleod* [2008] UKPC 64.
[128] Law Commission, *Marital Property Agreements* (Law Commission, 2011), para. 5.19.
[129] R. George, P. Harris and J. Herring, 'Pre-Nuptial Agreements: For Better or for Worse?' (2009) 39 *Family Law* 934.

1 Costs

The argument that prenups will save costs is doubtful. First, there would be the upfront costs of entering into a pre-marriage contract, which would require extensive legal advice and drafting. For the more than half of couples who do not divorce this will be completely wasted expenditure. Secondly, even for those who do divorce an agreement is unlikely to save much by way of costs. It should be borne in mind that there is nothing to stop a couple entering into it and abiding by it – regardless of its validity or fairness – should the marriage subsequently break down. There is no requirement that the division be approved by the court. But if either is unhappy with the provision agreed, there will be many points capable of dispute. Jurisdictions which have enforced pre-nups have faced substantial levels of litigation challenging them.[130] Indeed, pre-nups will open up a new source of litigation: claims that there was inadequate disclosure at the time of the agreement; that they were not given adequate advice at the time of entering the agreement; or that it should be invalid on the basis of misrepresentation, undue influence or unconscionability, as experience elsewhere demonstrates.[131] And if the court is to ascertain whether the agreement will lead to injustice the court will need to know all of the relevant facts and assess what order would be fair in order to determine whether there will be injustice. So a hefty lawyers' bill to get the pre-nup arranged in the first place and another hefty lawyers' bill to undo it when you divorce. No wonder pre-nups are so popular among the lawyers![132] And perhaps no wonder so few people choose to enter them.[133]

2 Certainty

Supporters of pre-nups claim they will increase certainty. However, this may be questioned. If a pre-nup is challenged then many of the problems which beset the current law would still need to be resolved: non-disclosure of assets; attempts to dispose of assets; excessive expenditure etc. In fact there will be increased uncertainty because the court will need to determine what order they would make if no pre-nup existed using the current uncertain law and then decide how big a departure from that a pre-nup can make, providing yet more uncertainty. As Rix LJ acknowledged in *Radmacher v Granatino*,[134] 'it may be difficult to say what is meant by fairness: is it fairness in the contents of the contract, in the circumstances of its making, or in the circumstances which have come about?' Further, there would be all the uncertainty as to whether the agreement would be regarded as binding or not. What kind of changes in predicted circumstances might justify a departure from the pre-nup? There may be disputes over the interpretation of the terms of the contract. If the contract refers to each retaining ownership of their

---

[130] B. Fehlberg and B. Smyth, 'Binding Pre-Nuptial Agreements in Australia: The First Year' (2002) 16 *International Journal of Law, Policy and the Family* 127.

[131] See e.g. Fehlberg and Smyth, 'Binding Pre-Nuptial Agreements in Australia: The First Year'.

[132] George, Harris and Herring, 'Pre-Nuptial Agreements: For Better or for Worse?'.

[133] Hitchings, 'From Pre-Nups to Post-Nups: Dealing with Marital Property Agreements'.

[134] [2010] UKSC 42, at para. 71.

own property, that may simply open up a new set of uncertainties over who owns what. At least under the current law the court does not normally determine issues of ownership on divorce or dissolution. The list goes on. So far from producing predictability it would in fact increase uncertainty.

3 Drafting difficulties

Pre-nups are impossible to draft. It is hard enough to assess what is a fair distribution of the assets when the facts are known. Trying to predict what will happen in an uncertain future is impossible. How can a couple negotiate a fair division of assets when they don't know what life will bring them? One may become seriously disabled; caring for their children may take its toll on their earning capacity; the wealth of one may be decimated in a stock market crash; another may become unexpectedly successful. The imponderables are too many. As one of us has written elsewhere:

Relationships are unpredictable and messy. The sacrifices called for can be unpredictable and obligations without limit. Ask any partner caring for their demented loved one. To seek to tie these down at the start of the relationship in some form of 'once and for all' summation of their claims against each other, ignores the realities of intimate relationships.[135]

4 Fairness at the time of signing

There must be grave concerns over the fairness of pre-nups at the time of their making. First, there is inequality of legal advice. While a richer spouse will be able to have *substantial* legal representation, the less well-off will struggle to fund independent advice. Second, there will be the emotional inequality. The position for the poorer spouse is enviable. If they stand up for a fair settlement, then they will appear to be simply 'gold diggers'; if they do not the agreement is likely to be to their disadvantage. Third, if there are significant differences in the parties' wealth the less well-off spouse is likely to be less familiar with financial information and less adept at negotiation skills.

5 The interests of others

Most significantly, financial orders on divorce are not just about the interests of the spouses; there are important interests of the state too.[136] Even putting it at its strongest, we might assume that parties who reach agreement are able to take due account of their own interests, but we cannot assume that they can take or have taken due account of the interests of the state or the interests of others. Intimate relationships, especially those involving children, create inequalities in the parties' economic positions. Through the obligations of support which marriage creates, the state has sought to provide some protection from the risks faced by

---

[135] J. Herring, 'Relational Autonomy and Family Law', in Wallbank, Choudhry and Herring, (eds) *Rights, Gender and Family Law*, p. 270.

[136] Herring, 'Why Financial Orders on Divorce Should Be Unfair'.

those entering intimate relationships. In *White v White*[137] and *Miller; McFarlane*, the House of Lords developed the law on ancillary relief to ensure that orders met the needs of the parties; provided compensation for any losses caused by the marriage; and shared, at least, the fruits of the partnership. These were important principles needed to combat gender discrimination and prevent exploitation of the wife's labour. Yet in *Radmacher*, the Supreme Court tells us that the couple can agree to by-pass this protection. This is remarkable. There are few, if any, other areas of law where a person can engage in gender discrimination because the other person has consented to the treatment. For so long, marriage has been a vehicle for oppression and disadvantage for women, and it is unfortunate that, so soon after having amended the law on ancillary relief so that marriage can be a tool for protecting women's interests, the court should allow men to create agreements which remove that protection. Lady Hale was brave indeed to be explicit about the gendered nature of this decision:

> Would any self-respecting young woman sign up to an agreement which assumed that she would be the only one who might otherwise have a claim, thus placing no limit on the claims that might be made against her, and then limited her claim to a pre-determined sum for each year of marriage regardless of the circumstances, as if her wifely services were being bought by the year? Yet that is what these precedents do. In short, there is a gender dimension to the issue which some may think ill-suited to decision by a court consisting of eight men and one woman. (para 137)

6 Pre- and post-nups

It could also be argued that the distinction between a pre-nup and a post-nup endorsed in *MacLeod*[138] (but rejected in Radmacher) is entirely appropriate. As the Law Commission noted:

> We agree that before marriage there may be great pressure to sign an agreement rather than having a wedding cancelled. Equally, either party is still free to walk away. After the wedding the financially weaker party has ancillary relief rights and thereby considerable protection; but he or she may not know this; and the pressure to comply may be tremendous. He or she may be unwilling to displease a dearly-loved spouse. The parties may have now made the emotional as well as financial investment of buying a home together and having children. The agreement may be the price of the continuation of the marriage or civil partnership at a point when one party would otherwise be willing to contemplate divorce or dissolution.[139]

The Law Commission in fact went on to reason that the vulnerability that a party may feel depends on the circumstances of the case. There may be some cases where the pressures for a post-nuptial agreement will be greater than a pre-nup

---

[137] [2000] 3 FCR 555.
[138] [2008] UKPC 64.
[139] At para. 3.79.

and some where they are less. However, the fact that the parties are now married and the one has a clear claim against the other makes a huge difference. The fact that some post-nups may be a result of pressure is not a reason for making pre-nups enforceable, but a reason for making not only pre-nups but some post-nups unenforceable.

7 The nature of marriage

A final issue concerns the nature of marriage.[140] Lady Hale noted that the traditional view was that marriage was a status:

> Marriage is, of course, a contract, in the sense that each party must agree to enter into it and once entered both are bound by its legal consequences. But it is also a status. This means two things. First, the parties are not entirely free to determine all its legal consequences for themselves. They contract into the package which the law of the land lays down. Secondly, their marriage also has legal consequences for other people and for the state. (para 132)

However, the approach taken by the majority makes it hard to see marriage in these terms. Along with the mutual duty of support which marriage creates, and reflective of it, the court's redistributive powers over property on divorce have become by far the most significant legal consequence of marriage. If the couple can contract out of these powers with an ante-nuptial agreement then we are moving to a position where marriage ceases to have any particular legal meaning. It becomes difficult to promote marriage, if its legal effect depends substantially on the agreement of the parties.

Some commentators got carried away in the heat of the moment and announced that *Radmacher* was 'The death knell of marriage'.[141] That is surely an exaggeration. Although *Radmacher* marks a shift away from marriage as a status to marriage as a contract, it should not be forgotten that only a few marriages will involve a pre-nup. The majority was clear that the court would not be bound by an agreement if it was unfair, suggesting that marriage is more than a contract. However, this argument may not be compelling. There are other examples of contracts which can be vitiated because of unfair terms (see e.g. Unfair Contract Terms Act 1977; Unfair Terms in Consumer Contracts Regulations 1999), but no- one suggests they are not contracts. A marriage contract in that regard would be no different.

CONCLUSION

In *Charman v Charman*[142] Sir Mark Potter suggested that 'London is regularly described in the press as the "divorce capital of the world"'. That has even been

---

[140] J. Herring, R. George and P. Harris, 'Ante-nuptial Agreements: Fairness, Equality And Presumptions' (2011) 127 *LQR* 335.

[141] J. Herring, '20: 10: 2010: The Death Knell Of Marriage' (2010) *New Law Journal* 1511.

[142] [2007] EWCA Civ 503.

posited as a reason why it would be a good idea if prenups were made enforceable. However, even if London is the 'divorce capital of the world' that is not necessarily a bad thing. Being the financial capital of the world is not a bad thing. It may simply reflect the fact that English law is more egalitarian and progressive than other countries.

Yet, perhaps, therein lies the problem. While to some people the law as developed in *White v White* and the case-law following that decision is a major step in combating discrimination and injustice, to others it is profoundly unfair. In this area of the law, do we recognize principles which the law should uphold for all marriages, or should people be allowed to set the terms of their relationship themselves?

Lady Hale, in *MacLeod v MacLeod*,[143] suggested that the desire for pre-nuptial agreements might be motivated by 'a perception that equality in marriage is wrong in principle'. It is easy to see why adopting such a view would lead one to oppose pre-marriage contracts.

The complaints of uncertainty may be exaggerated. The complexity of the issues raised by big-money ancillary relief questions should not be overestimated. Any attempt to produce a clear formula to deal with these cases is unlikely to be sufficiently nuanced to provide the certainty so many crave. At least it would do so at the cost of unfairness in individual cases. In fact Emma Hitchings[144] in her study of 'everyday' cases found little uncertainty in the law. She writes:

> I would suggest that the findings in this study do not support the argument that the law of ancillary relief is uncertain and chaotic. At the everyday level at least, there does not appear to be a pressing need for additional principle to increase certainty of outcome. In the everyday case where needs dominate, the findings demonstrate that the advice given to clients is pretty consistent, subject to local court culture and the practicalities of the individual's case.

Further Reading

R. Bailey-Harris, 'Dividing the Assets on Breakdown of Relationships Outside Marriage: Challenges for Reformers', in R. Bailey-Harris (ed.) *Dividing the Assets on Family Breakdown* (Jordans, 1998).

E. Cooke, 'Miller/Mcfarlane: Law in Search of a Definition', (2007) 19 *Child and Family Law Quarterly* 98.

J. Eekelaar, 'Post-Divorce Financial Obligations', in S. Katz, J. Eekelaar and M. Maclean (eds) *Cross Currents* (Oxford University Press, 2000).

J. Eekelaar, 'Property and Financial Settlement on Divorce – Sharing and Compensating' (2006) 36 *Family Law* 754.

L. Ellman, 'Do Americans Play Football?' (2005) 19 *International Journal of Law, Policy and the Family* 257.

---

[143] [2008] UKPC 64, at [33].

[144] E. Hitchings, 'Chaos or Consistency?', in Miles and Probert (eds) *Sharing Lives, Dividing Assets*, p. 204.

R. George, P. Harris and J. Herring, 'Pre-Nuptial Agreements: For Better or for Worse?' (2009) 39 *Family Law* 934.

L. Glennon, 'The Limitations of Equality Discourses on the Contours of Intimate Obligations', in J. Wallbank, S. Choudhry and J. Herring (eds) *Rights, Gender and Family Law* (Routledge, 2010).

J. Herring, 'Why Financial Orders on Divorce should be Unfair', (2005) 19 *International Journal of Law, Policy and the Family* 218.

J. Miles, 'Principle Or Pragmatism in Ancillary Relief: The Virtues of Firting with Academic Theories and Other Jurisdictions' (2005) 19 *International Journal of Law, Policy and the Family* 242.

J. Miles, '*Charman v Charman* (no. 4) [2007] EWCA Civ 503 – Making Sense of Need, Compensation and Equal Sharing after Miller; Mcfarlane' (2008) 20 *Child and Family Law Quarterly* 378.

K. O'Donovan, 'Flirting with academic categorisations' (2005) 17 *Child and Family Law Quarterly* 415.

P. Perry, G. Douglas, M. Murch et al. (2000) *How Parents Cope Financially on Marriage Breakdown* (Joseph Rowntree, 2000).

N. Wikeley, *Child Support: Law and Policy* (Hart Publishing, 2006).

INDEX